Transnational
Latina/o Communities

Latin American Perspectives in the Classroom
Series Editor: Ronald Chilcote

Forthcoming

Transnational Latina/o Communities

Politics, Processes, and Cultures

Edited by
Carlos G. Vélez-Ibáñez and Anna Sampaio

with
Manolo González-Estay

ROWMAN & LITTLEFIELD PUBLISHERS, INC.
Lanham • Boulder • New York • Oxford

ROWMAN & LITTLEFIELD PUBLISHERS, INC.

Published in the United States of America
by Rowman & Littlefield Publishers, Inc.
4720 Boston Way, Lanham, Maryland 20706
www.rowmanlittlefield.com

12 Hid's Copse Road
Cumnor Hill, Oxford OX2 9JJ, England

British Library Cataloguing in Publication Information Available

Library of Congress Cataloging-in-Publication Data

Transnational Latina/o communities : politics, processes, and cultures / edited by Carlos Vélez-Ibáñez and Anna Sampaio with Manolo González-Estay.
   p. cm.
Includes bibliographical references and index.
ISBN 0-7425-1702-0 (cloth : alk. paper)—ISBN 0-7425-1703-9 (pbk. : alk. paper)
   1. Hispanic Americans—Ethnic identity. 2. Hispanic Americans—Social conditions. 3. Immigrants—United States—Social conditions. 4. Transnationalism. 5. United States—Relations—Latin America. 6. Latin America—Relations—United States. 7. United States—Emigration and immigration. 8. Latin America—Emigration and immigration. I. Vélez-Ibáñez, Carlos G., 1936– II. Sampaio, Anna, 1969– III. González-Estay, Manolo, 1970–

E184.S75 T73 2001
305.868'073—dc21

2001044380

Printed in the United States of America

∞™ The paper used in this publication meets the minimum requirements of American National Standard for Information Sciences—Permanence of Paper for Printed Library Materials, ANSI/NISO Z39.48-1992.

051104-6600 D2

We dedicate this work to Fred Lopez, who organized the first issue on Latina/os for *Latin American Perspectives* and whose too early death robbed us all of his fine counsel and intellectual contribution.

Contents

Series Introduction

Since its inception, *Latin American Perspectives* has worked to make its material available for classroom use. Our goal has been to introduce students to some of the important themes and issues about Latin America that have appeared in the journal and make them accessible to students. Our pedagogical plan has been to trim individual articles to their essential core, reorganize them into teachable groups—each preceded by a contextualizing commentary—and add a general introductory essay. To ensure that our material is effectively oriented for classroom use, all articles have been reviewed by three to four *LAP* editors, included the volume editors and myself.

This project was inspired by the late Fred López, who in the early 1990s organized a special issue of the journal around Latino issues that he had hoped to extend into a book. Drawn from his vision, this volume includes one piece from the original collection, along with new and important related work. Anna Sampaio and Carlos G. Vélez-Ibáñez have worked diligently to organize a comprehensive set of essays for the classroom. Their introductions lead the reader into the subject matter so that students can delve into the issues and controversies surrounding this dynamic theme.

Ronald H. Chilcote
Series Editor

Acknowledgments

The coeditors would like to thank the editorial collective of *Latin American Perspectives* for their patience and forbearance in bringing this work to fruition. We would be remiss if we did not especially thank Ron Chilcote, Professor Emeritus of Economics of the University of California at Riverside, who also served as senior volume editor of the series, for his invaluable assistance, belief, and unwavering support. We are particularly grateful to William Aviles, Ralph Armbruster-Sandoval, Bernadete Ramos Beserra, Michael Kearney, Enrique Ochoa, Manuel Pastor, Marta Savigliano, Jeff Tobin, and Jan Rus for sharing their invaluable insights and expertise. In addition, we would like to extend special appreciation to those who work tirelessly and selflessly in the *LAP* office to ensure that everything from collective meetings to final edits is done efficiently and skillfully; for this we recognize Fran Chilcote, Sarah C. Varner, Sean Dillingham, and Erin Estrada.

We would also like to extend our heartful gratitude to the collection of people at Rowman & Littlefield who have worked diligently and patiently over the course of a year to see this book come to fruition. In particular, Susan McEachern, acquisitions editor, oversaw the development of this book from initial proposal to final product with disciplined and gracious leadership. Assistant managing editor Janice Braunstein took care to guide us through some of the most arduous day-to-day operations with the steady persistence needed to balance our sometimes chaotic tendencies. Jennifer Huppert's talents in graphic design were apparent in the stunning book cover. Finally, Alden Perkins, associate editor, guided us through the final stage of production (just as we were thinking we'd never see the end) with skill and confidence.

Barbara Metzger provided expert copyediting. Dominic Rissolo was instrumental in completing the copyediting process, and we are especially indebted to him for his knowledge of Latin America, from history to popular culture.

Kudos go to our unknown reviewers, whose comments helped shape the final version of this work and aided our conceptual, analytical, and empirical musings immeasurably. Whoever you are, a profound and respectful "gracias."

We also thank the Ernesto Galarza Applied Research Center of the University of California at Riverside for its energetic and material support of the project and the Center for U.S.-Mexican Studies of the University of California at San Diego for facilities support during the 1999-2000 Visiting Scholar period, without which Carlos Vélez-Ibáñez would not have had the opportunity to work on the project. In addition, we would like to recognize the department of political science at the University of Colorado at Denver, where Anna Sampaio has spent the past two years working on the book and benefiting from the creative insights of her colleagues and her Latino politics students. Most important has been the support of the University of California at Riverside generously provided by Executive Vice Chancellor David Warren and Chancellor Raymond Orbach, both extraordinarily strong advocates of faculty's being allowed time and material support to fulfill their scholarly goals.

To Maria Luz Cruz Torres, Assistant Professor of Anthropology at the University of California at Riverside, who readily provided one of the coeditors many of the insights of Puerto Ricans, his profound professional and personal gratitude.

Ultimately, we are most indebted to the colleagues whose work appears in this collection not only for their patience and their inspiration but for their ability to imagine new possibilities in Latina/o scholarship and the leadership they take in sharing this with all of us.

Introduction

Processes, New Prospects, and Approaches

Carlos G. Vélez-Ibáñez and Anna Sampaio

One of the best ways to begin to understand the cultures of the Latina/o populations of the United States is to consider the term as it has been used and appropriated over time. The term "Latino" (Spanish *Latino Americano*), according to David Bushnell (1970: 3) was first used by the Colombian publicist José María Torres Caicedo in 1856 (Miguel Tinker Salas, personal communication, 2001). "Latin" was used in the United States, especially in films from the 1920s through the 1960s as a cover designation that masked the origin of Mexicans and Puerto Ricans superseding the word "Spanish" to accomplish the same function.

"Mexican" was a word of opprobrium in the United States even before the 1846–1848 Mexican war and is associated with cheap labor to this day. However, especially during the eugenics period of the 1920s–1940s in the United States, the population was considered inferior because of "admixture" (Vélez-Ibáñez, 1996: 83–84). For some Mexicans this period was important in distinguishing them as "white," with the word "Spanish" being used to distinguish whiter, middle/upper-class Mexicans from their allegedly darker, working-class "Mexican" brethren. Of course, the actual variation of melanin in the Mexican population is probably as great as that between Anglos. Any cultural value given to darker or whiter is a social creation, since difference of skin color can have no biological or genetic value except as a positively adaptive function.[1]

"Puerto Rican" was equally if not more negatively cast on the East Coast of the United States, especially after large-scale Puerto Rican migration in the 1950s. The term "Puerto Rican" was made questionable by a racialist ideology that positively valued lighter-skinned Puerto Ricans against those with more melanin and devalued the partial African origins of Puerto Ricans. Like

1

Mexicans, Puerto Ricans were perceived as cheap labor and initially filled secondary and tertiary jobs, with the result that "whiteness" and class became intertwined. "Puerto Rican" became a negative designation denoting dark/African/working-class status while "Spanish" was its opposite.

In both cases, parts of both populations internalized these racialisms in order to fit a more positively rewarded stereotype that reinforced existing racialisms dating back to the caste system. This was a sixteenth-century Spanish colonial invention that sought to divide admixed populations according to physical characteristics and to limit their legal rights. Those "purest" were the Iberian-born Spaniards, and those at lower levels allegedly reflected their degrees of admixture.[2] For both Mexicans and Puerto Ricans, the inherited melanin/caste ideology combined to varying degrees with the U.S. melanin/class designation. Both categories are important for understanding hierarchical dimensions of power and inequality during the colonial periods and later between and among Anglos, Mexicans, and Puerto Ricans as well as other Latina/os.

More recently, the U.S. Bureau of the Census has introduced "Hispanic" to capture the various segments of the Spanish-speaking population. "Latina/o" (but not "Latin" in American usage) is used by a segment of the U.S.–born of Mexican, Puerto Rican, and Latin American origin as a term of cultural recognition and positive designation of social place. For this part of the population, "Hispanic" lacks legitimacy and authenticity and is a national imposition. In either case, both "Latino" and "Hispanic" tend to homogenize origins, lineality, and geographic associations, but the former term is a self-designation term rather than imposed and Spanish rather than English. We use the word "Latina/o" to refer to all persons residing in the United States whose cultural and national origin is from Mexico, the Spanish-speaking Caribbean, or Latin America. We recognize that while this definition locates the population within geographical boundaries, Latina/o populations often operate in transnational and transgeographic settings. We begin, then, by unpacking the term, distinguishing populations by historical, cultural, and national origin and, where appropriate, geographical context.

HISTORICAL ORIGINS

"Latino" populations have their genesis in colonial enterprises that are in reality "transnational," although both nations and the term are nineteenth-century phenomena. The sixteenth and twenty-first centuries share transcontinental and transoceanic economic, political, and demographic movements that are the consequences of capital's moving about without reference to geographic or political borders in an effort to capture human labor, physical space, and material goods. In the sixteenth century, such investments led to vast human and material exploitation and appropriation. In the Americas, two grand empires (Spain and England) and a few less grand (Portugal, Holland, and France) sought control over vast territories from Tierra del Fuego to the shores of the Pacific and Atlantic Oceans.

"Latinos" for almost three hundred years saw few or no "national" differences, since they were all part of the Spanish colony. In the Southwestern United States the term "Españoles Mexicanos," meaning a subject of Spain but born in New Spain or Mexico, was the favored designation. It was not until the nineteenth century that "national" entities became differentiated after the independence movements in Mexico (which at the time included large parts of North America, Central America, and South America). Puerto Rico, which gained independence from Spain in 1897, was quickly incorporated into the United States as a condition of the Treaty of Paris in 1898. The Foraker Act, passed by Congress in 1907 (giving the United States the power to establish a president and executive council on the island), further solidified this new colonial relationship and bound the territory inextricably to the United States (Jennings, 1988; Rodriguez, 1997).

These new nations were quickly penetrated by capital and by political and colonial intervention from the United States and Europe. Thereafter there developed continuous transcontinental and transoceanic relations in which the expropriation of material, land, and human beings tied these national economies to U.S. and European markets in a type of economic colonialism and indirect rule that largely supported dictators such as Porfirio Diaz of Mexico (1876–1910) and dozens of others throughout the twentieth century in Nicaragua, El Salvador, Panama, Honduras, Venezuela, Chile, Argentina, Peru, Bolivia, Brazil, Paraguay, and Colombia.

In the case of Mexico, U.S. invasion and expropriation of land and population has created 150 years of asymmetrical transnational economic and political relations with political borders often crossed by capital, goods, and human beings. Three different versions of the U.S.-Mexican political border were imposed by the United States, and crossing and recrossing of "Mexicans" is a simple outcome of proximity and asymmetry. Varying forms of political economy have developed, ranging from the early extractive industries of U.S. and foreign interests of the nineteenth century to today's North American Free Trade Agreement (NAFTA)-generated "open market" structures. Augmented by occasional revolutions, the movement of Mexicans across borders is directly related to the asymmetry of the two countries' economies and their expulsion when economic conditions in the United States defined them as undesirable (Vélez-Ibáñez, 1996: 82–83).

All over Latin America, from the nineteenth century to the present, transnational mining, agricultural, banking, construction, assembly, clothing, electronic, and information interests have been developed without particular allegiance to their national origins. Such corporations are constantly seeking out places, spaces, peoples, and material to appropriate and exploit at the lowest possible cost with the highest possible return. As they expand, populations are forced to move and regions previously unconnected to the First World become the material and resource backyards for transnational investment and expropriation.

The United States and its surrogates (Cuba, Chile, the Dominican Republic, Guatemala, Nicaragua, Panama, and El Salvador) have historically subjected Latin American countries to these processes punctuated often by direct or indirect armed interventions. These interventions are often accompanied by ideological convictions such as the "free-market" or "free-trade" megascripts and together create the conditions for transcontinental human movements from all such afflicted areas and especially so from Latin America. Thus the movement in the 1960s of Dominicans into the United States emerged as the direct consequence of a failed popular uprising of an American-supported dictatorship and of the American invasion of 1965 and stimulated the Diasporas of thousands of Dominicans.[3] Similarly by 1990, 1.2 million Salvadorans were counted by the Census while only 21,000 had been enumerated 10 years before. Such dramatic increases are the direct consequence of Salvadorans fleeing the latest version of a long historical conflict between Salvadoran oligarchies, the Catholic Church hierarchy, and a U.S.-trained army against indigenous populations, peasants, middle class, and Salvadoran revolutionaries buttressed by both Marxist and localized Catholic liberation theologies. Similarly, in the same period, Guatemalan and Nicaraguan political refugees largely accounted for most of the demographic growth as the aftermath of long periods of political and economic unrest in Guatemala and Nicaragua directly associated with U.S. military assistance programs, U.S. protection of American corporations in agricultural production, and U.S. ideological convictions favoring capitalist transnational strategies.

Yet for many such populations, migration has meant migrating to similar structural conditions in Washington, D.C., Los Angeles, New York, Miami, Atlanta, Chicago, and sundry other cities. Simultaneously, other populations are canvassing out to suburban and rural areas seeking employment as agricultural laborers, gardeners, and housekeepers; service workers in restaurants, stores, and hotels; and as caretakers of children, the elderly, and the infirm in homes, hospitals, and old age homes. It is these structural similarities to that which was left that have created a new cultural and political symbiosis with their points of origin. In the process, new cultural forms have emerged, ideologies have shifted, and the idea of spaces and places bound by nationality and origin have become blurred, and new forms of identity, multiculturality, and simultaneity of multiple experience have made their appearances.

Yet many of these characteristics are not limited to the present. What differentiates the transnational period from previous ones has three important dimensions: (1) the dependent and interdependent structural relations between economies, the fluidity of which is made possible by electronic and other means of communication;[4] (2) the massive migration of millions of persons and their continued communication with their points of origin; and (3) a totally unintended consequence of the first two, the billions of dollars in remittances that create local, regional, and national dependency upon those revenues and even more closely tie national economies to the sources of international capital in Europe, Asia, and the United States. Thus, the difference between the transnationalism of the late twentieth century and the imperialism of the nineteenth and early twentieth centuries is more a matter of agents and process than of outcome. While the movement of capital between colonial states in the early 1900s was a function largely of formal merchants, diplomats, and state departments, today's migration is fueled as much by the practices of individual migrants themselves (seeking to maintain a clear connection with their countries of origin) as it is by the trade policies or distribution of multinational corporations. Our approach to the study of Latina/o communities must therefore include consideration of these characteristics of contemporary transnationalism at almost every level.

From the point of view adopted here globalization is a form of intense capital expansion that is practically unlimited in time and space. Time and space are in fact overcome by the electronic carriers that facilitate financial and political policy decisions, and these decisions are driving millions of human beings to cross borders to other nations. This border crossing is attended by terrible costs of poverty, illness, and abuse. The process involves not only the continuing appropriation of value from the labor of millions but also the squeezing of populations into "devaluing" spaces (Nagengast and Vélez-Ibáñez, n.d.).

This migration, whether international, national, or regional, entails social dislocation, depopulation of local areas, cultural fracturing of the human developmental process, and virtually forced adaptation to new localities. Each of these consequences has severe impacts on the material provisioning of households and on the ability of households to predict the availability of future subsistence requirements so as to create relatively secure social platforms. (See WEDO, *Codes of Conduct for Transnational Corporations: Strategies Toward Democratic Global Governance* quoted in Hom, 1996: n. 43.) Appropriate provisioning includes not only wages but also security of income, protection of physical and mental health, and educational benefits. A stable social platform includes inherited historical relations and their cultural understandings, familial relations, and nonfamilial social, economic, and political relations and events.

Through the life cycle individuals learn, reject, and/or reconstitute relations and events, and these become the cultural basis for their social platforms. The earliest platform for the neonate is the suckling and bonding between mother and child. When a child's social platform develops in insecurity, uncertainty, conflict, and basic economic disparity without appropriate provisioning, the following generation may internalize all of the attending psychological and emotional ills, and its own children will become victims as well. Human beings are, however, amazingly plastic and inventive, and Latina/os are no exception. Innovation, negotiation, accommodation, and success are also possible.

Transnational global processes create world pathways for the movement of populations along with capital, goods, and communications, but these processes have no regard for appropriate provisioning to support stable familial social platforms. Populations seem to be reestablishing themselves in new places at the speed of an e-mail message and for Latina/os especially such movement is often a forced dislocation accompanied by extreme psychological and cultural uncertainty and indeterminacy. The consequences for many subsequent generations include disproportionate participation of youth in gangs, too early childbearing, lack of quality education, and high dropout rates (Vélez-Ibáñez, 1996: 186–199).

DEMOGRAPHICS OF LATINA/OS IN THE UNITED STATES

According to the 1990 U.S. Census, the total Latina/o population numbered 22 million, almost five times greater than 1960 (Grebler, Moore, and Guzmán, 1970). Of the 1990 population, Mexicans made up more than 13 million, 62 percent of the total Latina/o population. They had in fact increased by more than 50 percent between 1980 and 1990 (U.S. Bureau of the Census, 1993). Figure 1 shows the distribution of Latina/os by origin in 2000; of 32.8 million Latina/os, about 12 percent of the total U.S. population, Mexicans made up 66.1 percent, Central and South Americans 14.5 percent, Puerto Ricans 9.0 percent, Cubans 4.0 percent, and Other "Hispanics" 6.4 percent.[5] The non-Mexican percentages were not significantly different from those of 10 years before.

The Latina/o population will almost double by 2025 and double again by 2070 to make up almost 30 percent of the U.S. population.[6] While such growth is rooted in historical political factors, globalization influences its speed and intensity. This volume attends centrally to both the historical and the contemporary processes that are reflected in these demographics and to the political and cultural consistencies over time.

The growth described here has exacted a heavy human price. In few places are the costs of globalization more deeply felt than in the U.S. *colonias* that line the border between the United States and Mexico. Their physical and ecological disparities are similar to those suffered by migrants to cities all over Latin America forty years ago but now extend into the

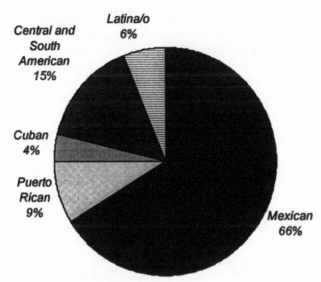

Figure 1.   Percentage Distribution of Latina/os by Type, 2000
Source: Current Population Survey, March 2000, P20–535

United States as well. As a microcosmic example, in the middle of a desert bowl, forty dwellings of assorted types lay spread over approximately eighty barren acres. About thirty of the dwellings are former trailers that have been converted to permanency and in some cases have been encased within family-built brick homes. Many of these dwellings have no access to sewerage, water, electricity, or gas, and all at one time or another have lacked all such services. Most residents bought their lots without any amenities or infrastructure for $4,000 each from owners who had paid one-fourth of that. Eventually the residents themselves create "miracle" communities out of nothing, and with the courage, tenacity, and know-how that those in dire need often display. They fight as *colonos* for basic water services and electricity and for the most part rely on septic tanks that often overflow or incomplete sewerage lines that allow partially filtered but untreated sewage to overflow and collect in pools. Needless to say, children suffer from high rates of gastric and pulmonary diseases, and over 80 percent of adults twenty-five or over suffer from traces of hepatitis A. For the most part, residents work on nearby farms for a minimum wage; a lucky few are employed in a nearby city as service workers or in construction. About a third of this population travels the migrant stream for three or four months a year to provide subsistence for their families when the crop cycle of the area slows. A very high percentage of residents fall below the poverty level, have low levels of educational attainment, and suffer from untreated health and nutritional problems, and the limits of opportunity tend to reproduce the long-term attendant problems of children working alongside their parents in the fields at too early an age.[7]

These conditions are found not in a Third World country but in a rural Southwestern U.S. state, a few thousand feet from the serpentine Rio Grande. In fact, more than eighteen hundred such communities arose in the early 1980s and now are inhabited by nine hundred thousand to a million residents of Mexican-origin in the border states of Texas and New Mexico. These communities are mini-reproductions of conditions in the residents' point of origin, and they depend on low-wage labor without health coverage, adequate legal protection, or job security. Inability to provision themselves forces approximately 25 percent of households into the underground economy, creating even greater anxiety and insecurity for their members.[8]

Similar conditions have emerged in rural agricultural contexts in California, Arizona, and, more recently, in places such as Kansas, South Carolina, and Oregon, where residents struggle daily not to succumb to conditions that would easily overwhelm even the most seasoned survivor. Mexicans are also reoccupying California rural towns abandoned by non-Latina/os over the past 30 years as the young moved out and their parents followed them to other states or to suburban sites nearby (see Palerm in this volume for a detailed analysis of the reoccupation process in Santa Maria, California). This process is a double-edged sword; while towns are being reoccupied, businesses reborn, and local government revived, poverty, low income, poor housing, and decaying institutions are also being reestablished. There is similar nascent growth of Mexican populations in rural Iowa, Indiana, and Alabama in mostly farming communities where local institutions have been hard-pressed to adjust to the educational and cultural needs of the newcomers. Yet even in these "non-Mexican" regions, Mexican-oriented restaurants, stores, and other services are being developed by migrants who have been contractors for fellow migrants, or in some cases, participants in the underground economy.[9]

These recent developments are but a small part of much larger demographic changes across the Southwest and throughout the United States. In fact, the great majority of the Latina/o population is urban and part of a great movement from south to north, especially since World War II. The size and scope of this movement rivals the great trek westward in the nineteenth century (Gonzalez, 2000: xi). When high birth rates (U.S. Bureau of the Census, 2000b) are figured into this mix, the Latinization of large parts of the United States is guaranteed.

Entire urban landscapes in large metropolitan areas such as Los Angeles, Santa Fe, San Antonio, San Diego, Tucson, San Francisco, and Albuquerque are increasingly being occupied by entering Mexicans and other Latina/os joining populations established since the eighteenth century.[10] Others cities, such as Phoenix, Dallas, Houston, and Long Beach, have greatly expanded, especially between 1970 and 1980 when the Latina/o population virtually doubled. In urban border areas like those of Brownsville-Harlingen, El Paso, and Laredo, Mexicans make up over 60 percent of the population. The Los Angeles-Long Beach area has the highest number of "Latino" households, of which the great majority is of Mexican origin (U.S. Bureau of the Census, 1995)[11] (see Rocco in this volume on changing neighborhoods in Los Angeles).

Atlanta, Miami, Chicago, and New York and New Jersey are relocation centers for many of these populations, which follow in the footsteps of Puerto Ricans in New York and New Jersey, previous generations of Mexicans and Puerto Ricans in Chicago, and Cubans in Florida. As evidenced by the burgeoning numbers of Dominicans in New York, many of these new immigrants move into largely African-American neighborhoods, quickly turning these into culturally mixed arenas in which schools, churches, stores, governing bodies, and electoral politics become new grounds of social and cultural change, intermarriage, conflict, economic relations, and shifts in the U.S. discourse on ethnic relations. Salvadorans in Los Angeles, Peruvians in Washington, DC, Guatemalans in San Francisco, and Nicaraguans in Miami migrate to structural conditions reminiscent of those they have left.

In 1998, slightly more than 27 percent of the U.S. population of Mexican origin, a large percentage of them recent migrants to cities, lived in poverty. Slightly over 30 percent of the population of Puerto Rican origin and 20 percent of that of Central and South American origin suffered from poverty. Cubans, considered "golden exiles," had a poverty rate only slightly higher (13.6 percent) than the general non-Latina/o population (11 percent). Removing the Cuban statistic, Latina/os in the United States would have suffered a poverty rate of 25 percent in 1998 (U.S. Bureau of the Census, 1999a). This is significant because it was only 5 percent lower in the midst of a booming economy than it had been in 1993 (U.S. Bureau of the Census, 1994).

In 1999, the percentage of Latina/os with incomes less than $10,000 by cultural grouping is even larger than the percentage in poverty (Figure 2). The hardship this imposes is greater given the youth of these populations: 38 percent under eighteen for Mexicans and 35 percent for Puerto Ricans as compared with only 24 percent for Anglos (Figure 3). This is compounded by the fact that households are twice as large among Mexicans than among Anglos. The high percentage of Cubans with incomes less than $10,000 is primarily due to the large number of aged Cubans no longer in the workforce, with 18 percent being over age sixty-five as compared with 4 and 7 percent for Mexicans and Puerto Ricans (Figures 4 and 5). Even the Anglos' 14 percent is less than the Cubans'.

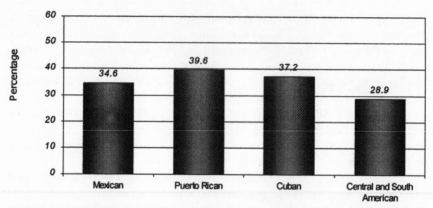

Figure 2.   Percentage of Latina/os (15 Years and Older) with Income Less Than $10,000 in 1998, by Origin

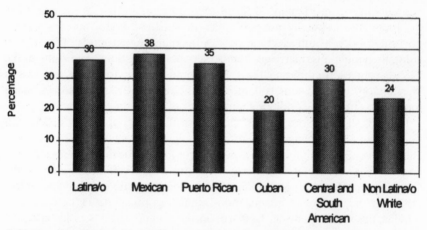

Figure 3.   Percentage of Population under Age 18 by Latina/o Origin, 1999

But the percentages are especially troubling with regard to children living below the poverty level. More than 35.4 percent of Mexican children and a startling 43.6 percent of Puerto Rican children were below the poverty line in 1999, as were 26.6 percent of Central and South American children and 16.6 percent of Cuban children. Only 10.6 percent of non-Latina/o white children were so characterized (U.S. Bureau of the Census, 1999b).

For the most part, however, Latina/os suffer from low wages and under-employment rather than unemployment. In part, this poverty is associated with limited number of blue-collar jobs and the decline in wages in these jobs. For example, real earnings in the clothing and furniture industries in Los Angeles decreased more than $6,000 a year between 1970 and 1990.[12]

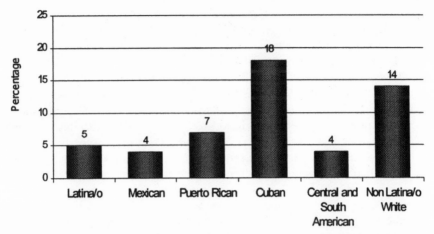

Figure 4. Percentage of Population Aged 65 and Over by Latina/o Origin, 1999

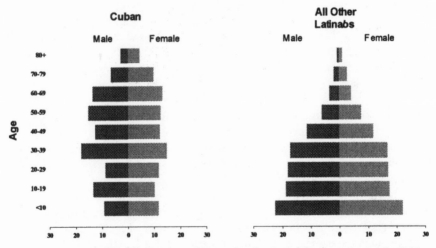

Figure 5. Age Distribution by Sex and Type of Latina/o Origin (in percentage), 1999
Source: Current Population Survey, March 1999, PGP-2

Yet what is often not emphasized sufficiently is that while the vast majority of Latina/os—73 percent Mexicans, 70 percent Puerto Ricans, and 80.1 percent Central and South Americans—fall above the poverty line, the problem lies in their lower wages and limited opportunities for upward mobility in comparison to the non-Latina/o white population (U.S. Bureau of the Census, 1999c).

In 1998 only 25.8 percent of the Mexican population, 38.8 percent of Puerto Ricans, and 30 percent of Central and South Americans earned

$25,000 or more. Almost 50 percent of the non-Latina/o population and almost 45 percent of Cubans earned in that range. Among Mexicans and Central Americans, first-generation migrants are younger and have fewer marketable skills. In part, however, the income discrepancy can be explained in terms of lower levels of education, especially among first-generation migrants. Of foreign-born Mexicans twenty-five years and over, more than 50 percent had less than a ninth-grade education; 25 percent of Central Americans and only 14.1 percent of "Caribbean" populations fell into this category (U.S. Bureau of the Census, 1997a). Younger workers will also earn less, and, as we have seen, a greater proportion of the Latina/o population is under eighteen than in the general non-Latino white population where the figure is 25.3 percent (U.S. Bureau of the Census, 1999c). Thus age, education, and foreign birth all affect income.

If these phenomena were limited to the first generation of migrants, then this income disparity could be understood as a temporary condition that would improve over time. Paradoxically, however, some age groups of third- or fourth-generation Mexicans acquire slightly less schooling than did their parents and thus are likely to earn less. Even more disturbing, while for Mexicans especially there is a direct relationship between educational attainment and income, recent studies indicate that this effect is no longer a certain pathway to higher income (Rumbaut, 1998: 17). In 1999, the median income for whites in California was $27,000 a year, (Lopez, Ramirez, and Rochin, 1999: 9). Asians were close behind, at $24,000, and African Americans at $23,000, but Latina/os, the largest minority group in California and largely of Mexican origin, had a median income of only $14,500. In many states, moreover, 76 percent of the Latina/o population has had no college education, compared with 49 percent of Anglos, and the dropout rate from secondary school is still at 50 percent (U.S. Bureau of the Census, 1997b).

Amazingly, these indicators of poverty, underemployment, and lack of educational opportunity among Latina/os coexist with increasing upward mobility. While there has been ample documentation of "elite" Mexicans and Latinos since the earliest communities were established, the rapid increase in the numbers of professional and managerial Latinos, particularly in the same instance as we have seen some of the most devastating poverty, is unique. This phenomenon, of course, is part of the much broader disparity between the very affluent and those earning low wages that has been especially characteristic of the way previously discussed in which communications and finances have created greater gaps.

Between 1975 and 1990 the numbers of Latina/os earning over $75,000 a year tripled, and the combined numbers earning $50,000 and $75,000 a year made up 20 percent of the Latina/o population (U.S. Department of Commerce, 1996: Tables 709, 729). The growth in this income sector is also apparent in their increased presence in universities, professional programs, and graduate programs. While the largest segment of the Latina/o population averaged fewer years of formal education between 1980 and 1990 than in previous decades, the numbers completing bachelor's degrees, master's degrees, and doctoral degrees increased (U.S. Department of Education, 1996: Tables 7, 202-203). What is particularly significant about this trend is that it represents not only the achievements of the second and third generation but also the migration of upper-income Mexicans and Central and South Americans encouraged by changes in immigration laws and by the increased flow of capital between these regions. In short, the changes in our economic climate have produced unprecedented prosperity for some and devastating poverty for many. The congregation of the population in the larger urban centers has produced "demographic pits"[13] whose inhabitants may have less hopeful futures than past generations.

Rumbaut and Cornelius (1995: 46-47) point to a negative association between length of residence in the United States and scholastic achievement and aspirations. They state that even though time in the United States is strongly associated with the acquisition of English language skills and should be a positively selective factor for educational attainment, in fact both longer residence and being born in the United States are correlated to reduced academic achievement and positive aspirations.

APPROACHES TO UNDERSTANDING

The Latina/o population will continue to grow, and Latina/o studies as an essential intellectual and policy enterprise within the academy must continue to grow with it. What has not been clear is how these very heterogeneous populations should be approached theoretically and methodologically. For example, we know that for Latina/os intermarriage is an important factor nationally, and the way in which Latina/o studies engage this phenomenon is important. Intermarriage between Puerto Ricans and non-Latina/o populations such as Anglos and African Americans accounts for at least 35.4 percent of marriages of Puerto Ricans. Another 9.7 percent intermarry with other Latina/o populations, and the remaining 55 percent marry other Puerto Ricans. For Mexican-origin populations, 28.3 percent intermarry with non-Latina/os while 2.3 percent marry other Latina/os so that almost 70 percent marry others of Mexican origin. Cubans marry other Cubans less frequently (63.2 percent), while 25.7 percent marry non-Latina/os. The remaining 11.1 percent marry other Latina/os: much higher than the Mexican rate, but only slightly higher than the Puerto Rican (U.S. Bureau of the Census, 1998).

However, even these rates may be deceiving and may change, depending on the actual physical location of the populations and the generations in question. A recent study conducted at Fordham sampled 21,000 New York

City marriage records and found that Cubans in New York marry out at much higher rates than do Puerto Ricans (Edmondson, 1996). It may be surmised that the higher intermarriage rate of Cubans with non-Latina/os in New York, which contrasts with the national figures, is due to significant demographic presence of other Cubans and Latina/os in areas such as Miami—especially Nicaraguans, Salvadorans, and, increasingly, Mexicans.

And what of the children of these intermarriages of all types? They account for almost 22 percent of the offspring due to intermarriage among the Mexican populations, 38.4 percent among Puerto Ricans and almost 37 percent among Cubans. Are these children to be considered, as some have suggested, as "hybrids," doubly rich, triply hyphenated, or ensconced within the general term of "Latino" or "Hispanic?" [14] Do the dense, cross-border households in the desert localities of the Southwest United States, such as Tucson—only 60 miles from the border—guarantee the continued Mexicanization of such offspring? The almost total integration of non-Mexican spouses into very dense Mexican social networks also argues against facile acculturation models of one-way movement from Mexican to "American" cultural assimilation (Vélez-Ibáñez, 1996: 149; see Cabán in this volume on the attempted forced assimilation of Puerto Ricans on the island).

Similarly, how do offspring born in New York of Puerto Rican and African American parents negotiate different cultural paths when they travel to Puerto Rico for their annual Christmas and summer visits? Here phenotypic heterogeneity is as common as an evening breeze from the ocean and similarly taken for granted. The rigidity of a group phenotypic classification based on the socially created notion of "race" in the United States is supplanted by a Puerto Rican ideology of hazy phenotypic individual differences between persons in which group stereotype is deemphasized and individual variation is noted. This group-versus-individual premise creates a very different dynamic between individuals and eventually groups in the Puerto Rican case, even though Europeanized "whiteness" is viewed more positively than African "darkness." Yet this dynamic may be changing because of an even greater emphasis on phenotypic characteristics of groups with the recent migration of Dominicans to Puerto Rico, where they are subject to the same racist stereotypes from which Puerto Ricans suffer in the United States (Duany, 2000: 15-16).

Nevertheless, in the U.S. case all individuals, regardless of actual phenotypic characteristics, are regarded as "black" if they are known to have one "drop" of African ancestry.[15] Thus, individuals have to break down the group definition to move beyond white and black. For Puerto Rican/African American offspring born in the United States these dynamics assume profound emotional, cultural, and psychological importance in their various returns to Puerto Rico and the United States (see Cruz-Janzen in this volume on the development of "Latinegra" identity).

THEORETICAL VIEWS OF POWER, RELATIONSHIPS, PROCESS, SCRIPTS, AND CULTURE

These demographic discussions and ethnographic examples are of such salience and complexity that a more "processual" approach to the study of Latina/o communities is called for. By "processual" we mean focusing on unfolding historical relations between and within populations and within social fields and arenas that may be local, regional, national, and transnational without necessarily reducing the analysis to physical boundaries (see Rocco in this volume for an insightful critique of postmodernist theory for the remapping of Latina/os and Latina/o studies).

This more fluid approach focuses on central questions of contestation over physical, natural, and material resources, property, and goods between and within populations. From such contestation emerge important questions of the movement of capital, investment, expropriation, and the creation or diminution of labor or surplus value. These, in turn, strongly influence the power relations between populations at a variety of levels of human organization and determine the legitimacy and the character of the power associated with relations of gender, class, and ethnicity. As Wolf (1999: 66) has so eloquently stated the case, "Power is brought into play differently in the relational world of families, communities, regions, activity systems, institutions, nations, and between nations." This approach is event-centered and traces the decisions, maneuvers, resources, relationships, and constructs of cultures used at these various organizational levels, from the household to the transnational setting, and the manner in which these unfold within the gender, class, and ethnic relations of power (Vélez-Ibáñez, 1983a: 9; see Sampaio in this volume for an extended discussion of the often complex and at times difficult relations between transnational political policies and national political borders and Oboler for discussion of class differentiation among Latina/os).

THE DEVELOPMENT OF CULTURAL SCRIPTS AND MEGASCRIPTS AND THEIR TRADITIONAL COUNTERPARTS

Such power relations, however, need to be articulated and legitimated through structured references, recognition, symbols, rituals, practices, and expectations. Schools and institutions of many sorts, communications, media, and supralocal juridical, legislative, and executive corporate networks and nodes provide central and created "cultural scripts" for each of the dimensions cited by Wolf, and where appropriation is greatest such cultural scripts are often contested, negotiated, or rejected (see Nájera-Ramírez in this volume for an analysis of the "traditional" cultural form of the *charreada* as a mode of resistance to imposed "cultural scripts"), but also often assimilated and accepted as true and "natural." Each of these potential temporary conclusions may reinforce, reproduce, eliminate, and/or partially support the relationships of power at each organizational level, between levels, and between and among relations of gender, class, and ethnicity. This is, however, an ongoing process for the simple reason that human populations are not automatons but agents that often reject and internalize their subordination in the "name" of something else such as the "nation," "General Motors," "Jesus," "the doctor," or "father."

These scripts underwrite local, institutional, or transnational relations of power and economy by seeming to cohere between the most abstract order of organization, such as the transnational corporation, and the local household, and correspond to the "appropriate" definitions of the relations of gender, class, and ethnicity. Over time, these scripts become "megascripts" at the most centralized and powerful levels—nations, transnational entities such as the World Trade Organization, and international bodies such as OPEC. Versions of these megascripts are distributed to varying degrees of success, through the means described above. (See Part II for further development of the "megascript").

When coherence breaks down because of the resistance, negotiation, or rebellion expressed by the concerned populations, a reordering of the status quo will emerge. However, such reordering probably will not "cohere," given the simple contradictions that emerge as accommodations are offered, resolutions attempted, and satisfaction temporarily found. (See Pérez in this volume for a discussion of the apparent contradictions of cultural understanding in Chicago that are, in fact, transnational constructions that speak to the seeming "incoherence" of various cultural scripts).

Used in this way, "culture" has a much more dynamic meaning than the common definitional sense, as the following section illustrates. The word "script" allows for an interactive and changing process that involves both agency and internalization, both resistance and accommodation in the same space and place. Which of these factors are more or less influential is often an empirical question.

But how does "culture" as a heuristic device fit critically within this processual approach? For many Latina/o scholars this central question has to be answered from a historical point of view. In fact, "culture" continues to be a focus of contention with regard to its analytical usefulness and its capacity for outlining the various shapes of identity and reference.

The traditional focus on culture often relied on an assumption of unchanging essential characteristics of "a" culture that induced people to follow traditional practices like some sort of frozen road map. This "culturological" approach often reduced Latina/o populations to simple caricatures following patterns of familism, extended kinship, male domination, religiosity, present-time orientation, linguistic conservatism, and a provincialism that did not allow for interaction across "ethnic boundaries" (Vélez-Ibáñez, 1983: 9-10).[16] Homogeneity was the hallmark of culture in this approach (see Oboler in this volume for a fresh theoretical point of view on ethnicity, culture, and identity).

In the United States especially, the underlying text was that immigrant populations were "un-American," and educational institutions were mandated to force them to abandon their "traditional" characteristics and values. Assimilation was the assumption that rationalized such a shift. This idea was strongly embedded in U.S. political and policy premises and was in fact part of the folklore whereby all foreign cultural groups eventually became part of the mainstream. This national cultural prism was expressed in the English language, nucleated family systems, achievement motivation, individualism, Protestantism, representative democracy, and covertly and overtly preferred group phenotypes. Without any reference to relations of power between "traditional" Latina/o groups and the mainstream, the preferred groups were expected to achieve closure on their historical cultural orientations by being erased.

THE EMERGENCE OF A LATINA/O CRITIQUE

For many Latina/os this utopian assimilationist view was either theoretically questionable or empirically unsatisfying.[17] A number of anthropological and culturologically oriented works of the 1960s became special targets, concerned as they were with "traditional" Mexican values, ideas, and behaviors, the "culture of poverty," present-time orientation, lack of delayed gratification, and a cultural propensity for criminal behavior.[18]

Julian Samora and Patricia Vandel Simon (1977), Octavio Romano (1968), and Nick Vaca (1970a; 1970b) laid out the deficiencies of anthropology and the social sciences in terms of their underlying epistemological and logical formulae. They pointed to issues of ahistoricism and the lack of validity and replicability of many social science studies, and Romano especially was highly critical of one-shot, one-year, bounded and encapsulated "community" studies displaying an "as if" present of unchanging behaviors attributable to "culture."

One aspect of these early critiques was an insistence on more rigid systematic fieldwork, including attention to representativeness, sampling, and an eye to either a grounded theory or some broader theoretical framework within which to understand the specificity of what we wanted to examine. What Latina/o critics questioned was not the nomothetic model, but its inappropriate application or lack of application, resulting in timeless, synchronic, and bounded renditions of Mexican populations. Failure to appreciate power and coherence was particularly questioned, and Vine Deloria's

Custer Died for Your Sins: An Indian Manifesto (1969) was very important for many. Similarly, Margaret Mead's debate with James Baldwin in *A Rap on Race* (1971) crystallized aspects of African American–Anglo relations, but it especially laid out the limits of traditional thinking about culture and questions of cultural relativity and its lack of recognition of the power of subordinate/superordinate relations.

For many Latina/o graduate students in the early 1970s, a "Latina/o" filter sought out analytical processes rather than things; understanding relationships and connections rather than boundaries and looking from the inside out rather than from the top down became part of the operating procedure in the social sciences. As Diego Vigil and Robert Alvarez (personal communications, June 27 and December 15, 1997)[19] have pointed out, this array in part emerged from aspects of recalled daily experience. Put simply, many had not assimilated as was expected, and cross-border and cross-water connections with kin in Mexico, Puerto Rico, and other parts of Latin America remained significant.

These critiques coincided with others in Puerto Rican studies, Mexican American studies, Chicano studies, and Latino studies in the 1970s. They attempted to unpack the multilayered political and cultural impositions on these populations by institutions and communication media from books to film. These "cohering" institutions themselves were part of broader structural processes that seemed to be worldwide and were considered as "colonial" projects. International political conditions in Africa, Latin America, the Caribbean, and Asia had spawned various movements in pursuit of freedom from foreign economic and political domination or repressive national governments. Cuba served as the model for both kinds of movements, and in the infancy of that revolution many in Latin America and some Latina/os in the United States felt an admiration if not adoration for its leadership. Puerto Ricans had fought for national status since the "Grito de Lares" in the nineteenth century against Spain, and in the same century the anticolonial struggle was renewed against the United States. Various Puerto Rican political movements that antedated the Cuban Revolution served as background for the political and academic assertions of Puerto Ricans in the United States. As early as 1936 more than ten thousand Puerto Ricans in New York marched for Puerto Rican independence (see Cabán in this volume on U.S. colonialism in Puerto Rico).

Many Puerto Rican intellectuals and academics in the United States regarded themselves as subject to a type of "internal colonialism," especially with regard to language loss, cultural assimilation, and economic exploitation. Internal colonialism was considered an analogue of international colonialism in which territory, population, and material resources were controlled by force and the metropolis was the controlling colonial power. In the case of Puerto Ricans, the island was the colonized entity and most forms of production were in the hands of colonial agents or their surrogates. Puerto Ricans in New York were basically fleeing to the metropolis as the direct consequence of these colonial relations, and these relations were partially duplicated in the city in the sense that Puerto Ricans were concentrated in particular areas such as the Bronx and political and economic control was in the hands of non-Puerto Ricans or their surrogates. The resulting poverty, undereducation, overrepresentation in the underground economy, unhealthful living conditions, and identity crises were predictable consequences. In an interesting manner, this model echoes our transnational model of analysis in insisting that the structural conditions of the migrating populations in their points of origin are duplicated in their new place of residence.

In the United States, especially on the eastern seaboard, Puerto Ricans struggled for independence as well, but for many experiencing U.S. forms of racism and cultural discrimination it gave a different cast to their analytical frameworks. For many Puerto Ricans racial, ethnic, and class stratification became an important urban condition along with freedom from an oppressive rural existence on the island. Other Puerto Ricans who joined the agricultural migrant stream for higher wages in Florida and followed the crop road to New Jersey during the 1940s and early 1950s became simply migrant statistics rather than part of a problem to be solved because of their origin. However, since the vast majority of Puerto Ricans after 1950 congregated in New York City, job discrimination, political underrepresentation, and poor education became central to the political and intellectual interests of Puerto Ricans in the city with an eye to the independence movements on the island.

For Mexicans, three different historical processes/events created the present border between Mexico and the United States and the related phenomena of Mexicans crossing and recrossing it. The first was the 1836 revolt of Texans against Mexico, with the annexation of Texas by the United States ten years later. The second was the Mexican War of 1846–1848, in which the United States invaded Mexico and eventually forcibly incorporated parts of Colorado, New Mexico, and California into its territory. The third was the Gadsden Purchase of 1853, whereby land in southern Arizona was purchased from Mexico by the United States. While it seemed on the surface to be a voluntary sale, it was preceded by unmistakable indications that there would be unpleasant consequences for Mexico if the transaction were not consummated (Park, 1961: 27). Given these historical events and almost two hundred years of asymmetrical synergy between Mexico and the United States in labor, land, and economy, Mexican scholars of the United States equally embraced much of the colonial model, slightly revamped as "internal colonialism."[20] Associated with this model were issues of land loss, mythic origins, and borderlands identities as well as the central issues of job discrimination, undereducation, poor housing, low wages, and poor health.

By the 1980s the idea of "internal colonialism" had been supplanted by others. Among the most important intellectual developments in social science devoted to Latina/o issues was the theorizing resulting from the formation of the Inter-University Program for Latino Research in the early 1980s. By 1993 the program was calling for a serious questioning of the capacity of the social sciences to meet the myriad needs and issues concerning the Latina/o population on opposite coasts of the United States. Almost at the same time, Bonilla (1998) points out the Gulbenkian Foundation found the social sciences to be floundering without direction and confined to small academic niches of questionable relevance. Dissatisfaction led to a very extended discussion of theoretical approaches that might move beyond the traditional culturological, assimilationist, functionalist, and other utopian versions. Bonilla (1998: ix) underscores four major areas emphasized in the various discussions and conferences on the topic:

> the emergent forms of global and transnational interdependence; the negative impact and demographic repercussions within the United States, especially in Latino communities, of economic and political restructuring; changing concepts of and social bases for community formation, citizenship, political participation, and human rights as individuals are obliged to construct identities in more than one sociopolitical setting; and fresh pathways into international relations and issue-oriented social movements and organizations among these highly mobile populations.

Yet there are also elements of transnational theory to which the contributions to this volume are attentive. It is obvious that broad interdependent binational, transnational, and global questions have become an important part of the conversation regarding Latina/os and Latin Americans. This emerges from the understanding that a new economic hegemony was created in the late twentieth century in which the United States is a central player and in which the production of goods and need for services and labor are part of an exchange system between parts of Latin America and the United States. In fact, this exchange relationship is an interdependent one in which inequality in one nation is replicated and created by an international market in the other. According to Pastor (1998: 18), "The inequality that faces both Latin Americans and Latinos, particularly urban residents, is partly the result of internationally induced economic restructuring. In this sense, integration into global economies has had uneven effects for both Latin and Latino Americans." These include the exporting of Fordist technology, bottling up technological innovation in Latin America and "re- and deindustrialization" in urban centers in the United States with a concomitant overcapitalization of finance and communication ventures (see Pastor, 1998: 18-20; Vélez-Ibáñez, n.d.; see also Zamudio in this volume suggesting that these new socioeconomic formations require a rethinking of both labor theory and specific strategies and organizing tactics).

As Pastor (1998: 20) states the case, "The poor of Latin America meet with poor Latinos in the same place and space." These transnational dynamics require different ways of thinking about Latina/os in the United States, employing cultural frameworks that concentrate on coherence, stasis, reproduction, and essential cultural understandings of difference (see Zavella in this volume on the transnational aspects of gendered relations of work in the food-packing industry and the impact of globalization on Mexican women in both the United States and Mexico).

REEXAMINING TRANSNATIONAL POLITICS, PROCESSES, AND CULTURES

Bonilla's excellent guide and Pastor's suggestions for new theoretical approaches have so far been taken up only in part. Much of the transnational approach has focused on migration (Basch, Szanton-Blank, and Glick Schiller, 1994; Guarnizo and Smith, 1998; Kearney, 1991; 1995; Ong and Nonini, 1997; Rouse, 1989; 1991). It has also emphasized the cultural production that emerges in transnational space and the exchange of material goods and symbolic representations (Gupta, 1992; Marcus, 1995). An important part of this focus is the manner in which voluntary associations, social movements, and political protest and organizations have filled the newly created transnational or "hyperspace" (Kearney, 1995). For the most part these works have concentrated on the creation of political identities in such settings and conflated these with the social identities of the actors. This conflation has left out the nonparticipants and the daily created and negotiated hyperspaces in which persons must attend on a daily basis to household provisioning, establishing stable social platforms for the next generation, and negotiating with institutional, work, and service realities. For the most part, those left out are women, men, and children who must constantly reorganize themselves in unstable hyperspaces and often rely on tested methods of reducing the indeterminacy typical of such contexts. The contributions to this volume in part attend to these nonparticipants.

We come away with a conviction that no matter how globalization processes unfold, local-level formations are not just reproductions but contestations, negotiations, and adaptations that are not reducible to a single theoretical construct—materialist, symbolic, or empirical. To use a more current phrase: most local-level niches operate in fields characterized by routine struggles between "prosaic state force and economic grand structures and networked defiance" (Heyman, 1998: 51). The latter may be represented by political organizations in struggles for simple amenities like water, electricity, and sewerage systems in New Mexico, by economic practices such as the rotating credit associations called *tandas,* largely in the hands of women,[21] by extended modular households that build and create entire communities from nothing, by networks of Latinas confronting educational authorities throughout the United States in pursuit of quality education, by the creation of new art forms and the replication of traditional ones, and by the creation of funds of knowledge vital to the development of hearth and home.

Heyman (1994: 51) argues that large-scale national and international political and economic institutions help create cultural niches and modes of action that strengthen transnational existences, as they appear in localized arenas and develop cultural places and spaces where they should not exist. Thus in some of the *colonias* of the Southwest, almost a third of households are engaged in a "niche" underground economy in which relatives are recruited from their places of origin and distributed to labor contractors all the way to Kansas, Mississippi, Alabama, and Arkansas. The cost to relatives for this service is a third that charged to others, and the migrants themselves feel safety within the kinship relations that make their transnational transport possible. This niche economy operates only a few miles from strict border control checkpoints and the sources of constant institutional observation and intervention. Needless to say, the underlying cultural bases for social relations are being extended from the central Mexican states in which workers are recruited to the *colonias* and on to the agricultural and animal production sites in the Plains, the Southeast, and the Midwest (Vélez-Ibáñez et al., n.d.).

These practices are part of much larger cultural nexuses too often dismissed as unimportant, exotic behaviors rather than being seen as forms that speak to the very basis of a human and social identity. These are, in fact, locally derived scripts that often oppose those created by educational and political institutions. They may develop from transnational localities, and the medium of transmission may vary from extended transnational households to voluntary associations and from cross-border rotating credit associations to the underground networks just described.[22]

At the local level these scripts encompass physical and cultural spaces the content of which ranges from the colors used to paint a home to the recreational, ritual, and familial sites selected for use, enhancements, and change. And while the example may seem trivial, in fact such declarations of space use may create community upheavals when the new spatial and perceptual definitions introduced are not based on the proper "ethnic community" script. One of us painted his home a Mexican pink in the midst of the placid gray-blues and pastel hues of the surrounding homes and replaced the perfectly groomed grass with unpatterned red, purple, and yellow flowers and a Mexican colonial fountain.[23] The resulting upheaval generated a series of newspaper articles and letters to the editor, one of which declared that the city in Southern California where the controversy took place was not "Mexico or Spain." Ironically, Juan Bautista de Anza in 1776 had passed through the area on his way to found the settlement and presidio of San Francisco, and his trail is marked by a number of street and place-names in his honor.

These phenomena contradict the very basis for geographically derived statuses such as citizenship, nationality, cultural identities, spatial and perceptual definitions, and political borders. This last generates political issues such as what constitutes representative governance, individual rights, legal protection, and collective organizing and, most importantly, contradicts the right to be governed by national entities based on geographically defined constructs. Such constructs do not conform to the social and cultural reality of many of the populations discussed in this volume.

The processual method helps provide the means to trace the various dimensions of such phenomena and engage multiple theoretical pathways. In this volume, the contributors adopt a number of different theoretical points of view, but this method guides even the most theoretically oriented discussions. The emphasis is on process rather than on traditional theoretical constructs.

TRADITIONAL ANALYTICAL FRAMES

The traditional analysis that focuses on acculturation as measured by language change, cultural identity, and social relations simply reproduces frameworks tied to a national ideology of monoculturalism and assimilation which is the analogue of the ideological conviction of nationalism. Such traditional approaches fail to consider the bidirectionality of cultural processes, the creation of localized and regional cultural and linguistic forms, the emergence of multidimensional social identities based on class, intermarriage, and binationalism, and the development of localized scripts and localities in the midst of institutional and national repressive policies, actions, and megascripts.

Similarly, a strictly materialist approach that accentuates the totalizing force of capitalism of Latina/o populations is insufficiently supported. While world capitalism does in fact tend toward the flattening out of cultural systems into analogues of itself, localities, communities, and networks of niches simply are not erased. This approach clearly provides useful analytical tools, especially in relation to the devaluing of labor value and the asymmetry of class relations, but it overlooks the amazing ability of populations to deal with the destructive effects of globalizing economies and their various "distributions of sadness" (Vélez-Ibáñez, 1996: 182-206): the statistical overrepresentation in low-paid jobs, prisons, and jails, high-risk behaviors such as gang membership and drug use, specific mental and physical health disorders and problems, and even war. For the most part, this approach fails to test the limits of human creativity and to recognize the reality of agency and of consistent cultural reformulation and contestation.

As Leacock and Lee (1982: 6-7) have pointed out,

> The materialist approach's invaluable contribution is that Marxist methodology resolves the conflict between generalizing and particularizing emphases, for it both enables fine-grained analyses of underlying determinant relations in specific instances and articulates these analyses with a comprehensive general theory of human history.
>
> While committed to the importance of historical and cultural specificity, a dialectical and historical-materialist approach requires the search for underlying regularities or "laws." While committed to the significance of social cohesion, the approach calls for definition of the basic disharmonies, conflicts, or "contradictions" within socio-economic structures that impel change.

The Marxist approach often fails to attend to agency and resistance as well as accommodation within these broader socioeconomic structures. While it seeks out underlying relations in specific instances, it incompletely recognizes innovation and creativity in the process, often failing to acknowledge the tendency to create social and cultural places and spaces in spite of determinant relations. Its emphasis on changes in class formations as globalizing and transnational processes that collect more and more adherents to the megascripts of unmatched wealth and consumerism is, however, an invaluable intellectual and theoretical tool. Examining class relations in the abstract and in the empirical world simultaneously, it reveals details of these processes without which history becomes only the telling of one script after another. Accompanied by the processual method, class analysis not only reveals the myriad scripts that rationalize the basic relations of power and value among different populations but also pinpoints the loci of power, the strategies of contestation that need to be developed, and the probable outcomes of these strategies.

Yet a materialist approach that focuses only on class relations often fails to deal with the realities of the "naturalizing" processes that affect gender and cultural scripts. It does not contend with the power relations between populations and within the same population that reproduce sexism and subordination of women to men. Both gender and cultural relations are more than class. The naturalizing processes whereby the exploitation of women or of Mexicans as commodities is made acceptable originate in subtle and even unspoken messages and behaviors that are not reducible to class expectations. A rigorous processually oriented analysis can capture these messages and render a much more accurate account of the relations of power and their genesis.

Somewhat similar to the materialist approach, but lacking its dynamic theoretical machinery concerning the creation of labor value, is a "structural" approach that defines ethnicity as an artifact of labor market integration and residential proximity. From this sociological "structural" point of view, there is a direct relationship between immigration history, the availability of wages, spatial context, technology, and the structure of the organization of production and the emergence of ethnicity (Nelson and Tienda, 1997: 9). Residential isolation and participation in segmented labor leads to interaction and the creation of cultural bonds, relationships, and finally ethnic identity in the same residential area. As Yancey, Erikson, and Juliani (1976: 392) put it, "Ethnicity may have relatively little to do with Europe, Asia, or Africa, but much more to do with the requirements of survival and the structure of opportunity in this country."

This point of view, although partially supported by empirical data, is in the present transnational period only partly explanatory. It fails to recognize the importance of the reality of often-crossed political borders, cross-border households, intensive informal and underground economies, and networks and webs of migration and relations that occupy spaces and places that are in fact borderless, nonresidential, and, because of communications and rapid travel, almost simultaneous. These both maintain linguistic and cultural knowledge and create new versions of both, such as augmented Hispanicized English and Americanized Spanish.

The limitations of this structural approach are in part epistemologically associated with the assimilationist model, which ultimately erases "ethnic" populations by equating proximity of residence and labor market participation with cultural and social relations. It seems to suggest that by a change in the labor market and residential moves out of their neighborhoods, these populations will come to be characterized by nucleated households, frequent divorce, few children, and monolingualism. In fact, such erasure does not have to occur, despite the elimination of "structural" factors. There are countless examples of Latina/o populations in the United States maintaining long-distance social relations by travel, communication via the Internet, visits, and sojourner and circular migration. The creation of Latina/o studies programs and the explosion of creative literature and art over the past thirty-five years contradict this view.[24] The contributions to this volume stress an understanding of culture and ethnicity not merely as an artifact of place and pay but as the result of populations' contesting the impacts of economic globalization and the structural impediments created by monolingual schooling, misrepresentations in the media, the commoditization of identity, and an emphasis on a one-dimensional "ethnic" identity.

Among the most promising theoretical points of view for understanding Latina/os is the postmodernist model, which has contributed to a strong analytical emphasis on multiculturalism and multidimensional forms of analysis including such constructs as critical race theory.[25] As Rocco (this volume) asserts, critical race theory critiques notions of progress and points out that Western ideas of inclusion have depended on the exclusion of marginalized peoples. The premise of Western ideas of mobility, advancement, economic betterment, and the eventual elimination of class by the efforts of a few creates the basis for the exploitation of populations defined as lazy, as commodities, or as cheap labor or assigned to subordinate positions because of presumed intellectual and social limitations. The postmodernist critique would suggest that processes such as class mobility guarantee inequality and marginalization. The state creates the institutional means by which this process is made possible and guarantees a stratified society. Yet the postmodernist approach largely precludes any extended understanding of class conflict, the relations of such conflict to the massive accumulation of wealth, and people's inventiveness, creativity, and sheer determination. It largely fails to provide a substantiated analysis of the way in which Latina/os must negotiate, contradict, and sometimes overcome their overrepresentation in the distribution of sadnesses.

The contributions to this volume strongly suggest that these approaches must be informed by the broad questions of transnational economy that basically undermine national theories of culture, society, polity, and economy. At the same time, they must attend to the manner in which affected populations manage the formal, informal, and underground economies, and therefore contestation, negotiation, and local invention and practice must also become part of Latina/o studies. No single theoretical venture can be successful in the midst of the constant movement of populations and resources and the rapid changes in cultural scripts based on localized actions and behaviors of persons tied to each other by short- and long-term relations and interests. We suggest that the analytical "glue" that is most helpful for integrating an array of analytical tools and theories is a processual approach coupled with a class analysis in which human actions and behaviors are assumed not to follow any predetermined course and not to lead to any obvious solution.

ORGANIZATION OF THE VOLUME

The volume has three parts: Part I, "Reconceptualizing Latina/o Studies and the Study of Latina/o Subjects," Part II, "Cultural Processes and Changing Forms of Ethnic Identity," and Part III, "Transforming Work, Labor, Community, and Citizenship." Each part is provided with an introductory guide to the chapters in the book.

In part I, Anna Sampaio's "Transforming Chicana/o and Latina/o Politics: Globalization and the Formulation of Transnational Resistance in the United States and Chiapas" is a significant example of the manner in which the processual approach handles the difficult analytical relations between transnational political policies designed for economic unification and their impacts on national political borders. These impacts lead to a reconfiguration of the idea of traditional national citizenship, the development of understandings dealing with the creation of transnational localities, and the disturbance of coherent cultural scripts at local, regional, national, and transnational levels. This fluidity creates a need for attention to the multidirectionality of transnational cultural scripts in which borders at best are something to cross.

Suzanne Oboler's "The Politics of Labeling: Latino/a Cultural Identities of Self and Others" focuses on the emergent processual properties of identity among Latina/os. She describes the way in which class and race background shape the meaning and social value that individuals attribute to self-identifying terms and points out that the relationship between Latina/os and others is central to their identity and ethos. Identity, she says, echoing Stuart Hall, is emergent and always in relation to multiple versions of self, regardless of the homogenizing effect of "Americanization."

Raymond A. Rocco's "Reframing Postmodernist Constructions of Difference: Subaltern Spaces, Power, and Citizenship" argues that in transnational contexts coherence at many levels may become so fluid that new conceptualizations are needed to capture the dynamics of the situation. More important, he broadens the scope of the discourse on citizenship to include the experiences of immigrants as central to the process of defining (and redefining) Latina/o communities and civil society. His examination of the ongoing tensions between Latina/os and newly arrived Latin Americans is equally significant because it reveals the changing boundaries and definitions of the United States and Latin America and the changing roles of occupants of both of these spaces.

In part II, Pedro Cabán's "The Colonizing Mission of the United States in Puerto Rico, 1898-1930" is a historical analysis of attempts at the Americanization of Puerto Rico and the role in these efforts of an underlying national script designed to provide an amenable and pliable population for capitalist expansion and use. This thirty-two-year-long process, which combined major "cohering" U.S. institutions including the Department of Education, the Interior Department, and the Office of the Attorney General, imposed legal, juridical, educational, labor, and social models leading to Americanization throughout the island in an exact copy of the Spanish colonization of five hundred years before. However, this imposition created the basis for its own contradiction: the development of Puerto Rican nationalism and cultural identity.

Marta Cruz-Jansen's "Ethnic Identity and Racial Formations: Race and Racism American-Style and *a lo latino*" begins from a multiracial and multiethnic position to describe the formation of Latina/o identities in the United States and links contemporary Latina/os with the history of race and ethnicity in Latin America. Ultimately, however, Cruz-Jansen's strongest contribution is her unfolding processual testimonial as a *Latinegra*, a Latina whose racial heritage is largely African. This perspective goes a long way toward producing a fresh multidimensional understanding of Latina/os in the United States and introduces a complex, processual and dialectical discussion of race, class, and ethnicity that explains the multidimensionality of this population.

Olga Nájera-Ramírez's "Haciendo patria: The *charreada* and the Formation of a Mexican Transnational Identity" examines the Mexican rodeo as a
means of *haciendo cultura y patria* among Mexicans on both sides of the
border. Although the physical properties of this performance are similar in
Mexico and the United States, Nájera-Ramírez points to its different meanings
for these two populations, paying particular attention to the way in which it
constitutes a form of oppositional politics in the United States. Using ethno-
graphics and historical data, she demonstrates that the *charreada*'s performance in the United States becomes a political gesture aimed at constructing a
viable social space for expression and valorizing Mexican identity in the face
of contemporary anti-Mexican discourse. Her work is significant in that it sit-
uates this process in the larger context of shifting cultural commodities in
global capital that dissolve the boundaries between Mexicans and Mexican
Americans and contribute to the traffic of people and processes as well as
culture and ideas.

Gina M. Pérez's "'*La tierra*'s Always Perceived as Woman': Imagining Urban Communities in Chicago's Puerto Rican Community" uses multidimensional methods of exposition to show how "traditional" scripts that reflect a
mythic rural existence in Puerto Rico are used in the mobilization of ideas
concerning hearth, home, and culture and in the gendered definition of "cultural work" in response to the large-scale Mexicanization of Chicago, resistance to Americanization, and the refashioning of important links to an imagined and real motherland.

In part III, "Transforming Work, Labor, Community, and Citizenship," Margaret Zamudio's "Segmentation, Conflict, Community, and Coalitions:
Lessons from the New Labor Movement" examines the condition of Latina/o
workers in the context of the restructuring of the U.S. economy. Except for
the United Farm Workers, no labor union in recent history has been as successful in appealing to and organizing Latina/o workers as Local 11 of the
Hotel Employees' and Restaurant Employees' Union, an organization whose
work is highlighted in her case study of labor practices at Los Angeles's New
Otani Hotel. She makes excellent use of ethnographic data to preserve the
voices of her subjects, and her opposition to more orthodox readings of segmented labor market theory is processually analyzed and effectively coun-
ters the traditional interpretation of racial/ethnic issues as merely epiphenomenal to the structure of occupational segmentation. Her approach opens
up opportunities for reexamining how race, racism, and racial identities inform aspects of working life from employers' hiring, promotion, and assignment practices to the possibilities for interethnic and interracial coalitions
among workers themselves.

Patricia Zavella's "Engendering Transnationalism in Food Processing: Peripheral Vision on Both Sides of the U.S.-Mexican Border" examines the
class, ethnic, regional, and engendered dynamics encountered by Mexican

food-processing workers in Watsonville, California, and Irapuato, Mexico. She highlights the gendered dimensions of work in the food-packing industry and the impact of increasing globalization (and especially the relocation of one major food-processing employer in Watsonville) on Mexican women in the United States and Mexico. Finally, she examines the ways in which workers have adapted to and overcome the obstacles created by deterritorialization through the formations of transnational communities that escape the boundaries of the new capitalist order.

Juan Vicente Palerm's "Immigrant and Migrant Farmworkers in the Santa Maria Valley" offers an important analysis of the reintensification of California agribusiness and its effect on the new farmworker communities emerging throughout the rural portion of the state. In particular, Palerm demonstrates the need to retheorize rural farmworking communities processually in light of changing trends in the economy of agriculture and the resulting changes in the settlement patterns and practices of this population. His contribution ties the actual energy and labor needs of changes in production strategies to the need for more labor resources and points out that the recruitment of such labor is not accompanied by the provision of appropriate housing, familial support, and security.

Raymond A. Rocco's "Citizenship, Civil Society, and the Latina/o City" examines the convergence of race, class, and culture in a discussion of the nature of citizenship in light of the emergence of new immigrants and new political/economic formations. Specifically, Rocco offers a critique of the burgeoning literature on citizenship, noting its fascination with globalization and multiculturalism as new constructs of citizenship and its failure to examine the institutional nature of these processes. He maintains that while class and the distribution of capital are still fundamental to our understandings of globalization, current political and social theorists have not appreciated the way in which the nature of class itself has been altered and therefore undervalue issues such as immigration and ethnicity. He also points out that to the extent that immigration and ethnicity have been theorized within a global framework, it has tended to be as forms of "otherness" rather than as globalized elements with their own local manifestations. To address this problem, which he sees as an obstacle to theory building around the citizenship or civic practices of emerging Latina/o communities in Los Angeles, he explores theories of civil society that promote new explorations of citizenship and redefines the discourse of contemporary political participation as emergent and processual. He supports his assessments with case studies of Latina/o associational organizations in Southeast Los Angeles.

The final argument points out the limitations of past understandings that have not benefited from processual analysis. Alternative methodologies are recommended that link human identities and power and economic relations to broader processes but recognize that the local and the supralocal are intimately linked and populations must negotiate these creatively. Local-level niches and the scripts produced are not necessarily carbon copies of those that have induced their emergence; experimentation and originality constantly intervene in their creation.

NOTES

1. Melanin content is merely the selective phenotypic trait most generally thought to confer an evolutionary advantage. The positive adaptive qualities of more or less melanin are associated with latitudes according to intensity of sunlight with darker skin protecting against the damage of sunlight and lighter skin absorbing the sunlight needed for the synthesis of vitamin D. In Europe, the farther south one goes, the greater the melanin. In North Africa, melanin intensity also increases as one moves south, reaching its maximum at the equator. The same process holds in Asia, with color hues in southern India matching those of equatorial Africa (see Rensberger, 1994). Children with more melanin in higher latitudes had the probability of developing rickets—a bone-deforming disease caused by a lack of vitamin D—before fortified milk was available.

2. The justification for the Spanish caste system was highly problematic to begin with, especially given Spain's seven hundred years of Moorish occupation, the heterogeneous origins of inhabitants of the Iberian Peninsula, and the fact that no such system can remain in force for long. There is simply no justification of any sort for any racialist stratified system.

3. This paragraph is partly a compression of data and historical information found in Gonzalez (2000: 117-148).

4. The speed of electronic communication is itself the consequence of enormous capital investment.

5. Therrien and Ramirez, 2000; U.S. Bureau of the Census, 2000a. "Hispanic" is the census designation for any person of Spanish-speaking origin whether from Latin America, the Caribbean, or Spain.

6. U.S. Bureau of the Census, 2000a; 2000b. We have substituted "Latina/o" for "Hispanic."

7. This description is based on fieldwork conducted by Vélez-Ibáñez in five *colonias* in a Southwestern state on the Mexican-U.S. border. The word *colonia* has a legal definition in Mexico and the United States, but for the latter it refers to a settlement situated within fifty miles of the U.S.-Mexican border that is characterized by low-cost land, nonexistent infrastructure, mostly modular housing that is locally or familially constructed, and an absence of roads, schools, fire protection, health facilities, and police. The *colonia* in Mexico and in Mexican neighborhoods in the United States is a locality primarily composed of Mexican or Spanish-speaking populations that may or not have the characteristics just listed. Thus the Colonia Chapultepec in Mexico City probably has more millionaires per capita than any other part of Latin America and would not fit the appropriated U.S. term. The appropriation of the term in the United States by federal authorities has served a number of economic and po-

litical interests, especially in already established townships that suffered lack of infrastructure and redefined themselves according to the federal definition.

8. This percentage is an estimate based on fieldwork conducted by Vélez-Ibáñez between 1998 and 2001.

9. In a work in press (Vélez-Ibáñez, Nunez, and Rissolo, 2002) Vélez-Ibáñez will argue that these processes are possible only in a highly segregated labor market.

10. Many of these traditional cities were founded in different historical periods as the Spanish colonies expanded from Mexico beginning in the sixteenth century. Santa Fe, for example, was founded in 1610, three years after Jamestown, and Albuquerque one hundred years later. San Antonio was founded in 1731, San Diego as a garrison, in 1769, Tucson and San Francisco in 1776, and Los Angeles in 1781.

11. Mexicans have always preferred to settle in the Southwest and since 1960 have especially settled in urban areas. In 1910 only 5.7 percent of the population of Mexican origin lived outside of the Southwest. By 1960, however, this figure had increased to 12.8 percent, and in 1990 it was 16.4 percent. Illinois has been the preferred state outside of the Southwest for the past twenty-five years (see Grebler, Moore, and Guzmán, 1970: 112; Bean and Tienda, 1987: 80; U.S. Bureau of the Census, 1990). Of over 20 million persons of Mexican origin in 2000, over 15 million live in the five Southwestern states of Arizona, California, Nevada, New Mexico, and Texas. Over 1 million Mexican-origin persons reside in Illinois, while the rest are distributed over the entire U.S., with Vermont attracting the lowest number (U.S. Bureau of the Census, 2000b).

12. How much undocumented migration accounts for a depression of wages is not known for this sector.

13. "Demographic pits" is a metaphor for dense urban settlements to which Mexican and Latina/o migrants have concentrated as a result of the deindustrialization/ reindustrialization process. High employment, low wages, and minimal job security characterize the labor sectors in these areas, while poor housing, decaying institutions, limited transportation, and high levels of personal safety result from their high density. See Vélez-Ibáñez, "'The Border Crossed Us and We Cross the Border': The Emergence of the Commoditization and Devalorization of the Mexican Population of the Southwest United States," in press.

14. Conceptually the notions of race, nationality, and ethnicity are problematic since all such categories are historical, social, political, and economic constructions. Certainly the U.S. Census Bureau is finding its categories increasingly archaic.

15. The perennial confusion between biology and culture is prominent in this discussion. Sixteenth-century racialist ideologies promoted "purity of blood" as a means of establishing claims to inheritance. This often got mixed up with the cultural practices of different populations, with the result that indigenous populations of Africa, Asia, and the Americas were considered both biologically inferior and characterized by exotic cultural practices that were compared to devil worship. It followed that intermarriage or concubinage between European and indigenous populations would create offspring bearing the worst characteristics of both biology and culture.

16. At the same time, Steward et al. (1956) were attentive to cultural heterogeneity, class formation, and their relationship to the demands of international commodity markets and the global reorganization of productive relations.

17. Three paragraphs of this section appear in Vélez-Ibáñez (1998).

18. The educational literature in the 1960s and early 1970s took up the idea that Mexican children suffered from an inability to delay gratification and that Mexican culture was present-time oriented. The two constructs dovetailed nicely, since parents who cannot or will not plan for the future cannot save for a rainy day, and it follows that their children will be taught to gratify themselves immediately. Emerging from the anthropological works by Clyde Kluckhohn on New Mexican villages and George Foster's idea of "the image of the limited good" and reinforced by Oscar Lewis's notion of a "culture of poverty," they encouraged the idea that Mexican children in the United States were destined to fail given that U.S. educational institutions were constructed with opposite "value orientations," delayed gratification and an emphasis on individual achievement in mind. Celia Heller took up the task of providing a unified field theory that attached some of these concepts to a cultural propensity of Mexican youth to commit crimes. All in all, a tortured construct termed "culturally disadvantaged" then took root, from which were developed many other constructs to account for the behavior of Mexican children. Then educational authorities were required to create a watered-down "culturally appropriate" curriculum for these "disadvantaged" students who suffered from Mexican value orientations. Mexican students found themselves in "special" education classes that, in time, made them special—unable to handle the simplest of composition assignments and without many times being challenged beyond "consumer math." It was implicit that algebra would be reserved for the "culturally appropriate" students. What many of us observed even as youngsters were the behavioral consequences: economic despair, racialist and ethnocentric relationships, miseducation and "tracking," and a type of political manipulation of our communities which would have delighted the famous Mayor Daley of Chicago.

19. This conversation reminded Vélez-Ibáñez of the motivating force of internal dissatisfaction. He can recall visiting one of his future graduate professors at UCSD and stating rather arrogantly that he intended to provide badly needed correctives to the way "my people" were being described. In hindsight, Professor F.G. Bailey treated his pronouncement with extraordinary kindness and a puckish twinkle and then proceeded to test the depths of his convictions. After much training, he guided Vélez-Ibáñez towards developing much greater analytical force and depth to treat what he felt but did not know.

20. For the application of the concept to U.S. Mexican populations, see Barrera, Muñoz, and Ornelas (1972).

21. Oscar Lewis (1959; 1961; 1968) first reported their existence in the *vecindades* of Mexico City but did little analysis, while Kurtz collected data between 1968 and 1969 in Tijuana, B.C., and the adjoining border community of San Ysidro, California (Kurtz, 1973; Kurtz and Showman, 1978). Yet rotating credit associations were not associated with Mexicans in the United States until the analysis by Vélez-Ibáñez (1983b). *Bonds of Mutual Trust: The Cultural Systems of Urban Mexican/Chicano Rotating Credit Associations,* New Brunswick: Rutgers University Press.

22. These familial smuggling networks devote themselves to bringing only relatives in order to avoid the many dangers of border crossing. There may be ranches along the U.S.-Mexican border to which persons are brought and crossed over using back roads and then proceed into various border rural areas of the United States. The kin smugglers basically charge $750 per person for the service but with almost guar-

anteed security, given their kin and point-of-origin ties. Whole villages in some rural states of central Mexico have been largely stripped of their working-age populations.

23. While Vélez-Ibáñez and his wife were away conducting fieldwork in Mexico, the painter was interrupted by irate non-Mexican neighbors who threatened to sue the painter personally if he continued. On their return they found half of their house painted pink and the rest the original pasty yellow. The issue was resolved by Vélez-Ibáñez placing "bills of comportment" on the doors of the offending trespassers and instructing the painter to videotape verbal and physical threats.

24. Literature and art are not simply the expression of ethnicity and rage but the use of cultural symbols, styles, social relations, economy, and psychological orientation as intersected by race and gender as well. For Latina/os this process has been expressed in murals across the southwestern United States (Vélez-Ibáñez, 1996: 213-264).

25. The major emphasis of critical race theory is the construction of race as an analytical and causal relation that explains the statuses, positions, and dynamic political and power differences between populations and nations. However, this construction cannot capture the complex economic and political relations that result in the use of a melanin-related term or process to exclude populations, as the critique by Antonia Darder and Rodolfo D. Torres (1999) has indicated.

REFERENCES

Allensworth, Elaine and Refugio I. Rochín. 1995. *Rural California Communities: Trends in Latino Population and Community Life*. East Lansing: Julian Samora Research Institute, Michigan State University.

Barrera, Mario, Carlos Muñoz, and Charles Ornelas. 1972. "The Barrio as Internal Colony," pp. 465–498 in Harlan Hahn (ed.), *People and Politics in Urban Society*. Los Angeles: Sage.

Basch, Linda, Cristina Szanton-Blanc, and Nina Glick Schiller. 1994. *Nations Unbound: Transnational Projects, Postcolonial Predicaments, and Deterritorialized Nation-States*. Langhorne, PA: Gordon and Breach Science Publishers.

Bean, Frank and Marta Tienda. 1987. *The Hispanic Population of the United States*. New York: Russell Sage Foundation.

Bonilla, Frank. 1998. "Rethinking Latino/Latin American Interdependence: New Knowing, New Practice," pp. 217–218 in Frank Bonilla, Edwin Melendez, Rebecca Morales, and Maria de Los Angeles Torres (eds.), *Borderless Borders: U.S. Latinos, Latin Americans, and the Paradox of Interdependence*. Philadelphia: Temple University Press.

Bushnell, David. 1970. *The Liberator Simón Bolívar: Man and Image*. New York: Knopf.

Darder, Antonia and Rodolfo D. Torres. 1999. "Latinos and Society: Culture, Politics, and Class," pp. 3–26 in Antonia Darder and Rodolfo D. Torres (eds.), *The Latino Studies Reader: Culture, Economy, and Society*. Malden, MA: Blackwell Press.

Deloria, Vine. 1969. *Custer Died for Your Sins: An Indian Manifesto*. New York: Macmillan.

Duany, Jorge. 2000. "Nation on the Move: The Construction of Cultural Identities in Puerto Rico and the Diaspora." *American Ethnologist* 27: 5-30.

Edmondson, Brad. 1996. "Tying the Knot in the Melting Pot." *The Numbers News.* www.marketingtools.com/publications/fc/96_nn/9607_nn/9607NN04.htm.

Gonzalez, Juan. 2000. *Harvest of Empire: A History of Latinos in America.* New York: Viking.

Grebler, Leo, Joan Moore, and Ralph Guzmán. 1970. *The Mexican American People: The Nation's Second-Largest Minority.* New York: Free Press.

Guarnizo, Luis and M. P. Smith. 1998. *Transnationalisms from Below.* New Brunswick, NJ: Transaction Publishers.

Gupta, Akhil. 1992. "The Song of the Non-Aligned World: Transnational Identities and the Re-Inscription of Space in Late Capital." *Cultural Anthropology* 7(1): 63-79.

Heyman, Josiah M. 1998. *Finding a Moral Heart for U.S. Immigration Policy: An Anthropological Perspective.* Arlington, VA: American Anthropological Association.

Hom, Sharon. 1996. "Commentary: Repositioning Human Rights, Discourse on 'Asian' Perspectives." *Buffalo Journal of International Law* 3: 209-234.

Jennings, James. 1988. "The Puerto Rican Community: Its Political Background," pp. 65–79 in F. Chris Garcia (ed.), *Latinos and the Political System.* Notre Dame, IN: University of Notre Dame Press.

Kearney, Michael. 1991. "Borders and Boundaries at the End of Empire." *Journal of Historical Sociology* 4(1): 52-74.

_____. 1995. "The Local and the Global: The Anthropology of Globalization and Transnationalism." *Annual Review of Anthropology* 24: 547-565.

Kurtz, Donald F. 1973. "The Rotating Credit Association: An Adaptation to Poverty." *Human Organization* 3: 249-58.

Kurtz, Donald F. and Margaret Showman. 1978. "The *Tanda*: A Rotating Credit Association in Mexico." *Ethnology* 17: 65-74.

Leacock, Eleanor and Richard Lee. 1982. *Politics and History in Band Societies.* Cambridge and New York: Cambridge University Press.

Lewis, Oscar. 1959. *Five Families.* New York: Basic Books.

_____. 1961. *Children of Sanchez.* New York: Random House.

_____. 1968. *La vida.* New York: Random House.

Lopez, Elias, Enrique Ramirez, and Refugio I. Rochin. 1999. *Latinos and Economic Development in California.* Sacramento: State Library Research Bureau.

Marcus, George. 1995. "Ethnography in/of the World System: The Emergence of Multi-Sited Ethnography." *Annual Review of Anthropology* 24: 95-117.

Mead, Margaret and James Baldwin. 1971. *A Rap on Race.* Philadelphia: Lippincott.

Migration Dialogue. 2000. Migration New: Remittances. www.Migration.ucdavis.edu/ Data/remit.on.www/remittances.html. 2000.

Nagengast, Carol and Carlos Vélez-Ibáñez. n.d. "Introduction: The Scholar as Activist," in Carol Nagengast and Carlos Vélez-Ibáñez (eds.), *Human Rights, Power, and Difference: Expanding Contemporary Interpretations of Human Rights in Theory and Practice.* Washington, DC: Publications of the Society for Applied Anthropology. In press.

Nelson, Candace and Marta Tienda. 1997. "The Structuring of Hispanic Ethnicity: Historical and Contemporary Perspectives," pp. 8–29 in Mary Romero, Pierrette Hondagneu-Sotelo, and Vilma Ortiz (eds.), *Challenging Fronteras: Structuring Latina/os and Latino Lives in the U.S.* New York: Routledge.

Ong, Aihwa and Donald M. Nonini. 1997. *Ungrounded Empires: The Cultural Politics of Modern Chinese Transnationalism*. New York: Routledge.

Park, Joseph F. 1961. "The History of Mexican Labor in Arizona during the Territorial Period." Master's thesis, Department of History, University of Arizona.

Pastor, Manuel Jr. 1998. "Interdependence, Inequality, and Identity: Linking Latinos and Latin Americans," pp. 17–33 in Frank Bonilla, Edwin Melendez, Rebecca Morales, and Maria de los Angeles Torres (eds.), *Borderless Borders: U.S. Latino, Latin Americans, and the Paradox of Interdependence*. Philadelphia: Temple University Press.

Ramirez, Melissa and Roberto R. Ramirez. 2000. *The Hispanic Population in the United States: March 2000*. Current Population Reports, P20535.

Rensberger, Boyce. 1994. "Racial Odyssey," pp. 57–63 in Aaron Podolefsky and Peter J. Brown (eds.), *Applying Anthropology: An Introductory Reader*. Mountain View, CA: Mayfield Press.

Rodriguez, Clara E. 1997. "A Summary of Puerto Rican Migration to the United States," pp. 101–113 in Mary Romero, Pierrette Hondagneu-Sotelo, and Vilma Ortiz (eds.), *Challenging Fronteras: Structuring Latina/os and Latino Lives in the U.S.* New York: Routledge.

Romano, Octavio. 1968. "The Anthropology and Sociology of the Mexican-Americans: The Distortion of Mexican-American History." *El Grito* 1 (Fall): 13-26.

Rouse, Roger. 1989. "Mexican Migration to the United States: Family Relations in the Development of a Transnational Migrant Circuit." Ph.D. diss., Stanford University.

———. 1991. "Mexican Migration and the Social Space of Postmodernism." *Diaspora* 1(1): 8-23.

Rumbaut, Ruben. 1998. "Immigrants Continue to Shape America." *NEXO: Newsletter of the Julian Samora Research Institute* 6(3): 1-24.

Rumbaut, Ruben and Wayne Cornelius. 1995. *California's Immigrant Children: Theory, Research and Implications for Policy*. La Jolla, CA: Center for U.S.-Mexican Studies.

Samora, Julian and Patricia Vandel Simon. 1977. *A History of the Mexican-American People*. Notre Dame, IN: University of Notre Dame Press.

Steward, Julian, Robert A. Manners, Eric R. Wolf, Elena Padilla Seda, Sidney W. Mintz, and R. L. Scheele. 1956. *The People of Puerto Rico*. Urbana: University of Illinois Press.

Therrien, Melissa and R. R. Ramirez. 2000. *The Hispanic Population in the United States: March 2000, P20-535*. Washington, DC: U.S. Bureau of the Census.

U.S. Bureau of the Census. 1990. *Race and Hispanic Origin, 1990 Census Profile*. Washington, DC.

———. 1993. *Hispanic Americans Today. Current Population Reports, P23-183*. Washington, DC.

———. 1994. *Selected Economic Characteristics of All Persons and Hispanic Persons, by Type of Origin*. www.census.gov/population/socdemo/hispanic/cps94/syntab-2.txt. 94.

———. 1995. *Housing in Metropolitan Areas—Hispanic Origin Households*. Washington, DC.

———. 1997a. *Educational Attainment of the Foreign-Born Population 25 Years and Over by Region of Birth and Gender*. Washington, DC.

_____. 1997b. *Poverty by Race-Ethnicity Including Unrelated Persons*. Washington, DC.

_____. 1998. *Hispanic Origin of Couples: 1990, Table 3, 1990 Census of Population and Housing, Public Use Microdata Samples, Internet Release, June 10, 1998*. http://www.jointcenter.org/databank/families/marital/intemargs/origin.txt.

_____. 1999a. *Population by Poverty Status in 1998, Selected Age Categories, Hispanic Origin and Race, and Sex*. www.census.gov/population/socdemo/hispanic/cps/12.2.tr. 99.

_____. 1999b. *Population Age 15 Years and Over by Total Money Earnings in 1998, Hispanic Origin and Race, and Sex*. www.census.gov/population/hispanic/cps98/tab11.2txt. 99.

_____. 1999c. *Population by Age, Hispanic Origin and Race, and Sex*. www.census.gov/population/socdemo/hispanic/cps99/tab01-2.txt. 99.

_____. 2000a. *The Hispanic Population of the United States: Population Characteristics 1999*. www.census.gov/prod/2000pubs/p20-527.pdf. 2000.

_____. 2000b. *Projections of the Resident Population by Race, Hispanic Origin, and Nativity: Middle Series, 2000 to 2025 and 2050 to 2070*. www.census.gov/population/www/projections/natsum-T.5.html. 2000.

_____. 2000c. *The Hispanic Population, Census Brief 2000*. Washington, DC.

U.S. Department of Commerce. 1996. *Statistical Abstract of the United States 1996*. Washington, DC.

U.S. Department of Education. 1996. *Digest of Education Statistics*. Washington, DC.: Office of Educational Research and Improvement.

Vaca, Nick. 1970a. "The Mexican-American in the Social Sciences: 1912–1970. Part 1, 1912–1935." *El Grito* 3(3): 3-24.

_____. 1970b. "The Mexican-American in the Social Sciences: 1912–1970. Part 2, 1936–1970." *El Grito* 4(1): 17-51.

Vélez-Ibáñez, Carlos G. 1983a. *Rituals of Marginality: Politics, Process, and Culture Change in Central Urban Mexico, 1969-1974*. Berkeley: University of California Press.

_____. 1983b. *Bonds of Mutual Trust: The Cultural Systems of Urban Mexican/Chicano Rotating Credit Associations*. New Brunswick, NJ: Rutgers University Press.

_____. 1995. "Plural Strategies of Survival and Cultural Formation in U.S. Mexican Households in a Region of Dynamic Transformation: The U.S. Borderlands," pp. 193–234 in Shepard Foreman (ed.), *Diagnosing America: Anthropology and Public Engagement*. Ann Arbor: University of Michigan Press.

_____. 1996. *Border Visions: The Cultures of the Mexicans of the Southwest United States*. Tucson: University of Arizona Press.

_____. 1998. *Chicano Drivers of Ideas in Anthropology Across Space and Place: The Synergy of Anthropology and Chicano Studies*. East Lansing: Julian Zamora Research Institute, Michigan State University.

_____. n.d. "'The Border Crossed Us and We Cross the Border': The Emergence of the Commoditization and Devalorization of the Mexican Population of the Southwest United States," in Carol Nagengast and Carlos G. Vélez-Ibáñez (eds.), *Human Rights, Power, and Difference: Expanding Contemporary Interpretations of Human Rights in Theory and Practice*. Washington, DC: Publications of the Society for Applied Anthropology. In press.

Vélez-Ibáñez, Carlos G., G. Nunez, and D. Rissolo. 2002. "Off the Backs of Others: The Political Ecology of Credit, Debit, and Class Formation and Transformation among the *Colonias* of New Mexico and Elsewhere," in R. Carson and L. Fernandez (eds.), *Both Sides of the Border: Transboundary Environmental Management Issues Facing Mexico and the United States*. Amsterdam: Kluwer Academic Publishers and IGCC.

Wolf, Eric R. 1999. *Envisioning Power: Ideologies of Dominance and Crisis*. Berkeley: University of California Press.

Yancey, William, Eugene Erikson, and Richard Juliani. 1976. "Emergent Ethnicity: A Review and Reformation." *American Sociological Review* 41: 391–403.

I

RECONCEPTUALIZING LATINA/O STUDIES AND THE STUDY OF LATINA/O SUBJECTS

Latina/o studies has long served as an academic marker, providing us with the analytical tools to understand and evaluate the signs of our times. From early case studies of Mexicans in the U.S. Southwest and the depictions of Puerto Rican urban life through the shifting paradigms presented by those employing nationalist, Marxist, feminist, and other oppositional strategies, scholars and activists in the field have both reported on the conditions prevailing in Latina/o communities and helped to shape the future of those communities. Today, the radical restructuring of our political, economic, and cultural milieu once again requires that we reevaluate our methodological and ideological approaches to studying Latina/os.

In particular, in the past thirty years we have seen several Latin America countries alter their economies to favor the unobstructed flow of capital and commerce across the region. In places such as Mexico, Chile, Peru, and Venezuela such liberalization has been accompanied by the proliferation of trade agreements aimed at reducing tariffs and trade barriers and increasing the circulation of goods and people. And while these changes have produced favorable results for industry and professionals, the effects have often been less so for the traditionally subordinated poor, working-class, and indigenous peoples of the region. The impacts can be measured in large part by the unprecedented waves of migration to the United States and the surge of rebellions in places such as Chiapas, Haiti, and Ecuador. These changes have begun to transform Latina/o communities in the United States in profound and unexpected ways.

Two important processes in this transnational era create community outcomes very different from those in previous periods. The first is migration and its impact on the cultural and social life of the receiving communities.

The second is the dependence of the communities of origin on resources and remittances from migrants. In many cases these two processes have worked to create new economic and political opportunities that revitalize moribund towns and villages and create new infrastructures in urban contexts.

While the contributors in this section examine migration of this period in detail, it is worth discussing the question of remittances here, particularly as they impact the relationships between communities in the United States and Mexico. In particular, the levels of remittances sent from the United States to Mexico between 1979 and 1995 demonstrate the remarkable degree of dependence on worker wages, which have increased over 400 percent in this period (Table I.1). From all sources in that same period, Mexico received almost $40 billion in remittances.[1] In 2002, the annual remittance had jumped to more than $9.3 billion (Thompson 2002: 5).

Similarly, in El Salvador remittances have increased from $11 million in 1976 to over $6 billion in 1995 (Table I.2), in Guatemala from $14 million in 1977 to almost $7 billion in 1995, in Nicaragua from $4 million in 1975 to $75 million in 1995, and in Colombia from $22 million in 1970 to total remittances of $6 billion twenty-five years later. The Dominican case is as dramatic, with an increase from $25 million in 1970 to nearly $800 million in 1995 (Table I.3).

Table I.1   Remittances 1979–1995, Mexico

Year	Workers' Remittances (Millions US$)	Compensation of Employees (Millions US$)	Migrant Transfers (Millions US$)	Total (Millions US$)
1979	0	177	0	177
1980	698	341	0	1,039
1981	859	361	0	1,220
1982	844	382	0	1,226
1983	984	407	0	1,391
1984	1,127	434	0	1,561
1985	1,157	459	0	1,616
1986	1,290	481	0	1,771
1987	1,478	507	0	1,985
1988	1,897	542	0	2,439
1989	2,213	580	0	2,793
1990	2,492	606	0	3,098
1991	2,414	616	0	3,030
1992	3,070	630	0	3,700
1993	3,332	647	0	3,979
1994	3,694	647	0	4,341
1995	3,672	695	0	4,367
TOTAL				39,733

Source: IMF Balance of Payments Statistics Yearbook.

Table I.2   Remittances 1979–1995, El Salvador

Year	Workers' Remittances (Millions US$)	Compensation of Employees (Millions US$)	Migrant Transfers (Millions US$)	Total (Millions US$)
1976	0	11	0	11
1977	34	20	0	54
1978	45	23	0	68
1979	49	51	0	100
1980	11	38	0	49
1981	42	30	0	72
1982	78	34	0	112
1983	92	23	0	115
1984	114	45	0	159
1985	126	31	0	157
1986	139	19	0	157
1987	167	19	0	187
1988	194	16	0	211
1989	228	10	0	238
1990	357	9	0	366
1991	467	8	0	475
1992	687	7	0	694
1993	789	5	0	795
1994	967	5	0	972
1995	1,061	3	0	1,064
TOTAL				6,057

Source: IMF Balance of Payments Statistics Yearbook.

In each of these cases, a phenomenal increase in migrating populations has attended these economic transfers. Simultaneously, revitalization of broken neighborhoods in New York and Los Angeles by Guatemalans, Salvadorans, Mexicans, and Dominicans has created new and stable economic and social platforms from which new generations emerge.

For rural communities and urban networks, remittances in Mexico account for up to 25 percent of household income and are crucial for infrastructure in villages and towns throughout the country. In fact, remittances are Mexico's third-largest source of income (Thompson 2002: 5). In the United States, Mexican voluntary associations such as hometown beneficent organizations, religious sodalities, and migrant associations maintain and develop membership rolls and censuses of migrating members. Small collections from members are amassed to ensure consistent financing of hometown schools, churches, and lands they may still hold. Remittances are also used as funding sources for further household and kin migration, in some cases until rural areas are emptied of entire generations.

In urban settings remittances are invested in small businesses, in financing younger siblings' educational costs, in constructing self-built homes, and in

Table I.3   Remittances 1970–1995, Dominican Republic

Year	Workers' Remittances (Millions US$)	Compensation of Employees (Millions US$)	Migrant Transfers (Millions US$)	Total (Millions US$)
1970	25	0	0	25
1971	14	0	0	14
1972	24	0	0	24
1973	24	0	0	24
1974	27	0	0	27
1975	28	0	0	28
1976	112	0	0	112
1977	124	0	0	124
1978	132	0	0	132
1979	161	0	0	161
1980	183	0	0	183
1981	183	0	0	183
1982	190	0	0	190
1983	195	0	0	195
1984	205	0	0	205
1985	242	0	0	242
1986	225	0	0	225
1987	273	0	0	273
1988	289	0	0	289
1989	300	0	0	300
1990	315	0	0	315
1991	329	0	0	329
1992	347	0	0	347
1993	721	1	0	722
1994	757	1	0	758
1995	794	2	0	796
TOTAL				6,224

Source: *IMF Balance of Payments Statistics Yearbook.*

purchasing automobiles and small trucks. Migrants closer to the border use their U.S. earnings to buy merchandise for resale in Mexico—like perfumes, tires, auto parts, boat motors, and hundreds of other items too expensive to purchase in Mexican stores.

However, at the household level the transnational ties between networks and communities continue to expand. In Mexico, sixty-one percent of Mexican households have a relative currently residing in the United States, and 73 percent of Mexican households have some social connection with someone in the United States.[2] Important implications of all this are (1) that the presence of a former or current migrant in the household doubles the probability of undocumented migration and (2) that at least 10 percent of Mexican households have claims to a greencard because of someone already present in the United States.[3]

The creation and expansion of Mexican transnational rural and urban networks in the United States as a consequence of these relationships can be shown in a number of ways. We have already described the emergence of more than eighteen hundred *colonias* in areas largely devoid of residential occupation. Equally important is the re-Mexicanization and revitalization of many rural towns and villages in such states as California and New Mexico, where mobile non-Mexican residents have abandoned rural towns and villages for jobs and professions elsewhere.

Allensworth and Rochin (1996: 7) recently sampled 126 California agriculturally based communities in which a minimum of 15 percent of residents were "Latino" (more than 90 percent of whom were of Mexican origin) in 1980 and compared their growth between 1980 and 1990. According to this study, in fifteen communities the non-Mexican population increased by more than 50 percent while the Mexican population increased by the same percentage. In forty-five communities Anglo and Mexican populations increased between 1 and 50 percent, and 64 communities lost Anglos while experiencing a 50 percent increase of Mexicans. Therefore, the main causative factor in demographic change seems to be Anglos' leaving when they become adults and their parents eventually following. However, the consequence of this demographic change has been the revitalization of moribund Anglo communities reoccupied by Mexicans in the aftermath of accelerated migration in the post-1980s. Such reoccupation creates new foundations for transnational relations, further migration, and continuous movement of populations in and out of these communities with changes in the economy.

The maintenance and expansion of social, economic, political, residential, and cultural ties in the United States and Mexico through immigration, remittances, and the reoccupation of towns raise new questions regarding the changing political and economic climate that the contributors to this section address. As they note, in evaluating these changes we are required to assess the methodological and ideological tools available for understanding these changes and their impacts on Latina/o communities. Thus, in this section we are treated to variations of a theory regarding the formation of these communities and the changing forms of political participation that they display. Central to it is the recognition that incompleteness is an important part of being human, especially when events and processes push populations to migrate in the midst of massive economic and social disruptions. New theoretical approaches must be employed to understand the fluidity of social and cultural categories in the context of globalization, migration, the creation of transnational relationships, and the asymmetry of political and economic relationships in multiple settings.

We have pointed out that our theoretical lenses must include a processual approach that captures the transnationalization process in which Latina/os are engaged, and we have suggested that the stretching of space and place beyond borders requires multiple versions of behavior, social relations, and identity but at the same time involves the creation of relationships and points of contact that seemingly emulate "traditional" forms.

Even in the midst of the most dynamic of indeterminate conditions, Latina/o populations seek settlement, conviviality, and reciprocal relationships based on the social supports created by kinship, friendship, and exchange. Thus, a central question that the three contributors implicitly address is how we can reconceptualize these communities while accounting for the parallel and often contradictory effects of globalization and transnational resistance—how to bring the most cogent theoretical models to bear on the processes by which institutional scripts, political domination, and the appropriation of labor power are confronted by localized modes of resistance.

In addressing these issues Sampaio explores the limits of nationalism as a political and academic strategy (particularly in the movement toward globalized capital and the formation of binational communities) while avoiding the homogenizing rhetoric prevalent in much of the human rights discourse rooted in the First World. As a political scientist engaged in feminist and minority-group discourse, Sampaio traces the transnational political relations between Chiapas and the United States and thus makes a valuable contribution to an approach unhampered by political boundaries.

Rocco mirrors this discussion in his assessment of postmodernist and postcolonialist tools. In this introduction to his study of Central American migrants in Los Angeles, he carves out a transnational dialogue of resistance that includes both postmodernism and the empirical sciences, offering critiques and suggestions for both. Suzanne Oboler refines these debates in a concentrated discussion of the formation of Latina/o subjectivity and our notion of "otherness." By exploring the formation of U.S. versus Latin American identities among Latina/os, Oboler artfully demonstrates that even the most benevolent exercises in self-determination often have the unintended consequence of assigning subordinate roles to members of the communities they seek to empower. In this way, each of the contributors brings home the importance of considering how we should map Latina/o studies in this new millennium and how Latina/o subjects are to be constructed in this new landscape.

NOTES

1. Remittances are the monies that migrants return to their countries of origin. If labor is considered an export, then remittances are the part of the payment for exporting labor services that returns to the country of origin. Three streams of money flowing into countries are included in remittances and published annually by the International Monetary Fund in its *Balance of Payments Statistics Yearbook*: workers'

remittances, compensation of employees, and migrant transfers. "Workers' remittances" are the monetary transfers sent home by workers abroad during the course of a year. "Compensation of employees" (previously "labor income") refers to the gross earnings of foreigners residing abroad for fewer than twelve months, including the value of in-kind benefits such as housing and payroll taxes. Finally, "migrant transfers" refers to the net worth of migrants who move from one country to another (e.g., the value of IBM stock owned by a migrant who moves from France to Germany gets transferred in international accounting from France to Germany).

Total remittances increased from less than $2 billion in 1970 to $70 billion in 1995. Between 1970 and 1995, total remittances reached nearly $1 trillion. Over the past fifteen years workers' remittances have accounted for almost two-thirds of total remittances, while compensation of employees accounted for 25 percent and migrant transfers 10 percent. The workers' remittances share of total remittances peaked in the early 1980s at over 70 percent. In 1995, the country receiving the most workers' remittances was Portugal, with $3.8 billion, followed by Mexico ($3.7 billion), Turkey ($3.3 billion), and Egypt ($3.2 billion). In addition, eight developing countries accounted for half of 1995 workers' remittances: Mexico ($3.7 billion), Turkey ($3.3 billion), Egypt ($3.2 billion), Brazil ($2.9 billion), Morocco ($1.9 billion), Bangladesh ($1.2 billion), Yemen ($1.1 billion), and El Salvador ($1.1 billion). Consequently, five countries paid 80 percent of workers' remittances in 1995: Saudi Arabia ($16.6 billion), the United States ($12.2 billion), Germany ($5.3 billion), France ($3.1 billion), and the UK ($2.7 billion). Kuwait paid $1.8 billion and Oman $1.3 billion in workers' remittances in 1995.

Remittances are very important for many island economies. In 1994, total remittances were equivalent to more than 100 percent of merchandise exports for the Dominican Republic and over 75 percent of merchandise exports in El Salvador. In Mexico, total remittances were equivalent to 12 percent of merchandise exports in 1994. Total remittances have not declined as migration streams have "matured" in many labor-exporting nations. There are many reasons for this, including the fact that the willingness of migrants to remit depends on economic and savings policies in the host and home countries, exchange rate and risk factors, and the availability and efficiency of transfer facilities. In some emigration countries, changed economic policies encouraged migrants to send home more remittances; in other cases, simply making it easier or cheaper to send money home has increased and/or sustained remittances (http://Migration.ucdavis. edu/Data/remit.on. www/about Remit html, 10/28/2000).

2. http://Migration.ucdavis.edu/Data/remit.on. www/about Remit html, 10/28/2000.
3. http://Migration.ucdavis.edu/Data/remit.on. www/about Remit html, 10/28/2000.

REFERENCES

Allenworth, Elaine M. and Refugio I. Rochin. 1996. *White Exodus, Latino Repopulation, and Community Well-being: Trends in California's Rural Communities.* Julian Somora Latino Research Institute Research Report 13.

Thompson, Ginger. 2002. Paychecks in U.S. fuel Mexico's economy. *The Press Enterprise* (Riverside, CA), 1 April 2002.

1

Transforming Chicana/o and Latina/o Politics: Globalization and the Formation of Transnational Resistance in the United States and Chiapas

Anna Sampaio

> Mexican identity . . . can no longer be explained without the experience of "the other side," and vice versa. As a socio-cultural phenomenon, Los Angeles simply cannot be understood without taking Mexico City into account, its southernmost neighborhood. Between both cities runs the greatest migratory axis on the planet, and the conceptual freeway with the greatest number of accidents.
>
> —Guillermo Gómez-Peña, p. 137, 1998

In 1993 Congress passed the North American Free Trade Agreement (NAFTA), with great anticipation at home and abroad that the newly formed regional alliance between Mexico, the United States, and Canada would increase productivity, reduce inefficiency, and strengthen the states' economies. However, the agreement was not met with universal enthusiasm. Among many of the rural poor, *campesinos*, working classes, racial minorities, and indigenous populations of all three states, NAFTA's passage signaled an unprecedented move toward globalization and mounting economic pressures (Mander and Goldsmith, 1996). In particular, in Chiapas, Mexico, peasants, *campesinos*/farmers, and indigenous populations had for some time been under the weight of neoliberal economic strategies intensified by the austerity programs adopted by Carlos Salinas in the 1980s (Collier, 1994; Harvey, 1990). These *campesinos* and indigenous communities had been notably impacted by privatization and deregulation. In effect, they had seen their own farms and communities displaced and deterritorialized in the move toward regional economic integration and knew that NAFTA's passage would only expedite this process (Kearney, 1996).[1] Such sentiments were reflected in an interview conducted with Subcomandante

Marcos, one of the leaders of the 1994 indigenous and *campesinos* uprising (quoted in Katzenberger, 1995: 67):

> NAFTA is a death sentence for the indigenous people. NAFTA sets up competition among farmers, but how can our campesinos—who are mostly illiterate—compete with U.S. and Canadian farmers? And look at this rocky land we have here. How can we compete with the land in California or Canada? So the people of Chiapas, as well as the people of Oaxaca, Veracruz, Quintana Roo, Guerrero, and Sonora, were the sacrificial lambs of NAFTA.

In the same year that NAFTA was to be implemented, California voters, responding to the recession that still engulfed the state and the perceived threat of growing numbers of immigrants from the south, passed an initiative that would have barred undocumented immigrants from access to a range of public services, including public schools, subsidized health clinics, and social security, and curtailed access for documented immigrants as well. While most of Proposition 187's measures never went into effect and were eventually overturned in the U.S. District Court, its passage served as a critical rallying point in the mounting anti-immigrant/anti-Latina/o campaign that would effectively bring all Latina/os in the state under criminal suspicion (*Los Angeles Times*, September 14, 1999). Angry activists organized rallies, marches, and sit-ins throughout the state. In Mexico City, according to the *New York Times,* forty masked men ransacked a McDonald's restaurant to demonstrate their outrage. "Yankee Go Home!", "Solidarity with the Immigrants!", and "No to 187!" were among the messages left on the restaurant's windows.

These events demonstrate that the restructuring of domestic economies in favor of greater flexibility for multinational capital has dramatically impacted both local and national economies and the social and cultural fabric of those inscribed in these trade agreements. In essence, globalization has placed unprecedented pressure on the poor, working-class, rural, and indigenous communities of both the United States and Mexico and required new strategies of resistance. What is more, these incidents demonstrate the unexpected ways in which people's lives and their struggles to resist the pressures of this new global matrix have been reconfigured and interwoven in unexpected ways. It has become evident that what occurs on this side of the border can no longer be considered strictly in terms of nation-state sovereignty, divorced from what happens to those across the border. In the effort to erase tariffs, taxes, and trade restrictions for capital, agreements such as NAFTA have also transformed traditional state boundaries and necessitated a remapping of this increasingly transnational space.

For Chicana/os and Latina/os in the United States, immigrants moving between these countries, and Mexican rural working-class and indigenous populations, globalization has integrated communities in new ways. While globalization has altered the popular perception of national and cultural identities for Chicana/os and Latina/os in the United States and Mexicans throughout Mexico,[2] it has equally impacted the structure of gendered relationships in these locations as the feminization of poverty has been aggravated by the restricted opportunities afforded traditionally marginalized women. In addition, while the new global matrix has exacerbated the uneven development between the First and the Third World, it has also engendered new spaces for resistance.

In this study, I examine the impact of globalization on the economic and political context of Chicana/os and Latina/os in the United States and indigenous peoples in Chiapas, Mexico, with a view to showing how this economic process has transformed people's political subjectivities. I focus particular attention on the socioeconomic conditions of Chicana/os and Latina/os in the United States and of the conditions for indigenous peoples and *campesinos* in Chiapas for two reasons. First, the two populations have comparable socioeconomic and political positions relative to their national populations. That is, on key indicators such as average income, occupational mobility, educational attainment, and overall health, both have consistently been ranked in the lowest percentile. Both populations are linked to forms of colonialism not only in the traditional terms of imposition of economic/political/sociocultural control from some external source but also in their relationship to a neocolonialism represented by the intensification of globalization. Among indigenous Chiapanecos the pattern of colonial control was clearly established with the onslaught of the Spanish conquistadores and the continuing battles to maintain elements of Mayan tradition (including political autonomy) in their relations with the Mexican state, with multinationals vying for land and resources, and with cattle ranchers and plantation owners in the region. For Chicana/os and Latina/os the relationship to colonial structures has best been articulated as an "internal colony," one in which these populations have been concentrated in urban barrios and subjected to systematic forms of repression and loss of autonomy (Barrera, 1979). As a consequence, both of these populations have been effectively pushed outside the realm of traditional governmental institutions and public policy making and positioned largely as second-class citizens.[3]

Second, in some forms of resistance Chicana/os and Latina/os in the United States have increasingly responded to the call for solidarity put out by the Zapatistas when they began their rebellion in Chiapas in 1994. While hundreds of Chicana/os and Latina/os from the United States have gone to Chiapas to witness the rebellion, a better indicator of this affinity has been the adoption of cultural symbols, the creation of "sister communities" and support organizations in the United States, and a gravitation to a political philosophy and a political identity that emphasize a common struggle in the war against globalization.[4]

I examine the changing socioeconomic conditions that have affected these populations' political sensibilities and the terrain on which they resist them, and the impact of the feminization of poverty. In particular, I consider the way in which women's experiences of these transnational transformations have opened up possibilities for resistance. I conclude with a detailed discussion of an example of this altered political subjectivity in the context of transnational resistance—the formation of a coalition of Chicanas/Latinas/Mestizas called Hermanas en La Lucha. Ultimately, the aim of this study is to demonstrate that traditional formations of Chicana/o and Latina/o subjectivity inscribed in the context of a nation-state analysis have become increasingly obsolete with the changes to their daily lives introduced by globalization and increasingly supplanted by the emergence of binational and transnational communities. In conducting such an examination I am equally suggesting that the terrain on which Chicana/o and Latina/o studies has been conceived is increasingly ill-equipped to capture these changing political and economic dynamics and requires remapping.

SHIFTING PARADIGMS IN CHICANA/O AND LATINA/O POLITICAL SUBJECTIVITY

The expression of political subjectivity amongst Chicana/o and Latina/o activists has a long history of challenging idealized notions of citizenship and participation, particularly those of Americanization efforts at promoting assimilation and those implying biological or cultural inferiority (Sanchez, 1990; 1993). Thus, when Chicana/o activists such as Rodolfo González of the Crusade for Justice led high-school students in a massive walkout in Denver, Colorado, in 1968, or marched in the Vietnam War moratorium on August 29, 1969, they were redefining notions of American citizenship; seeking not merely to add Mexicans to a well-seasoned "melting pot" but to construct a new form of civic identity that began from the experiences of a nonwhite population. In particular, these activists practiced a more engaged and transformative leadership that ultimately sought to displace the political and ethnic hierarchy of the country with the growing numbers of politically conscious Chicana/os and Latina/os (Acuña, 1988; Cabán, 1998).

Furthermore, in the process of building a new and explicitly nonwhite America, participants in the Chicana/o movement centered their activities on educational institutions. Schools became a significant site for organizing because they represented a collection of intellectuals who had the space to engage in such debates about alienation and because many Chicana/o movement activists saw them as the foundations of civic engagement in the United States and therefore a central venue for addressing the larger questions about citizenship and belonging. Consequently, the work of many in the movement was aimed at reconstructing citizenship from a cultural vantage point and reforming the very process of inculcating it. The formation of Chicana/o and Latina/o studies across the country and the scholarship of popular academics in this discipline took on a decidedly *nationalist* tone, emphasizing the particular racial formations at work in the United States that had produced internal colonies of Mexican Americans (Acuña, 1972; Barrera, 1979; Gómez-Quiñones, 1971; 1974; 1978; Muñoz, 1970).

As the study of Chicana/os and Latina/os has expanded to include more sophisticated studies of gender, region, and generation, and analyses of participation and political behavior, the focus of the field is still on internal *nation-state* struggles. While the mapping of Chicana/o and Latina/o politics in this manner has proved strategically efficient (suggesting a type of homogeneity does not exist) and relevant to analyses of particular case studies or political behavior (e.g., voting), it has obscured the manner in which Chicana/o and Latina/o communities are "simultaneously engaged in a struggle for inclusion and ethnic affirmation within the U.S. while seeking to maintain some voice in affairs 'back home'" (Bonilla, 1993: 182, as quoted in Cabán, 1998).

The focus on North American political relationships in Chicana/o and Latina/o politics has detracted from the examination of ongoing changes in global capital in the 1980s and 1990s and the way in which the demographics of Chicana/o and Latina/o communities in the United States have been directly affected by efforts at increased regional and global economic integration. Three factors in particular have substantively impacted this trend toward globalization: the employment of neoliberal economic policies in Latin America, the deregulation of U.S. domestic markets, and the increased mobilization of capital and people across national borders (Sampaio, 2001). I will briefly examine these changes and the possibilities that emerge for studying Chicana/os and Latina/os in a transnational framework.

Globalization and Regional Integration

At no time has the movement toward globalization been more apparent than in the past two decades, as countries in Latin America (including Argentina, Brazil, Chile, Mexico, Panama, and Venezuela) have embarked upon a path of political and economic modernization via neoliberal strategies. Within a relatively short period of time these countries have adopted neoliberal economic theory[5] and begun a series of transitions including the devaluation of their national currencies, the reduction of import tariffs and other trade restrictions, the privatization of public resources, and the deregulation of financial and industrial sectors in an effort to minimize the role of government in the economy while strengthening private business. As a result, these countries expected to achieve greater productivity and reduced inefficiency by curtailing the costs of imported capital and transforming local economies to favor exports.

The effects of these efforts aimed at bolstering economic growth and regional integration are evident in levels of trade and the traffic in goods, services, and peoples across the region in the past decade. In particular, reports from the U.S. Department of Commerce document the rapid growth of state economies in countries favoring neoliberal economic plans such as Brazil, Chile, Colombia, El Salvador, Peru, and Venezuela. Between 1990 and 1996, as the U.S. economy grew, the gross national products (GNP) of these countries grew comparably (*Statistical Abstract of the United States*, 1998: Tables 1324, 1347, 1348).[6] Furthermore, the levels of trade between the United States and Latin America (particularly Central and South America) from 1990 to the present show a steady increase in NAFTA imports and exports, resulting in an overall level of trade which surpasses the balance of U.S. trade with the rest of the world (Center for the Study of Western Hemisphere Trade, 1999).

More recent examples of these efforts can be found in a host of trade agreements such as the Caribbean Basin Initiative, Caricom, and MERCOSUR (NAFTA's Caribbean and Central and South American counterparts, respectively).[7] This shift in economic policies is also apparent in the day-to-day operations of farms such as those in Chile's desert regions; an area that had been the province of small subsistence farmers has been transformed in the past ten years into an agricultural haven where the main fruits produced are harvested almost exclusively for foreign markets (González-Estay, 1998).

However, in the decades since Latin America embarked upon these political and economic transformations, the limitations of this strategy have become apparent, especially in the increased polarization of citizens and the increasing numbers of migrants/immigrants displaced from local labor markets. Morales (1998) reports that while poverty levels climbed throughout most of Latin America to reach 41 percent in 1980, the percentage of Latin Americans living in poverty continued to grow, reaching nearly 50 percent by 1990. Moreover, recent reports from Mexico estimate a level of poverty as high as 66 percent (Sassen, 1998). The impact of these efforts extends far beyond the boundaries of Latin America; the United States witnessed an unprecedented surge of immigration from Mexico and Central and South America and an increase in the levels of poverty, underemployment, and wage deflation among U.S. Chicana/os and Latina/os.

In particular, while there was a significant increase in the overall migration of Latin American residents to the United States in the 1980s, immigration has increased dramatically in the past decade with the intensification of globalization and the increasing displacement of working-class, poor and peasant populations from land, employment, and access to necessary resources. While Immigration and Naturalization Service (INS) reports documented 1,653,300 migrants from Mexico entering the United States between 1981 and 1990 (approximately 183,700 migrants per year), there were over 1,651,400 Mexican migrants entering the United States between 1991 and

1996 (approximately 330,280 migrants a year). When we compare these numbers to the rate of immigration in the history of the Southwest, we find that between 1820 and 1996 total Mexican migration was 5,542,625 (averaging 31,492 migrants per year), while between 1981 and 1996 it was 3,304,682 (averaging 220,312 migrants per year). Comparable increases are apparent among immigrants from Central and South America (INS Statistics, U.S. Immigration and Naturalization Service, 1999).[8]

The percentage of immigrants who entered the United States undocumented in this period also grew; by 1996 an estimated 2,700,000 undocumented immigrants from Mexico were residing in the United States and the largest increases in undocumented immigration were emerging from Mexico, Guatemala, El Salvador, and Honduras (INS Statistics, U.S. Immigration and Naturalization Homepage, 1999). Furthermore, these immigrants were disproportionately women, from Latin America (Mexico in particular), poor, and between the ages of fifteen and twenty-nine (INS Statistics, U.S. Immigration and Naturalization Service Homepage, 1999). There is also evidence to suggest that these migrants were increasingly younger, less well educated, and poorer than previous waves of migrants, indicating on some level a form of displacement more profound than in previous periods (Chapa, 1998).

Ultimately, the privatization and rollback of government subsidies (such as those on oil, gas, and tortillas) inherent in neoliberal strategies across Latin America were key factors in the migratory shift from Latin America to the United States. In particular, information exports from the United States, such as innovative technologies in agricultural production, produced changes in the manufacturing and distribution of agricultural commodities, thereby undermining broad sectors of Latin American farmers and ranch owners, as well as rural *campesinos*, and increasing the "push" toward migration. In certain instances, for example, in southern Mexico, Guatemala, and parts of Central America, these economic changes were coupled with ongoing civil strife (often remnants of the civil wars which had begun in the mid-1970s), resulting in the flight of thousands (Hamilton and Chinchilla, 1997; Portes and Stepik, 1997).

However, while the process of economic integration served as a key catalyst for the migration described here, this is not to suggest that globalization's impact in this period was felt solely by those in Latin America. Nor is it to suggest that the only impact globalization had on Chicana/os and Latina/os in the United States was to change the demographic makeup of traditional neighborhoods by adding more recent immigrants to the mix. In socioeconomic terms the intensification of economic integration between the United States and Mexico impacted the wage and occupational opportunities of Chicana/os and Latina/os (sometimes in contradictory ways), restricted their prospects for economic mobility, and served as an underlying element in the anti-immigrant/anti-Latina/o campaign that culminated in the mid-'90s.

In terms of wages, occupation, and economic mobility, Chicana/os and Latina/os in the United States witnessed a persistent decrease in wages and benefits commensurate with the intensification of globalization in the region. Between 1975 and 1989 average earnings growth among Latina/os slowed to the point of stagnation and income inequality grew. Moreover, although Latina/os have made up a greater percentage of the workforce in the past ten years, their real wages have decreased (the median household income for Hispanics dropped from $27,421 in 1990 to $26,628 in 1997) or remained stagnant (the weekly income of Hispanic women from 1990 to 1998 grew at a slower rate than inflation) (*Statistical Abstract of the United States,* 1999: Tables 742, 702). In addition, while the median income of African Americans (both men and women) and Anglos increased between 1990 and 1996, the median income of Hispanics decreased in the same period (*Statistical Abstract of the United States,* 1998: Table 753).[9]

In 1992 the rate of job displacement among Chicano and Latino workers surpassed the rates of Anglos and African Americans, and by 1995 unemployment rates among Latinos surpassed that of African Americans for the first time in American history (Levy, quoted in Chapa, 1998: 77-78). Among Latinas, a slightly different pattern emerged; while more Latinas have entered the labor force in the past twenty years, they have been disproportionately concentrated in service industries offering slightly more than minimum wage and few to no benefits. In addition, while unemployment among Latinas decreased, the percentage of Latinas living in poverty increased from 22 percent in 1980 to 27 percent in 1998 (*Statistical Abstract of the United States,* 1999: Tables 768, 769). These signals indicate that while Chicanas and Latinas increasingly worked to expand the flow of capital into their own homes, they struggled to keep from losing what little economic ground they had achieved. Moreover, this shift in the types of work, income, and opportunities for Latina/os has led to the formation of a new class of underemployed working poor (Chapa, 1998). While this pattern of wage deflation and increased occupational insecurity impacted virtually all working class laborers in the United States in the 1990s, Chicana/os and Latina/os proved to be particularly vulnerable to its impacts as the downturn was compounded by an anti-immigrant movement that included all Chicana/os and Latina/os (not just immigrants) in its path.[10]

Specifically, with the onset of a recession and a weakened currency, Chicana/os and Latina/os were bombarded by a nativism that culminated in 1994-1996 with the passage of anti-immigrant legislation at both the state and federal level and a concerted effort to restrict the rights of documented and undocumented immigrants.[11] In its implementation, U.S.-born Chicana/os and Latina/os, as well as the immigrant population explicitly targeted in these laws, became subject to a host of racist expressions including verbal attacks on radio talk shows, racial profiling by state and local law enforcement officers, racist billboards in various Southwestern cities, and a range of verbal, emotional, and physical assaults waged by citizen groups empowered by these laws. Clearly, the economic insecurity introduced in this region by the intensification of globalization served as an important underlying factor in this racist hysteria.

THE FORMATION OF BINATIONAL
AND TRANSNATIONAL LATINA/O COMMUNITIES

Collectively these socioeconomic changes indicate a radical restructuring of national economies, but they also indicate a restructuring of individual labor, family life, and community among Chicana/os and Latina/os in the United States and Latin America. For many these changes are felt in terms of alienation, isolation, and fragmentation—what some have termed the "postmodern condition" (Aronowitz, 1981; Jameson, 1984; 1991; Laclau and Mouffe, 1985; Lyotard, 1984; Soja, 1989). What marks this stage is a sense of schizophrenic decentering and fragmentation reflected in a disproportionate emphasis on local events and localized knowledge, in Jameson's (1991: 413) terms a "multidimensional set of radically discontinuous realities." It has also reconfigured traditional forms of cultural and political expression in unexpected ways.

Obvious manifestations of these changing cultural sensibilities among Chicana/os and Latina/os are readily available in popular culture, where traditional standards such as oldies, mariachis, salsa, merengue, and cumbia have been continually supplanted by the fusion of sounds characteristic of *rock en español* bands such as Los Fabulosos Cadillacs (Argentina), Café Tacuba (Mexico City), Plastilina Mosh (Monterrey, Mexico), and Ozomatli (Los Angeles). Additional indicators of these shifting patterns of culture, identity, and political subjectivity can be found in the increasing numbers of Mexicans and Mexican Americans participating in Mexican politics (such as the 1999 Consulta Nacional, organized by the Los-Angeles based National Commission on Democracy in Mexico); the extension of binational citizenship in Brazil, Mexico, and Peru; and the decision of unions such as the Union of Needletrades, Industrial and Textile Employees (UNITE) to develop cross-border organizing strategies in the struggle against transnational corporations such as Guess Jeans (Silverstein, 1997; Ritchie, 1996).

Ultimately, these practices point to the formation of a binational or transnational cultural and political identity, one not easily understood in terms of paradigms emphasizing the nation-state. Nowhere has the realization of these new identities become more apparent than in the experiences of immigrants and in the emerging literature on the process of immigration between Latin America and the United States (Bonilla, 1993; Hondagneu-Sotelo, 1994;

Massey, 1986; Sassen, 1988; Ueda, 1994; see also Zavella in this volume). In general, these studies have attempted to shift the focus by examining the flow of transnational capital, the social location of immigrants in the context of the economic process of globalization, and their relationships to each other and to the changing national landscape. As Glick Schiller, Basch, and Szanton-Blanc (1994; 1995) point out, immigrants continually build familial and social networks that bridge the boundaries of multiple nations and which situate them in a transnational space between countries. Specifically, they argue (1995: 48):

> Transmigrants are immigrants whose daily lives depend on multiple and constant interconnections across international borders and whose public identities are configured in relationship to more than one nation-state. . . . They are not sojourners because they settle and become incorporated in the economy and political institutions, localities and patterns of daily life of the country in which they reside. However, at the very same time, they are engaged elsewhere in the sense that they maintain connections, build institutions, conduct transactions, and influence local and national events in countries from which they emigrated.

Moreover, Latin American immigrants are compelled to build and maintain these social networks not merely out of nostalgia for their home countries, but because they provide supportive structures in the midst of a global climate that is unsupportive of its poor and working-class immigrant populations. In both the United States and Europe, contemporary immigration policies have not only made the process of immigration more costly, more time-consuming, and generally more difficult for the poor and working-class populations migrating to the metropoles but have also resulted in the removal or suspension of immigrant rights and access to basic social services.[12] This racism has contributed to a heightened sense of political and economic insecurity for immigrants and their descendants.

Building social networks helps immigrants to strengthen their economic position in their new homes while securing resources and social position with family and community members back home. Furthermore, these connections have provided immigrants with opportunities to have their children cared for by family members in their home countries, to continue participating in family decisions, to make regular return trips, and to build homes and small businesses even while they engage in similar activities in their new locations (Rubenstein, 1982; Thomas-Hope, 1985; Gmelch, 1992). Thus, by constructing such transnational networks families and individual immigrants are able to "maximize the utilization of labor and resources in multiple settings and survive within situations of economic uncertainty and subordination" (Basch, Glick Schiller, and Szanton Blan, 1995: 54).

Finally, it should be clear that while industrial centers such as the United States have experienced periods of concentrated immigration coupled with intensive trade and expanded markets, the formation of contemporary transnational communities and the altered political subjectivity they embody are distinct. In particular, today's immigration is prompted by a massive restructuring of national economies that surpasses the scope of trade and integration of earlier decades. The closest comparison in U.S. history occurred at the turn of the century; however, this earlier version was characterized largely by the exchange of goods among small merchants, while contemporary globalization is structured by mergers of multinational industries and entire nation-states. Furthermore, the building of transnational networks is facilitated not strictly by trained merchants, official diplomats, or elites (as was the case in the late nineteenth century) but also by working-class immigrants via processes such as registering as binational citizens. Finally, these patterns of integration are expedited by the expansion of conventional communication media and the development of a host of new technologies that structure our very concepts of space and distance (Cabán, 1998; Poster, 1990).

BUILDING TRANSNATIONAL RESISTANCE

Recently, activists have appropriated and expanded on this understanding of globalization and the formation of transnational spaces of resistance to it. One such organization is Hermanas en la Lucha/Sisters in Struggle, a coalition of Chicanas/Latinas/Mestizas based in Denver, Colorado, whose goal is to form alliances with indigenous women outside the United States.

> We are the mothers and sisters, daughters and wives that have come together through the strength of our indigenous ancestors, women working in sisterhood to support each other in our struggles, learn what our sisters have to teach, pass our knowledge to future generations, and to join forces in order to empower our communities locally and continentally. . . . we are different yet the same; we struggle together for self-determination, justice and the right to exist as who we were, who we are, and who we will always be . . .

In forming this organization, the women borrowed a number of theoretical principles from the history of Chicana feminist activism (Garcia, 1990; 1997; Pesquera and de la Torre, 1993; Sandoval, 1991). Specifically, they recognized the history of discrimination that devalued not only the experiences of Chicana/os and Latina/os but also those of women and working-class communities, leading to the development of a "triple oppression" among women of color (Segura, 1986). The women recognized their own perspectives as a function of their experiences with race, class, and gender formations.

More important, Las Hermanas sought to link their struggles with the histories of other women (especially indigenous women) in Latin America generally and Mexico in particular. They argued that non-indigenous

Chicanas/Latinas shared a social, political, and economic location with women in Mexico by virtue of the relationship to colonialism, globalization, and racial, gendered, and class subordination. In particular, they targeted the struggle of women in Chiapas, in part because they saw their struggles for resistance as having important parallels with their own battles in the United States and felt confident that changes in this pattern would emerge only through some type of transnational alliance. Thus, their expression of feminism moved beyond a strictly First World perspective and struggled to identify areas of commonality that could address the alienation and ultimately erasure to which both populations of women had been exposed (Grewal and Kaplan, 1997; Mohanty, 1991; Johnson-Odim, 1991). As one woman put it (interview with Jillann Mills, August 6, 1999),

> We wanted the organization to be more. . . . We wanted it to encompass a lot more possibilities . . . and as women on this continent we've had to deal with the brunt of the problems that come from colonization and we wanted to develop a network or a co-op for dealing with these problems in a proactive way. We try to be proactive. What we want to do is help build the infrastructure of our community continentally. . . . I think it's time we take a new approach to the problem, and that's what we're trying to do with Hermanas. We're trying to select different projects that will help us grow and help our community grow and work on those projects. I'm kind of hoping that . . . Hermanas can be one of those organizations that begins the healing of our community as a whole.

Finally, in forming the organization and seeking connections with other women in struggle, Hermanas en la Lucha were actively seeking creative and productive ways to resist these forms of subordination. For them the recognition of the historical and contemporary struggles of women of color did not preclude an expression of agency. Moreover, much like the women in Chiapas, their own brand of feminist consciousness emerged principally from their experiences and attempts to negotiate with the misogyny of the Chicano movement in Denver, the racism of much of the women's liberation movement, and the daily battle for simple dignity (Pardo, 1998). In their construction this organization moved away from classic depictions of Third World women as colonized and "overdetermined"—a depiction frequently juxtaposed with the image of First World women as active, engaged, and enlightened (Kaplan, 1997; Sandoval, 1991; Narayan, 1997). In this way, the sensibilities of the Chicanas/Latinas in the group reflected a type of mestiza consciousness articulated by Gloria Anzaldua (1987: 80):

> As a *mestiza*, I have no country, my homeland cast me out; yet all countries are mine because I am every woman's sister or potential lover. . . . I am cultureless because, as a feminist, I challenge the collective cultural/religious male-derived beliefs of Indo-Hispanics and Anglos; yet, I am cultured because I am partici-

pating in the creation of yet another culture, a new story to explain the world and our participation in it, a new value system with images and symbols that connect us to each other and to the planet.

And yet, despite the notion that their efforts to develop alternatives to globalization that are rooted in the specificity of women of color signaled an important political and theoretical shift among both Chicana/Latina activists in the United States and international women's movements, their efforts were not without shortcomings. In particular, there were obvious distinctions of privilege (e.g., easy travel access) that were not always recognized by the women themselves. In one episode the women ended up in a lengthy and heated debate while they were staying in one of the Zapatista communities over how long their stay should be (they had committed to four nights, and some wanted to leave after the first), the cultural and linguistic shock some women were experiencing, and the sense some women had that they were imposing a burden on the community. While the questions raised in these discussions were never fully resolved, they spoke to a larger effort on behalf of the women to negotiate the commonalities of their struggles without erasing the specificity of their experiences and without replicating the hierarchy of privileges that underlay so many of their relationships as Chicanas/Latinas with white women in the United States.[13]

However, in spite of these shortcomings and the geographical, political, and cultural disparities that divided these women, there is some evidence that their "shared differences" were recognized by some of the Zapatista women. Specifically, in an interview I conducted with Margarita López Díaz, one of the women weavers who later came to visit Las Hermanas in Denver, she noted:

This [racism and discrimination against indigenous people] is very, very strong and what I've seen on this trip is that racism against indigenous peoples exists not only in Chiapas or in Mexico, but there is racism here in the U.S. as well. And it is important to note that the same thing that happens there [in Chiapas] also happens here [in the United States]. . . . And the women of my cooperative or other women in the region don't know that racism exists or that there are indigenous people here. Thus, it is very important for us Chiapanecas to see that in all parts of the world these same things are happening.

THE BREAD PROJECT

Theoretically, Hermanas en la Lucha both borrowed from the cultural nationalist movements in their philosophical and political practices (e.g., the reclaiming of indigenous past) and distinguished itself from previous expressions of

Chicana/o and Latina/o political subjectivity by focusing on a transnational subjectivity. Politically, the group sought to make this altered identity a reality by working to form a collaborative relationship of support with indigenous women of Chiapas—to become what one woman from the highlands termed *transnationalistas de solidaridad* (transnationalists in solidarity). Specifically, the group first began to organize around the effort to help women in the Mayetik[14] coffee cooperative in the Municipio of El Bosque to build ovens in their communities. The cooperative had been organized four years earlier for the purpose of encouraging Zapatista communities to build a sustainable economic system that promoted fair trade. It brought together twenty-four "communities in resistance" in the highlands to assist in the growing, harvesting, and processing of their coffee, a mainstay for most families in those communities. Together, men and women of the cooperative grew their coffee, established a fair price for their product (including the cost of the actual production [water, fertilizer, tools], the value of the labor, and the value of the expertise, experience, and abilities that the worker brings to the production process), and developed networks of buyers for their product. Over the years the cooperative had been very successful in creating a fair-trade network with buyers and a critical mass of consumers in Mexico, and establishing contracts in the United States, Japan, Italy, Germany, and Sweden. In effect, the cooperative had found a way to protect the goals of the Zapatista struggle in promoting indigenous rights and an end to exploitative economic practices while using the possibilities opened up through globalization to develop an alternative economic model.

However, while the cooperative has successfully created an economic base, the gendered division of labor and authority in the organization had led several of the women to feel that they needed a project of their own.[15] As a result, the women of the twenty-four communities of Mayetik organized to build community ovens to bake their own bread. This effort, which would become known among Las Hermanas simply as the bread project, reflected both the daily politics of survival in the communities of the highlands (many of the women expressed an interest in building ovens so that they would not have to purchase overpriced, nutritionally deficient bread and tortillas from the local government-owned stores), and the effort to create collective economic change (the women also expressed an interest in selling the products at the markets in San Cristóbal and someday forming a women's cooperative around the bread making). The women recognized that to make the project work they would need financial support as well as training, and it was in this context that they turned to Las Hermanas.

These were largely corn-based communities and did not have much experience in making flour-based products such as flour tortillas and *pan dulce* (Mexican sweet bread). Las Hermanas performed a unique service both in helping the women raise the necessary funds and in sharing the culturally specific tradition of bread making that for many was a mark of their own gendered division of labor in the United States.

Las Hermanas organized for over a year around the bread project. What was interesting about their collaboration was that they approached their fund-raising with the same philosophy as their mission statement. They did not simply solicit funds from corporate charities but looked for opportunities to organize the Chicana/o and Latina/o communities in Denver around the larger Zapatista struggle. In this way, they sought to extend their own consciousness as *transnationalistas en solidaridad* to the communities of Chicana/os and Latina/os in Denver and produce change in these communities as well. In addition, they brought to their organizing efforts not only a broader transnational framework but also a sense of accountability, reminding Denver residents that their own actions as consumers and as citizens were directly related to the Zapatista struggle. They achieved this through such activities as a *flor y canto* (a type of cultural variety show that includes poetry, storytelling, song, dance, and other expressive performances), a short video depicting the struggle of indigenous women in the United States and Chiapas (which they showed to local community-based organizations and community development corporations and in high schools, college classrooms, and student organizing meetings and distributed widely among friends), Sunday community breakfasts, and dances.

Their most financially and strategically successful fund-raiser was the *flor y canto* celebration held in a gymnasium in the heart of Denver's Latina/o community. Preparing for this event, the women recruited students from their college classes (many of them Anglo) and for weeks visited local *taquerias*, restaurants, artists' studios, and stores in the Latina/o community discussing the Zapatista struggle and soliciting everything from $2 donations to food, plates, drinks, artwork (for raffles), and other accessories for the event. In addition, they invited these and other local vendors to set up their own tables at the *flor y canto*. For the performance, the women lined up a range of performers reflecting the complexity of cultural formations described earlier. The evening culminated with a presentation of the video Las Hermanas had created, and a discussion about the role of women in the Zapatista military and the significance of the Zapatista struggle to their own communities. Finally, they were concerned to make the event accessible to everyone in the Latina/o community and therefore charged no admission (they did charge for food, drinks, and a raffle) and conducted the evening in both English and Spanish. As a result, the mix of students, community members, parents, friends, shop owners, vendors, and activists was far broader than for other events sponsored in Denver's Chicana/o and Latina/o community.

Ultimately, the women of Las Hermanas raised enough money to build seven ovens (along with providing material for bread in six communities) and to facilitate workshops on bread making in several of the communities.

The experience of raising the money and working with the women of Chiapas proved to be a truly transformative process for those involved. As one woman commented, "I started the bread project thinking I was going to raise money and help organize these communities in Chiapas, but I realized that the women [of Chiapas] were really teaching and organizing us. . . . They taught us how to use our indigenous traditions to organize collectively and to find ways of being inclusive" (Larrea, 2000).[16]

This project depicts one way in which women have expanded the space of globalization to build a transnational collaborative network of resistance and support. Las Hermanas is a unique example of the way in which individual lives (both in the United States and in Mexico) have been altered by globalization. In response to this globalization, both of these populations of women have asserted counterhegemonic political practices that have transformed their own lives and those of their communities. In this way, their work mirrors the description of transnational feminist politics articulated by Caren Kaplan (1997: 139):

A transnational feminist politics of location in the best sense of these terms refers us to the model of coalition, or, to affiliation. As a practice of affiliation, a politics of location identifies the grounds for historically specific differences and similarities between women in diverse and asymmetrical relations, creating alternative histories, identities, and possibilities for alliances.

CONCLUSION

The need to move beyond a strictly nation-state approach in both social science research and Chicana/o and Latina/o political subjectivity becomes increasingly apparent with the dissolution of traditional state powers. In response to shifting demographics and the desire for regional economic integration, states have become committed to opening up domestic markets, transferring regulatory capacities to private industry, and generally scaling back the size of government with the elimination of social welfare programs. In the aftermath of these changes, countries such as the United States have been forced to negotiate with multinational corporations and manufacturing giants to sustain manufacturing centers in the United States or risk increased job displacement and possibly recession (Ong, Bonacich, and Cheng, 1994). Nation-states have also had to negotiate and often compete with a proliferation of nongovernmental organizations over domestic policies such as immigration law and citizenship status.

Thus, the move toward regional economic unification transformed traditional nation-state borders, weakening their capacity to restrict the flow of capital, commodified culture, and professional immigrants and strengthening their capacity to restrict poor immigrants and alternative economic models of development. This weakening of traditional state borders has lent itself to a reconceptualizing of the positionality of individuals in both locations and a challenge to the traditional constructions of citizenship within the state. Moreover, recent research on immigrants and the flow of capital and culture has led to a new understanding of the enhanced flexibility and fluidity of identity between these spaces and the notion of the binational or transnational migrant.

Thus, globalization and the transnational networks established by economic integration have produced a context in which the familiar knowledge about Chicana/o subjectivity drawn from nationalist discourse and social science research on the individual or the national level is becoming incomplete at best. It is in this context of increased globalization (specifically the increased traffic of goods, services, customs, and especially people) and a commensurate re-structuring of Chicana/o and Latina/o communities in the U.S. (specifically with overall decreases in per capita income and education and changes in demographic statistics to include greater numbers of Latin American immigrants and first-generation Latinas/os) that we are called upon to reexamine the usefulness of a strictly nation-state analysis in the study of Chicana/os and Latina/os. To begin a reexamination of Chicana/o and Latina/o political subjectivity we must consider the impact of political strategies such as the efforts toward naturalization on both the immediate surroundings as well as political environments beyond these borders. To researchers and scholars working in Chicana/o and Latina/o communities this means that we must find a way to capture the international and transnational boundaries of this Chicana/o and Latina/o diaspora. More importantly, in discussing the creation of an oppositional consciousness in Chicana/o and Latina/o communities it is no longer sufficient to consider the experiences of Chicana/os and Latina/os, we must examine the way actions taken in favor or against minority communities in the United States impact the conditions of Latin Americans and other members of developing nations.

Furthermore, the path of influence can no longer be viewed as unidirectional, with the bulk of goods, services, people, and cultural processes moving from Latin America (and other parts of the Third World) to the United States, and economic policy and development strategies traveling from the United States to Latin America (Rouse, 1991; Kearney, 1996). Rather, the push toward regional economic integration and the transformation of Latina/o communities into transnational locations suggests a more symbiotic relationship in which influence is multidirectional.[17]

Finally, we must begin to consider the formation of political subjectivities that reflect the social locations of people rather than a unified racial or gendered consciousness. Moreover, it is not sufficient to recognize the difference in history and relationship to globalization in forming alliances, we are equally called upon to recognize our own relative privilege in the relationships we form with other women and men and the ways in which we are accountable to each other. Ultimately, while this movement toward globalization promises to de-centralize Chicana/o and Latina/o collective consciousness, it also stretches the imagination and possibilities for the linking of oppositional discourse to the struggles that have long been waged outside our own borders. It is this frame-work of resistance to hegemonic economic consolidation, coupled with the specificity of our own day-to-day struggles, that promises the most fruitful analyses of the future of Chicana/os and Latina/os opposition movements.

NOTES

1. In 1992, in preparation for NAFTA's passage, Mexico's legislature revoked Article 27 of the country's constitution. The move, considered by many to be one of the galvanizing features of the 1994 Chiapas rebellion, eliminated the state's *ejido* system of land distribution and replaced it with a system of private ownership that was more compatible with that of the United States. In borrowing the term "deterritorialization" I mean to suggest that for many of the indigenous people, rural poor, and *campesinos* of the country the changes in economic structure not only forced them to move from their communities but systematically undermined their ability to own, farm, and maintain any land.

2. One key indicator of the change in political identity among Chicana/os and Latina/os has been the opportunity to obtain dual citizenship and/or become more intimately involved in the politics of their homelands.

3. While the indigenous communities of Mexico have been largely neglected in terms of their representation in government assemblies and by elected officials, this is not universally true for Latina/os in the United States. While the vast majority of this population (particularly Mexican Americans and Puerto Ricans, who represent more than two-thirds of the total Latina/o population) are working-class and will not participate in electoral politics, Chicana/os and Latina/os have had some success in gaining electoral leverage, with an increasing number occupying elected office. It is still the case, however, that only about one-third of the Latina/o population will vote in a presidential election, and the specific interests that register as important in their home communities are often ignored. In addition, the position of second-class citizenship becomes even clearer when we discuss the growing population of immigrants who are increasingly barred from governmental structures, cultural institutions, and employment because of a combination of de jure (e.g., English-only language requirements) and de facto restrictions (Schmidt, 2000). Thus, in drawing comparisons between indigenous Chiapanecos and Chicana/os in the United States I mean to imply not an exact comparison but a parallel "relative deprivation" that manifests itself in regionally specific forms (Vélez-Ibáñez, 1996).

4. One of the best indicators of this affinity is the development of web pages in Chicana/o and Latina/o politics that discuss the Zapatista struggle, make use of cultural symbols rooted in the Zapatista rebellion, or serve as organizing tools for humanitarian projects in Chiapas. For a sampling of some of these pages see La Voz de Aztlán (www.aztlan.net) and the Azteca web page (www.mexica.net).

5. For a more elaborate examination of the effect of U.S. economic theory on changes in Latin America, particularly the cadre of social scientists from University of Chicago School of Economics (the "Chicago boys"), which provided both theoretical foundations and technical assistance for Chile's neoliberal experiment, see Collins and Lear (1995: 37-46)

6. Of particular significance here is the absence of Mexico in these growth patterns. Whereas reports from the Department of Commerce indicated significant growth in Mexico's economy at the beginning of the decade, this pattern collapsed shortly after the passage of the NAFTA in 1994, when the emergence of rebel forces in the state of Chiapas and the flight of nervous investors forced the rapid devaluation of the Mexican peso and the near collapse of the state's financial institutions. Steady increases in the levels of imports from Mexico to the United States were reported throughout this decade (*Statistical Abstract of the United States*, 1998: Tables 1302, 1304).

7. As Bonilla (1998) mentions, these efforts at economic integration are also apparent in the 1994 "Summit of the Americas," in which presidents and heads of state from throughout the region endorsed a broad range of economic measures intended to encourage greater regional integration.

8. Between 1981 and 1990, the INS recorded the entrance of 455,900 immigrants from South America and 458,700 from Central America. Between 1991 and 1996 the numbers of South American immigrants totaled 344,000 (an increase of approximately 18,000 immigrants per year), while the numbers of Central Americans in the same period rose to 342,800 (with a comparable rise of approximately 17,500 per year) (INS Statistics, U.S. Immigration and Naturalization Service Homepage, 1999). However, among foreign-born Latina/os by far the largest and most significant increase in this period occurred among immigrants from the Dominican Republic. The total flow of Dominican immigrants between 1981 and 1990 reached 251,800; however, between 1991 and 1996 the number of Dominican immigrants totaled 258,100. In essence, the percentage of immigrants from the Dominican Republic virtually doubled beginning in the 1990s, significantly increasing the total population of Dominicans in the United States (*Statistical Abstract of the United States*, 1998: Tables 5-11).

9. Ironically, economic integration also created new opportunities for a professional-managerial class of Latin American entrepreneurs, sales representatives, consultants, engineers, and other highly educated workers to enter the U.S. and European economies (Chapa, 1998). The migration of this elite class of workers subsequently aided in the expansion of a U.S. Chicana/o and Latina/o middle class; however, the experience of these workers differed greatly from that of the larger percentage of working-class immigrants who were increasingly younger, less well educated, and poorer (Sampaio, 2001).

10. The persistent wage deflation among Latina/os and their overrepresentation in service industries documented here must be evaluated in conjunction with the undermining of traditional avenues of economic mobility in the past decade. In particular, since the early 1990s there has been a nationwide effort to rescind programs such as affirmative action and race/gender-based scholarships that promote opportunities in college admissions, retention, hiring, and promotions for women and racial minorities. In California, Texas, and Colorado these efforts have been matched by a push to undo programs of bilingual education and of ethnic and gender studies.

In the same period, the percentage of Latinas in single-headed households has increased (*Statistical Abstract of the United States*, 1999: Table 82), as has the percentage of single Latinas caring for children with no spousal support. This has been compounded by the repeal of state-sponsored support programs, the most notable of these being the dismantling of Aid to Families with Dependent Children in 1996 and its replacement by Temporary Aid to Needy Families, which imposed more restrictive conditions for receiving government assistance and dramatically reduced the length of time an individual could receive such support. While no single factor mentioned here (the rescinding of affirmative action and race/gender-based scholarships, the increase of single Latina headed households with children and no spousal support, and the reduction of state-sponsored support) can be linked directly to globalization, their combined effect in the context of a restructured political economy that has restricted opportunities for Latinas in the United States has been a concentrated underclass status akin to those that we have seen among women in Latin America.

11. In 1996 alone Congress passed a number of bills that would negatively impact Latina/o immigrant communities in the United States, including the Illegal Immigration Reform and Immigrant Responsibility Act, the Personal Responsibility and Work Opportunity Reconciliation Act, and the Antiterrorism and Effective Death Penalty Act.

12. It should be clear that while this is increasingly the case for poor and working-class immigrants, Congress has taken steps to ensure easy entrance for the host of professional-managerial immigrants who come to work as consultants, engineers, middle managers, and other professionals.

13. In another heated episode, the women in the organization debated what role (if any) men should play in the group. While Hermanas en la Lucha was originally formed from a small coalition of women, two men who were related to one of the women later joined the organization and began making demands of the women's time that many felt unwarranted. When some of the women discussed making "most wanted" banners of the men in their communities who could be identified as spouse abusers, one of these men exhibited verbally abusive behavior at the women's meetings. After a number of contentious discussions on the topic and some severed relationships between women in the organization, Las Hermanas eventually decided to eliminate men from the core of the organization.

14. As with informants' names, the name of the coffee cooperative has been changed to protect the communities.

15. Coffee production is a very labor-intensive process, involving long periods of picking, washing, depulping, drying, raking, and packaging. In the communities I have visited, the men were largely responsible for the maintenance of the coffee plants and the harvesting of the coffee, but the remaining processing elements were disproportionately women's work and tended to take place in or around the home. Ultimately, day-to-day authority over the distribution of resources related to coffee came to reside with the men, although decisions that affected the entire cooperative were discussed and decided on the basis of consensus.

16. Hermanas en la Lucha has continued to work with the women of the highlands to raise money for additional ovens in their communities and to help form a women's weaving cooperative that would continue the process of building fair-trade networks.

17. A recent example of the multidirectional nature of transnational culture is the emergence of *la chupacabra* as a feature of U.S. and Mexican popular culture. Be-

ginning as a myth about roving goat-suckers in rural Puerto Rico in 1995, it soon appeared in newspapers and oral histories in northern Mexico, and then in reported sightings (depicted in music and on T-shirts) in Mexico City. Ultimately, it was "sighted" in San Diego and Los Angeles, and by the end of 1997 it had become the subject of one of the country's most popular television programs, *The X-Files*. Since then the series has been rebroadcast over Univision to countries all over Latin America, including Puerto Rico and Northern Mexico.

REFERENCES

Acuña, Rodolfo. 1972. *Occupied America: The Chicano's Struggle Toward Liberation*. San Francisco: Canfield Press.

———. 1988. *Occupied America: The Chicano's Struggle Toward Liberation*. 3rd Ed. New York: Harper & Row.

Anzaldúa, Gloria. 1987. *Borderlands/La Frontera: The New Mestiza*. San Francisco, CA: Aunt Lute Books.

Aronowitz, Stanley. 1981. *The Crisis in Historical Materialism: Class, Politics, and Culture in Marxist Theory*. New York: Praeger.

Barrera, Mario. 1979. *Race and Class in the Southwest: A Theory of Racial Inequality*. Notre Dame, IN: University of Notre Dame Press.

Basch, Linda G., Glick Schiller, Nina, and Szanton Blan, Cristina, 1994. *Nations Unbound: Transnational Projects, Postcolonial Predicaments, and Deterritorialized Nation-States*. New York: Routledge.

Benjamin, Medea. 1995. "Interview: Subcomandante Marcos," in Elaine Katzenberger, (ed.), *First World, Ha Ha Ha!: The Zapatista Challenge*. San Francisco: City Lights.

Bonilla, Frank. 1993. "Migrants, Citizenship, and Social Pacts," in Edwin Meléndez and Edgardo Meléndez (eds.), *Colonial Dilemma: Critical Perspectives on Contemporary Puerto Rico*. Boston: South End Press.

———. 1998. "Changing the Americas from Within the United States," in Frank Bonilla, Edwin Meléndez, Rebecca Morales, and María de los Angeles Torres (eds.), *Borderless Borders: U.S. Latinos, Latin Americans, and the Paradox of Interdependence*. Philadelphia: Temple University Press.

Cabán, Pedro. 1998. "The New Synthesis of Latin American and Latino Studies," in Frank Bonilla, Edwin Meléndez, Rebecca Morales, and María de los Angeles Torres (eds.), *Borderless Borders: U.S. Latinos, Latin Americans and the Paradox of Interdependence*. Philadelphia: Temple University Press.

Center for the Study of Western Hemisphere Trade. 1999. "Tracking U.S. Trade." http://lanic.utexas.edu/cswht/tradeindex/index.html. March 14.

Chapa, Jorge. 1998. "The Burden of Interdependence: Demographic, Economic, and Social Prospects for Latinos in the Reconfigured U.S. Economy," in Frank Bonilla, Edwin Meléndez, Rebecca Morales, and María de los Angeles Torres (eds.), *Borderless Borders: U.S. Latinos, Latin Americans and the Paradox of Interdependence*. Philadelphia: Temple University Press.

Collier, George. 1994. "The Rebellion in Chiapas and the Legacy of Energy Development," *Mexican Studies/Estudios Mexicanos* 10(2).

Collins, Joseph and John Lear. 1995. *Chile's Free-Market Miracle: A Second Look*. Oakland: Institute for Food and Development Policy.

Comisíon Nacional por la Democracia en México. 1996. "¡Celebramos la lucha de las mujeres! ¡Celebramos la lucha de las mujeres zapatistas!" El Paso, Texas.

Foucault, Michel. 1977. *Power/Knowledge: Selected Interviews and Other Writings, 1972–1977.* New York: Pantheon Books.

García, Alma. 1990. "The Development of Chicana Feminist Discourse, 1970–1980," in Ellen C. Dubois and Vicki L. Ruiz (eds.), *Unequal Sisters: A Multicultural Reader in U.S. Women's History.* New York and London: Routledge.

———. 1997. "Introduction," in Alma Garcia (ed.), *Chicana Feminist Thought: The Basic Historical Writings.* New York: Routledge.

Glick Schiller, Nina, Linda Basch, and Cristina Szanton Blan. 1995. "From Immigrant to Transmigrant: Theorizing Transnational Migration." *Anthropological Quarterly,* 68: 48-63.

Gmelch, George. 1992. *Double Passage: The Lives of Caribbean Migrants Abroad and Back Home.* Ann Arbor: University of Michigan Press.

Gomez-Pena, Guillermo. 1998. "1995—Terreno Peligroso/Danger Zone: Cultural Relations Between Chicanos and Mexicans at the End of the Century," in *Borderless Borders: U.S. Latinos, Latin Americans, and the Paradox of Interdependence,* Frank Bonilla, Edwin Melendez, Rebecca Morales, and Maria de los Angeles Torres (eds.). Philadelphia: Temple University Press.

Gómez-Quiñones, Juan. 1971. "Toward a Perspective on Chicano History," *Aztlán,* 2 (2): 1-49.

———. 1974. "On the State of Chicano History: Observations on Its Development, Interpretations, and Theory, 1970-1974." *Western Historical Quarterly,* 7 (2): 156-185.

———. 1978. *Mexican Students Por La Raza: The Chicano Student Movement in Southern California, 1967–1977.* Santa Barbara, CA: Editorial La Causa.

González-Estay, Manolo. 1998. "The Californization of Chilean Farms: Preliminary Study of the Social Consequences of Chilean Campesinos in a Global System of Production." Paper presented at the Twenty-first International Congress of the Latin American Studies Association, September.

Grewal, Inderpal and Caren Kaplan. 1997. "Transnational Feminist Practices and the Questions of Postmodernity," in Inderpal Grewal and Caren Kaplan (eds.), *Scattered Hegemonies: Postmodernity, and Transnational Feminist Practices.* Minneapolis: University of Minnesota.

Hamilton, Nora and Norma Stoltz Chinchilla. 1997. "Central American Migration: A Framework for Analysis," in Mary Romero, Pierrette Hondagneu-Sotelo, and Vilma Ortiz (eds.), *Challenging Fronteras: Structuring Latina and Latino Lives in the U.S.* New York: Routledge.

Harvey, Neil. 1990. "Peasant Strategies and Corporatism in Chiapas," in Joe Foweraker and Ann Craig (eds.), *Popular Movements and Political Change in Mexico.* Boulder, CO: Lynne Rienner.

Hondagneu-Sotelo, Pierrette. 1994. *Gendered Transitions: Mexican Experiences of Immigration.* Berkeley: University of California Press.

Huerta, Alberto. 1995. "Seeds of a Revolt," in Elaine Katzenberger (ed.), *First World, Ha Ha Ha! The Zapatista Challenge.* San Francisco: City Lights.

INS Statistics, U.S. Immigration and Naturalization Service Homepage. 1999. http://www.ins.usdoj.gov/stats/annual. March.

Jameson, Frederic. 1984. "Postmodernism or The Cultural Logic of Late Capitalism." *New Left Review* 146.

———. 1991. *Postmodernism, or The Cultural Logic of Late Capitalism*. Durham, NC: Duke University Press.

Johnson-Odim, Cheryl. 1991. "Common Themes, Different Contexts: Third World Women and Feminism," in Chandra Talpade Mohanty, Ann Russo, and Lourdes Torres (eds.), *Third World Women and the Politics of Feminism*. Bloomington: Indiana University Press.

Kaplan, Caren. 1997. "The Politics of Location as Transnational Feminist Critical Practice," in Inderpal Grewal and Caren Kaplan (eds.), *Scattered Hegemonies: Postmodernity, and Transnational Feminist Practices*. Minneapolis: University of Minnesota.

Katzenberger, Elaine. 1995. "Living Conditions," in Elaine Katzenberger (ed.), *First World, Ha Ha Ha! The Zapatista Challenge*. San Francisco: City Lights.

Kearney, Michael. 1996. *Reconceptualizing the Peasantry: Anthropology in Global Perspective*. Boulder, CO: Westview Press.

Laclau, Ernesto and Chantal Mouffe. 1985. *Hegemony and Socialist Strategy: Towards a Radical Democratic Politics*. London: Verso.

Larrea, Monica. 2000. "Building Transnational Feminist Resistance." Paper presented at International Women's Week, Boulder, CO, March 8.

Legorreta Gómez, María del Carmen. 1994. *La República de Agascalientes a Zacatecas*.

Los Socios de la Unión 'Tierra Tzotzil'. 1990. *La historia de cómo compramos nuestra finca*. Chiapas: INAREMAC.

Lyotard, Jean-François. 1984. *The Postmodern Condition: A Report on Knowledge*. Minneapolis: University of Minnesota Press.

Mander, Jerry and Edward Goldsmith (eds.). 1996. *The Case Against the Global Economy: And for a Turn Toward the Local*. San Francisco: Sierra Club Books.

Massey, Douglas. 1986. "The Social Organization of Mexican Immigration to the United States." *Annals of the American Academy of Political and Social Science* 487 (September).

Mohanty, Chandra Talpade. 1991. "Cartographies of Struggle: Third World Women and the Politics of Feminism," in Chandra Talpade Mohanty, Ann Russo, and Lourdes Torres (eds.), *Third World Women and the Politics of Feminism*. Bloomington: Indiana University Press.

Morales, Rebecca. 1998. "Dependence or Interdependence: Issues and Policy Choices Facing Latin Americans and Latinos," in Frank Bonilla, Edwin Meléndez, Rebecca Morales, and María de los Angeles Torres (eds.), *Borderless Borders: U.S. Latinos, Latin Americans and the Paradox of Interdependence*. Philadelphia: Temple University Press.

Mercer, Kobena. 1990. "Welcome to the Jungle: Identity and Diversity in Postmodern Politics," in Jonathan Rutherford (ed.), *Identity: Community, Culture, and Difference*. London: Lawrence and Wishart.

Muñoz, Carlos. 1970. "Toward a Chicano Perspective of Political Analysis." *Aztlan* 1(2).

———. 1983. "The Quest for a Paradigm: The Development of Chicano Studies and Intellectuals," in National Association for Chicano Studies (ed.), *History, Culture, and Society: Chicano Studies in the 1980s*. Ypsilanti, MI: Bilingual Press/Editorial Bilingue.

———. 1989. *Youth, Identity, Power: The Chicano Movement.* London and New York: Verso.

Narayan, Uma. 1997a. "Contesting Cultures 'Westernization,' Respect for Cultures, and Third-World Feminists," in Linda Nicholson (ed.), *The Second Wave: A Reader in Feminist Theory.* New York and London: Routledge.

———. 1997b. *Dislocating Cultures: Identities, Traditions, and Third-World Feminism.* New York and London: Routledge.

Ong, Paul, Edna Bonacich, and Lucie Cheng (eds.). 1994. *The New Asian Immigration in Los Angeles and Global Restructuring.* Philadelphia: Temple University Press.

Pardo, Mary. 1998. *Mexican American Women Activists: Identity and Resistance in Two Los Angeles Communities.* Philadelphia: Temple University Press.

Pesquera, Beatríz and Adela de la Torre. 1993. "Introduction," in Adela de la Torre and Beatríz M. Pesquera (eds.), *Building With Our Hands: New Directions in Chicana Studies.* Berkeley: University of California Press.

Poniatowska, Elena. 1995. "Women, Mexico, and Chiapas," in Elaine Katzenberger (ed.), *First World, Ha Ha Ha! The Zapatista Challenge.* San Francisco: City Lights.

Poster, Mark. 1990. *The Mode of Information: Poststructuralism and Social Context.* Chicago: University of Chicago Press.

Portes, Alejandro and Alex Stepick. 1997. "A Repeat Performance? The Nicaraguan Exodus," in Mary Romero, Pierrette Hondagneu-Sotelo, and Vilma Ortiz (eds.), *Challenging Fronteras: Structuring Latina and Latino Lives in the U.S.* New York: Routledge.

Ritchie, Mark. 1996. "Cross-Border Organizing," in *The Case Against the Global Economy: And for a Turn Toward the Local.* San Francisco: Sierra Club Books.

Rouse, Roger. 1991. "Mexican Migration and the Social Space of Postmodernism." *Diaspora* 1(1): 8-23.

Rubenstein, Hymie. 1982. "Return Migration to the English-Speaking Caribbean: Review and Commentary," in William F. Stinner, Klaus de Albuquerque, and Roy S. Bruce-Laporte (eds.), *Return Migration and Remittances: Developing a Caribbean Perspective.* Research Institute on Immigration and Ethnic Studies: Smithsonian Institution, Occasional Papers, No.3.

Rus, Diana. 1997. *Mujeres de Tierra Fria.* Chiapas: Universidad de Ciencias y Artes del Estado de Chiapas.

Rus, Jan. 1995. "Local Adaptation to Global Change: The Reordering of Native Society in Highland Chiapas, Mexico, 1974–1994." *European Review of Latin American and Caribbean Studies* 58 (June).

Sanchez, George J. 1990. "'Go After the Women': Americanization and the Mexican Immigrant Woman, 1915-1929," in *Unequal Sisters: A Multicultural Reader in U.S. Women's History.* New York and London: Routledge.

———. 1993. *Becoming Mexican American: Ethnicity, Culture, and Identity in Chicano Los Angeles, 1900-1945.* New York: Oxford University Press.

Sampaio, Anna. 2001. "Crossing Disciplinary Borders: Re-examining Latina/o Studies and Latin American Studies." *Latino Studies Journal,* 12 (1): 3–35.

Sandoval, Chela. 1991. "U.S. Third World Feminism: The Theory and Method of Oppositional Consciousness in the Postmodern World." *Genders,* No. 10 (Spring).

Sassen, Saskia. 1988. *The Mobility of Labor and Capital: A Study in International Investment and Labor Flow.* Cambridge, MA: Harvard University Press.

———. 1998. "The Transnationalization of Immigration Policy," in Frank Bonilla, Edwin Meléndez, Rebecca Morales, and María de los Angeles Torres (eds.), *Borderless Borders: U.S. Latinos, Latin Americans, and the Paradox of Interdependence.* Philadelphia: Temple University Press.

Schmidt, Ron. 2000. *Language Policy and Identity Politics in the United States.* Philadelphia: Temple University Press.

Segura, Denise. 1986. "Chicanas and Triple Oppression in the Labor Force," in *Chicana Voices: Intersections of Class, Race, and Gender,* Teresa Cordova, Norma Cantu, Gilberto Cardenas, Juan Garcia, and Christine M. Sierra (eds.). Austin, TX: The Center for Mexican American Studies.

Silverstein, Stuart. 1997. "A UNITEd Effort," *Los Angeles Times,* February 16.

Soja, Edward W. 1989. *Postmodern Geographies: The Reassertion of Space in Critical Social Theory.* London and New York: Verso.

Spivak, Gayatri. 1997. "'In a Word': Interview," in Linda Nicholson (ed.), *The Second Wave: A Reader in Feminist Theory.* New York and London: Routledge.

Statistical Abstract of the United States. 1998. Washington, DC: U.S. Department of Commerce.

Statistical Abstract of the United States. 1999. Washington, DC: U.S. Department of Commerce.

Suro, Roberto. 1998. *Strangers Among Us: How Latino Immigration is Transforming America.* New York: Knopf.

Thomas-Hope, Elizabeth M. 1985. "Return Migration and Its Implications for Caribbean Development: The Unexplored Connection," in Robert Pastor (ed.), *Migration and Development in the Caribbean: The Unexplored Connection.* Boulder, CO: Westview Press.

Ueda, Reed. 1994. *Postwar Immigrant America: A Social History.* New York: St. Martin's Press.

Vélez-Ibáñez, Carlos G. 1996. *Border Visions: Mexican Cultures of the Southwest United States.* Tucson: University of Arizona Press.

Womack, John. 1999. "Chiapas, the Bishop of San Cristóbal, and the Zapatista Revolt," in *Rebellion in Chiapas.* New York: New Press.

2

The Politics of Labeling: Latino/a Cultural Identities of Self and Others

Suzanne Oboler

"I am what I am." Thus begins "Ending Poem," by Aurora Levins-Morales and Rosario Morales (1986: 212–13), a mother-and-daughter statement that reaffirms the existence of the self and is almost a challenge to those who question the existence in the United States of a Latina identity and culture. It supports the critique by Eliana Ortega and Nancy Saporta-Sternbach (1989: 3) of the claim that minority literatures express a search for identity rather than a "paradigm of self-affirmation in the Latina writer, a self-perception and self-definition." Certainly the Moraleses' "Ending Poem" would support Ortega and Saporta-Sternbach's view that among U.S. Latina writers, the issue is more a question of searching for "the expression or articulation of that identity, but not for . . . identity itself." Throughout the poem, mother and daughter alternate in their affirmation of their respective identities and use historical, geographical, ancestral, culinary, and other cultural aspects to characterize their (Latina) selves.

Still, reading the Moraleses' poem, one is struck by the ways in which *both* self (I am what I am) and other (I am not what I am not) are fundamental to the construction of the identities of these individual Latinas—and, one might say, to the ethos of the (Latino) group:

I am not African.
Africa waters the roots of my tree, but I cannot return.
I am not Taina. *I am a late leaf of that ancient tree*
and my roots reach into the soil of two Americas.
Taino is in me, but there is no way back.

I am not European, though I have dreamt of those cities.
Europe lives in me but I have no home there.[1]

Characterizations of the self necessarily evoke those of the other, and there are many "others" to be portrayed, re-created, and redefined in the process of constructing and affirming the Latina self. As Ortega and Saporta-Sternbach have argued (1989: 14), "In constructing herself as a subject, a Latina must dismantle the representation of stereotypes of her self, constructed, framed, and projected by the dominant ideology." The need to dismantle stereotypes is well known and can be traced to the dichotomizing of self and other apparent, for example, in the essentializing practices of classical anthropology. Recent critiques of traditional anthropology suggest that the study of the other has been as much about the affirmation of the anthropologist's self as about the construction of the native's otherness.[2] If this is true, then one might ask, how are the dichotomies of self versus other problematized when dealing with bicultural or multicultural peoples? Is not the affirmation of the self, and the examination of stereotypes of it, also the affirmation of the internalized (stereotyped) others within it (Lorde, 1990; Fanon, 1967; Anzaldúa, 1990)?[3]

One could argue, for example, that these various "others" are also (although certainly not only) aspects of the ethos of the Latino/a[4] ethnic group. Let me enumerate some of them: (1) There is the Latino as gendered other, (2) there is the Latino self as a Hispanic other, (3) then there is the notion of Latino as a class-specific other. (4) There is the Latino self as a racial other—whether that racial other is called *Mestizo/a*, the nonwhite, the white-Hispanic, the person of color, la *raza*, etc. (5) There is the Latino self as an American other—and, within that otherness, one must distinguish whether one is referring to the self as U.S. citizen or as a member of the population of the Americas as a whole. (6) There is the Latino self as a Latin American national other: the Puerto Rican self, the Mexican self, the Chicano/a, Colombian, Peruvian, Dominican, etc.[5] The question is how, if at all, is this internalized identity-tension between self and other(s) articulated and dealt with by those who identify themselves or are designated as Latinos in the United States? Are they indeed affirming the self, even as they redefine the other(s)? And if so, how?

These questions are important if we are to better understand the notion of Latinos as constituting a "social movement" (Flores and Yudice, 1990). Given the varying meanings in daily life in U.S. society of ethnic/racial identities—whether self-defined or imposed—there is a need to further explore the construction of Latino identity and "ethnic consciousness" both within and beyond the context of the "situational ethnicity" that Felix Padilla (1985) has described in his important study on "Latinismo" among Mexican Americans and Puerto Ricans in Chicago.[6] Indeed, the fact that with the gradual dissemination of the term Hispanic since the 1970s a significant number of second- and later-generation Latinos have grown up identified and self-identifying as Latinos or Hispanics raises the question whether Latinismo can be viewed, in certain regions around the country, solely as a "situational" identity, particularly in urban areas like New York City.[7] Preliminary observations among second and later generations of Chicanos, Puerto Ricans, Cubans, Dominicans, and Central and South Americans raised in the United States appear to suggest that for some, Latinismo is not only or necessarily "situational." Latino-Americans are growing up in the borderlands of at least two cultures and are affected by and aware of the discrimination and prejudice against them as *Latinos*. It is therefore not surprising that some might want to take the term farther by constructing their identities as a group in this country.[8] The result seems to be the creation of new Latino histories and traditions that may in effect be eroding these later generations' consciousness of the historical discrimination against Mexican-Americans and Puerto Ricans since 1848 and 1898, respectively, and of the differences in modes of incorporation into the U.S. economy between these groups and the Latin American and Caribbean immigrants arriving in the past two decades.

I will therefore focus on some of the internalized others within and against which the Latino/a self is asserted in the United States to suggest (1) that class and race background and values shape the meaning and social value individuals attribute to the terms they adopt to define both self and other and (2) that, at least in the present conjuncture, both self and other are fundamental to the formation of the ethos of the Latino/a ethnic group in the United States. I will explore the self/other dichotomy through an analysis of interviews with middle- and working-class Latinos currently living and working in New York City.[9]

THE LATINO/A AS OTHER

The Gendered Other

Gender ideologies throughout the world have traditionally privileged men with better employment possibilities (Leacock and Safa, 1986). Latin American societies have been no exception to this rule. Indeed, in spite of the economic realities on the continent, Latin American societies continue to hold that a respectable woman's place is in the home (Brown, 1975; Rubbo, 1975).[10] Discussing women and work in the United States, Rubin (1976: 171) has pointed out that "historically, it has been a source of status in working-class communities for a woman to be able to say 'I don't *have* to work.'" This observation is applicable to Latin America, although status considerations there are not limited to working-class communities. As one male informant whose social status was middle-class in his home country explained:

> I had to work for so many people in the family that it got very difficult for me because in Colombia, the wife doesn't work. When one reaches a certain position, the wife becomes the gracious hostess. She's the one who takes care of the children, she's the person who collaborates, but she doesn't really produce any money

through work . . . the social side has to be kept up. There are those who say, "How can so-and-so's wife go to work! It's impossible!" (Francisco, Colombia)

While immigration had directly affected men's perceptions of women's traditional roles, it was the women I interviewed who provided the best interpretations of the types of cultural adjustments men have to make when women enter the workforce here in the United States: "It's harder for men because they have to forget their *machismo* and depend on themselves here" (Soledad, Colombia). The women reported that many men begin to help with the household chores, which may lead some to feel that their masculinity and pride is undermined in the immigration process—a finding confirmed in Pessar's (1987) study of Dominican households in the United States. Both the men and the women I interviewed agreed that men had better job opportunities here in the United States, but only the women expressed negative feelings about men's working lives: "He's got to pay the rent, the big bills. They have to have two jobs here. It's easier to buy a house there than it is here. Come to think of it, he hasn't gone up in life as I have" (Milagros, Peru).

Coming from a male-privileged employment context, the women incorporate these changes into their own sense of self, challenging the stereotyped gendered other within. As a result of immigration, a woman's sense of self begins to shift back and forth between her previous "othered" socialization and values and the "new self" constructed in a daily life of active participation in the workforce, which often (as noted by Pessar and Grasmuck, 1991) results in her becoming the primary or at least an equal contributing member of her household.

Comparing their juggling of work and household chores here and in their own countries, some women explained why life for them was easier here: "It's better because you don't have to wash all day long, and you can get clothes that don't have to be ironed. You can study. Back home, I wouldn't be able to do what I do here" (Milagros, Peru). This woman added that the ability to pay some of the bills gave her a new sense of freedom and of self. It also made her feel that she had bettered herself. But for some of the women life here raised other issues: "It's not better here because here mothers have to leave their children with someone outside of their circle of family and friends to go to work" (María, Dominican Republic). The need to rely on people other than family and friends is a forced departure from the traditional cultural patterns of the Latin American extended family. Dealing with this break—and with the struggle not only for daily survival but also to recognize oneself and adapt to changes in gender roles, values, and expectations—is at the heart of both immigrant men's and women's lives in the United States.

Still, people with ties to Latin America and the Caribbean in this country are not seen merely as men and women struggling with the changes in their gender values brought on by immigration. Rather, regardless of the way or time of their arrival in U.S. society, they are identified as Hispanic men and women, and this identity interacts with their experiences here in the United States and hence also challenges their already shifting sense of self.

The Hispanic Other

Over the past two decades, the term Hispanic has come into general use in the United States to refer to all people in this country whose ancestry is predominantly from one or more Spanish-speaking countries. The term therefore assigns people of a variety of national backgrounds to a single "ethnic" category. It encompasses great racial and class diversity, obscures gender differences, and even includes people whose primary language is not Spanish (Flores, 1985; Hayes-Bautista and Chapa, 1987; Giménez, 1989). The Hispanic othered-self is, through its implicit homogenization, a denial of the diversity of national, linguistic, social, historical, cultural, gendered, racial, political, and religious experiences of at least 25 million people. Despite this, the term Hispanic is increasingly used, as Trevino (1987) notes, by Hispanics and non-Hispanics alike to establish the idea of a homogeneous Hispanic ethnic group.

Not surprisingly, the term has caused much confusion among government agencies, scholars, the media, and the public at large. It directly affects both policy decisions and the individual selves of many immigrants, residents, and citizens with ties to Latin America and the Caribbean. In failing to do justice to the variety of backgrounds and conditions of the individuals to whom it has been applied, the term Hispanic can have the effect of denying their sense of self. This became clear in my interviews with Latinos as they sought to define themselves in relation to the Hispanic other attributed to them. Informants rejected the term Hispanic as a self-identifier, but this rejection took many forms and was particularly differentiated in terms of social class.

The Class-Specific Other

One of the revealing points that emerged again and again in the interviews was the extent to which people's sense of self contrasted, sometimes dramatically, with the connotations they attributed to the label Hispanic. While many informants had been forced by immigration to reexamine their gender roles and values, they did so through the prism of the values shaped in their own countries. And, although all of the informants were working in the garment industry in New York City and so had what are here considered traditional working-class occupations, not all of them had had working-class occupations or status in their own countries. Social class values were clearly a determinant of both their sense of self and the ways in which they positioned themselves in a society that applied to them a label with negative connotations.

People with a middle-class background immediately pointed out that the term was derogatory, but they recognized that, derogatory or not, that is what they were called. One informant, for example, explained the term this way: "They invented the word Hispanic to discriminate against us. We are at the bottom of the pile here" (Francisco, Colombia). Another middle-class person said, "I'm Colombian, but in the census I wrote Hispanic. That's what they call us here."

In contrast, working-class informants appeared reluctant to call them-selves Hispanic or even to discuss the term in relation to themselves. They clearly saw it as identifying a group of people with negative attributes, and they implied that these people had absolutely nothing to do with them. Not surprisingly, many informants simply distanced themselves from the term and asserted their sense of self in terms of their continental and national ori-gins: "It's wrong to call us Hispanic, because that word applies to the Spaniards. We're not Spaniards. We're from Latin America" (Alicia, Colom-bia). Others explicitly recognized the existence of the Hispanic as other by expressing deep disapproval of those they identified as Hispanics in this so-ciety. Thus, one person began by denying any knowledge of the meaning of the term and ended up by specifying its negative connotations. In her inter-pretation, Hispanic was a term that "they" (i.e., mainstream U.S. society) used as a synonym for "pigs," people who were "dirty," had "bad habits," lacked morals, and were "noisy." She concluded, "So because of those two or three families, they call us all Hispanics" (Rosa, El Salvador).

Hence this informant expressed her fear of being labeled Hispanic and openly distanced herself from the term. That is very different from the middle-class perception that "Hispanics are at the bottom of the pile here." This sug-gests that while middle-class informants may recognize themselves as His-panic and simultaneously distance themselves from the label by *sociological* interpretation, working-class people interpret the implications of the label for their sense of self in strictly *personal* terms.[11]

The Racial Other

One key aspect of the effects of the imposition of a homogenizing label that classifies people with ties to Latin America and the Caribbean in ethnic terms is the ways in which the informants adopted U.S. racial/ethnic classifi-cations to articulate their sense of self. Again, the informants' responses cor-responded to the values stemming from their social class positions in their own countries, including not only class-based values but also the *culturally specific* racial prejudices that accompanied them in Latin America. Thus, for example, when asked to comment on whether his life had changed in the United States, one worker who had middle-class status in his native country first established his class background, pointing out that there was considerable social distance between him and the other Latin Americans with whom he worked in the factory:

> They [i.e., "Americans"] exploit us with very low salaries, and they delude us into thinking that life is owning a car. Here it's common for people to have car— you can get one dirt-cheap; there's no status in it. You see, having an acceptable car, a good house does bring you status in any South American country. They delude people who could never have had a car in their own country. But the comforts of a good kitchen, of being able to wash your plates, of having a dish-washer, a refrigerator, a good sound system, a television—none of that is really life. There is no pride in acquiring any of it for anyone who comes here with an education (Francisco, Colombia).

This informant proceeded to speak of the shift in his social status using the U.S. racial/ethnic hierarchy:

> The fact is that they've got us [Latin Americans] poorer here. . . . The problem is that we Latin Americans are considered the lowest race here. We are only here to work at the bottom. Because there's a bad policy here in the U.S. There are around 32 or 33 million of us, and yet we are considered a minority. The per-centage of Greeks, Germans, Poles is very low, yet they have special privileges that we don't have.

In comparing his position and aspirations with those of the Latin American working-class immigrants with whom he worked and not with those of other middle-class immigrants like himself, the informant was adopting the U.S. ethnic/racial system of classification. On the one hand, he was distancing himself from the other workers as a middle-class person "with an education." On the other hand, as a middle-class person himself, he was claiming the same rights accorded to what he perceived as the white middle class ("Greeks, Germans, Poles") and, in the process, excluding African-Americans and other minorities from the "special privileges" accorded to the (white) middle class. Moreover, his discourse seems to suggest a desire for incorpo-ration into U.S. society—an incorporation that he defined in terms of access to the rights and privileges of the (white) middle class.

While the middle-class informants tended to measure themselves in terms of social status—comparing themselves to people whom they considered their equals in this country—working-class people seemed to assess them-selves in material terms, that is, by comparing what they had achieved here with what they had had back home: "I'm much better off here than there. Af-ter paying all the bills, it's almost the same here [as in the Dominican Re-public], but you are more comfortable here."

Still, like the middle-class informants, these working-class people also knew that they were identified as Hispanic and were aware of the prejudice against them. Not surprisingly, their sense of self as members of U.S. society was shaped by their awareness of the barriers to their incorporation, which dictated the ways they positioned their selves in the United States:

> I would like my children to go into the U.S. army. You know why? Because what I've achieved here I've gotten thanks in part to this country. I did it with my efforts, but they gave me the opportunity to come, to survive. So to show my gratitude I would like that. . . . The problem is that in the army, or in the navy, Hispanics are always given the worst jobs. If my daughter is educated and qualified, why should the Americans give her the worst positions just because she's Hispanic? (María, Dominican Republic)

In this statement, María expressed not only her ability to integrate into U.S. society but also the limits to her doing so, as defined by the label Hispanic and its connotations. Although she recognizes that her daughter is qualified, she fears the latter will never be considered to be American because she will always be treated as a Hispanic.

The American Other

Although second- and later-generation Latin Americans may never be considered "American," it is important to keep in mind that the identity of Latin America as a unified continent has itself long been debated and is yet to be fully forged (Oddone, 1987; Giordano and Torres, 1986). Thus, it is perhaps not surprising that the notion of exploring the existence of an identity shared by Latin American people (and the meaning of that identity) was new to some informants, regardless of their time of arrival in the United States.

> I went to the factory the very next day after our last conversation and asked my colleagues at work what they understood by Hispanic. I asked an Ecuadorian, a Dominican, and a Puerto Rican. They all gave the same answer. They said it was because we all speak Spanish. . . . They didn't seem to care what the Americans call us. But I think it's interesting. I think we should know why they call us Hispanic. So I began to think about it (Rosa, El Salvador).

Asked whether she thought of herself as Hispanic, Rosa answered:

> No, I don't. I'm Central American. Because you know there's the North Americans and the Central Americans and the South Americans. We're all Americans, right? But then we have to differentiate ourselves. Some are in the North, some in the Center, and others in the South, right? So when someone asks me what I am, I say, "I'm Salvadoran. I'm Central American from El Salvador," and that's it. A Colombian can say, "I'm South American, from Colombia."

As did most informants, Rosa defined herself in terms of her nationality. Her reluctance to use the term Hispanic was at least partly due to her negative perception of the term. At the same time, contextualizing her national identity in terms of the continent's geography, narrowing the latter down to particular nationalities, was an approach echoed by most other informants as they sought to assert their identities in the U.S. context.

The Latin American National Other

For most informants, the Hispanic was in many ways the external other. At the same time, through its negation, the label Hispanic became the basis on which the self was being constructed. Thus, several informants rejected the application of Hispanic to themselves and others from the Latin American and Caribbean region: "I will call myself by my nationality, no matter where I live" (Irene, Ecuador); "We should be called South Americans, or Central Americans. It depends on where you're from" (Julián, Peru). Indeed, for many of the informants, the root of the problem with the term Hispanic was the discrimination attached to the grouping of all Spanish-speaking people and their awareness that labels such as this one efface what are for them obvious national, ethnic, and social distinctions.[12] Thus, for example, for the most part, the informants perceived the erasure of their national differences as being caused by the ignorance of non-Hispanic Americans about Latin America and the Caribbean: "Neither Americans or Europeans know much about geography. In this respect they are very ignorant. That's why they group us all together. They don't know the difference, because they don't know their geography" (Soledad, Colombia). The extent to which the informants resented what they perceived as Americans' lack of knowledge about their culture can be seen in the relationship they established between the ways they defined their identity in the U.S. context and their attempts to be specific about the continent's geography:

> We are all of us Americans (Julián, Peru).
> I never call people from this country "Americans." I use that word for everyone from Alaska to Patagonia. In my city—I can only speak of my city, because, you know, each one has its own customs—we call them *yanquis* or *gringos*, but not Americans.
> I only know one America. Its geographical position may be North America, Central America, or South America. But we're all American. Colombia isn't located in Europe, it isn't located in Asia, and it isn't in Africa, either. So if they take the name of the entire continent for their country, what is left for ours? What is the name of the continent that Colombia is on? (Alicia, Colombia).

Comments such as this point to the tension that has historically existed between the populations of the Latin American and Caribbean nations, on the one hand, and the United States on the other. For some informants, the tension is overtly political: "I'm American only by accident, because

Puerto Rico is a territory of the United States. I don't think that's by choice, because they've got American bases there" (Juan, New York–born Puerto Rican). Asked about his American citizenship and passport, Juan continued to deny that he was American, explaining, "I'm Americanized, but I'm not American"—by which he means "I believe like they say, work hard, you get ahead, you get whatever you want, you get your house, your cars, your mortgages." Thus he refuses the identity of American, recognizing that it has been imposed in much the same way as the identity of Hispanic: "From whites you came up with the word Hispanic. . . . Puerto Ricans never call each other Hispanic." Not surprisingly, then, Juan defined his identity in (Puerto Rico) national rather than ethnic (Hispanic or Latino) terms: "First I'd say I'm Puerto Rican. I would consider myself that because that's what I was taught to believe in. . . . you know, to be proud of your nationality. You're proud of what you are and what the people in your country fought for."

For the most part, among the non-Puerto Rican informants, the tension between the "two Americas" is further manifested in the need to recognize the boundaries of the identity of the other—whether that other be a Latin American national or a U.S. citizen—in the process of shaping one's own identity in the U.S. context: "I once had a discussion with a Puerto Rican who said to me, 'I'm American,' and I answered, 'I'm as American as you are, because there is only one America'" (María, Dominican Republic). Thus Latinos specify their national origins especially among themselves: "If I introduce you to someone I would say, 'This is my friend, she's from Peru.' Or else I'd say, 'She's South American, or Peruvian'" (Verónica, Dominican Republic).

Indeed, regardless of their social class, informants did not necessarily understand the purpose of grouping everyone collectively as Hispanics:

> It just doesn't sound right to me. For example, if I'm with my people, I might say "South Americans," as others would say "Central Americans" or "Caribbeans." . . . we're not just a lump, we know who everyone is—because even though we may use the same language, our cultures are different, and we have to think about what we're going to say to different people and how we're going to say it (Soledad, Colombia).

Thus, while mainstream U.S. society tends to erase the differences among populations with ties to Latin America and the Caribbean through a label such as Hispanic, my informants are more concerned with focusing their assertion of self in relation to other Latin American nationalities in the United States. Although they are fully aware of their commonalities (e.g., language use, geographical origins), they also affirm their respective selves through pointing to, and emphasizing, the distinctions—both subtle and otherwise—among themselves.

DEFINING THE SELF: RACE, CLASS, NATIONAL ORIGIN, AND LANGUAGE

In defining the meaning of the term Hispanic for themselves, most inform-ants showed themselves to be conscious of the differences among the vari-ous Latin American and Caribbean nationalities yet aware of the prejudices that indiscriminately group Hispanics in the United States. It is not surprising, then, that they speculated about the weight of the various aspects of the def-inition that they identified, ranging from the geographical to the linguistic, national, and racial. Inevitably, they included their life experiences as immi-grants as they tried to make sense of these various aspects in defining their selves vis à vis the value of the term Hispanic in their lives.

Some made specific reference to the term's linguistic element: "They call us Hispanics because we speak Spanish" (Julián, Peru). Others related the term specifically to nationality: "I don't really know what Hispanic means: I think it's all the people who come from Latin America, but I'm not sure. I know that people who are born here in the United States aren't Hispanic. So, for example, one of my children, the one born in Peru, is Hispanic; the other isn't because she was born in this country" (Milagros, Peru). Asked how she would categorize the child born in the United States, Milagros didn't hesitate to answer: "Well, if she was born here, of course she's an American." Thus she views the term Hispanic as having a precise regional connotation, although she perceives its meaning to be strictly tied to people's birthplaces rather than to their ethnicity. Another version of this approach combined the regional and the linguistic elements of the term: "It's an undefined group name given to all the countries where Spanish is spoken" (Mónica, Domini-can Republic).

Cynicism was also not absent from some of the informants' explanations of the origins and meaning of the term:

> White people have a name for everybody else. From whites you came up with the word Hispanics, and spic. I mean, Puerto Ricans never call each other His-panic. They never called each other spics. They never did. When they said Hispanics, that's just a group of people that they've put together that speaks Spanish. . . .
>
> They just count all Latin people in one bunch. They do it to the blacks, too. I mean, come on, there're more than just blacks. You got your American blacks, you got your African, your Jamaican; then you got your Puerto Rican blacks; some guys are darker than me. Then you got your Dominican blacks, you got white people that are dark-skinned. . . .
>
> So you got your Hispanics over here, which includes whatever race you want to put in it south of the border. Then you got your blacks, anything from the Congo down. Then you got your whites, which is Americans . . . (Juan, New York–born Puerto Rican)

In view of the prevalence of race-related representations in New York City, it is perhaps not surprising that a New York-born Puerto Rican discussed the meaning of Hispanic in strictly racial/ethnic terms. Although Juan recognized the diversity within the various groups, he also had a firm perception of a two-tiered racial hierarchy made up of whites and everybody else in the United States. He defined Hispanic as including "whatever race you want to put in it south of the border," while singling out whites as Americans. Indeed, although he clearly rejected Hispanic as a term of self-identification and focused instead on his nationality rather than race, Juan nevertheless implicitly recognized that in this society his nationality and his race were conflated. Hence, as a Puerto Rican, his identity in this society was not white.

Interpreting the weight of the various components of the term Hispanic—race, class, national origins, and language—becomes an essential part of informants' self-definitions and strategies of survival. Perhaps the clearest example of the extent to which this is true can be seen in one informant's description of the problems raised for Hispanics by the 1990 census questionnaire:

> If I were black and I spoke Spanish, I don't know how I would have answered that census questionnaire. They put black down as a race and separated it from people who speak Spanish, and they didn't have anything down for mestizos or for white Latin Americans. So when I was answering the census I said to myself, "Whoever did this made a lot of mistakes. Whoever did the census form wasn't educated enough about race." Because how could someone who is really black but speaks Spanish write down that he's black? I kept wondering about that (Soledad, Colombia).

This criticism of the separation of race and language points to the prejudices Latin Americans confront in themselves as they come to terms with the prevalence of racial over national classifications in the United States. In fact, it illustrates Latin Americans' *public* assignment of greater social value to cultural/linguistic attributes (speaking Spanish) than to skin color.

What emerges from this study is the extent to which informants drew on their social and cultural backgrounds and their life experiences as they tried to come to terms with the label Hispanic. Juan's cynicism about the classification of Hispanics was the result of his lived experience as a Puerto Rican in the racially charged environment of New York City, where he grew up. Soledad's questions stemmed from her own socially and culturally shaped Latin American perception that "whoever did the census form wasn't educated enough about race." Where she comes from, Colombia, as in all other Latin American countries, the discourse on race distinctions has more gradations, and each gradation is strictly related to the individual's social class position (Wade, 1985).

U.S. LATINOS: BEING AND BECOMING

The interviews in this study show that the way in which people with ties to Latin America and the Caribbean choose to identify themselves in this country is less a cultural imperative than a reflection of their direct experiences and their need at a given conjuncture in their lives. It also expresses their expectations of and strategies for incorporation into the U.S. social structure. While as Latin Americans they may insist that they are as American as the *gringos*, their confrontation with race and class representations in U.S. society forces them to incorporate both these dimensions into their imagining of the "American community" (Anderson, 1983) and their construction of a sense of self in relation to the label Hispanic and the racial, class, national, and linguistic others attributed to them.

Whereas the middle-class informants tended to project their integration into this society and immediately adopt U.S. categories to measure their progress here, the working-class informants appeared more divided and ambivalent. They tended to continue to assess their sense of self in relation to their progress in terms of the standards of their old society—how much better off they were here.

Both groups knew that they were classified as Hispanic, but the way in which they positioned themselves in relation to this classification differed. Working-class informants positively evaluated their lives in this country relative to what they perceived to be their life chances in their home countries, but they were not naive about the extent to which they could advance in economic terms in U.S. society. The ambivalence they expressed toward the United States reflects an awareness of the limits imposed on their upward mobility by what they perceived as the prejudice and discrimination against Hispanics. The prejudiced, "low-class," and negative connotations of the term Hispanic seemed to place a ceiling on how far they could rise. For them, ambivalence had become a way of positioning themselves in relation to both the old and the new society. In contrast to the working-class informants, the middle-class Latinos I interviewed appeared to expect immediate incorporation into U.S. society on the grounds of their class, their education, and their social status in their own countries. Their sense of self and positioning vis-à-vis their new society did not *necessarily* correspond to that of the working-class informants.

Thus, in constructing the Latino self and a Latino social movement in the struggle for social justice in the United States, it is important to acknowledge the many "others" within—and against—which Latinos' identities and sense of self are being forgotten. "I am what I am" is a dare, a challenge to all those who would question the existence of a Latina/o self in the United States. But it is also a reminder that identity is, as Stuart Hall (1990: 222) has argued, "'production,' which is never complete, always in process." The homogenizing quality of the label Hispanic is the result of mainstream U.S. society's indifference to the distinctions within the Latino/a population—whether the indifference refers to the diverse races, classes, languages, nationalities, linguistic or gendered experiences of the more than 25 million people identified as Hispanics or Latinos/as currently living in the United States. Yet the richness of the Latino ethos lies precisely in incorporating the individual life histories and experiences as processes of being and becoming—in recognizing and acknowledging the internalized others in the process of defining the self.

Padilla (1985: 167) points to the need for research focusing on "the collective and emergent character" of Latino/a ethnic behavior. Although that behavior clearly depends on the extent to which Latino/a interests can be politically articulated, aspects of personal identity may promote and/or hinder it. Given the diversity of national, racial, and class-based histories and experiences within the populations with ties to Latin American and the Caribbean, to identify oneself as a Latino/a is a conscious choice not only acknowledging one's history and sociocultural background but also recognizing the need to struggle for social justice. In this sense, more than solely a culturally dictated fact of life, identifying oneself as Latino/a and participating in a Latino social movement is a *political* decision. By making that decision in these terms, those who recognize one another as Latinos through their ideological advocacy of social justice will be able to express the strength of *la comunidad* with greater force. They will also be more likely to assert, as do the Moraleses in their poem, that "We are whole."

NOTES

In the title of this chapter, I use the word "politics" in the sense of a "political ethos" or "political culture," following the definition of the Chilean political scientist Norberto Lechner (1987, my translation): "The set of shared beliefs and values which, in influencing the practice of strategic actors (reinforcing and reproducing it in daily life), constitutes the common ground—the political culture—upon which proposals to conserve or transform reality are presented." I thank Keitha Fine and Dicxon Valderruten for their many suggestions on earlier versions of this paper and María Celia Paoli, Elitza Bachvarova, and Anani Dzidzienyo for their helpful comments on the present version.

1. "Ending Poem," in *Getting Home Alive* by Aurora Levins-Morales and Rosario Morales, copyright © 1986 by Firebrand Books, Ithaca, New York. Used by permission.

2. The question of the other has been central to the debates on what West (1990) has called "the new cultural politics of difference." For varying perspectives and approaches to theorizing "the other" in anthropology and literary and cultural studies, see Clifford (1988), Clifford and Marcus (1986), Spivak (1987), Said (1983), Bhabha (1989; 1990), and Hall (1990). For a useful overview and critique of the recent debates on these various approaches to multiculturalism and cultural studies in the United States, see Chicago Cultural Studies Group (1992).

3. West (1990) has noted the need to explore "blackness-whiteness" in order "to conceive of the profoundly hybrid character of what we mean by 'race,' 'ethnicity,' and 'nationality'" (see also Morrison, 1992; Bhabha, 1989).

4. Latino/a was coined as an alternative to the term Hispanic imposed by government agencies and the society at large in the 1970s and 1980s. Like Hispanic, ethnic, minority, marginal, alternative, and Third World, it is "inaccurate and loaded with ideological implications" (Gómez-Peña, 1989). Hayes-Bautista and Chapa (1987), Treviño (1987), and Giménez (1989) have discussed the implications of a standardized terminology for people with ties to Latin America and the Caribbean.

5. Language, generation, religion, and sexual preference are additional ways of understanding Latino/a "othering."

6. According to Padilla (1985: 163), "Latinismo is *political ethnicity*, a manipulative device for the pursuit of collective political, economic, and social interests in society."

7. Padilla's analysis of the emergence of Latinismo among Puerto Ricans and Mexican-Americans focuses on "situations involving inequality experienced in common by Puerto Rican and Mexican American groups" in Chicago (1985: 68). His pioneering study focuses on Latino ethnic consciousness resulting from interest-group articulation. Of particular relevance here is his discussion of the implications of regional differences in the United States. His point that Latino interests may sometimes conflict with the interests of national groups is also well taken. As he notes, the fact that different national-origin groups are settling in different areas of the United States and have diverse needs and historically rooted reasons for being in this country requires more localized research into the different possibilities for and meanings of Latino identity as well as of Latinismo as situational ethnicity.

8. For some, the term "Latino" is taking on a clearly nationalist connotation. As one second-generation Colombian youth recently told me, "I'm not American; but I'm not Colombian either. My nationality is Latino."

9. In-depth interviews were conducted over a two-year period with 22 immigrants from nine countries—men and women, old and young, of different genders, races, classes, and generations—who were garment workers in New York City (Oboler, forthcoming).

10. Latin American gender ideologies notwithstanding, only one of the informants had never worked outside the home in her country—attesting both to the difficult economic conditions in the Latin American countries (MacEwan, 1985) and the increasing integration of Third World women into the development process as a result of change in the world economic order (Leacock and Safa, 1986; Fuentes and Ehrenreich, 1983; Portocarrero, 1990).

11. The complexity of self-identifying through an imposed ethnic label can be seen in this and other informants' responses. The distance they place between themselves and the term "Hispanic" should not, however, be mistaken for a rejection of themselves (or others) as Latin American and Caribbean people or a lack of pride in or awareness of their cultures and language. As workers in ethnically diverse factories and members of an ethnically conscious society, they were fully conscious of their geographical, cultural, and linguistic commonalities. Moreover, in the workplace, for example, these commonalities would of course differentiate them as a group from their non-Latino coworkers.

88 *Suzanne Oboler*

12. The extent to which differences are erased by the other depends on how socially and culturally "distant" the other is from the self. For many people with ties to Latin America and the Caribbean, "the American" (the external referential other) may be perceived as much more distant from the cultural experience of a Latino/a self than another Latin American national. Closer distinctions (the internal boundary), however, are essential for constituting the cultural horizon of the Latino/a self, and in specifying this strategic internal boundary class, gender, and race biases are easily identifiable. Hence, many informants were prone to erase the differences among those they designated as "Americans" while stressing the subtle distinctions between self and other within the Latino population. I thank Teresa Caldeira for discussion and clarification of this idea.

REFERENCES

Anderson, B. 1983. *Imagined Communities: Reflections on the Origin and Spread of Nationalism*. New York: Verso.

Anzaldúa, G. 1990. "How to Tame a Wild Tongue," pp. 203-212 in R. Ferguson et al. (eds.), *Out There: Marginalization and Contemporary Cultures*. New York and Cambridge, MA: New Museum of Contemporary Art/MIT Press.

Bhabha, H. K. 1989. "Remembering Fanon: Self, Psyche, and the Colonial Condition," pp. 131-150 in B. Kruger and P. Mariani (eds.), *Remaking History*. Seattle: Bay Press.

———. 1990. "The Other Question: Difference, Discrimination, and the Discourse of Colonialism," pp. 71-89 in R. Ferguson et al. (eds.), *Out There: Marginalization and Contemporary Cultures*. New York and Cambridge, MA: New Museum of Contemporary Art/MIT Press.

Brown, S. E. 1975. "Love Unites Them and Hunger Separates Them: Poor Women in the Dominican Republic," pp. 322-332 in R. Rapp (ed.), *Toward an Anthropology of Women*. New York: Monthly Review Press.

Chicago Cultural Studies Group. 1992. "Critical Multiculturalism." *Critical Inquiry* 18: 530-555.

Clifford, J. 1988. *The Predicament of Culture: Twentieth-Century Ethnography, Literature, and Art*. Cambridge, MA: Harvard University Press.

Clifford, J. and G. Marcus (eds.). 1986. *Writing Culture: The Poetics and Politics of Ethnography*. Berkeley and Los Angeles: University of California Press.

Fanon, F. 1967. *Black Skin, White Masks*. New York: Grove Press.

Flores, J. 1985. "'Qué assimilated, brother, yo soy Assimilao': The Structuring of Puerto Rican identity in the U.S." *Journal of Ethnic Studies* 13(3): 1-16.

Flores, J. and G. Yudice. 1990. "Living Borders/*Buscando América*: Languages of Latino Self-Formation." *Social Text* 8(2): 57-84.

Fuentes, A. and B. Ehrenreich. 1983. *Women in the Global Factory*. Boston: Institute for New Communications/South End Press.

Giménez, M. E. 1989. "'Latino/Hispanic'—Who Needs a Name? The Case Against a Standardized Terminology." *International Journal of Health Services* 19: 557-571.

Giordano, J. and D. Torres (eds.). 1986. *La identidad cultural de Hispanoamérica: Discusión actual*. Santiago de Chile: Monografías del Maitén.

Gómez-Peña, G. 1989. "The Multicultural Paradigm: An Open Letter to the National Arts Community." *High Performance* (Fall 1989): 20.

Hall, S. 1990. "Cultural Identity and Diaspora," pp. 222-237 in J. Rutherford (ed.), *Identity, Community, Culture, Difference.* London: Lawrence and Wishart.

Hayes-Bautista, D. E. and J. Chapa. 1987. "Latino Terminology: Conceptual Bases for Standardized Terminology." *American Journal of Public Health* 77: 61-68.

Leacock, E. and H. I. Safa (eds.). 1986. *Women's Work.* South Hadley, MA: Bergin and Garvey.

Lechner, N. 1987. *Cultura política.* Santiago: CLACSO/FLACSO.

Levins-Morales, A. and R. Morales. 1986. *Getting Home Alive.* Ithaca, NY: Firebrand Books.

Lorde, A. 1990. "Age, Race, Class, and Sex: Women Redefining Difference," in R. Ferguson et al. (eds.), *Out There: Marginalization and Contemporary Cultures.* New York and Cambridge, MA: New Museum of Contemporary Art/MIT Press.

MacEwen, A. 1985. "The Current Crisis in Latin America and the International Economy." *Monthly Review* 36: 1-17.

Morrison, T. 1992. *Playing in the Dark: Whiteness and the Literary Imagination.* Cambridge, MA: Harvard University Press.

Oboler, S. 1995. *Ethnic Labels, Latino Lives: Identity and the Politics of (Re)presentation in the United States.* Minneapolis: University of Minnesota Press.

Oddone, J. M. 1987. "Regionalismo y nacionalismo," pp. 201–238 in L. Zea (ed.), *América Latina en sus ideas.* Mexico City: Siglo XXI/UNESCO.

Ortega, E. and N. Saporta-Sternbach. 1989. "At the Threshold of the Unnamed: Literary Discourse in the Eighties," pp. 2–26 in A. Horno-Delgado et al. (eds.), *Breaking Boundaries: Latina Writings and Critical Readings.* Amherst: University of Massachusetts Press.

Padilla, F. 1985. *Latino Ethnic Consciousness: The Case of Mexican Americans and Puerto Ricans in Chicago.* Notre Dame, IN: University of Notre Dame Press.

Pessar, P. 1987. "The Dominicans: Women in the Household and the Garment Industry," pp. 103–130 in N. Foner (ed.), *New Immigrants in New York.* New York: Columbia University Press.

Pessar, P. and S. Grasmuck. 1991. *Between Two Islands.* Berkeley: University of California Press.

Portocarrero, P. (ed.) 1990. *Mujer en desarrollo: Balance y propuestas.* Lima: Flora Tristán.

Rubbo, A. 1975. "The Spread of Capitalism in Rural Colombia: Effects on Poor Women," pp. 333–357 in R. Rapp (ed.), *Toward an Anthropology of Women.* New York: Monthly Review Press.

Rubin. L. B. 1976. *Worlds of Pain.* New York: Basic Books.

Said, E. 1983. *The World, the Text, and the Critic.* Cambridge, MA: Harvard University Press.

Spivak, G. C. 1987. *In Other Worlds: Essays in Cultural Politics.* New York: Routledge.

Trevino, F. M. 1987. "Standardized Terminology for Standardized Populations." *American Journal of Public Health* 77: 69-72.

Wade, P. 1985. "Race and Class: The Case of South American Blacks." *Ethnic and Racial Studies* 8: 233-249.

West, C. 1990. "The New Cultural Politics of Difference," in R. Ferguson et al. (ed.), *Out There: Marginalization and Contemporary Cultures.* New York and Cambridge, MA: New Museum of Contemporary Art/MIT Press.

3

Reframing Postmodernist Constructions of Difference: Subaltern Spaces, Power, and Citizenship

Raymond A. Rocco

One of the fundamental concerns that served as the basis for the establishment and early development of Latina/o studies was to understand the nature, dimensions, and dynamics of the historical disempowerment and exclusion of Latina/o communities. This theme of exclusion has continued to be central in the various contestations of traditional constructions of Latinas/os and a principal ideological point of reference for Latina/o struggles, but there have been considerable differences in the constructs of empowerment and/or inclusion that underlie the many approaches that have characterized the historical development of the field. Many theoretical formulations, traditions, and interests have influenced the way in which these concerns and debates have been framed, but clearly the most attractive have been those that have focused on modes of exclusion.

It is precisely postmodernism's contestation and critique of the modernist conceptions of progress and emancipation as culturally bounded and exclusivist that has led some scholars to consider this framework useful for deepening our understanding of the development of Latina/o communities. In this chapter, I want to assess the challenges and possible contributions of postmodernism by considering it from the perspective of understanding the institutional and structural obstacles to Latina/o empowerment that I found in my studies of the effect of economic restructuring on the transformation of Latina/o communities in Los Angeles that has occurred in the past twenty-five years.[1]

APPROPRIATING THE POSTMODERN

The first difficulty encountered in addressing the issue is the variety of positions and conceptualizations of the postmodern. Most social and cultural theorists agree that the global pattern of relationships between societies is in a period of transition, and, as Grewal and Kaplan point out, "there is also significant consensus over the transnationalization of accumulation, shifts that challenge the older, conventional boundaries of national economies, identities, and cultures" (1994: 8). However, postmodernists have focused on different dimensions of these changes. Thus postmodernism has been theorized as a cultural phenomenon, social theory, philosophical stance, and architectural movement, and distinctions have been made between postmodernity, postmodernism, and postmodernization. The different characteristics, conditions, and qualities of the postmodern, then, reflect the particular field or area of engagement, and the concept has been applied in fields as varied as art, fiction, photography, drama, architecture, literary criticism, music, geography, anthropology, and sociology (Featherstone, 1988: 431). Despite the differences in subjects, emphasis, and interpretations, what is necessarily part of all discussions, debates, and theorizations of postmodernism is, as indicated, the notion of transition and either implicit or explicit problematizing of the notion of modernity. The rise of modernity is generally regarded as having begun with the Renaissance, and it is contrasted with the structures of traditional social and cultural order. For social theorists such as Weber, Tönnies and Simmel, modernization "implies the progressive economic and administrative rationalization and differentiation of the social world: processes which brought into being the modern capitalist-industrial state" (Featherstone, 1988: 197–98). Marshall Berman (1983) focuses on both the role of the city and the societal transformation represented by capitalism as the existential contexts for the experience of the modern. As Philip Cooke (1988: 67) puts it, modernity is forged by

> . . . the unleashing of competitive capitalism with its mass migrations, disruptive social rhythms, urban explosions, industrial transformations, and technical as well as political innovations. This process of sociospatial *modernization . . .* is what uproots the subject from the stability of pre-modern life, either by enveloping or magnetizing the person into its field of forces. But this uprooting from tradition challenges the subject by liberating but also disorienting cognition.

The range of cultural forms that emerged from this transformation included a sense of purpose, direction, and progress, the primacy of reason, centering of the subject, selection and ordering as organizing principles that reason could discern and reveal, linear causality, and grand narratives or foundational frameworks as the mode of organizing thought and analysis. Progress and emancipation were advanced as universally valid normative goals that greatly influenced the way that political visions and movements were framed and promoted. The premise of all forms of postmodernist thought is that this configuration of elements and relationships has begun or already changed in fundamental ways in the contemporary period.

Postmodernist projects attempt to delineate the dimensions and parameters of the modern period of these changes both to express and to understand the new social processes, cultural forms, institutional configurations, and modes of analysis and thought and the emergence of a social order with its own distinctive organizing principles. Postmodernist thought rejects the basic ground of the Enlightenment project based on the primacy of reason, the centrality of the subject, and the belief in the existence of propositions or rules of universal validity that govern nature, society, and cultural forms. It rejects, as well, the Enlightenment's reliance on grand narratives or totalistic theories to advance specific conceptions of progress and emancipation and argues that those narratives and theories are rooted in a model of reality based on linear, one-dimensional concepts of causality—on the idea that the key to understanding and explaining reality is the discovery of one fundamental defining, central force or universal characteristic. Postmodernists advocate modes of analysis that acknowledge the complexity of multiple causation rooted in the historically specific conditions of local and particular sites. The variation in the configurations of social practices, cultural formations, and institutional contexts makes the search for universal laws or patterns of economic development, political struggle, or cultural change, a futile and misguided effort. Rather, the emphasis should be on complexity, specificity, plurality, and difference, and the role of subjectivity and agency is problematized and usually decentered. Thus, despite a lack of consensus on the precise and "correct" meaning of "postmodernism," these characteristics do seem to define a general field of postmodern qualities. The sociologist Bryan Turner provides the following useful although not necessarily comprehensive summary (1994: 154):

> . . . an increasing fragmentation and differentiation of culture as a consequence of the pluralization of life-styles and the differentiation of social structure; the employment of irony, allegory, pastiche, and montage as argumentative styles and as components of rhetoric; the erosion of traditional "grand narratives" of legitimation in politics and society; the celebration of the idea of difference and heterogeneity (against sameness and standardization) as minimal normative guidelines in politics and morality; the globalization of postmodern culture with the emergence of global networks of communication through satellites, which are associated with military surveillance; the emergence of a central emphasis on flexibility and self-consciousness in personality and life-style; a partial erosion of the idea of coherence as a norm of personality; and the decline of "industrial society" and its replacement by "post-Fordism" and "post-industrialism."

While these general elements seem to inform most postmodernist approaches, there are also important differences in the ways in which they have been applied and understood and in their political implications. Thus, for example, a distinction between "ludic" and "oppositional" postmodernisms has been proposed by a number of scholars (O'Brien and Penna, 1996: 192; McLaren, 1994: 198–200). The former (associated with the works of Lyotard, Derrida, and Baudrillard) "constitutes a moment of self-reflexivity in deconstructing Western metanarratives . . . that is decidedly limited in its ability to transform oppressive social and political regimes of power [and] . . . focuses on the fabulous combinatory potential of signs in the production of meaning and occupies itself with a reality that is constituted by the continual playfulness of the signifier and the heterogeneity of differences" (McLaren, 1994: 198). Because of this emphasis on the abstract level of philosophical discourse, this approach has often been dismissed as a distraction from confronting the material basis of economic and political disempowerment and inequality. In particular, some of the political opposition to postmodernism arises from the "reluctance to abandon historically and culturally sedimented ideas about progress, emancipation and societal management" that characterize the "modernist project" (O'Brien and Penna, 1996: 186).

An alternative formulation of postmodernism has been advanced as providing basic explanations of the processes of marginalization and exploitation. In fact, this conceptualization (O'Brien and Penna, 1996: 191) is proposed precisely as a means to focus on the ways in which processes of exclusion and exploitation have been obscured and legitimated because it refuses

> . . . to take modern visions of progress, inclusion and identity at face value. By paying close attention to those who have been excluded from the visions . . . postmodern investigations have documented the invasions, occupations and confrontations that have formed the channels for social, political and economic modernization and the crucial contributions that have been made by those marginalized constituencies.

It is this version of postmodernism, emphasizing the extent to which Western notions of inclusion depend on the exclusion of marginalized peoples, that has been most attractive to Latina/o scholars. The following section focuses on how this perspective has influenced the constructions of these processes and representations of marginalization.

DIFFERENCE REFRAMED:
POSTCOLONIALISM AND SPATIALIZATION

From a postmodernist perspective, no one concept can adequately define the fundamental axis of interpretation and analysis. Rather, the positions, concepts, and arguments that define postmodernism are intertwined in different combinations with varying emphases in its proponents' analyses. However, as indicated before, the notions of fragmentation, multiplicity, plurality, complexity, specificity, and difference do appear to be common characteristics of most theorizations of the postmodern. These are precisely the types of categories that initially seem best to describe the varied dimensions of a city like Los Angeles. My study of the transformation of Latina/o communities in Los Angeles linked the regional changes in economic relations and formations with ethnographic studies of a broad variety of institutional sites and more than ninety family histories. Thus I examined economic institutional structures and patterns, social, cultural, and economic networks, and the household strategies of adaptation, resistance, and survival. In attempting to interpret these different levels of interaction, I found that these were extremely complex and fragmented and that the multiplicity and plurality of peoples and cultures exploded any notion of clear boundaries. The differences of class, immigrant status, gender, country of origin, race, ethnicity— are all clearly visible in the patterns of everyday life, in the streets, restaurants, parks, beaches, shopping centers, malls, swap meets, schools, and churches—hence the initial appeal of the postmodernist project for elaborating an approach that emphasizes precisely these dimensions. However, as we have seen these dimensions of difference have been framed, interpreted, and applied in very different types of analysis and arguments. What I want to focus on here is the framing and development of these elements in several approaches that resonate with the transitions, transformations, and restructuring that characterize the urban reality with which my research is concerned. These approaches have constructed and interpreted the dimensions of difference along a conceptual axis characterized as "hybridity," "borders," "margins," the "in-between," and "third-space," which, despite the different inflections and emphasis, I want for the sake of convenience to refer to as "subaltern spaces." A sense of these notions is revealed by a brief review of their development and application in postcolonial thought, theories of spatialization, and in some cultural studies texts.

Although the animating project is quite different, postcolonial thought shares some characteristics with postmodernist approaches, partly because they are both grounded in a critique of the Enlightenment and its legacy, modernity. In his careful assessment of postcolonialism, Scott (1996: 7) writes:

> This colonialist discourse grounds its own authority in justificatory apparatuses derived from the Enlightenment project, and thus depends on the assumption of a transcendentalist and universalist Reason, a progressive unfolding of Universal History, and a sovereign rational and self-transparent subject. Constituting, as I have suggested, one wing of a broader assault on the assumptions of the Enlightenment, postcolonial criticism's oppositional strategy has entailed a rejection of these justificatory or legitimizing assumptions.

As is indicated by this observation, the referent for this oppositional strategy is a more specific historical configuration than is the case in a good deal

of postmodernist theory. The colonizing-decolonizing axis is the focus for
the reexamination and critique of the articulation between the former colonial subjects and the former colonial metropole. At the center of this project
is a critique of the way in which Eurocentric constructions of this articulation
conceptualize "difference." Focusing on the disjunctions between Eurocentric and Third World constructions of cultural formations and configurations,
postcolonialists problematize the notion of difference and elaborate theoretical constructs to capture the complexity of the conditions of articulation.

A number of similar conceptualizations have emerged from this critique,
some focusing on the colonial relations between societies and some on the
nature of the relations between populations of Third World origin in Eurocentric First World cities. Constructs such as hybridity, margins, borders, and
third-space have emerged at the center of a collective effort to rethink, retheorize, and rearticulate these relations. Although elaborated in different registers and with different emphases, they revolve around the same theoretical
and historical axis that has emerged from "the serious calling into question
of white/Western dominance by the groundswell of movements of resistance, and the emergence of struggles for collective self-determination most
frequently articulated in nationalist terms" (Frankenberg and Mani, 1993:
293). At the root of these struggles is a radical cultural disjunction superim-
posed on what have been structural relations of domination. The clash of Eurocentric and Third World peoples is a centuries-old story, but the specific
mode of engagement has varied with each set of countries and over historical phases and stages. Hybridity, borders, third-space, and margins are all attempts to theorize the complexity of these relations in terms that reject the
privileging of the West and describe the institutional locations of Third World
peoples. Without conflating these terms and the complex theoretical frameworks within which they have been elaborated, or assuming a sameness of
content, it can nevertheless be said that they operate within a field of constructs that overlap considerably. Lavie and Swedenburg (1996: 154) point
out this overlap in a recent essay on boundaries:

> A jumble of cultural-political practices and forms of resistance have emerged that
> have variously been named hybrid, border, or diasporic. The most creative and
> dynamic of these resistances are located on the borders of essentialism and con-
> juncturalism. They refuse the binarism of identity politics versus post-modernist
> fragmentation. . . . We name this terrain of practice and theory, this zone of shift-
> ing and mobile resistances that refuse fixity yet practice their own arbitrary pro-
> visional closures, the third timespace.

Soja reviews a group of affiliated positions that he designates "third-space"
and provides the following description, which, although advanced in the
discussion of the work of bell hooks, captures the thrust of his own conceptualization: "[hooks] attempts to move beyond the modernist binary

oppositions of race, gender, and class into the multiplicity of *other* spaces
that difference makes" (1996: 96). In their study of popular culture in Latin
America, Rowe and Schelling propose a useful definition of cultural hybridity as "the ways in which forms become separated from existing practices and recombine with new forms in new practices" (1991: 231), but this
deceptively simple definition does not convey the complexity of both the
processes involved and the modes of theorizing them. Theorists such as
Bhabha, Spivak, and Said have sought to delineate these in great detail and
with great sophistication. These conceptualizations all reject binary theoretical constructions and the privileging of monocausal factors and insist
on the notions of multiple subjectivities and voice, on complex modes of
positioning.

These concepts and the frameworks they are nested in are clearly not
without difficulties. They have been the subject of wide-ranging critique
from a variety of positions, and their shortcomings have been amply delineated. While it would be useful to review these, I want instead to follow a
line of critique that I have found helpful in exploring their usefulness for interpreting the specifics of Latina/o community transformation in Los Angeles. My point of departure is the argument advanced by Hall (1996) and by
Frankenberg and Mani (1993) that, while the notions of the margins, borders,
hybridity, and third-space seek to address fundamentally important phenomena, they are even more complex than many formulations maintain.
What is called for is careful delineation of the problems that arise in applying these concepts to issues of, for example, periodization, historical appropriateness and correlation, and both historical and institutional contextualization. For those of us exploring these themes within the context of the
United States, Frankenberg and Mani's critique of postcolonial theorizations
is especially helpful. They point out that terms like "postcolonialism" need to
be situated in the particular historical circumstances and experiences that are
being addressed, and they focus on the appropriateness of the concept of
postcolonialism for comprehending the U.S. situation. They provide the following summary of the historical and political elements that such an en-
deavor would have to account for (1993: 293):

> White settler colony, multiracial society. Colonization of Native Americans,
> Africans imported as slaves, Mexicans incorporated by a border moving south,
> Asians imported and migrating to labor, white Europeans migrating to labor. US im-
> perialist foreign policy brings new immigrants who are "here because the US
> was/is there," among them Central Americans, Koreans, Filipinos, Vietnamese, and
> Cambodians. The particular relation of past territorial domination and current racial
> composition that is discernible in Britain, and which lends a particular meaning to
> the term "postcolonial," does not, we feel, obtain here. Other characterizations,
> other periodizations, seem necessary in naming for this place the shifts expressed
> by the term "postcolonial" in the British and Indian cases.

They suggest the use of the term "post–Civil Rights" as a possible way to talk about the U.S. case but immediately indicate their reservations about its adequacy (1993: 293):

> Let us emphasize at the outset that we use the term "post Civil Rights" broadly, to refer to the impact of struggles by African Americans, American Indians, La Raza, and Asian American communities that stretched from the mid 1950s to the 1970s. . . . However, the name, "post Civil Rights," would only grasp one strand of our description of the US. The term would have to be conjugated with another, one that would name the experience of recent immigrants/refugees borne here on the trails of US imperialist adventures, groups whose stories are unfolding in a tense, complicated relation—at times compatible, at times contradictory—with post Civil Rights USA.

It is in these substantially different, particular (local) historical and institutional circumstances that one encounters a major difficulty in characterizing and theorizing notions of borders, margins, third-space, and hybridity. Two dimensions of this problematic in particular need to be addressed and disentangled: the connection between the colonizing-decolonizing contexts and histories that are the root of much of the theorizing about these concepts and the connection between the long-standing populations from formerly colonized countries and the most recent immigrants from both the same countries and from different regions and substantially different cultural contexts. Again, Frankenberg and Mani (1993: 202, my emphasis) put the issue succinctly and clearly: referring to recent immigrants to the United States,

> Their travel to the U.S. has been occasioned by a history related to, but distinct from, that of people of color already here. Their historical experiences stretch existing categories—"Hispanic," "Asian"—inflecting them with new meanings. Relations between recent immigrants/refugees and those already here, whether whites or people of color, are constituted through discourses that draw heavily on colonial and racist rhetoric both in form and content. . . . *Nothing but the most complex and historically specific conceptions of identity and subjectivity can sufficiently grasp the present situation and articulate a politics adequate to it."*

The question arises whether the notion of subaltern spaces has been theorized in ways that can adequately account for the realities of the substantive experiences, particular networks, modes of engagement, and relations of political configurations that revolve around substantive historical and institutional axes and moments. To repeat, "nothing but the most complex and historically specific conceptions of identity and subjectivity can sufficiently grasp the present situation and articulate a politics adequate to it." My premise here is that while some of the formulations move in the right direction and articulate positions that are adequate at one level of theory, they are failing to provide institutional grounding for these concepts. To use a phrase from a recent essay by the Argentine theorist Walter Mignolo (1997), they have not for the most part established a theoretical basis for elaborating the multiple institutional configurations and manifestations in terms of which "colonial legacies [are] at work in the present." Thus, in developing my analysis of the transformation of Latina/o communities in Los Angeles, one of the most difficult dimensions to explain is the dynamic between recent immigrants and those already here, who have a long history of engagement with U.S. culture and the U.S. system of subordination and power. These are two different yet complexly related trajectories or axes of engagement, and they provide conditions and opportunities for cultural and political strategies that have qualitatively distinct centers of gravity.

In addition, we need to suspect that some of the accents, emphases and limitations of the theorization of subaltern spaces have to do with another factor that is less often discussed. It is clear that the critical examination of both colonialism and decolonization is hardly a new focus of attention, particularly in decolonized Third World countries, but it appears that the reason it has become a major preoccupation in the present historical moment of the Eurocentric academy has less to do with theory than with demographics. It is the enormous and rapid migration of Third World peoples into the heart of Euro-U.S. cities that has burst the boundaries of canonical paradigms. The pervasiveness of radical cultural differences in the major Euro-U.S. metropolitan centers has sounded a dissonant chord for some and brought welcome decentering for others, but it can hardly be ignored by anyone. The world has changed, and sooner or later theory had to confront it. The grounding of this particular theoretical enterprise in this reality requires not only that the outlines of these spaces be delineated but, to paraphrase Michael Kearney's critique of ethnography, the theorizing "must situate the production and consumption of representations of [subaltern spaces] within the relationships that join [the theoretical self to the subaltern] other it presumes to represent" (1996: 3). There needs to be, in other words, an accounting as well of the ways in which the theorizing itself may function as a "strategy of containment" (Dowling, 1984: 76–93).

Both of these dimensions—expanding and deepening the boundaries of the conceptions of subaltern spaces and including the self-reflexive moment as part of that enterprise—can be advanced by specifying their institutional grounding.[2] With regard to the former dimension, the necessity to move in this direction is reflected in the following (Lavie and Swedenburg, 1996: 168–69).

Third spaces, third texts, third scenarios are concepts articulated in the interdisciplinary field of Minority Discourse through usage of Cultural Studies methodologies. Thus the cultural materials currently analyzed by using the modalities of "the third" are highly stylized domains of knowledge, framed as dramatic, literary, cinematic, artistic and musical texts. Bridging Ethnography, Cultural Studies, and Minority Discourse will be possible if we return to the primary daily realities from which such textual representations are derived. *We call for reconceptualization, from lived identities and physical places, not just from texts, of the multiplicities of identity and place.* As they are forced into constantly shifting configurations of partial overlap, their ragged edges cannot be smoothed out. Identity and place perpetually create both new outer borders, where the overlap has not occurred, and inner borders between the areas of overlap and vestigial spaces of non-overlap.

The "lived identities" and realities of these hybrid and third spaces, margins, borders, and spaces "in-between" are not random, epiphenomenal, or transient. They are institutional spaces, structures of cultural, economic, and political practices, that determine the conditions, strategies, and options for social and political action. And their quality as spaces of the hybrid, border, or margin is directly linked to the variety of changes in the nature of the relationship between territory, space, identity, and community that have resulted from the processes of transnationalization. What I am positing here is not a simple, linear causal relationship but a complex set of interdependent and multidimensional constellations of institutional practices.

Theorizations of subaltern spaces, then, must be reconfigured to incorporate these institutional spaces as necessary, inherent dimensions of the organic discursive and material complexes that constitute societal relations. I am not calling for a return to binary or totalistic constructs of society or a rejection of the premise articulated by Bhabha (1995: 208): "It is only when we understand that all cultural statements and systems are constructed in this contradictory and ambivalent space of enunciation, that we begin to understand why hierarchical claims to the inherent originality or 'purity' of cultures are untenable, even before we resort to empirical historical instances that demonstrate their hybridity." In other words, the articulation of theorization is not reducible to or dependent in a mechanistic or reductive manner on empirical "reality." Rather, it is a constitutive element of that reality (constitutive and not causal, which would return us to the tradition of idealism). Therefore it is not sufficient to situate the subaltern spaces within the "transnational" or "global" context. Rather, the modes of discourse and frames of representations of subaltern spaces themselves need to be part of the process of contextualization.

This is not a novel position. Thus, for example, Dirlik argues that "with rare exceptions, postcolonial critics have been silent on the relationship of the idea of postcolonialism to its context in contemporary capitalism; indeed, they have suppressed the necessity of considering such a possible relationship by repudiating a foundational role to capitalism in history" (1994: 331). And in a much earlier critique Benita Parry points out that postcolonial writers like Spivak and Bhabha share a "programme marked by the exorbitation of discourse and a related incuriosity about the enabling socioeconomic and political institutions and other forms of social praxis" (1995: 43).

Now, fragmentation, cultural disjunction, and the emergence of subaltern spaces that contest U.S.-Eurocentric representations and dominance are indeed found in urban centers such as Los Angeles, and my effort to understand and explain the transformation of Latina/o communities since the late 1960s has required that I examine the degree to which these are particular local expressions of processes that are global in nature. In doing so, I have found notions of borders, margins, third-space, and hybridity useful in that they establish a discourse that accommodates the complexity of the consequences of the transformations in social formation, within the past thirty years known as globalization, restructuring, and transnationalization. My argument here, however, is that these constructs can promote a better approximation of that complexity only if they organically incorporate the fundamental institutional dimensions of that formation. And what, then, are these?

As I have indicated, it has been the rapid and massive migrations of people from Asia, Latin America, and Africa to European and U.S. megacities, their impact on cultural, economic, and political institutional relationships, and the construction and interpretation of these as perceived threats to the maintenance of the cultural ground of national identity that have occasioned the preoccupation with theorizing "difference." And the sustained work of scholars like Sassen on the latest phase of changes in the world economy leaves little doubt that these migrations are an integral part of the configuration of that restructuring. These latest migrations have been promoted by the economic and state policies, practices, and strategies that have come to characterize this process of global restructuring (see Sassen, 1988; Castles and Miller, 1993).

One of the significant characteristics of this process has been the particular form that the transnationalization of capital has taken since the late 1960s.[3] The specific institutional grounding, then, for the field of forces, practices, and theorizations that is the axis of postmodernist and postcolonial theoretical constructions of subaltern spaces is the particular configuration of interrelated processes of the restructuring of global capitalism variously described as globalization and transnationalization. To recognize the centrality and influence of these processes does not necessarily privilege them or reduce the theorization of subaltern spaces to mere ideological expressions, although that has been evident in some studies. It is precisely to avoid this facile dismissal of the complex reality that the theorizations of subaltern spaces attempt to account for that I have sought to delineate a more structurally rooted elaboration of them. To ignore them or construct them in institutionally ungrounded ways leads to an incomplete analysis at best and the obfuscation of the reality of domination at worst.

Thus, margins, borders, and third-spaces need to be framed and contextualized as components and expressions of the ways in which these processes of transnationalization are being lived. Nederveen Pieterse observes that "hybrid formations constituted by the interpenetration of diverse logics manifest themselves in *hybrid sites* and spaces. . . . Global cities and ethnic mélange neighborhoods within them (such as Jackson Heights in Queens, New York) are other hybrid spaces in the global landscape" (1995: 51). The emergence of these new types of institutional spaces or sites challenges traditional ways of understanding and explaining culture, identity, and community, primarily because they are expressions of a different relationship between space and place that characterizes the dynamics of transnationalism. The degree, extent, and pervasiveness of the changes in patterns of social relations, cultural configurations, and forms that are part of transnationalization have disrupted long-established boundaries based on representations and constructions of those populations constructed when "they" were "there" and "we" were "here." The viability and adequacy of these constructions have been undermined now that "they" are "here" and challenging the notion of who the "we" are. Thus, although the focus of analysis of these concepts of subaltern spaces has been on those marginalized in different ways, in fact the emergence of transnationalism has impacted long-established populations as well. Thus the meaning of, and hence the stability and orientation provided by, established notions of "here" and "there," of "we" and "them," have been fundamentally problematized.[4] Gupta and Ferguson (1992: 10) have advanced a convincing critique of contemporary forms of cultural analysis that continue to assume an isomorphic relationship between nations, territory, space and identities:

> In a world of diaspora, transnational culture flows, and mass movements of populations, old-fashioned attempts to map the globe as a set of culture regions or homelands are bewildered by a dazzling array of postcolonial simulacra, doublings and redoublings, as India and Pakistan apparently reappear in post-colonial simulation in London, prerevolution Tehran rises from the ashes of Los Angeles, and a thousand similar cultural dreams are played out in urban and rural settings all across the globe.

And while they appreciate the effort to describe this dislodging of identities from a fixed and stable territorial "place" through the notion of "deterritorialization," they opt instead to characterize this dimension as "reterritorialization" to avoid the connotation that space and place are no longer significant dimensions of social formations. Space and place still matter but in a different way.

What all this means is that the processes and various dimensions and manifestations of transnationalization require that we rethink the concept of what constitutes a nation—of the role of territory and the nature of the claims of sovereignty and how these are related to the processes of community and identity formation. And as the particular configuration of these change, so too must the complex ways in which these dimensions are incorporated into the institutional structures of the state and of civil society.

CITIZENSHIP AND SUBALTERN SPACES

How are we to understand and articulate the linkages between the issues of difference and the various constructions of subaltern spaces raised by postmodernism and postcolonialism and the political realm? I propose that the types of changes I referred to above with regard to nation, identity, community, territory, and the state are precisely what the discourses of citizenship attempt to articulate. In particular, I want to turn to an approach recently developed by the historical sociologist Margaret Somers that I believe allows us to address the issues of difference, transnationalism, and the complex sets of relationships examined by the literature on subaltern spaces.

While this framework for conceptualizing citizenship does not directly address the issues involved in the discussion of subaltern spaces, it does provide a basis for addressing the lack of institutional grounding that limits most constructions of these issues. The position is developed most clearly and thoroughly in an article entitled "Citizenship and the Place of the Public Sphere: Law, Community, and Political Cultures in the Transition to Democracy" (Somers, 1993).[5] Somers's point of departure is the premise that the conceptions of citizenship developed in most traditions, although they are constructed differently, tend to have in common a definition of citizenship as a status or attribute of a category of persons (see Axtmann, 1996, for discussion). She tries to demonstrate that this approach leads to a static analysis that makes it extremely difficult to understand the dependence of citizenship practices on the particular and historically specific articulation of several institutional relationships. She writes that: "Instead, I propose that citizenship be defined as an 'instituted process,' i.e., citizenship is a set of institutionally embedded social practices" (1993: 589) and continues:

> Thus, citizenship is reconceptualized as the outcome of political, legal, and symbolic practices enacted through relational matrices of universal membership rules and legal institutions that are activated in combination with the particularistic political cultures of different types of civil societies. As such, citizenship practices are also a source of political identity—the translation of this identity into a rights-based positive citizenship identity depends entirely on the contexts of activation. . . . Quasi-democratic citizenship rights can emerge only in certain institution-specific relational settings and only in the context of particular social practices, namely, practices that support popular public spheres. . . . Theorizing about citizenship must . . . include a sociology of public spheres and their relationships to the associational practices of civil society.

The institutional sites of civil society are most effectively construed, Somers contends, in terms of a "relational/network and institutional analysis," in which institutions are understood as "organizational and symbolic practices that operate within networks of rules, structural ties, public narratives, and binding relationships that are embedded in time and space" and in which the relational approach "disaggregates social categories and reconfigures them into institutional and relational clusters in which people, power, and organizations are positioned and connected" (1993: 595). Instead of using the concept of "society" to frame the issue of citizenship, Somers uses the term *relational setting*, which she defines as "a patterned matrix of institutional relationships among cultural, economic, social, and political practices. . . . A relational setting has no governing entity according to which the entire setting can be categorized; it can only be characterized by deciphering its spatial and network patterns and its temporal processes" (1993: 595). This approach generates a different way of linking citizenship to the dimensions of subjectivity and agency. Instead of "categorical" attributes being the source of legal and political standing and action, "identity" becomes the axis conceptualizing the source of political action. Identities are

> not derived from attributes imputed from a stage of societal development (e.g., pre-industrial or modern) or a social category (e.g., traditional artisan, factory laborer, or working-class wife), but by actors' places in the multiple relationships in which they are embedded. . . . It is no longer assumed that a group of people has any particular relationship to citizenship simply because one aspect of their identity is categorized as the "working class." "Social categories" presume internally stable properties such that, under normal conditions, entities within that category will act appropriately, whereas "identities" embed the actors within relationships and stories that shift over time and space. Social action thus loses its categorical stability, and class embeddedness becomes more important than class attributes. Thus, citizenship identities are investigated by looking at actors' places in their relational settings (1993: 595).

I have taken the liberty of quoting extensively in order to provide a sense of the major conceptual and theoretical elements of an approach that may be unfamiliar to many.

What Somers has provided is a way to situate and explain concepts and practices such as "citizenship," which are advanced as universal within the nation-state, in terms of specific and local institutional relations and to understand these as constituting the articulations between state and civil society. And she provides a way to assess, at least in a general way, the degree to which various social and cultural practices in civil society might be claims to rights. Thus the nature of the activities and practices that express claims to citizenship depends on the institutional mix of factors, and this allows for the possibility (and likelihood) that these claims will take different forms.

Somers focuses on the set of practices that constitute the "public sphere," understood as "a contested participatory site in which actors with overlapping identities as legal subjects, citizens, economic actors, and family and community members form a public body and engage in negotiations and contestations over political and social life" (1993: 589). Yet the theoretical basis for linking other dimensions (such as those listed) of civil society to the institutional axis of citizenship is established.

Somers's conception of the core components of citizenship as "membership, participation, association, inclusion/exclusion, national identity and . . . the rule of law" (1993: 609) is consistent with much of the literature. What is different is that she has elaborated a way of linking these dimensions to the specific forms they take in particular institutional sites or "relational settings" within civil society. These spaces are precisely the sites where the positionalities identified as subaltern spaces are realized as a range of discursive and material practices. It is here that transnational practices and subjectivities and the particular ways in which space and place are reconfigured by those practices take form. It is within these spaces, I would argue, that we can determine the degree to which subaltern practices constitute what are often implicit claims to rights. Thus, for example, in my study of community transformation in Los Angeles, Latinas/os who lived in spaces and settings that fit the characteristics elaborated by notions of hybridity, third-space, margins, and borders were making claims within the relational settings (or specific institutional sites) of civil society that often revolved around the core components of citizenship identified by Somers. In other words, they were engaging in practices within relational settings of civil society that can under specific conditions be construed as claims about membership in the community—about having access to institutional settings, resources, and opportunities (e.g. in seeking educational opportunities), about the freedom to develop and maintain culturally based associational networks—that challenge the criteria for inclusion/exclusion and constitute affirmations of spaces of cultural identity. Ethnographic studies of these sites of hybridity and borders, and the life histories of households that have developed strategies in response to the impact of transnationalization, have revealed a number of such practices, which, although they are not necessarily construed as or intended by the actors as "political," are in effect contestations of established boundaries, rules, and constructions of "citizenship."[6]

CONCLUSION

As we have seen, the issues and problematics of postmodernist discourse represent a very broad range of concerns that challenge many of the basic assumptions of the social sciences and the humanities. This discourse has initiated a serious rethinking of the ways in which these fields have constructed concepts such as society, cultures, subjectivity, theoretical discourse, representation, and others that have emerged from a long tradition rooted in the Enlightenment. And this is precisely the problem from the postmodernist perspective, for the traditional approaches reflect a world and a reality that have long since ceased to exist. The privileging of the subject (centering), binary ways of framing concepts and theories, and the assumption of single and fixed patterns of causality have all been severely criticized. In their place postmodernist approaches posit a multiplicity of subject positions and of causal relations and patterns, fragmented and decentered practices, and the need to explore the complexity of representational practices. One of the dimensions of postmodernist analysis is the attempt to explain the fluidity and dynamism of the often radical disjunction of cultures that seems prevalent today. While postcolonial approaches differ in many ways from postmodernist analysis, they have overlapping concerns. Thus we find writers in both frameworks theorizing the spaces created by those radical disjunctions, spaces of "difference," variously called hybrid, borders, margins, and third-space, that I have called "subaltern spaces." And these are important explorations for all of those attempting to establish a grounding for strategies of empowerment and social change to promote the construction of "new architectures of power." Yet, as Stuart Hall points out, "It is only too tempting to fall into the trap of assuming that, because essentialism has been deconstructed *theoretically*, therefore, it has been displaced *politically*" (1996: 249). My argument has been that the theorizations of these subaltern spaces are limited politically because most lack any serious effort to ground either the theorization itself or the spaces in the institutional contexts within which they occur. I have proposed that one way to address this political limitation is to resituate the discourse of subaltern spaces within an approach to the problematic of citizenship that links citizenship and civil society. This approach allows us to focus on prefigurative oppositional practices, that is, practices that are not normally constructed as having any direct political significance or standing but make claims that in effect challenge the existing relations of disempowerment. In this way, it establishes a means to elaborate the political dimensions of the transnationalization of identities, spaces, and communities that is an essential component of the postmodernist challenge.

NOTES

1. For examples of work on this, see Moore and Pinderhughes (1993), Lamphere (1992), and Lamphere, Zavella, and Gonzales (1994).

2. Merod (1987) has presented a strong case for the need for this type of institutional grounding with regard to the field of literary criticism.

3. Rouse (1995: 357) has argued that the major transformations of the past two decades are "best understood *not* as a move from modernity to postmodernity" but as a shift from "multinational processes of capital accumulation to the growing dominance of processes organized along transnational lines."

4. Here I am summarizing Gupta and Ferguson's (1992) discussion of the issue.

5. Different dimensions of this approach are elaborated in Somers (1992; 1993; 1995) and in Somers and Gibson (1994). An emphasis on the sociological and institutional dimensions of citizenship is also reflected in the work of Bryan Roberts (1995 and 1996) and in most of the articles published in issues of the journals *Public Culture* (8[2], 1996) and the *International Journal of Urban and Regional Research* (20[1], 1996) devoted to exploring the theme of "citizenship and the city."

6. For a more detailed analysis of theses practices and themes, see Rocco (1996). I am currently finishing a book-length manuscript that includes a full discussion of the three levels of analysis, the theoretical framework linking them, and the presentation and analysis of the results of ethnographic studies of specific institutional sites and of the narrative structures and themes of the family histories of Latina/o households in Southeast Los Angeles, the center of the Fordist industrial activity in Los Angeles between 1940 and 1980.

REFERENCES

Axtmann, Roland. 1996. *Liberal Democracy into the Twenty-First Century: Globalization, Integration, and the Nation-State*. Manchester: Manchester University Press.

Berman, Marshall. 1983. *All That Is Solid Melts into Air*. London: Verso.

Bhabha, Homi K. 1995. "Cultural Diversity and Cultural Differences," pp. 206–9 in Bill Ashcroft, Gareth Griffiths, and Helen Tiffin (eds.), *The Post-Colonial Studies Reader*. New York: Routledge.

Castles, Stephen and Mark J. Miller. 1993. *The Age of Migration: International Population Movements in the Modern World*. New York: The Guilford Press.

Cooke, Philip. 1988. "Modernity, Postmodernity and the City," pp. 62–80 in Michael Peter Smith (ed.), *Power, Community, and the City*. New Brunswick, NJ: Transaction Books.

Dirlik, Arif. 1994. "The Postcolonial Aura: Third World Criticism in the Age of Global Capitalism." *Critical Inquiry* 20: 328–56.

Dowling, William C. Jameson. 1984. *Althusser, Marx: An Introduction to the "Political Unconscious."* Ithaca, NY: Cornell University Press.

Featherstone, Mike. 1988. "In Pursuit of the Postmodern: An Introduction." *Theory, Culture and Society* 5: 195–216.

Frankenberg, Ruth and Lati Mani. 1993. "Crosscurrents, Crosstalk: Race, 'Postcoloniality' and the Politics of Location." *Cultural Studies* 7: 292–310.

Grewal, Inderpal and Caren Kaplan. 1994. "Introduction: Transnational Feminist Practices and Questions of Postmodernity," pp. 1–33 in Inderpal Grewal and Caren Kaplan (eds.), *Scattered Hegemonies: Postmodernity and Transnational Feminist Practices*. Minneapolis: University of Minnesota Press.

Gupta, Akhil and James Ferguson. 1992. "Beyond 'Culture': Space, Identity, and the Politics of Difference." *Cultural Anthropology* 7: 6–23.

Hall, Stuart. 1996. "When was 'the Post-Colonial'? Thinking at the Limit," pp. 242–60 in Iain Chambers and Lidia Curti (eds.), *The Post-Colonial Question: Common Skies, Divided Horizons*. New York: Routledge.

Kearney, Michael. 1996. *Reconceptualizing the Peasantry: Anthropology in Global Perspective*. Boulder, CO: Westview Press.

Lamphere, Louise (ed.). 1992. *Structuring Diversity: Ethnographic Perspectives on the New Immigration*. Chicago: University of Chicago Press.

Lamphere, Louise, Patricia Zavella, and Felipe Gonzales. 1994. *Sunbelt Working Mothers: Reconciling Family and Factory*. Ithaca, NY: Cornell University Press.

Lavie, Smadar and Ted Swedenburg. 1996. "Between and Among the Boundaries of Culture: Bridging Text and Lived Experience in the Third Timespace." *Cultural Studies* 10:154–79.

McLaren, Peter. 1994. "Multiculturalism and the Postmodern Critique: Toward a Pedagogy of Resistance and Transformation," pp. 192–222 in Henry A. Giroux and Peter McLaren (eds.), *Between Borders: Pedagogy and the Politics of Cultural Studies*. New York: Routledge.

Merod, Jim. 1987. *The Political Responsibility of the Critic*. Ithaca, NY: Cornell University Press.

Mignolo, Walter. 1997. "The Allocation and Relocation of Identities: Colonialism, Nationalism, Transnationalism." Paper presented at workshop "Hybrid Cultures and Transnational Identities," University of California, Los Angeles, March.

Moore, Joan and Raquel Pinderhughes (ed.). 1993. *In the Barrios: Latinos and the Underclass Debate*. New York: Russell Sage Foundation.

Nederveen Pieterse, Jan. 1995. "Globalization as Hybridization," pp. 45–68 in Mike Featherstone, Scott Lash, and Roland Robertson (eds.), *Global Modernities*. Thousand Oaks, CA: Sage.

O'Brien, Martin and Sue Penna. 1996. "Postmodern Theory and Politics: Perspectives on Citizenship and Social Justice." *Innovation: The European Journal of Social Science* 9: 185–203.

Parry, Benita. 1995. "Problems in Current Theories of Colonial Discourse," pp. 36–44 in Bill Ashcroft, Gareth Griffiths, and Helen Tiffin (eds.), *The Post-Colonial Studies Reader*. New York: Routledge.

Roberts, Bryan R. 1995. *The Making of Citizens: Cities of Peasants Revisited*. London: Arnold.

———. 1996. "The Social Context of Citizenship in Latin America." *International Journal of Urban and Regional Research* 20: 38–65.

Rocco, Raymond A. 1996. "Latino Los Angeles: Reframing Boundaries/Borders." pp. 365–89 in Allen J. Scott and Edward W. Soja (eds.), *The City: Los Angeles and Urban Theory at the End of the Twentieth Century*. Berkeley: University of California Press.

Rouse, Roger. 1995. "Thinking through Transnationalism: Notes on the Cultural Politics of Class Relations in the Contemporary United States." *Public Culture* 7: 353–402.

Rowe, William and Vivian Schelling. 1991. *Memory and Modernity: Popular Culture in Latin America*. London: Verso.

Sassen, Saskia. 1988. *The Mobility of Labor and Capital: A Study in International Investment and Labor Flow*. New York: Cambridge University Press.

Scott, David. 1996. "The Aftermaths of Sovereignty: Postcolonial Criticism and the Claims of Political Modernity." *Social Text* 48 (14): 1–26.

Shklar, Judith N. 1991. *American Citizenship: The Quest for Inclusion*. Cambridge, MA.: Harvard University Press.

Shohat, Ella. 1992. "Notes on the 'Post-Colonial.'" *Social Text* 31–32:99–113.

Smith, Michael Peter. 1994. "Can You Imagine? Transnational Migration and the Globalization of Grassroots Politics." *Social Text* 39:15–34.

Soja, Edward W. 1996. *Thirdspace: Journeys to Los Angeles and Other Real and Imagined Places*. Cambridge, MA: Blackwell.

Somers, Margaret R. 1992. "Narrativity, Narrative Identity, and Social Action: Rethinking English Working-class Formation." *Social Science History* 16: 591–630.

———. 1993. "Citizenship and the Place of the Public Sphere: Law, Community, and Political Culture in the Transition to Democracy." *American Sociological Review* 58: 587–620.

———. 1995. "What's Political or Cultural about Political Culture and the Public Sphere? Toward an Historical Sociology of Concept Formation." *Sociological Theory* 13: 113–44.

Somers, Margaret R., and Gloria D. Gibson. 1994. "Reclaiming the Epistemological 'Other': Narrative and the Social Constitution of Identity," pp. 37–99 in Craig Calhoun (ed.), *Social Theory and the Politics of Identity*. Oxford: Blackwell.

Turner, Bryan S. 1994. "Postmodern Culture/Modern Citizens," pp. 153–68 in Bart van Steenbergen (ed.), *The Condition of Citizenship*. Thousand Oaks, CA: Sage.

van Steenbergen, Bart (ed.). 1994. *The Condition of Citizenship*. Thousand Oaks, Ca. Sage.

II

CULTURAL PROCESSES
AND CHANGING FORMS
OF ETHNIC IDENTITY

We have introduced the idea of cultural scripts to denote values, beliefs, and operational guides that are distributed according to class, gender, ethnicity, and racialized evaluations of phenotypic characteristics.[1] These scripts are created historically by many means and sources including national and international fonts, educational and political institutions, and occupational and professional organizations and organized at many different levels from the household to the transnational corporations. They are transmitted to varying degrees linguistically, symbolically, and ritually and through expressive cultural forms such as music, drama, myths, and literature and through film, art, television, theater, and print.

But there are megascripts derived from supralocal settings such as government, corporations, large-scale institutions such as the Internet, and institutions such as universities that not only serve as the means of transmission but also provide the content of national and international discourses. These supralocal institutions are seldom "value free" or neutral but represent the means by which political control expands, "appropriate" social organization is accepted as normal, and the economic appropriation of labor and value is maintained. Nations have perennially fostered political myths as part of the megascripts that legitimate their control and their current economic structures by reference to heroic pasts, and unique political ideas such as representative government, individual rights, and equal access to education, health, and a livelihood for its "citizens" while all others, deemed "illegal aliens," are denied such privileges and rights. Megascripts may be internalized as the only acceptable guides for reflection and action, becoming part of group and individual funds of knowledge. They can seldom become totally hegemonic and therefore populations that are reduced to subaltern or subordinated status will often reject their premises and practices and turn to others inherited from other sources or develop syncretic forms.

One of the central concerns of this section is the way in which Latina/o populations maneuver, negotiate, adapt, resist, create, and develop localized, regional, and sometimes national scripts about identity and the ability to live a decent life. Localized scripts emerge in conjunction with household funds of knowledge that have both strategic and tactical functions and are sometimes in direct opposition to these larger scripted references. These profoundly positive creations may serve as household and community social platforms from which following generations may emerge whole and capable of filtering the traumas of institutional racialism, sexism, classism, and ethnocentrism.

Among the recurrent megascripts are those involved in the colonization of populations and the broad economic "flattening" processes specific to expanding capitalism in its current transnational version. This is made clear by Cabán's historical treatment of the enforced acculturation of Puerto Rico, which depicts the eventual failure of "Americanization" programs and its paradoxical contribution to the development of Puerto Rican nationalism. This colonial cultural experiment, reminiscent of the Americanization programs for Native Americans of the same period and the linguistic and cultural erasure of Mexicans in the Southwest after the Mexican War, created political and cultural national dynamics that remain important in the new millennium, as the Vieques Island case illustrates.

Cruz-Jensen's uncompromising essay breaks down the psychocultural megascripts of racialism in Latin America that are derived from Spanish colonial and U.S. domination. Her sometimes personal and always enlightening piece clearly explains the oppression that racialism creates and the elaborate denial and defense mechanisms that give it strength. Her experiential and intellectual opposition to this complex megascript is part of hundreds of years of cultural and political resistance to being reduced to a melanin category.

Nájera-Ramírez shows us how a seemingly "traditional" national expressive form, the Mexican rodeo, crosscuts the cultural dislocation created by a political border that dissects a regional identity. The *charreada* reflects a changing cultural script with regard to gender and class relationships in the United States but also becomes part of a struggle against Mexicans being made mere subjects in the dominant regimes of representation and constructed only as the "other."

Pérez illustrates how Puerto Ricans in Chicago have been redefined from model "ethnics" to a low-caste, criminally-inclined, and poverty-stricken stereotype. In opposition to this script have emerged new mythic and revitalizing scripts employing traditional Puerto Rican national symbols of an idealized hearth and home and of the *jíbaro* (the traditional agricultural Puerto Rican hero). These represent the quest for a sense of Puerto Rican identity, place, and space in the midst of urban Chicago and in contention with other Latina/o populations that are creating alternative Mexican scripts in the same area. While this seems like a search for a single pristine cultural script of "Puerto Ricanness," it is in actuality a means of filtering the impact of delocalization, linguistic and cultural erasure, and the psychocultural uncertainty and indeterminacy created by dislocation and resettlement. In the Puerto Rican case the process becomes even more problematic as part of a diaspora that is politically undivided but bordered by class, ethnic, and racial scripts in the context of continued colonializing relations between Puerto Rico and the United States.

Each contribution provides important insights into the many ways in which urban, rural, national, and transnational Latina/o populations struggle to retain, develop, and create cultural scripts that provide alternative interpretations and options to those posed by supralocal others.

NOTE

1. These last are primarily focused on melanin differences, with whiteness usually communicated as the preferred light filter, and other physiognomic characteristics such as nose, mouth, and hair preferences. Discourses are then reduced to a quasi-explanatory reference to "white blood" and "black blood," these constructs being societally provided a "social value." What follows from such premises is the incorporation of entire populations into stratified racialized castes based on imposed categories of human worth. Genotypic biological descriptors have nothing to do with the social constructs about race, although they can reinforce racial categories. Most biological anthropologists in these areas of study analyze genetic typings to derive an estimate of genotypic mixing based on allele or haplotype frequencies to see if the distribution of frequencies is influential genetically. Such work has nothing to do with "racial" memory, cultural affinity, or any sort of magical relationship, nor do they fix a "racial" distribution of "blood" among cultural populations. These are red blood allele frequencies, not socially derived racial markers (Vélez-Ibáñez, 1996: 312, n 20).

4

The Colonizing Mission
of the United States in Puerto Rico,
1898–1930

Pedro A. Cabán

In the summer of 1898 the United States attained its long-standing goal of acquiring strategic insular possessions in the Pacific and the Caribbean. Moreover, with its decisive defeat of Spain, U.S. expansionists could rightly claim that their nation had achieved imperial status. But the United States not only appropriated far-flung exotic islands but also claimed sovereignty over approximately 10 million inhabitants of the lands ceded by Spain.[1] The sobering question that confronted the United States after the euphoria of military victory was the legal status and political rights of these subject peoples. Eventually it devised a complicated structure of laws that prescribed a distinctive citizenship status for the subjects of each of its territorial possessions (Smith, 1997: 428).

While the inhabitants of the territories were all perceived to be so racially and culturally different as to justify their permanent exclusion from the American polity, U.S. empire builders believed that effective colonial rule required that they be Americanized. Colonial administrations embarked on ambitious campaigns to transform the legal systems and codes of Puerto Rico, Cuba, and the Philippines and to install a program of universal public education of which English-language instruction was the cornerstone. While Americanization, or the colonizing mission, was never a coherent policy, it did identify the general outlines of the institutional transformation and political change that the colonial governors were expected to undertake. Colonial officials were permitted, indeed expected, to modify the content of the Americanization programs to adjust to local conditions.

The purpose of this chapter is to examine the methods and goals of the colonizing mission in Puerto Rico during the first thirty years of U.S. rule. I document the contradictions inherent in the mission, some of the more salient episodes of opposition, and ultimately the failure of the colonial authorities to attain their imperial objectives. I am more interested in specifying the content of this program and how it was related to larger imperial objectives and explaining how paradoxically it created a space for opposition than in examining the complex history of the diverse and elaborate attempts by Puerto Ricans to deter, modify, or benefit from the Americanization campaign.[2] I discuss two colonial administrations that Congress imposed on Puerto Rico. The Foraker Act, in effect from 1900 to 1917, set up a civilian colonial administration that accelerated the transformation of Puerto Rican life inaugurated during the period of military occupation. The Jones Act modified the least democratic and most authoritarian features of the previous regime but sustained its pursuit of Americanization of the subject population. Although the legislation established seemingly different structures for colonial rule, in both regimes three departments were pivotal for carrying out the colonizing mission of the central government during these three decades: the Departments of Education and Interior and the Office of the Attorney General.

AMERICANIZATION AND THE AMERICAN CENTURY

When Henry Luce prophesied the start of an "American century—America's century as a dominant power" in 1941, the United States had had territorial possessions and colonies in the Caribbean and the Pacific since 1898. Scholars differ as to the reasons the United States embarked on war with Spain over a century ago, but they concur that by the waning years of the nineteenth century the country was rapidly emerging as an economic power with global aspirations. Ever conscious of European designs on the Caribbean and expanded commercial presence in the Americas, the United States was determined to demonstrate to its competitors that the Western Hemisphere was its exclusive sphere of influence. An influential and highly active coalition of manufacturers and export agricultural producers lobbied for an aggressive foreign trade policy, while an ultranationalist cadre of expansionists in government, the media, and the academy demanded decisive military action against Spain, the last vestige of European power in the Americas.

This alliance between internationalist corporate capital and an evolving imperialist state was in its infancy when the United States embarked on a war with the decaying Spanish empire. Over a century later, the same array of public and private power drives the Summit of the Americas and its goal of neoliberal trade liberalization. The expansionism of the late nineteenth century was built on an ideological edifice of virulent nationalist social Darwinism. Imperialists preached that the superiority of U.S. institutions was divinely ordained and that the nation had a moral imperative to implant these institutions and the values they embodied throughout the hemisphere. The contemporary justification for a U.S.–dominated regime of free trade and investment no longer relies on racially constituted dogma. Yet it is undeniable that a celebratory, almost chauvinistic, conviction of the superiority of the United States, particularly the democratic republicanism that is embedded in the free-enterprise mentality, underpins the discourse on U.S.–led hemisphere globalization.

The imperialism of the late nineteenth century required modernizing the political institutions in the "host country" and creating the sociopolitical environment that would permit the rational implantation of capitalist production relations (Sklar, 1988: 81). Americanization in Puerto Rico and other U.S. territorial holdings entailed very similar processes of transformation of political institutions, property relations, and class structure. The contemporary discourse on globalization underscores the indispensability of liberal democratic political institutions because they harmonize with capitalist economic organization and practice.[3] It is a familiar argument to those who have studied the history of late nineteenth-century and early twentieth-century U.S. colonial rule and imperialism. In Puerto Rico, colonial officials had the extraordinary opportunity to implant those institutions and practices they believed were necessary to effect the colony's transformation into an appendage of the metropolitan economy. While such overt intervention has disappeared since the demise of the Soviet Union, the political corollary of globalization is the extension of formal democratic systems—preferably the one that prevails in the United States—because these have demonstrated their adaptability to the requirements of highly internationalized capital.

In 1898 the United States exacted Puerto Rico from Spain as indemnification for having lost the war. For almost two years Puerto Rico was a "department" under the jurisdiction of the War Department. During this brief period of military rule the foundations for a radical and sustained transformation of Puerto Rico's political institutions, legal codes, and education system were firmly established (see Berbusse, 1966; Santiago-Valles, 1994; Cabán, 1999). On May 1, 1900, the Foraker Act established a civil colonial administration in Puerto Rico. By far the most important feature of this administration was the Executive Council. It was to be responsible for overhauling Puerto Rico's political and judicial institutions, installing an insular constabulary, modernizing the infrastructure, and installing a system of public education. In the following pages I will examine three key Executive Council agencies that were responsible for these tasks: the Department of Education, the Interior Department, and the Office of the Attorney General. U.S. colonial officials were confident that the Executive Council would transform Puerto Rico's institutions and people so that the island-nation would assume its required role in the American century. Since Americanization entailed the implantation of government and judicial institutions patterned on those of the United States, the Foraker Act was the first stage of the colonizing mission.

THE IDEA OF AMERICANIZATION

The U.S. acquisition of Puerto Rico and other insular Spanish possessions—the Philippines, Guam, and Cuba—was a unique event in the history of U.S. territorial expansion. First, it was the result of conquest of a European nation that had claimed sovereignty over the inhabitants of the islands for over four hundred years. These established overseas societies possessed definable cultures, languages, values, and political systems, but they were different from each other and each posed distinct challenges to U.S. colonial officials. Puerto Rico and Cuba, for example, were perceived as partially European societies, while the Pacific islands were popularly viewed as exotic and somewhat more primitive. Nonetheless, by virtue of their cultural, linguistic, and racial characteristics the people of the former Spanish possessions were judged inferior and would be excluded from the body politic of the United States. U.S. colonial officials believed that through a campaign of Americanization these strange and exotic peoples would be converted into semiliterate, loyal subjects who would apprehend the legitimacy of U.S. sovereignty and accept the new political and economic order that would be imposed on their societies. Although they would be educated and incorporated into colonial administration and partially assimilated into the norms and values of U.S. society, they would forever be barred from full and equal participation in the U.S. polity. Politically excluded, these possessions were nevertheless to be fully incorporated into the circuit of U.S. production and trade as sugar producers and markets for the industrial and agricultural products of the North.

The rationale for Americanization was popularly portrayed as a noble and selfless effort to bestow on the unfortunate primitive peoples the possessions and virtues of U.S. civilization. Yet Americanization was driven by a strategic and economic calculus that was pivotal to the United States' aspirations for hemispheric hegemony and national security. Political stability and social order were vital in these militarily strategic insular possessions. Since the islands were destined to be either territories under de facto regulation or formal territorial possessions for an unspecified period, their inhabitants had to be socialized into accepting as legitimate their subordination and exclusion from the U.S. body politic. The insular possessions were quickly to take on an important role in the remarkable expansion of the U.S. economy during the first decades of the twentieth century.

Before the war with Spain, expansionists had envisaged U.S. control of sugarcane producing islands in the Pacific and Caribbean and an escape from dependency on imported European beet sugar. By stabilizing and modernizing the financial and revenue-generating institutions and adopting business practices and corporate legal codes from the mainland, colonial officials laid the foundations for a rapid transition to capitalism in the underdeveloped and war-torn possessions. Such a transformation was not merely economically beneficial but politically necessary since the ideology of commercial expansion closely associated capitalism with democracy. Finally, U.S. empire builders learned from the experience of their European predecessors and quickly moved to create an indigenous cadre of political leaders and managers who would participate in the task of transforming the colonies.

While Americanization was never more than a broadly conceived, loosely defined conception that rationalized the necessity to transform subject peoples and their institutions in the service of empire, U.S. officials aspired to convert Puerto Rico into a commercial bridge to Latin America and its people into ambassadors for U.S. interests in the hemisphere. Not withstanding these grandiose aspirations, which should be viewed with a measure of skepticism, Puerto Rico was an invaluable strategic commercial and military asset, and the loyalty of its people to the new sovereign had to be secured.

Americanization was predicated on belief in the superiority of Anglo-Saxon cultural and industrial capabilities.[4] According to the Senator Albert Beveridge, a vocal ultranationalist of the 1890s, the United States was "an industrial civilization" and had reached such "a state of enlightenment and power" that "its duty to the world as one of its civilizing powers" was to embark on a "period of colonial administration" (Beveridge, 1907: 3–5). The proponents of Americanization argued that the United States, because of its Anglo-Saxon heritage, was the epitome of industrial modernity and possessed the most developed form of republican democracy. As practiced in the overseas possessions, Americanization required English-language instruction to provide the subject peoples a functional knowledge of the customs, national character, and political principles of the new sovereign. Because it was a process specifically devised by the central government to influence the political behavior and attitudes of a subject people, Americanization in the insular possessions differed from its practice in the United States (see Cabán, n.d.).[5] It was more comprehensive because it called for the systematic replacement of Spanish legal systems and political institutions. The War Department, especially the Bureau of Insular Affairs, its specialized agency for colonial administration, periodically had jurisdiction over Puerto Rico, but the bureau's influence in setting colonial policy was always compelling.

Although some enthusiastic officials called for the virtual eradication of indigenous culture and language, others recognized that it was not only futile but unwise to adopt such a radical approach.[6] Education Commissioner Edward Falkner may well have most accurately assessed the objective of Americanization in Puerto Rico in describing it as "our national social laboratory" (Falkner, 1905: 159–60). While the process of replacing Puerto Rico's institutions was important, Falkner believed that "the primary object of our administration in Puerto Rico should be to infuse into the political, social and economic life of the Puerto Rican people the spirit, rather than the form of American institutions" (Falkner, 1908: 171).

The political education of Puerto Ricans was a key goal of the Americanization discourse (U.S. Department of State, 1905: 41). Although colonial managers never formally defined what political education entailed, they propagated the notion that Puerto Ricans were woefully unprepared to exercise self-government. This presumed incapacity justified restrictive colonial rule and careful oversight of Puerto Rican political behavior (see Go, 2000; Clark, 1973). Expressing this imperial arrogance, General George Davis, Puerto Rico's last military governor, assured Secretary of War Elihu Root that "the knowledge which I possess of the inhabitants of this island . . . forces me to the conviction that, [self-government] would be a disaster to them and to the best interest of their fair island" (U.S. Department of War, 1900: 75). In 1899 Root justified strict colonial rule by arguing that Puerto Ricans "would inevitably fail without a course of tuition under a strong and guiding hand" (1916: 203). Governor Beekman Winthrop crisply reported that "the work of U.S. officials was to install American institutions and American governmental principles, and to educate the Puerto Rican on these lines" (U.S. Department of State, 1905: 41). Of course, U.S. officials would ultimately decide if and when Puerto Ricans had acquired the capabilities and temperament to exercise self-government in harmony with Anglo-Saxon principles of republican democracy. Ironically, the goal of "educating the natives in self-government" was stymied by the Bureau of Insular Affairs, which resisted relinquishing its centralized control over Puerto Rico. As late as 1932, when jurisdiction over Puerto Rico was transferred from the War Department to the Department of the Interior, the Bureau of Insular Affairs asserted that it could supervise the unincorporated territories more efficiently than their inhabitants (Clark, 1973: 233).

THE EXECUTIVE COUNCIL AND AMERICANIZATION

The appointed eleven-man Executive Council was a singular institution in U.S. territorial history in that it had both executive and legislative functions. It was the cabinet of the presidentially appointed governor and the upper chamber of the legislature. Six of its eleven members were male citizens of the United States, and each was assigned a cabinet post. No fewer than five Puerto Ricans were appointed to the council, although more than a decade would pass before any were put in charge of insular departments. Congress felt compelled to abandon the hallowed constitutional checks and balances here because it feared that otherwise the popularly elected lower house would be able to impede the work of the council. This arrangement also ensured that the Americanization of Puerto Rico would be closely directed by the central government, which virtually prohibited any Puerto Rican participation. According to William Willoughby, who served as council president,

"The greatest freedom was given to the newly constituted government to work out practically every question requiring the exercise of governmental authority." He wrote that the council constituted "the center or keystone to the whole system" of government (1902: 35; 1905: 98). Although the Executive Council was independent of the War Department, the Bureau of Insular Affairs worked closely with it in implementing the colonizing mission.

While the Executive Council's mandate for transformation was sweeping in its scope and touched virtually every area of Puerto Rican economic and political life, three functions predominated. These I identify as ideological, developmental, and coercive. These categories do not sufficiently convey the diverse and contradictory tendencies and policies that characterized the work of the Executive Council, and they were not mutually exclusive. Indeed, at times they were complementary. For example, laws favorable to foreign corporations were enacted and enforced by the attorney general and complemented the efforts of the Interior Department to attract U.S. investment, particularly in sugar. By broadly identifying general tendencies in the Americanization campaign, however, we can generate a clearer understanding of imperial thinking as it pertained to transforming the people of Puerto Rico into loyal wards of the empire and incorporating the island into the metropolitan economy. The ambitious program to remake Puerto Rico's institutions and people and to sustain the operations of the colonial administration was financed overwhelmingly from internal revenue sources.

The Department of Education was most directly involved in the ideological component of the Americanization process. One of its most important tasks was to teach the colonial subjects the language of the colonizer. The education commissioners set about to instill popular understanding and acceptance of U.S. norms, customs, and historical myths. They were keen to implant a patriotic spirit and socialize Puerto Ricans into accepting the superiority of U.S. institutions and way of life (see Negrón de Montilla, 1971; Osuna, 1949). The department was crucial in constructing and implanting a new and alien worldview divorced from the historical context of the Puerto Rican people's lived experiences.

The Department of the Interior, the director of health, and the director of public charities were charged with developing Puerto Rico's physical and human infrastructure. The director of public charities and the director of health were responsible for staving off mass starvation and destitution and eradicating the diseases that depleted Puerto Rico's workforce and endangered the lives of U.S. colonial officials. Officials were convinced that investments in education and vocational and industrial training would not only improve the material conditions of Puerto Rico's population but result in significant increases in the productivity of labor. Further investments in improved sanitary conditions, public health, and physical education would ensure an ample supply of healthy and energetic workers for the emerging industries. The Interior

Department modernized the country's infrastructure through ambitious public works projects: irrigation systems, hydroelectric plants, roads, warehouses and piers, and a telegraph system.

The attorney general was the chief legal officer and, like the commissioner of education, was appointed directly by the president. In addition to the attorney general, the coercive apparatus of the colonial state included the system of local courts, the bureau of prisons, the insular constabulary, the Porto Rico Regiment, and the federal district court. The courts were directly engaged in protecting private property, enforcing compliance with the laws, apprehending and prosecuting violators of the law, and enforcing commercial transactions and contracts. The courts and the body of jurisprudence that guided their conduct were among the most important institutions for advancing the Americanization of Puerto Rican society. Each Executive Council department employed its own staff of workers, and collectively this bureaucracy was the primary employer of the country's educated and professional strata. As Puerto Ricans were hired to work in the colonial administration, they became purveyors of the standards and values of the metropolitan power. The attorney general's office and the courts, as well as the insular police and the Porto Rico Regiment, were important agents for socialization and legitimated the new institutional order. Hundreds of Puerto Rican lawyers and judges acquired knowledge of a new body of jurisprudence and developed an understanding of U.S. legal codes and traditions. Thousands were trained for service as government clerks, technicians, managers, tax assessors, police officers, laborers, teachers, and so forth. In the midst of the increasing unemployment and widespread poverty that followed the U.S. occupation of Puerto Rico, these workers became dependent on the colonial state for their livelihood.

NEW LAWS AND NEW COURTS

A court system and a legal code patterned on those in the United States were among the most important institutions for advancing the Americanization of Puerto Rican society. Two months before General Nelson Miles landed in Guanica, Lawrence Lowell (who would become president of Harvard University) insisted in an influential article on the importance of implanting the "authority of American courts." It was chiefly by means of the courts and U.S. legal codes that the people of Puerto Rico "would acquire our political ideas and traditions" (1898: 58). Indeed, the military governors reported that Puerto Rico's legal system was strange and un-American and, according to one observer, "seriously obstructed the introduction of American ideas and methods" (Wilson, 1905: 105).

The Foraker Act set up a three-person commission appointed by the president to compile and revise Puerto Rico's laws. By 1902 the Spanish penal code and laws of civil and criminal procedures had been replaced with exact duplicates of the California and Montana codes. The commercial codes were amended according to the Louisiana Civil Code, while the codes of civil and criminal procedure were replaced with analogous legal codes from other states (Graffam, 1986: 115; Rivera Ramos, 2001: 70). (Governor William Hunt observed, "There is no more ready or more practical method of Americanizing our new possessions than by the enactment and enforcement of American laws, and the introduction and practice of American jurisprudence" [U.S. Department of State, 1904: 26]).

The Office of the Attorney General wielded considerable power. The supreme court, district courts, municipal courts, and justice of the peace courts all reported to the attorney general. In 1915 the Executive Council established a juvenile court system to try minors under the age of sixteen. One of the most controversial reforms was the extension of the U.S. federal district court system to Puerto Rico. The court was an important institution for socializing the population in the norms of the U.S. jurisprudence as well. Originally all the presidentially appointed judges were from the United States, and its proceedings were and continue to be conducted in English. The district court was bitterly opposed by Puerto Rico's political leaders, who saw it as an instrument of the metropolitan state to protect the interests of its citizens against claims brought by the colonial subjects. Various attempts were made to exclude Puerto Rico from the district court system. R. L. Rowe, an important colonial official, observed that "as a distinctly American tribunal it has done much to acquaint the native population, especially lawyers, with the procedure of American courts" (Rowe, 1904: 212).

Although subsequently much of the original legislation was modified, the initial alteration of the system of courts, civil and criminal law, and judicial procedures was swift and comprehensive. The task of overhauling the legal codes was greatly facilitated by the cooperation of the Puerto Rican Republican party. The Republicans were staunch supporters of the colonial regime and had exclusive control of the lower house of the legislature.[7] Within a decade of the acquisition of Puerto Rico, Willoughby announced that "in no other regard have institutions of Porto Rico existing under Spanish rule undergone so complete a change at the hands of the Americans as in respect to judicial organization and procedure" (1905: 107). Instead, Puerto Rico had "a complete system of practice in the courts, similar in its main features to that existing in the code states of the United States" (U.S. Department of State, 1905: 32).

Legal reform was key to establishing a favorable investment climate, which in turn was necessary for attracting U.S. corporations to Puerto Rico. It was commonly argued that U.S. men of business would further the Americanization of the island. Spanish commercial law was revised to reflect U.S. concepts of corporate rights and protection. In order to establish a favorable investment climate, the colonial state passed generous corporate tax laws modeled on those in industrial states. Indeed, since Puerto Rico was absorbed into the U.S. district court system, the full weight of federal legal protection was extended to U.S. firms operating in Puerto Rico. After these sweeping legal changes went into effect, Governor Allen informed potential investors, "Capitalists can be assured of protection to their property and investments, guaranteed in the form of government, in the tax laws, and in the reorganization of the courts, and capital is pretty sure to take care of itself" (Wood, Taft, and Allen, 1902: 366).

During the life of the Executive Council (1900–1917) expenditures for the coercive apparatus of the colonial state consumed about a quarter of the insular budget. Expenses for operating the penal institutions were the most rapidly increasing budget item (Cabán, 1999: 160). The rate of arrests increased over thirteenfold from 1899 to 1905 but declined slightly by 1916, when about 4.5 percent of the population was incarcerated (Santiago-Valles, 1994: 72).

PUBLIC EDUCATION AND AMERICANIZATION UNDER THE FORAKER ACT

The remarkable industrial and technological advancement of the United States during the Progressive era was popularly attributable not only to the dynamism of the Anglo-Saxon entrepreneurial spirit but to the system of universal public education. Among European governments the radical American idea that education was a right available to all and not a privilege reserved for an antiquarian elite was seen as a force behind the country's rapid emergence as a world power. The British journalist William Stead extolled the idea that "the superior education of the American common people was the secret of their growing ascendancy." In contrast to the elitism of much of European education, which was private and designed to preserve class privilege, the "universality of education in the United States is probably more calculated than all others to accelerate their progress towards a superior rank of civilization and power" (1902: 148).

Government interest in vocational education, especially manual training in the industrial arts, accelerated during the 1890s. By the end of the century the United States was a world leader in the manufacturing of machinery. The new economy demanded skilled workers, managers, and technicians, and the high schools were expected to provide this training. But industrialization required the immigration of millions of Europeans, many desperately poor and illiterate. While they provided the human labor power that fueled the industrial revolution, they also constituted a potential threat to national unity because of their alien political values and ignorance of the English language. Here as well, the public education system was expected to play a vital role.

Educators were developing an awareness of the centrality of public education in creating a sense of national identity among ethnically and linguistically heterogeneous European populations. State officials were also developing an appreciation for the systematic use of public education for political socialization. The Americanization of the foreigner became a project for local and federal government. The noted educator Ellwood P. Cubberley preached widely that the public schools should take "on the task of instilling into all a social and political consciousness that will lead to unity among the great diversity" (1918: 357). School authorities experimented with curricula that not only provided vocational training but included English-language instruction, civic education, patriotic exercises, and the transmission of values and beliefs through the study of U.S. history.

Given the importance of education to the development of the nation, it is not surprising that U.S. empire builders made universal public instruction the cornerstone of their Americanization campaigns in the former Spanish colonies. The appointments of Major John Eaton, who had served as the first commissioner of the U.S. Bureau of Education, and the influential educator Martin G. Brumbaugh as education commissioners demonstrated that Puerto Rico would be an important laboratory for testing the latest education theories—enculturation, vocational training, language acquisition, and political socialization. The education commissioner was appointed directly by the president and given unrestricted authority to design and administer Puerto Rico's public education system. The Department of Education was entrusted with the task of transforming a Spanish-speaking people with a four-hundred-year history and distinct culture into patriotic subjects conversant in the language of the colonizers, familiar with their political values, and trained for work in the new economic order. In addition, education officials tested the applicability of industrial arts, vocational training, and other manual education programs in Puerto Rico.

The department's mandate was extensive: (1) imparting English-language skills, (2) instilling civic values, patriotism, and adherence to the colonial regime, (3) training Puerto Ricans for managerial, supervisory, and technical positions in government and industry, (4) installing a gender-based educational program in which women were socialized and trained to perform tasks that would preserve the traditional male-centered family, (5) providing job-related skills in manual and industrial trades for the boys and needlework and domestic service for the girls, (6) preparing a select group of Puerto Ricans to assume high-level administrative positions in the government, and (7) conducting physical education and hygiene instruction.

The significance assigned to these various goals depended upon the priorities of the education commissioners. Invariably instruction emphasized instilling in youngsters a work ethic that was in harmony with the anticipated labor requirements of a new corporate order, as well as providing political socialization that emphasized the superiority of U.S. governmental organization and institutions. U.S. officials felt that the public education system would build loyalty for the United States by generating increased employment and earning power among the poverty-stricken rural population. An early government report noted the public schools were "organized to provide training for good citizenship, and one of the first essentials is that the individual shall be so trained as to support himself and those dependent upon him" (U.S. Department of State, 1903: 265). The increased earning capacity attributable to education and training would, according to one education commissioner, "convert our rural people into citizens capable of maintaining the sovereignty of the state" (quoted in Negrón de Montilla, 1971: 153).

School officials passionately enforced English-language instruction, and many considered this the department's most important educational task. Indeed, according to Commissioner Brumbaugh, "The first business of the American republic . . . is to give these Spanish-speaking races the symbols of the English language in which to express the knowledge and the culture which they already possess" (Brumbaugh, 1907: 65). Implicit in all this, of course, was the deeply prejudicial view that English-speaking peoples were the custodians of democracy and enlightened republicanism. Over the decades thousands of teachers were recruited in the United States and brought to the island to teach English to the students and teachers. In 1904 the Department of Education hired 120 teachers from the United States to provide English-language instruction (U.S. Department of State, 1904: 16). In 1917, 193 teachers came from the United States (U.S. Department of War, 1917: 461).

School officials aspired to educate an indigenous political elite that would be at the service of the colonial government. They emphasized the necessity of instilling "civic virtues" among members of Puerto Rico's "upper class, from which must be drawn the directors and administrators of public affairs." To this end, scholarships for young Puerto Rican men and women were provided in 1900 as "part of the plan for instituting American culture and American educational ideas into Porto Rico" (U.S. Department of State, 1903: 157). They would return to Puerto Rico to assume the role of ambassadors of the new sovereign and, with their newly burnished status as cosmopolitan and educated colonials, legitimate the material and social gains to be achieved by passively submitting to the assimilationist credo of Americanization. Racist constructions of Puerto Ricans as falling short of the vastly superior Anglo-Saxon intellect were at the core of American perceptions regarding the ability of Puerto Ricans for advanced education. According to key officials, the type of instruction that was required in Puerto Rico was "primarily and essentially one of training rather than of education, of character-building rather than scholastic instruction" (Willoughby, 1909: 162–65). While Puerto Ricans lacked the innate cerebral capabilities for abstract thought, they could be adequately trained to mimic the colonizer and perhaps learn to appreciate its higher moral character.

U.S. education officials understood that the school system had an explicit ideological role in the imperial project; it was, after all, an agency of Americanization. These men regularly organized activities and educational programs to foster patriotism for the United States. Commissioner Brumbaugh's first report emphasized the centrality of patriotic exercises in the curriculum. Rev. James H. Van Buren, the Protestant Episcopal bishop of Puerto Rico for over a decade (1902–1912), went so far as to write that "loyalty to American principles and standards is a leading feature of the public school curriculum in Porto Rico" (Van Buren, 1913: 151–52). Educational attainment was promoted as essential for fostering responsible citizenry. Elihu Root insisted that Puerto Ricans were incapable of self-government because of their Spanish cultural legacy and lack of education. The electoral franchise, he argued, should be limited to the minuscule percentage of the male population that was literate. He felt that with universal public education men "should acquire the suffrage on this basis as soon as they are capable of using it understandingly" (1916: 167). Paradoxically, he also endorsed the franchise for males, literate or otherwise, who paid taxes to the insular treasury. Root and others entertained grandiose aspirations to mold Puerto Rico's people into a bilingual community and convert the island into "a liaison point between English speaking and Spanish speaking America" (Clark et al., 1930: 90).

Officially, one of the objectives of the public education system was to prepare Puerto Ricans for eventual self-government. However, since educational instruction seldom went beyond the sixth grade for the vast majority of Puerto Rican children, the capacity for the society to exercise self-rule could not be demonstrated. Ultimately, it would be Congress that would determine whether Puerto Ricans would be granted the autonomy to conduct the affairs of state within their own country. Universal literacy was never a condition for admittance of territories as states into the union or, indeed, for individual states to govern within their boundaries. In reality, public education was perceived as a fundamentally conservative influence that would counter what were perceived as radical tendencies among the poor and illiterate rural and urban working class. Colonial officials were implanting a system of education that almost a century later Howard Zinn would refer to as "education for orthodoxy and obedience" (1992: 258).

Despite the goals of colonial officials and despite the fact that it consumed over a third of the insular budget, the system of public education failed both to prepare a literate and patriotic citizenry in sufficient numbers, and to produce young men and women with the skills that industry demanded. English-language instruction was consistently challenged by Puerto Ricans, who recoiled against the often crass and insensitive attitudes of school officials (see Negrón de Montilla, 1977). In 1915 the commissioner of education reported that the deplorable material conditions of the population were hazardous to colonial rule and could not be mollified by the educational system, whatever its effectiveness as a socializing agency. The commissioner observed with alarm, "The enormous mass of illiterates, in its primitive, uncured condition, is not safe timber to build the good ship of state. We realize that there are serious social and economic problems that have to be solved before the people of Puerto Rico reach the desired goal" (U.S. Department of War, 1915: 316).

The educational process in Puerto Rico was imbued with the ideological vision of exercising direct domination over the colonial subjects by persuasively devaluing and diminishing their identity. The everyday representation of Anglo-Saxon civilization as a desirable but ultimately unattainable goal for the inferior colonial subject was a conscious device for holding Puerto Ricans in a permanent state of subjugation. Referring to British imperial exercise of ideological domination in India, Edward Said called this "the quotidian processes of hegemony" (1993: 109).

BUILDING THE FOUNDATIONS FOR ECONOMIC EXPANSION

While public education harbored an explicit ideological project, it had an immediate and pragmatic goal as well. The Department of Education had a definite role in advancing Puerto Rico's conversion into a dependent of the metropolitan economy. The curriculum was designed in part to teach rudimentary skills and help turn out a healthy and obedient labor force for an economy dominated by sugar and tobacco production and needlework.

In the decision to employ public education to develop the island's human resources, two factors were probably decisive. First, such programs had been developed and employed with some success in a number of industrial states, and their adoption in Puerto Rico seemed appropriate given the anticipated direction of economic growth. Second, Puerto Rico had a demonstrated capacity as a sugar and tobacco producer and a "superabundance of labor." In fact, it was purportedly endowed with such a bounty of natural agricultural resources that one excited official was motivated to utter the preposterous claim that "the inhabitants can . . . exist without any remuneration" (U.S. Department of War, 1900: 36). Because of this "abundant labor force . . . Puerto Rico had a decided superiority over its natural competitors," [Cuba, Mexico, and Central America], "in the most essential element of industrial prosperity" (U.S. Department of Commerce and Labor, 1907: 10). But these same officials cautioned that Puerto Rico lacked the entrepreneurial talent and business acumen to develop industrially. The first colonial governor agreed that the country had "plenty of laborers and poor people generally" but what it desperately needed was "men with capital, energy, and enterprise to develop its latent industries . . . and make the country hum with the busy sound of commerce" (U.S. Department of State, 1901: 75).

Official reports portrayed a languorous island patiently waiting for its vast pool of labor to be efficiently exploited by these "men with capital." Dreams of a vast productive pool of labor were confounded by the reality that 90 percent of the population was afflicted with hookworm, a debilitating intestinal disease. Puerto Rico could not hope to develop industrially unless the deplorable health and sanitary conditions of the population were dramatically improved. Driven by a combination of humanitarian, strategic, and economic considerations, the colonial government set about to improve sanitation and health conditions. Accordingly, the government initiated a campaign to "stamp out the disease" in order to succeed in the "rehabilitation of the physique of the Puerto Rico laboring people" (U.S. Department of State, 1904: 28). The school system was recruited into this campaign to provide instruction on personal hygiene, sanitation, and nutrition as part of the larger campaign to eradicate hookworm. The epidemic-like status of hookworm persisted until the 1940s.

Employment opportunities for the island's impoverished masses did not increase during the steady transition to a corporate-dominated, export-oriented economy. In fact, in 1915 the Commission on Industrial Relations reported that "unemployment was very prevalent in the Island" and estimated that there were between two hundred thousand and three hundred thousand more workers available than jobs (Puerto Rico, Bureau of Labor, 1916: 9). According to the Bureau of Labor, "It may be said beyond any doubt that the most serious labor problem of Porto Rico . . . is unemployment. . . . It is absolutely necessary to take some steps . . . to diminish the great evils of unemployment" (U.S. Department of War, 1915: 428). Yet these same officials reluctantly had to acknowledge that the school system had failed to educate a self-reliant population with marketable skills for new labor markets. A special commission reported as early as 1912 that "although the Island schools are unquestionably helping to make good citizens, it is a grave question whether the present arrangements contribute materially to the making of home-makers, producers, skilled workers, self-reliant and efficient breadwinners" (cited in Clark et al., 1930: 83). Remarkably, despite the demonstrated inability of the education system to impart vital skills to the rural population and the documented failure of the corporate sector to absorb the massive surplus of labor, school authorities continued to request additional allocations for programs of dubious social value. In 1916, despite official acknowledgment of a surfeit of workers in virtually all labor categories, Commissioner Miller reported, "There is a demand for skilled labor—and unless industrial education is emphasized for the express purpose of training artisans skilled in various trades, serious labor troubles will probably ensue" (U.S. Department of War, 1916: 357).

Making healthy and reliable workers was an important component of the colonizing mission, but the Executive Council had a mandate to transform the physical landscape in preparation for a rapid transition to corporate-dominated export agriculture. In 1898 Puerto Rico's physical infrastructure was rudimentary and incapable of supporting a modern agricultural export economy. The council pursued the task of modernizing Puerto Rico's primitive and collapsing infrastructure with single-minded determination. It granted exclusive franchises to U.S. firms to build and maintain the roads and transportation, communications, and related facilities essential for economic development. Using the War Department as its fiscal agent, the colonial state issued bonds to generate millions of dollars in loans to finance this ambitious undertaking. A pattern of extensive colonial state engagement in sustaining a cheap, publicly financed and subsidized infrastructure was established during the council's seventeen-year life.

Puerto Rico's commercial development depended upon making the fertile interior of the country accessible to commerce and expanding the opportunities for the agricultural exploitation of these regions. Road construction and maintenance became the single most important—and costly—component of the ambitious program to rebuild Puerto Rico's infrastructure. According to Governor Allen, "It is an imperative necessity to devote every dollar which can be spared from the surplus revenue to the construction of permanent roads" (U.S. Department of War, 1901: 73). By 1910 approximately a thousand kilometers of first-class roads had been built, almost four times the amount built by the Spanish (Rigual, 1967: 90). Road construction and maintenance was the Interior Department's largest single expenditure in 1912, consuming over half of the department's budget and about one-tenth of all funds disbursed by the insular government (calculated from U.S. Department of War, 1912: 323–24).

The ambitious road construction and maintenance program helped dampen the acute unemployment problem, but the demand for jobs among the unemployed "was so great many have to be refused." Those fortunate enough to get hired received "30 cents per day—a small amount, but doing a great deal of good" (U.S. Department of War, 1901: 328). However, even these paltry expenses for labor were considered excessive as construction costs for the road-building program threatened to consume a dangerously large share of the state's revenues. In 1903 the department terminated the program to hire day laborers as a way of temporarily alleviating unemployment, but road building was too important for economic and military security to scale back. The agency sought to resolve its budgetary problems by relying on convict labor wherever possible as a cost-cutting measure, this despite the fact that unemployment hovered around 20 percent. The governor applauded the success of the convict labor program and its cost-efficiency. "Prisoners . . . are paid a wage of 5 cents per day," which amounted to "less than one fourth the wage paid free labor" (U.S. Department of War, 1914: 307). In 1915 the attorney general also happily reported that the convict labor program had saved the treasury over $76,000, about 10 percent of what the colonial government spent on salaries (calculated from U.S. Department of War, 1915: 33, 262). Prison maintenance expenses were amply reimbursed by the savings realized with convict labor. Given the profitability of this venture, the governor authorized the Interior Department to employ convict labor for road construction whenever possible. Despite its preference for imprisoned labor, the department reluctantly had to employ free wage labor, but, mindful of the wage structure in effect in the plantations, the government capped the daily pay of common laborers hired by state agencies at 45 cents. The law equalized wages in order "to protect the coffee and sugar districts from the loss of labor consequent on the payment of greatly increased wages by the government" (U.S. Department of War, 1904: 23).

The development of the sugar industry was an integral part of the U.S. colonizing mission. However, large-scale commercial sugarcane cultivation could not be undertaken profitably in the southern coastal plains, since the area lacked adequate water and rainfall. In 1908 the legislature authorized construction of an extensive irrigation system for the region. This project was directly beneficial to the United States, according to the chief engineer, because the country depended "heavily on Puerto Rico for its supplies of raw sugar" (U.S. Department of State, 1908: 184). The irrigation system became operational in 1914 and supplied water to twenty-four thousand acres in the southern coastal plain of Guayama (U.S. Department of War, 1914: 42). Naturally, sugarcane acreage prices soared, given the increased yields and reduced risk. In Guayama the value of cane land jumped from $99 in 1907 to between $350 and $400 an acre in 1917 (U.S. Department of State, 1908: 76; US Department of War, 1917: 336). The large sugar corporations were the primary beneficiaries of the new irrigation system. Small sugar producers, burdened by high property taxes, monopoly prices for railroad transit, and expensive imported fertilizers and other inputs, were highly motivated to sell their land to the U.S. absentee corporations that began to invest in the area. Guayama became one of the districts most characterized by the concentration of productive assets by absentee corporations.

The sale of insular bonds was routinely arranged by the Bureau of Insular Affairs of the War Department to obtain quick infusions of capital to finance public works projects. The purchasers of insular government and municipal bonds realized substantial earnings on these bonds, which were backed by the U.S. Treasury Department. As early as 1911 the total insular and municipal bond indebtedness for road construction and irrigation projects was $5.3 million—an unusual level of debt considering that the total receipts in that year were $6.8 million (U.S. Department of War, 1911: 41, 304). The colonial state's debt continued to increase and by 1918 had doubled, reaching $10.8

million (Clark et al., 1930: 326). The state turned to the bond market because it could not generate the necessary revenues to sustain the frantic pace of infrastructure development. However, debt financing had serious consequences for long-term development. The Brookings Institute reported that the borrowing policy had "been definitely harmful." It warned that "borrowing has been a great waste of public revenue by diverting it to the payment of interest, while the piling up of debt charges is almost certain to cause hardships for the country during future periods of reduced prosperity" (Clark et al., 1930: 304).

In 1916 the colonial administration realized that the revenue shortfall was jeopardizing its operations. Governor Yager warned that "the only solution" to the revenue problem was "to increase the tax on the property of the island which receives most of the benefits of government, and whose owners are the most able to pay for this support." He informed the legislature that "an unusually large percentage of the property of the island is owned by non-residents," and he criticized "these absent owners" because "they contribute practically nothing to the insular government which has done so much for them. The increase in the value of their property is almost wholly due to the improvements furnished by, and the fostering care of, the insular government" (U.S. Department of War, 1917: 261). Despite this generous treatment, the absentee sugar corporations delayed or refused to pay taxes and effectively orchestrated a tax boycott by engaging the government in protracted legal battles to block enforcement of the tax laws.

By 1918 an infrastructure had been built that included thousands of kilometers of roads, irrigation systems, dams and hydroelectric projects, railways and tramways, telegraph and telephone systems, and ports—many financed and built by the colonial state. These utilities were made readily available to absentee sugar corporations, often at highly subsidized rates. Puerto Rico's trade profile was altered as the island became a small but important market for industrial goods and technology that were used to build and maintain the infrastructure. Infrastructure development also facilitated the denationalization of productive assets by reducing the entry costs to U.S. firms—by lowering the costs for energy, transportation, and communications. Moreover, this early pattern of direct colonial state financing of infrastructure development is one of the permanent features of capitalist development under colonial management.

OTHER INSTITUTIONS FOR AMERICANIZING PUERTO RICO

The U.S. Army and the American Federation of Labor (AFL) were other institutions actively engaged in Americanizing Puerto Rico. In March 1899 an army battalion of Puerto Rican volunteers was formed under the command of U.S. army officers. According to U.S. officials, the Puerto Rican Regiment was an important institution for promoting the Americanization of the island. Army training was said to impose the "mental and moral discipline which comes from unremitting enforcement of those rules of conduct without which industrial and moral progress are impossible" (Rowe, 1901: 335). Even before the United States had invaded Puerto Rico, the Harvard law professor A. Lawrence Lowell had recommended that "natives of the island be recruited into the ranks" of the army and the navy because it was "a potent force in fostering the affection of the people of Puerto Rico for the United States. There is certainly nothing that stimulates loyalty to a flag so much as serving under it" (1898: 59). Governor William Hunt was "certain that the organization of the Porto Rican provisional regiment has been of material aid in the general work of education. Its existence has stimulated patriotism and aroused a pride in the honor of the flag" (U.S. Department of State, 1903: 15).

By 1900 the AFL was involved in the Puerto Rican labor scene. Puerto Rico's largest labor organization, the Federación Libre de Trabajadores (Free Federation of Labor—FLT) was an affiliate of Samuel Gompers's U.S. labor federation. In Puerto Rico as in the United States, the AFL effectively depoliticized industrial labor relations and focused workers' demands on immediate economic struggles. Under its guidance the FLT accepted the premise that Puerto Rico's workers should limit their demands to negotiating improvements in their material conditions within the industrial and political order imposed by the United States. To the extent that the workers were invested in collective bargaining with the employers and not confronting the agencies of the state that protected corporate interests, the FLT and the AFL allayed opposition to colonial rule. Indeed, according to Governor George Colton, by 1916 the AFL "was the most effective factor in Americanizing the people of Porto Rico" (U.S. House, 1924: 82). Samuel Gompers boasted that "there is no factor that has been of such value in Americanizing the people of Porto Rico than has the American labor movement, the American Federation of Labor" (U.S. Senate, 1916: 114, 113).

UNIONS AND THE POLICE

In March 1908 the Insular Police Service was established and placed under the general supervision of a three-person police commission appointed by the governor. The colonial authorities justified the routine deployment of the insular police during militant labor strikes as necessary to protect the property of large landowners. The political consequences of establishing a constabulary of poor Puerto Ricans under the direct command of the governor and commanded by a U.S. military officer were significant. Puerto Ricans in the employ of the colonizers were charged with preserving the very structure of property relations and social authority that was provoking widespread militancy.

As early as 1905 the police were ordered to handle "a strike situation in the sugar districts," but the most extensive and militant strikes broke out between 1915 and 1916, when eighteen thousand workers brought twenty-four of the thirty-nine largest plantations to a halt for three months (Fleagle, 1917: 114). The director of labor observed that the strike of agricultural workers "has been considered the most important in Puerto Rico since the American occupation" (U.S. Department of War, 1915: 424). These strikes were also among the most violent of the first two decades of colonial rule. Officials reported that "fires occurred and other kinds of damage were done all over the island during that period" and the "work of the police force was considerably increased during the past year by the strike of agricultural workers which began in January" (U.S. Department of War, 1915: 425; 1916: 18).

During these particularly violent strikes, many of the cane fields were torched and machinery and buildings destroyed by workers. Governor Yager reported that he "could not ignore the appeals for protection against such acts of lawlessness and disorder" (U.S. Department of War, 1915: 36). In the ensuing battles police killed five workers in Vieques and another in Ponce, dozens were wounded, and over three hundred workers were arrested (Iglesias Pantín, 1958: 188–89). Reports leave little doubt that the police used excessive force in suppressing these strikes.

Faced with uncompromising hostility from the sugar corporations and unresponsive colonial authorities, the FLT called on the AFL to come to its defense. The AFL successfully pressed its supporters in Congress to establish an industrial relations commission to investigate state violence against the strikers. According to the commission, the series of strikes "which began in January, 1915, was not only justified but was in the interests of the progress of the island. The long hours, low wages, and exploitation of laborers could not have been relieved except by organized action" (Marcus, 1919: 19). The commission concluded that the insular police were primarily responsible for the violence and criticized the actions of the local police magistrates (Mejías, 1946: 87). The labor bureau critically observed that "whatever the actions of the strikers may have been, there cannot be any justifiable cause for the actions of the police and of the municipal authorities," who "violated the individual rights of the strikers, often times treating them with unforgivable brutality" (Santiago-Valles, 1994: 114).

The FLT applied for federal government intervention to constrain the exploitative practices of the corporations, while inculpating the colonial authorities for violating the rights of workers, but at no time did it repudiate the sovereignty of the United States. In fact, it supported annexation for Puerto Rico because it believed only if it were a state in the union would workers be protected by federal labor legislation and constitutional guarantees.

THE JONES ACT:THE SECOND COLONIAL ADMINISTRATION

In 1917, after almost two decades of growing Puerto Rican frustration with the Foraker regime, Congress voted into law Puerto Rico's second organic act. The Jones Act was a wartime emergency measure enacted by Congress on the eve of U.S. entry into World War I. The imposition of political calm and loyalty in this troublesome insular possession was a crucial security objective for the United States as it made preparations for war in Europe. The metropolitan government saw the persistent challenges by Puerto Rico's dominant political party and other elites and increasing popular opposition to the colonial regime, particularly to the Executive Council, as evidence of the growing appeal of independence. The United States believed that the Jones Act would mollify these disgruntled voices while reasserting its imperial dominance over the island and its people. The Jones Act centralized power in the office of the governor and mandated continued U.S. presidential appointment of the commissioner of education and the attorney general. A Justice Department was established under the authority of the attorney general, who continued as the chief law enforcement officer and administrator of the system's penal administration and control. Nonetheless, the Jones Act was portrayed as an enlightened measure that significantly liberalized the colonial regime by eliminating the despised Executive Council and establishing a popularly elected upper house.

The Jones Act signaled the end of the aggressive Americanization campaign and introduced a new phase in the colonizing mission. Policy makers abandoned any serious idea they may have entertained regarding the use of Puerto Rico as a social laboratory for Americanization. After 1917 the goals of U.S. colonial rule in Puerto Rico were influenced by the island's changing economic and strategic roles in the American empire.

Puerto Rico emerged as an important sugar producer for the U.S. market and evolved into an even more crucial geo strategic asset during World War I. The European war had devastated sugar beet production and led to worldwide sugar shortages. Suddenly, the sugar-producing insular possessions of the United States became extraordinarily important to a U.S. economy that was becoming increasingly internationalized. As a result of escalating demand for sugar and tropical products, Puerto Rico became a particularly lucrative investment site for U.S. absentee firms. The inter-war period severely tested the ability of the United States to administer Puerto Rico peacefully. By 1932 mass sectors of the population languished in deplorable poverty and enervating disease and malnutrition. Puerto Rico's condition glaringly exposed the fallacy of economic theories that equated capitalist development with social equity. Consequently, Washington's goals in Puerto Rico were to preserve political stability, contain labor militancy, and defend the tarnished legitimacy of colonial rule.

The Jones Act is best known for conferring collective U.S. citizenship on the people of Puerto Rico. This grant of citizenship was novel because it gave Puerto Ricans few of the political and civil rights accorded native-born or naturalized citizens of the United States (see Smith, 1997; Cabranes, 1979: 96). According to General MacIntyre, chief of the Bureau of Insular Affairs, the purpose of granting citizenship to Puerto Ricans was "to make clear that Porto Rico is to remain permanently connected with the United States" (U.S. Department of War, 1916: 18). The grant of citizenship did not augment the already extraordinary plenary powers that Congress exercised over Puerto Rico and its people, but it did have the perverse psychological impact of dramatically demonstrating U.S. resolve to retain Puerto Rico as a colonial appendage.

Remarkably, while the Jones Act conferred collective naturalized citizenship on Puerto Ricans, it did not require literacy or fluency in the English language. Nonetheless, the public schools intensified English-language instruction in order to further the civic education of Puerto Ricans. Moreover, given the collapse of the insular labor market, public schools became immediately engaged in preparing a barely literate population for self-employment and petty commodity production. By the early to mid-1920s the colonizing mission, heralded with almost evangelical fervor as a moral campaign destined to elevate a dependent and inferior people to the status of Anglo-Saxon civilization, was essentially abandoned as an ideological project.

THE SCHOOLS AND CAPITALISM

Although corporate profits increased during and after World War I, Puerto Rico's economy degenerated into a morass of poverty and social immiseration that demonstrated the failure of the United States, despite its great wealth, to provide its colonial ward with economic security and social justice. By the 1930s corporate domination of the economy had provoked a social crisis that threatened the stability of Puerto Rico. Unemployment, landlessness and disease were so extensive as to place U.S. strategic and political objectives at risk. The superfluity of labor for capitalist production was one of the more serious potential challenges to social stability. The federal government was acutely aware of the unfolding social crisis in the island. Colonial officials repeatedly commented on the depressed wages that kept workers at barely subsistence levels and worried that unregulated market forces would create an unmanageable social crisis.

Puerto Rico experienced the brunt of the global depression of the 1930s. Salaries declined as the cost of imported food increased, and unemployment climbed. Absolute levels of poverty, malnutrition, landlessness, and disease escalated. Governor Theodore Roosevelt Jr. reported in 1930 that "more than

60 percent of our people are out of employment, either all or part of each year" (U.S. Department of War, 1930: 2). Congressman Johnson alerted his colleagues in 1930 that "the distress in Porto Rico among those citizens of ours is almost beyond words to express. More than 600,000 people of Porto Rico are woefully undernourished. . . . They work when they can, but there is so little work at so little pay—pennies not dollars" (U.S. House, 1930: 11345). Even for those lucky enough to find work, wages were often too low to meet their minimum needs. Governor Towner reported that "since 1915 the cost of the sugar laborer's diet has increased 48.6 percent, while his wages have increased but 26.5 per cent. . . . The fact remains that for agricultural laborers the wages paid have not increased as rapidly as the cost of living" (U.S. Department of War, 1925: 35). Puerto Rico's working population was not only poor but sickly and malnourished. Governor Roosevelt observed that the "death rate in this disease [tuberculosis] was higher than that of any other place in the Western Hemisphere, and four and one-half times the death rate in the continental United States" (U.S. Department of War, 1930: 1).

The public education system, after all, was supposed to prevent such conditions. The unconscionable unemployment levels, while ultimately a function of market forces, did expose the fiction in government declarations regarding the success of the education system. After decades of significant expenditures, which consumed almost a third of the insular budget, government officials were forced to admit that massive illiteracy continued to plague the population. In 1931 less than half of the 483,348 school-aged children were enrolled in the public schools, and of those enrolled in the rural schools 83 percent dropped out before completing the fourth grade. Since vocational training began in the second-unit schools, that is, after the sixth grade, only a small percentage of the rural children received adequate industrial and vocational instruction. According to officials, the literacy campaigns amounted "only to a smattering of the rudiments of an education which will probably wear off very soon after the children leave school" (U.S. Department of War, 1931: 69).

Despite these sobering assessments, colonial officials continued to dream of molding Puerto Rico's people into a bilingual community that would serve as a bridge between the United States and Latin America. Juan B. Huyke, the first Puerto Rican education commissioner, reported that bilingual education was emphasized because "Porto Rico is about halfway between North and South America," and it was a "proper location . . . for training of students for the important work of uniting the Americas" (U.S. Department of War, 1929: 375). By the mid-1920s the University of Puerto Rico envisioned itself as a pan-American university with specific diplomatic and economic responsibilities. The university was "to lend to the leaders in extra-governmental activities in North, Central and South America the bilingual, bicultural, and intercontinental resources of Porto Rico" (quoted in Rodríguez Fraticelli, 1991: 155).

By 1931 the hypothesized positive relationship between economic growth, increased demand for trained workers, and higher wages was severely shaken. The economy continued to demand contingents of cheap, relatively unskilled rural labor for employment in the sugar industry as field laborers. Even in the needlework industry, whose relatively skilled workers were trained in the public schools, wages were very low. The pool of unskilled labor required for the sugar-dominated corporate sector readily exceeded demand. The synergy between industry and the school system that had been advocated as a critical function of public education had essentially collapsed by the end of the 1920s. The education commissioner candidly admitted that "the efforts put forth in the past in the direction of vocational education have failed in many cases" (U.S. Department of War, 1931: 76).

Faced with the magnitude of the economic crisis of the early 1930s, the schools attempted to impart skills and knowledge that would assist impoverished families in their struggle to survive. A priority for the system was educating young people in some rudimentary skills so that they could exercise a measure of control over their lives in an economy that had left them behind. Programs in the common schools were expanded to train young people in carpentry, cooking, sewing, cultivation, and other skills that could provide livelihood. These schools were thought to be "the most promising agency . . . for improving the unsatisfactory conditions under which our peasants live and converting them from a liability into an asset" (U.S. Department of War, 1930: 105). In the early 1930s a gender-based curriculum offered boys courses in agriculture, carpentry, and shoe repair while girls were instructed in home economics and social work. Both boys and girls took industrial arts courses; for girls this meant primarily needlework. The purpose of this curriculum was to train the rural poor to eke out a bare living on the margins of the economy as independent commodity producers. If they were fortunate enough to generate a surplus, they could enter the market as petty commodity producers.

The rationale for this curriculum reveals much about the role of public education in developing human resources in light of the disastrous labor market conditions. The objective of the manual training and industrial trades was to "improve the quality of work and establish a standard for the products so that they may be marketable and thus become a dependable means of support." Shoemaking was directly related to the effort to protect the *jíbaro* from hookworm since the disease was contracted through the foot. The home economics curriculum emphasized cooking and sewing and was intended to teach the girls of the rural districts to do the things that would allow them to have a "more healthful and happy life with an appreciation for their homes" (U.S. Department of War, 1929: 390). Agricultural instruction consisted primarily of gardening with the aim of raising food crops so that families might be able to meet some of their nutritional needs. By participating in the petty commodity sector, employed workers could supplement their meager earnings from salaried work. The desperate need to improve sanitation and reduce the spread of contagious diseases prompted the curriculum in physical education and hygiene.

The educational curriculum reflected the bias of the patriarchally constituted social system of the United States. While Puerto Rico was experiencing wrenching economic dislocations, public school authorities employed the school system to re-inscribe women's reproductive role in the male-centered family. The gendered curriculum socialized youngsters into understanding and accepting the legitimacy of a gender-based division of labor within the system of generalized commodity production that was rapidly unfolding. Women were trained in activities and household tasks related to the economic reproduction of the family unit that were not necessarily required in the formal labor sector.

When the war in Europe virtually halted its lace and embroidery exports, manufacturers in the United States increased production, and many turned to Puerto Rico, where labor was abundant and cheap. In 1918, the needlework industry was targeted by the Department of Education for its capacity to employ huge numbers of unemployed young women. José Rosario, an official in the department, pointed to the "pressing duty of the rural schools to train the country girls to do this work in a more efficient way and so increase their income and the income of Porto Rico" (Rosario, n.d.: 691–92). School officials held conferences with manufacturers and designed special needlework courses that met the manufacturers' specifications. Private schools were also accredited in needlework, drawn work, and embroidery (U.S. Department of War, 1923: 182–83). By 1920, projected demand for skilled workers who were "expert in needlework" exceeded supply, and the legislature authorized hiring additional instructors in those municipalities where the prospects of employment were most favorable. Throughout the 1920s, demand for this skilled but very low-paid labor held steady. In 1931 the federal government financed vocational training in Puerto Rico and declared that "the principal emphasis will be laid upon training for jobs in the needle trades which are dominant industries in Porto Rico" (Society for the Advancement of Education, 1931: 558–59). Women constituted by far the majority of the labor in needlework, and their work, despite miserable pay, was skilled and demanding. The schools not only prepared women for incorporation into gender-segmented labor markets but sustained the needlework industry by providing fresh contingents of cheap female labor trained specifically for it.

As an instrument for the dissemination of an imperial ideology the school system appears to have been at best partially successful. Rarely was more than half of the eligible student population enrolled in any given year, and mandatory instruction was seldom enforced past the fourth year. Privately commissioned as well as government studies documented the failure of the school system to transmit knowledge and training in areas critical to economic growth and societal well-being. The needlework industry represents one of the few sectors in which the hoped-for synergy between the public school system and industry was realized.

The emergence of a vocal anti-American movement was a telling indication of the failure of the colonizing mission. Although the Nationalist party never posed a threat to U.S. colonial control, its violent activities galvanized the nation. The party's charismatic leader, Pedro Albizu Campos, threatened the legitimacy of colonial rule and attracted more adherents to the nationalist cause than the local elites were willing to tolerate.

The Nationalist party emerged as a militant reaction to the corruption and complacency of the Socialist and Republican Party coalition that controlled the legislature during the 1920s and early 1930s. But Albizu Campos directed his most vituperative diatribes against the U.S. government and absentee corporations. He lashed out against the colonialism that was impoverishing his people, and the local capitalist class that had amassed fortunes from this exploitation (Albizu Campos, 1979: 43). He imbued the nationalist movement with radicalism that resonated with ever-growing numbers of Puerto Ricans. He declared, "North American interests occupy a great part of our lands and are owners of almost eighty percent of the total wealth of the country; by virtue of this forced feudalism the majority of the electorate of this country are made dependent on its will" (Albizu Campos, 1930: 15).

By the early 1930s it seemed that the very process of Americanization was generating its antithesis, the formation of a nationalist vision of Puerto Rican identity and the emergence of political forces committed to promoting this identity. Unrestrained market forces had precipitated a social and economic crisis that persuaded the Democratic administration of Franklin Roosevelt in the early 1930s to intervene to save its crumbling Caribbean colonial possession. The modernization of the colonial state's coercive capabilities and its emphasis on protecting the rights of private property were elements of the colonizing mission. But opposition to the colonial order intensified virtually in unison with the growing social and economic immiseration. Opponents of the regime pointed to the growing contradiction between an official ideology of democracy and economic fairness and a colonial policy that increasingly relied on coercion and compulsion to enforce the rule of law.

THE MAKING AND UNMAKING OF THE COLONIAL SUBJECT

The arrival of an alien power that usurps a people's sovereignty is always traumatic for the colonized nation and historically has proven to be a wrenching and violent process. While the U.S. invasion and annexation of

Puerto Rico did not precipitate a social uprising or bloody confrontation between the colonizers and the indigenous peoples, it was a traumatic event. The speed and depth of Puerto Rico's transformation into a highly lucrative export platform for U.S. corporations ultimately destroyed a people's way of life. The change in sovereignty not only eradicated the sources of power and privilege of Puerto Rico's traditional political elite but also elevated to prominence other political actors who subscribed to the colonial enterprise.

U.S. officials gained enough support from key sectors to institute widespread institutional changes. Domestic capital and some of the professional strata that stood to gain under the new sovereignty worked closely with the colonial authorities (see Quintero Rivera, 1988). These sectors aspired to form a new economic and social order in which they would assume the perquisites of titular political authority. In the process they hoped to displace the traditional landed elite that had assumed prominence during the waning years of Spanish dominion. Support for U.S. sovereignty extended to other sectors. In a society wracked by unemployment, hunger, and disease, those fortunate enough to be employed by the colonial regime had privileged status. Puerto Rican participation in the colonial administration served to legitimate metropolitan rule and was used by U.S. officials as evidence that Puerto Ricans had consented to their own subordination. Despite these changes in the class composition and domestic political configuration, resistance did emerge to impede the U.S. effort to Americanize the Puerto Rican people.

The system of public education that had been heralded as the jewel of the Americanization program failed to achieve many of its objectives. Rather than preparing an educated, skilled, and loyal colonial subject, the school system was called upon to instruct the impoverished rural population in the skills they needed to survive. Capitalist development in Puerto Rico did not generate a significant demand for skilled labor. What the sugar and tobacco corporations needed was an unskilled, cheap, and complacent labor force—the younger and healthier, the better. Puerto Rico's experience under colonial management and capitalist development exposed the cupidity submerged in the ideological discourse that equated economic growth with political democracy and social equity.

The experiments in social engineering conducted in the great national laboratory that policy makers called Puerto Rico did not convert Puerto Ricans into a bicultural and bilingual people. Many of the broader goals of Americanization went unrealized. Admittedly, many of these goals were often ill-defined and grandiose, but the implied objective was to pacify the Puerto Ricans into accepting the superiority of the U.S. polity and its natural right to rule their lives. Although conflicting policy objectives and political aspirations in the federal government led to inconsistent and contradictory initiatives, the multiple instances of resistance to colonial authority revealed the durability of Puerto Rican national identity and the resiliency of its cultural sovereignty. Americanization was not only a generalized project to assimilate and transform an inferior people and its institutions but also a celebratory discourse on the power and wisdom of the American political system and American business. The hesitancy of Puerto Ricans to embrace this myth was a sobering realization to U.S. empire builders.

NOTES

1. Technically the United States did not have sovereignty over Cuba. Under Article 1 of the Treaty of Paris (1898) Spain relinquished sovereignty over Cuba, and the United States was to "assume and discharge the obligations that may under international law result from the fact of its occupation, for the protection of life and property."

2. For a lengthy examination of the complex and varied responses of different sectors in Puerto Rico to U.S. colonial policy, see Cabán (1999).

3. This idea of the concordance between democracy, market economies, and trade was a centerpiece of President George W. Bush's message at the 2001 Summit of the Americas: "Open trade reinforces the habit of liberty that sustains democracy over the long haul. Free enterprise requires liberty and enlarges liberty." Bush Comments at Summit of the Americas Working Session, April 21, 2001. http://usinfo.state.gov/regional/ar/summit/opening.htm.

4. Typified by Senator Albert Beveridge's statement: "And of all our race he has marked the American people as His chosen nation to finally lead in the regeneration of the world" (quoted in Smith 1997: 431).

5. According to Isaac Berkson, in his 1920 study on the Americanization of Europeans in the continental United States, "Newcomers from foreign lands must as quickly divest themselves of their old characteristics, and through intermarriage and complete taking over of the language customs, hopes, aspirations of the American type obliterate all ethnic distinctions. They must utterly forget the land of their birth and completely lose from their memory all recollection of its traditions in a single-minded adherence to American life in all its aspects" (Berkson, 1920).

6. For example, William Hunt, Puerto Rico's second appointed governor, believed that "every effort must be made not only to teach new doctrines and ideas, but at the same time to destroy the prejudices, ignorance and the false teachings of the past" (U.S. Department of State, 1904: 13).

7. See Trías Monge (1991: esp. 154-161) for the noted jurist's views on why the legal changes were effected so quickly and failed to provoke notable resistance. The opposition Federal party boycotted the elections of 1900 in part because Governor Allen did nothing to halt the campaign of physical intimidation against the party's candidates.

REFERENCES

Albizu Campos, Pedro. 1930. *Comercio, riqueza y soberania*. San Juan, PR: Editorial Nacionalista.

———. 1979. *La conciencia nacional puertorriqueña*. Mexico City: Siglo XXI Editores.

Berbusse, Edward J. 1966. *The United States in Puerto Rico: 1898–1900*. Chapel Hill, NC: University of North Carolina Press.

Berkson, Isaac B. 1920. *Theories of Americanization: A Critical Study*. New York: Columbia University Press.

Beveridge, Albert J. 1907. "The Development of a Colonial Policy for the United States." *Annals of the American Academy of Political and Social Science* 30: 3–15.

Brumbaugh, Martin G. 1907. "An Educational Policy for Spanish-American Civilization." *Annals of the American Academy of Political and Social Science* (July): 65–68.

Cabán, Pedro. 1999. *Constructing a Colonial People: Puerto Rico and the United States, 1898–1932*. Boulder, CO: Westview Press.

———. n.d. Immigrants and Subjects During the Progressive Era: Americanizing the Newcomer. *Revista Mejicana del Caribe*. In press.

Cabranes, José A. 1979. *Citizenship and the American Empire*. New Haven, CT: Yale University Press.

Clark, Truman. 1973. "Educating the Native in Self-Government: Puerto Rico and the United States, 1900–1933." *Pacific Historical Review* 42: 220–33.

Clark, Victor S., et. al. 1930. *Porto Rico and Its Problems*. Washington, DC: Brookings Institution.

Cubberley, Ellwood. 1918. *Public Education in the United States*. Boston: Houghton Mifflin.

Falkner, Roland P. 1905. "Porto Rican Problems." Paper presented at the Twenty-third Annual Lake Mohonk Conference of Friends of the Indian and Other Dependent Peoples, Lake Mohonk, NY.

———. 1908. "Progress in Puerto Rico." Paper presented at the Twenty-sixth Annual Lake Mohonk Conference of Friends of the Indian and Other Dependent Peoples, Lake Mohonk, NY.

Fleagle, Fred K. 1917. *Social Problems in Porto Rico*. New York: D. C. Heath.

Go, Julian. 2000. "Chains of Empire, Projects of State: Political Education and U.S. Colonial Rule in Puerto Rico and the Philippines." *Comparative Studies in Society and History* 42: 333–62.

Graffam, Richard. 1986. "The Federal Courts' Interpretation of Puerto Rican Law: Whose Law is It, Anyway?" *Revista del Colegio de Abogados de Puerto Rico* 47: 111–42.

Iglesias Pantín, Santiago. 1958. *Luchas emancipadoras: Crónicas de Puerto Rico*. San Juan, PR: Imprenta Venezuela.

Lowell, Lawrence A. 1898. "The Government of the Dependencies." *Handbook of the American Academy of Political and Social Science* (May): 45–59.

Marcus, Joseph. 1919. *Labor Conditions in Porto Rico*. Washington, DC: Government Printing Office.

Mejías, Félix. 1946. *Condiciones de vida de las clases jornaleras de Puerto Rico*. Río Piedras; PR: Junta Editora de la Universidad de Puerto Rico.

Negrón de Montilla, Aida. 1971. *Americanization in Puerto Rico and the Public-School System, 1900–1930*. Río Piedras, PR: Editorial Edil.

———. 1977. *La americanización de Puerto Rico y el sistema de instrucción pública, 1900–1930*. Río Piedras, PR: Editorial Universitaria.

Osuna, Juan José. 1949. *A History of Education in Puerto Rico*. Río Piedras. PR: Editorial de la Universidad de Puerto Rico.

Puerto Rico. Bureau of Labor. 1916. *Fourth Annual Report*. San Juan, PR: Bureau of Supplies, Printing and Transportation.

Quintero Rivera, Angel. 1988. *Patricios y plebeyos: Burgueses, hacendados, artesanos y obreros*. Río Piedras, PR: Ediciones Húracan.

Rigual, Néstor. 1967. *Reseña de los mensajes de los gobernadores de Puerto Rico 1900–1930*. Río Piedras, PR: Editorial Universitaria.

Rivera Ramos, Efrén. 2001. *The Legal Construction of Identity: The Judicial and Social Legacy of American Colonialism in Puerto Rico*. American Psychological Association.

Rodríguez Fraticelli, Carlos. 1991. "Colonial Politics and Education: The Pan-Americanization of the University of Puerto Rico." *Historia y Sociedad* (4): 138–66.

Root, Elihu. 1916. *The Military and Colonial Policy of the United States*. Collected and edited by Robert Macon and James Brown Scott. Cambridge, MA: Harvard University Press.

Rosario, José C. n.d. "Home Economics in the Rural Schools." *Bulletin of the Pan American Union* 61: 685–92.

Rowe, Leo S. 1901. "Military Training as a Factor in the Civic Restoration of Porto Rico." *The American Monthly Review of Reviews* 23: 334–35.

——. 1904. *The United States and Porto Rico*. New York: Longmans, Green.

Said, Edward. 1993. *Culture and Imperialism*. New York: Knopf.

Santiago-Valles, Kelvin A. 1994. *"Subject People" and Colonial Discourses: Economic Transformation and Social Disorder in Puerto Rico, 1898–1947*. Albany: State University of New York Press.

Sklar, Martin J. 1988. *The Corporate Reconstruction of American Capitalism, 1890–1916*. New York: St. Martin's Press.

Smith, Rogers M. 1997. *Civic Ideals: Conflicting Visions of Citizenship in U.S. History*. New Haven, CT: Yale University Press.

Society for the Advancement of Education. 1931. "The Vocational Education Program of Porto Rico." *School and Society* 33: 558–59.

Stead, W. T. 1902. *The Americanization of the World*. New York: Garland.

Trías Monge, José. 1991. *El choque de dos culturas jurídicas en Puerto Rico*. Austin, TX: Equity.

U.S. Department of Commerce and Labor. 1907. *Commercial Porto Rico in 1906*. Washington, DC: Government Printing Office.

U.S. Department of State. 1901. *First Annual Report of the Governor of Porto Rico*. Trans. Allen, Charles H. Washington, DC: Government Printing Office.

——. 1903–1905. *Annual Report of the Governor of Porto Rico*. Washington, DC: Government Printing Office.

——. 1904. *Fourth Annual Report of the Governor of Porto Rico*. Washington, DC: Government Printing Office.

——. 1908. *Eighth Annual Report of the Governor of Porto Rico*. Trans. Régis H. Post, Governor. Washington, DC: Government Printing Office.

U.S. Department of War. 1900. *Report of Brig. General George W. Davis on Civil Affairs of Puerto Rico, 1899*. Washington, DC: Government Printing Office.

——. 1901. *Military Government of Porto Rico from October 18, 1898 to April 30, 1900: Appendices to the Report of the Military Governor*. Washington, DC: Government Printing Office.

————. 1911. *Eleventh Report of the Governor of Porto Rico*. Washington, DC: Government Printing Office.

————. 1912. *Twelfth Annual Report of the Governor of Porto Rico*. Washington, DC: Government Printing Office.

————. 1914. *Fourteenth Annual Report of the Governor of Porto Rico*. Washington, DC: Government Printing Office.

————. 1915. *Fifteenth Annual Report of the Governor of Porto Rico*. Washington, DC: Government Printing Office.

————. 1916a. *Report of the Chief of Bureau of Insular Affairs*. Washington DC: Government Printing Office.

————. 1916b. *Sixteenth Annual Report of the Governor of Porto Rico*. Washington, DC: Government Printing Office.

————. 1917. *Seventeenth Annual Report of the Governor of Porto Rico*. Washington, DC: Government Printing Office.

————. 1923. *Twenty-Third Annual Report of the Governor of Porto Rico*. Washington, DC: Government Printing Office.

————. 1925. *Twenty-fifth Annual Report of the Governor of Porto Rico*. Washington, DC: Government Printing Office.

————. 1929–1931. *Annual Report of the Governor of Porto Rico*. Washington, DC: Government Printing Office.

U.S. Department of War, Bureau of Insular Affairs. 1915. *Report of the Chief of Bureau of Insular Affairs, Fifteenth Annual Report of the Governor of Puerto Rico*. Washington, DC: Government Printing Office.

U.S. House. Committee on Insular Affairs. 1924. *The Civil Government of Porto Rico: Hearings on H.R. 4087 and H.R. 6583*: 68th Cong. 1st. sess.

U.S. House. 1930. *Congressional Record* 72, January 18.

U.S. Senate. Committee on Pacific Islands and Porto Rico. 1916. *Government for Porto Rico: Hearings on S. 1217*, Pt. 1: 64th Cong. 1st. sess.

Van Buren, James H. 1913. "Problems in Porto Rico." Paper presented at the Thirty-first Annual Lake Mohonk Conference of Friends of the Indian and Other Dependent Peoples, Lake Mohonk, NY.

Willoughby, William F. 1902. "Two Years Legislation in Porto Rico: The Work of the First Legislative Assembly of Porto Rico, 1900–1902." *Atlantic Monthly* 90: 34–42.

————. 1905. *Territories and Dependencies of the United States: Their Government and Administration*. New York: Century.

————. 1909. "The Problem of Political Education in Porto Rico." Paper presented at the Twenty-seventh Annual Lake Mohonk Conference of the Friends of Indian and Other Dependent Peoples, Lake Mohonk, NY.

Wilson, Edward S. 1905. *Political Development of Porto Rico*. Columbus, OH: Fred J. Heer.

Wood, Leonard, William Taft, and Charles Allen. 1902. *Opportunities in the Colonies and Cuba*. New York: Lewis, Scriber.

Zinn, Howard. 1992. *A People's History of the United States*. New York: Harper Collins.

5

Ethnic Identity and Racial Formations: Race and Racism American-Style and *a lo latino*

Marta Cruz-Janzen

I am a Latinegra. Racism has been with me all my life. Born and raised a U.S. citizen in the U.S. Commonwealth of Puerto Rico, I completed most of my schooling on the island. In high school I moved back and forth between the island and the mainland. On the island, I became aware of Latina/o racism at an early age. On the mainland, U.S. racism was added to my consciousness and understanding. Today my life is affected not only by U.S. racism but also by Latina/o racism and the intersection of the two. Latina/o and U.S. racial ideologies seem to represent fundamentally divergent systems of social order. U.S. racism enforces the black-versus-white dichotomy; Latina/o racism appeases it. U.S. racism is sharp and clear; Latina/o racism is stratified and nebulous. The intersection of these doctrines unleashes a dilemma for Latina/os in the United States: What to do with a racial heritage shrouded in secrecy? What to do with a long history of blurred racial lines and deeply hidden family secrets in a world controlled by a rigid color line? I am rejected by both U.S. and Latina/o forms of racism. Latinas/os in Latin America accept me marginally; Latinas/os in the United States openly spurn me. The repudiation by Latinas/os has intensified over the years, and I know why. Through me Latinas/os see the blackness in themselves; I am a living reminder of the ancestors they thought they had left behind. Oppressors rely on their victims' shame and silence. Breaking the shackles of oppression requires telling what is really happening and addressing all the sources of racism. With this chapter I break my own psychological shackles of oppression. I explore the forces impacting racism in Latinas/os today, among them: (1) racism in Latin America, especially Mexico, Puerto Rico, and Cuba, (2) Spanish racism before colonization, (3) U.S. racism, and (4) the intersection of U.S. and Latina/o racial doctrines.

Mucho que poco, todos tenemos la mancha de platano (Much or little, we all have the plantain stain). Latina/o cultures are rich in oral traditions. Popular expressions bear witness to a long and complex history. Oral histories tell more and are often closer to the truth than what is written in books or discussed in polite society. This popular adage states what is known but not acknowledged in most Latina/o cultures—that everyone has some non-European blood. A green vegetable resembling a banana, the plantain is white inside but, when touched, quickly produces a stain that darkens to black and sets permanently. *La mancha de platano*—black and Indian heritage—may or may not be apparent but is present in all Latinas/os and cannot be washed away. When I was growing up, my father's [black] family called me *trigueña* (wheat-colored), whereas the favorite term of my mother's [white] family was *morena* (black), considered a step down. Sometimes, they both called me *negra*, or some variation of the term. When my black grandma called me *negrita* (little black) it was usually with pride and accompanied by a loving hug. When my white grandma called me *negra*, it signaled anger and impending punishment. Outside of the family the labels varied, but when *negra* was used it was as a derisive reminder of my race and lower status. In the latter instances, *negra* tended to be followed by *sucia* (immoral, but literally "dirty") or *parejera* (arrogant). *Parejero/a* is not used for whites, only for blacks and Indians. It denotes people who do not accept *su lugar* (their place) beneath whites and do not remain quiet like children or humbly obey (Zenon Cruz, 1975). An equivalent term, used in Mexico and many other parts of Latin America, is *igualada/o*. Both terms signify a false sense of equality and belonging among superiors.

It has always intrigued me that my father's birth certificate defines him as *mestizo*. The explanation for this was that because his parents, both black, were educated and middle-class they were *mejorando la raza* (improving the race). They had moved out of Barrio San Antón, the black quarters of the coastal town of Ponce, and lived in a predominantly white neighborhood. They maintained an impeccable home with a beautiful front garden and, aware of their neighbors' scrutiny, never ventured out unless well groomed. When I visited, though, I recall always playing alone, never having friends in the neighborhood. A white girl next door and I sometimes played together through the iron fence but never at each other's home. As I played in the front yard I saw children from across the street watching but knew that we could not get together. My black grandparents had five children. While concerned for all of them, they worried most about their two daughters; one attended the university, became a teacher, and taught in a remote rural school, while the other was considered fortunate for marrying a white man. San Antón was known as an *arrabal*, an impoverished slum beyond the city limits. Grandma was admired and respected there and often took me with her while distributing food and clothes. The differences in living conditions between my grandparents' neighborhood and San Antón were staggering: streets were narrow and unpaved, buildings were in disrepair and lacked indoor plumbing, most houses were makeshifts built of discarded wood and cardboard with zinc roofs. Distinctively, most residents were dark-skinned *puros prietos* (pure blacks).

My two sets of grandparents lived in what appeared to be two separate worlds. I do not recall a single time when they or their families visited each other. My siblings and I were shuttled between them on weekends and holidays. On one side we were *mejorando la raza*, on the other *una pena* (disgrace, sorrow, shame). On one side we were *trigueños finos* (wheat-colored and refined), on the other *morenos y prietos* (black and dark). My paternal black grandma reminded me to pinch my nose between my fingers each day to sharpen its roundness; my maternal white grandma wanted my *greñas* and *ceretas* (curly, wild hair) restrained at all times. Uninhibitedly, my mother's family voiced concerns for me and my siblings as black persons, and especially for me and my sisters as Latinegras in a white, male-dominated Latina/o society. Whereas my father "elevated" his family and himself by marrying a White, my mother was openly chastised for marrying *ese negro feo* (that ugly black), lowering herself and her entire family. Repeatedly, she was told, *Cada oveja con su pareja* (Each sheep with its pair), a reminder that interracial marriages were frowned upon even by the Catholic Church, which preached that we were all *ovejas de Dios* (God's sheep).

My mother's family understood that the presence of blacks in the family drastically reduced its options in life. Some members of her family who seemed to me to count their drops of pure Spanish blood even after generations simply disappeared from our lives. We were not invited to visit them and saw them rarely. It was apparent to me and my siblings that our own options in life were even more limited and that as Latinegras my sisters and I were in jeopardy. Comas-Diaz (1997) argues that there is a sociocultural glass ceiling for Latinegras/os, and particularly for Latinegras. Latina/o culture bestows greater status and patriarchal authority on all males, regardless of race or social status, being more forgiving of blackness in males (Oboler, 1995). Because of their powerlessness, Latinegras are further excluded racially (Comas-Diaz, 1996). Getting us girls *bien casadas* (properly married) is problematic because the role definition of females, especially mothers, in most Latin American cultures contributes to the rejection of Latinegras as proper wives and mothers. Latina mothers are expected to be present in the lives of their offspring, making their existence hard to hide. No such expectation applies to fathers, who are not censured for being absent. A Latinegra mother is undeniable proof of her children's inability to *mejorar la raza* (Comas-Diaz, 1996). My mother emphasized academics but did not want us to be teachers because in Puerto Rico black teachers were not assigned to city schools (Zenon Cruz, 1975). She feared that her daughters would end up as mistresses. Spanish literature has historically expressed Spanish men's obsession with African women as lovers. At various points in history, the words *negra* and "prostitute" have been synonymous and the black woman's body equated with a commodity for the taking. This image persists and is routinely depicted (Muhammad, 1995). Latinegras are still stereotyped as oversexed and promiscuous and as concubines. In a culture that simultaneously despises and desires black women, *mulattas* and *trigueñas* are particularly prized sexual objects.

In retrospect, I realize that having a white mother was an asset. Mom was better received in Puerto Rico than our father, and her presence eased our way into many opportunities. She was the family's ambassador, mediating between two worlds and handling neighbors, schools, and public matters. Yet I recall the cruel taunts of classmates, adults, and even teachers repeatedly calling me *negativo* (a reference to a photo negative) because of my dark complexion. I dreaded my father's visibility; he was superficially treated with respect, but behind his back peers, teachers, and others called him, among other things, *negro come coco* (coconut-eating black). I was advised to stay out of the sun to avoid getting darker: *Se te sube la sangre* (Your [black] blood will rise). Teachers made extremely disparaging remarks about the darker-skinned children right in front of me. I was supposed to believe that I was superior to darker-skinned persons but inferior to lighter-skinned ones and whites. Perlina was a bleaching detergent with a picture of black children dressed in white on the label; I was expected to accept being called a "bleached" person as a compliment. One memory remains vivid: On a hot day in fourth grade I stayed under a tree at recess. On returning to class the teacher declared: *¡Apesta a negro!* (It stinks like blacks). Because I was the only black child, the entire class turned to stare at me; children giggled, laughed hysterically, and smirked with disgust as the teacher opened windows. An inseparable friend, blonde with blue eyes, was unequivocally preferred. I was constantly reminded of the abyss separating us: "You may not be all black, but you're not blonde, either." In a play I was asked to be Cucarachita Martina (Cockroach Martina), a popular children's story character, because I was "black like a cockroach." Latinegras who used face powder were called *cucarachas empolvadas* (face-powdered cockroaches). I was also called *Lirio Blanco* (white lily), the name of a very debasing dark-skinned Latinegra character in a television comedy. The expression *una mosca en un vaso de leche* (a fly in a glass of milk) was used by peers to describe my standing out among whites. This expression was used to describe blacks who lived in white communities and, jeeringly, blacks who dressed in white. Consequently, in middle school I was denied participation in a school program because I "would look ridiculous" among all the white students, especially in the white dress selected.

LATINA/O RACISM

Racism is defined as the ability to limit individuals' choices and options on basis of their race, ethnicity, national origin, home language, or tribal affiliation. It has two interrelated components: structural inequality and personal prejudice (Wardle, 1998). Latina/o racism is complex and deeply ingrained. Fundamentally, it entails subliminal acceptance of the fictitious superiority of whites coupled with the fictitious inferiority of all others, with blacks and Indians at the bottom. In many Latin American countries blacks are seen as the lowest and most contemptible group. This dichotomy is paralleled by the general belief that racial improvement through racial purification is attainable in ascending stages. The notion of racial improvement involves the common conviction that incremental acquisition of whiteness, leading to hierarchical superiority, is desirable, possible, and essential. Belying this notion is the repressed reality of broad historical interracial mixing and the stratification of Latina/o whites. Superior to all are the *gente decente* (decent people), elite whites *puros de sangre* (pure blooded) or *limpios de sangre* (clean blooded). Beneath them are the social whites, those who are socially accepted as whites but have varying degrees of racial mixing. Latina/o white elites adamantly insist that they are "uncontaminated" by black or Indian blood. As with U.S. racism, membership in this white elite demands white racial purity. Whereas the general population accepts the notion of *mejorando la raza*, visible, known, and/or suspected non-white ancestry means exclusion from the elite. Although it is jokingly said that persons can be as white as their wealth, the truth is that Latinas/os of color can whiten themselves up to a certain point, beyond which they are excluded from the elite. Wealthy Latinegras/os are raised socially from the status of blacks but never accepted as full members of the white elite. Many light-skinned Latinas/os attempt to conceal their non white antecedents. The importance of family secrets in Latin American cultures helps explain why within-group racism is not a welcome topic and is often considered impolite and/or taboo. What is not stated is the fear that open discussions about race and racism may unveil personal and family secrets. The expression *La mona se viste de seda pero mona se queda* (The monkey may dress in silk but a monkey it remains) reveals the contradiction and hypocrisy of the Latin American notion of improving the race. It clearly states that the self-perception of social whites and other Latinas/os of color as members of the white elite is not shared by the white elite. Ultimately, elite white Latinas/os spurn all Latinas/os of color, including the social whites, perceived to be racially impure. Unlike U.S. racism, the black-versus-white dichotomy of Latina/o racism is buffered by an interracial middle layer topped by the social whites. Between the white elite and the purest blacks and Indians there are many strata with vague racial labels that act as filters, screening and processing the population and cushioning contacts.

Though Brazil is the country most frequently cited for its extensive racial labels and social stratification, similar systems persist throughout Latin America (Andrews, 1980). In contrast to the United States, where the "one-drop rule" (Nakashima, 1992) was historically used to identify persons of African American and European-American inheritance as full blacks, in most Latin American countries one drop of white blood makes a person whiter, or at least no longer black, in accordance to the policies of *blanqueamiento, mejorando la raza*. These policies promoted whiteness through the elimination of blacks and Indians (Muhammad, 1995). Mildly interpreted, they were designed to reduce or conceal the physical evidence of interracial parentage, proposing racial mixing that transformed Blacks and Indians into mulattoes and mestizos, then *criollos* (Creoles), and eventually social whites. They also encouraged extermination and outright massacres of black people have been recorded throughout Latin America. For example, in 1912 several thousand blacks and mulattoes were killed in Cuba (McGarrity and Cardenas, 1995). Blacks have been "disappeared" in Uruguay, Chile, and particularly Argentina in the pursuit of racial genocide (Comas-Diaz, 1996). *Blanqueamiento* called for the infusion of pure white genes, and more white European and especially Spaniard immigration to Latin America was encouraged (Andrews, 1980; Muhammad, 1995).

In Latin America, interracial parentage, education, and social status allowed for social mobility within the lower classes. Words such as *criollo, indio, mestizo, mulato, membrillo, pardo, grifo, jabao, requinto,* and *trigueño,* indicate interracial parentage. A mestizo is of Indian and white parentage. Mulattoes, also called *cholos,* are persons of African and white ancestry. The term "mulatto" contains a pejorative association with the mule, the sterile hybrid between a donkey and a horse. It is jokingly said that mulattoes cannot reproduce themselves because their offspring tend to *dar pa'tras* (kick back), or regain Negroid attributes. Mulattoes may be *pardos* (brownish) or *membrillos* (yellowish). A *pardo,* like a *zambo,* may be of black and Indian parentage. A *grifo* is light-skinned with Negroid hair; a *jabao* is medium-skinned with light-colored hair. *Requinto* is a pejorative term for persons, sometimes jeered at as *mulatos blancos* (white mulattoes), whose parents look white but who inherit detectable African features. They are ridiculed as *tapujos* (lies) and *chayotes.* A chayote is a fruit that is white inside and out, and has a rough, prickly surface, and the reference serves as a cruel reminder that whiteness inside-out still cannot hide blackness. *Moreno* evolved from *moro,* the black African Moor, and is considered a step up from *negro, prieto* or *retinto* (double-dyed). These last three terms are derisively used for the darkest blacks and publicly avoided.

Some designations have ambiguous definitions, perhaps intentionally. *Criollo* may refer either to a light-skinned person who looks like a Spaniard or to a descendant of Spaniards born and raised in Latin America. *Trigueños* (wheat-colored, tan, olive-skinned, swarthy), like *criollos,* are light-skinned persons of unspecified racial descent. The implication is of some racial mixing—somewhere. *Criollo* and *trigueño* have very broad applications, are used to avoid *negro*, and may be applied to a wide variety of persons from mulattoes, mestizos, and *pardos* to some darker Europeans including Sicilians, Andalusians, and Portuguese (Andrews, 1980). They elevate individuals by insinuating that they have escaped the "automatic assumption" of African inheritance and succeeded in crossing over to an intermediate nebulous category that includes many Europeans (Andrews, 1980). Acceptable and respectful ways of referring to people of black appearance, particularly those with education and economic mobility, involve euphemistically altering their racial status (McGarrity and Cardenas, 1995). Many Latin American countries have significant populations of Asians who are often considered superior to Blacks and Indians. Light-skinned Latinegros sometimes retain Negroid features resembling those of Asians and are elevated socially as *Chinos* (Chinese). Puerto Ricans joke that "there are more Indians today than when Columbus arrived" because of the high proportion of persons of interracial heritage, particularly African, who are characterized as Indians. Indians are becoming more visible throughout Latin America as persons of indigenous lineage, including the Taino of Puerto Rico and the Dominican Republic, reaffirm their roots. Still, being characterized as either Indian or mestizo allows Latinegros to avoid the stigma of their African past. Dark-skinned Latinegros may be elevated as mestizos, lighter-skinned ones as Indians. This system even allows for *indios claros* (light-skinned Indians) and *indios oscuros* (dark-skinned Indians). Under this elaborate plan, the label "indio" moves beyond racial categorization and skin color to signify a status that disavows African inheritance. Consequently, significant numbers of Latinegros attempt to escape their African past and connection to other blacks through the ascending status of Indians.

The term *negro* has acquired multiple meanings in Latin America. Among the lower classes it is used as a term of endearment, irrespective of racial background. Historically, many black females in Latin America were nannies and wet nurses and were seen as nurturers. The implication is that persons, particularly light skinned ones, who accept the nickname also accept a connection to blacks. Through the nickname they are perceived as generous, loving, loyal, and wise. In contrast, among Latinegros, especially dark-skinned ones, being called *negro* tends to be perceived as insulting; *moreno* is preferred. For centuries *negro* was equivalent to "slave", and although it is sometimes ostensibly used as praise and a sign of respect, it is more frequently perceived as a derisive put-down, particularly when directed at a dark-skinned person by a white—a reminder of the person's race, skin color, and social inferiority. According to McGarrity and Cardenas (1995), calling someone *prieto* or *negro* is likely to be combined with a disapproving voice and negative facial expressions. Again, this social mobility does not operate for the elite Latin American white upper class, where unequivocal white racial purity remains an inviolable requirement. Members of the elite upper class adhere rigidly to racial lines and social castes and do not accept being addressed as *negro* or *indio*, having their *pureza de sangre*—and superior status—called into question.

Dark-skinned Latin American blacks with "finer" features are elevated through such social referents as "Yardley," *esterlina* (sterling), *bien parecido* (good-looking), *fino* (refined), and *perfilado* (thin nose, lips, and face; well-groomed). Dark-skinned Latinos with strong "Negroid" features are the brunt of abusive, contemptuous, and vicious attacks. Labels such as *azurin* (blue-black), *bembon* (thick-lipped), *cafre* (contemptible), *congolele* (Congo), *maboya* (evil spirit), *negrete* (double black), *pasu* (raisin-like hair), and *betun* (shoe polish) are but a few of the prevalent dehumanizing terms. In Mexico, dark-skinned persons with Negroid features are taunted as *cucules* (ugly spirits). In Cuba and Puerto Rico the term used is *cucu* or *cuco*. *Moyeto* or *mayate*, another popular term, means "black and ugly." In Mexico, a *mayate* is a black beetle—in essence, a nuisance to be exterminated. A *cocolo* is a disliked and worthless dark-skinned person. In the United States Latinas/os refer to Africans and African Americans as *cocolos, cucos, morenos,* and *moyetos*. In this vein, Latinegros are differentiated from Africans and African Americans, who are considered inferior. Latinas/os are reluctant to deal with their African past because to do so would mean acknowledging a relation to Africa that is viewed as damaging their self-image and interfering with their struggle for acceptance (Zenon Cruz, 1974). Ironically, most Latin American cultures are sufficiently rich in African elements to be considered more African than African-American. *Trucutu*, another insulting label, was a popular cartoon character of the 1950s and 1960s, a very dark-skinned African cannibal or savage. The name evolved from the sound of beating an African hand drum: "tru-cu-tu, tru-cu-ta." The expression *Trucutu, trucuta. Y bueno que esta* (Trucutu, trucuta. It's so good) was an offensive reference to sex with blacks and was frequently directed at young Latinegras by white Latinos. This expression has resurfaced and has recently been used to sell products, including beer, to Latinos in the United States. Many Latinegros find it offensive and threatening that such demeaning portrayals are casually being brought back in this way. They feel that subliminally something more is being sold: the perception of Latinegros as sex-driven, promiscuous, and alcoholics.

Family lines and marriage are significant in a culture that has historically included extended families as well as genealogical and cultural connections through *compadrazgo*, the joining of families through oaths of honor, loyalty, and support for each other across multiple generations. In many Latin American countries other white Europeans, including U.S. Whites, are greatly admired, and marriage to them is encouraged. To marry a White, especially a Spaniard, European, or U.S. White, is *buscar pa'rriba* (looking up); to marry a darker person is *dañar la raza* (damaging the race). Whiteness brings privileges, and Nordic white looks are the ideal to emulate. Those who approximate the ideal are made to feel superior. Even within families, the lighter-skinned siblings are favored and treated preferentially: *¡Que niña/o tan bonita/o! ¡Parece Americano!* (What a beautiful child! Looks like an American [white]!) is frequently heard among Latinas/os. The politics of race and racism are enacted within families, pitting family members—parents, parents and children, and siblings—against each other.

A significant manifestation of Latin American racism is the historical negation of the black presence. The fact is that throughout Spain, across the Caribbean, and from Mexico all the way down to Argentina, Spaniards took significant numbers of African slaves. Rapidly, in most Latin American countries, Africans came to constitute a significant proportion or the majority of the population. Whites in Latin America and wherever black and Indian slavery has existed have written their history in their own terms. It should come as no surprise, then, that historical amnesia and perjury throughout much of Latin America, in census counts and even historical accounts, have systematically minimized or obliterated the presence and contributions of blacks and Indians. The plan has been either to assimilate them or to let them "die out" (Andrews, 1980). The darker one is and the closer one's roots are to Africa, the greater the oppression and repression. Most Latin American countries, while proclaiming racial democracy, have instituted a social, economic, and political structure that disenfranchise their African and Indian populations. An interracial population constitutes the majority and middle group. This middle group is superseded by the social whites, with the minority white Latin American elites, of various white European backgrounds and especially Spaniards, at the very top. Black and indigenous Latin Americans tend to be at the bottom, and their economic and social isolation contributes to their invisibility from the national conscience.

RACISM IN MEXICO, PUERTO RICO, AND CUBA

Aqui, el que no tiene dinga tiene mandinga. El que no tiene congo tiene carabali. Y pa' los que no saben na', ¿y tu abuela a'onde esta? (Here, those who don't have Dinga have Mandinga. Those who don't have Congo have Carabali. And for those who don't know anything, where's your grandma?). Carabalis, Congos, and Mandingas were African nations; Dingas and Ingas were Indians. This aphorism makes clear the preponderance of interracial bloodlines within the Latino world. At the same time, *Hoy dia los negros quieren ser blancos y los mulatos caballeros* (Nowadays blacks want to be whites and mulattoes knights) reveals the rancor of white Latinas/os over the social advances of Latinas/os of color.

Mexicans have a long history of interracial unions between Africans, Indians, and Spaniards. The contributions of Africans have influenced every aspect of

Mexican culture, history, and life. Esteban el Negro explored northern Mexico; the hit song "La Bamba" comes from the Bamba or Mbamba people of Veracruz, and the national *corrido* song style is partially African in origin; the muralist and painter Diego Rivera was of African descent. The African presence is apparent, but it is denied in Mexico and by Mexicans in the United States. In spite of their impressive contributions, Afro-Mexicans remain a marginalized group, not yet even recognized as full citizens (Muhammad, 1995). Mexican historians and academicians endorse the claim that the "discovery" of Mexico represented an encounter of two worlds, the Indian and the Spanish, with little if any mention of the Africans brought there (Muhammad, 1995). By the middle of the eighteenth century, Mexico's second-largest population group was largely of African extraction. In 1810 blacks represented 10.2 percent of the Mexican population (Muhammad, 1995). It is estimated that about two hundred thousand Spaniards and two hundred and fifty thousand Africans had migrated to Mexico up to 1810 (Forbes, 1992), and the African population was largely assimilated by the rapidly emerging interracial population. Although Mexico identifies itself as a nation of mestizos, the term "mestizo" is normally not used for identifiable Afro-Mexicans, who are instead referred to as *morenos*. The 1921 census was the last in which racial categories were used in Mexico. Today it is estimated that mestizos make up approximately 85–90 percent of the Mexican population and indigenous persons only 8–10 percent (Fernandez, 1992). There are no current data, demographic or otherwise, for Afro-Mexicans, but Miriam Jiménez Romón of New York's Schomburg Center for Research in Black Culture estimates that 75 percent of the population of Mexico has some African admixture (Muhammad, 1995). Mexicans will boast about their Spanish relatives and may even admit to Indian ones but will rarely admit to a black forebear. Whereas indigenous groups have gained national and international visibility and support, Afro-Mexicans remain suppressed and unheard. Contemporary social research in Mexico tends to exclude Afro-Mexican communities, and no major study on Mexican race relations has ever been done (Muhammad, 1995). Within the past decade anthropologists and others have visited Afro-Mexican communities and reported their deplorable living conditions and rampant illiteracy, their inadequate schools and medical facilities, and their lack of electricity, potable water, plumbing, sewerage, drainage, and paved streets. Visiting Mexico in 1988, I searched for and found Afro-Mexicans living in a clearly segregated shanty town outside of Guadalajara. The squalor of their homes and community was appalling. They openly talked about blatant racism and their financial and legal inability to migrate to the United States. These Afro-Mexicans have been ignored and neglected by government agencies; they receive little or no assistance (Muhammad, 1995).

Puerto Rico, after four centuries of Spanish colonial rule, had developed into a multiracial society. French people and multiracial Creoles went to Puerto Rico after the U.S. Louisiana Purchase from France and migrated from

Haiti when the slaves revolted (U.S. Commission on Civil Rights, 1976). Labor shortages throughout the island in the 1840s brought Chinese, Italians, Corsicans, Lebanese, Germans, Scots, Irish, and many others. As the twentieth century approached, the racial composition of Puerto Rico covered the spectrum from whites to blacks with a large in-between interracial group known as *trigueños* (U.S. Commission on Civil Rights, 1976). Racially speaking, most Puerto Ricans are of interracial black, Taino, and white origin. It is believed that racial mixing has touched at least 70 percent of Puerto Rico's population. With U.S. invasion of the island and installation of military rule in 1898, citizenship in 1917, and the establishment of the Commonwealth in 1952, U.S. whites became first-class citizens. Elite Puerto Rican whites were quick to ingratiate themselves with the new upper class by impressing them with their whiteness (Toplin, 1976). The advent of U.S. racism brought the exclusion of social whites who declared themselves white in official U.S. demographic surveys. Whereas the 1846 census reported 51.24 percent of the Puerto Rican population as African or Negro, in 1959 the count dropped to only 23 percent (Toplin, 1976). Members of Congress were not discreet in expressing their low opinion of Puerto Ricans and wondering how there could be so many whites in a "black man's country." Several were openly angered by the degree of racial mixture, stating that the "horror" of racial mixing had gone too far and prevented them from establishing clear racial categorization. They concluded that it was the "duty" of the United States to impose a strict color code on Puerto Rican society in order to ensure propagation of the white race, that is, the newly established elite (Toplin, 1976).

Racial prejudice increased with U.S. occupation of the island (Toplin, 1976; Zenon Cruz, 1974) and became prevalent in public places during the 1950s and 1960s. It persists in social clubs, public and private universities, businesses, banks, tourist facilities, public and private schools, and housing today. Although the local government stopped using racial classifications in 1950, the legal and penal systems, which remain predominantly white, continue to use them against black and dark-skinned poor urban youth (Santiago-Valles, 1995). Little if anything is done to correct the open racism, and many areas remain "hermetically closed" to the darker-skinned Puerto Rican (Toplin, 1976). The Puerto Rican elite, comprised mostly of the descendants of Spaniards with increasing numbers of U.S. whites and European immigrants, treat darker Puerto Ricans with visible contempt. Few Puerto Ricans of African descent explicitly identify as such because of a long history of discrimination and a present fear of police brutality and persecution (Santiago-Valles, 1995). Elite Puerto Ricans still claim that the Spanish white race prevailed in the island, making it the "whitest of all the Antilles," and seek closer ties with Spain (Santiago-Valles, 1995). The 1992 Columbus Quincentennial was celebrated with much emphasis on the Spanish roots of the island. Subsequent annual "Nuestra Hispanidad" (Our Hispanicism) celebrations have focused on Spain and white Puerto Ricans. There is a dearth of information about black and dark-skinned Puerto Ricans but a strong association between black and poor. Black and dark-skinned Puerto Ricans live disproportionately in slums under extremely deprived conditions. U.S. citizenship granted all Puerto Ricans, including those of black heritage, an open door to the continental United States. The enormous loss of jobs between 1940 and 1970 created a massive exodus of Puerto Ricans to the U.S. mainland (U.S. Commission on Civil Rights, 1976). This immense socioeconomic dislocation brought increased visibility to the predominantly black and interracial Puerto Ricans on the mainland.

The Cuban population has historically been African and Spanish (Fernandez, 1992). Almost all Cuban-born Latinas/os came to the United States as refugees from the Revolution of 1959 and the Mariel boatlift in 1980. Although the vast majority of Cubans today are black, most Cuban-Americans are white (McGarrity and Cardenas, 1995). Revolution refugees were mostly educated middle- and upper-class white Cubans with backgrounds in the professions, businesses, and government who soon became integrated into the U.S. middle class. The "less congenial" Marielos were mainly uneducated and poor lower-class black Cubans (Rivera, 1991). The long-standing racism of white Cubans against black Cubans is well known. In Cuba, blacks were excluded from certain schools, especially private Catholic schools, public beaches, hotels, restaurants, and parks. They could not rent homes in some areas (McGarrity and Cardenas, 1995). Before the Marielos, Cubans were welcomed in the United States and given preferential treatment with much transitional support. These elite Cubans were "proudly and adamantly white," uncontaminated, as they emphasized (McGarrity and Cardenas, 1995). Social and elite white Cuban Americans did not welcome the visibility brought on by the Marielos, the black compatriots they thought they had left behind in Cuba (Rivera, 1991). White Cubans are the most successful of the three major U.S. Latina/o groups; Mexicans follow, and Puerto Ricans, with more apparent African bloodlines, are the least (Forbes, 1992). This is not difficult to understand in the context of a racist, European white-dominated U.S. society.

SPANISH RACISM BEFORE COLONIZATION

Racism among and toward Latinas/os runs deep. Even today, in parts of Europe, Spain and Iberians are jeered: "Africa begins in the Pyrenees." The truth is that *negro* is a Spanish word, from the Latin *niger,* that is saturated with centuries-old European racial definitions. "Hispanic" is a term that predates both the Roman and the Moorish colonization of Spain (Fletcher, 1992). Then and now, the antithesis of *negro* is "Hispanic." Exploration of these antecedents begins unraveling the perceived superiority of white Hispanics over other dark-skinned and interracial Latinas/os. According to early Spanish historians, in ancient times the Iberian Peninsula was connected with Africa, allowing unobstructed movement from that southern continent. The River Ebro is the only major river in the peninsula that flows to the Mediterranean and is navigable by sea going craft for a considerable distance upstream, facilitating inland flows of Mediterranean and African peoples (Fletcher, 1992). The peninsula was first called Iberia after the River Ebro and was inhabited by the dark-skinned descendants of the African Maghribs who had settled in the mountains of Barbary on the Rock of Gibraltar in northern Africa (Fletcher, 1992; Wells, 1961). Much later the peninsula became known as Hispania after a Celtic conquerer ruler named Hispan (Fletcher, 1992). The Celts, or Hispanics, were a Nordic group from the Aran Islands that migrated down through Celtic Gaul (France), crossed the Pyrenees through the "Valle de Aran," pushed the Iberians west and south, and settled in the northwest coastal region of Catalonia. The Greeks and Romans held the Maghribs in contempt and derisively called them "Berbers" (Wells, 1961). In 218 b.c., when the Romans gained control of the peninsula, they officially established its name as Hispania (Crow, 1985), with its capital in Hispanic-controlled Tarragona. Eventually Hispania became España, the modern name for the Republic of Spain. The Maghribs or Berbers became regarded as barbarians—primitive, savage, and inhuman. Catalonians consider themselves different from the people of other parts of the peninsula. They still call themselves "Araneses," speak a distinct language, practice different customs, and have for centuries struggled for separate identity and independence from the rest of Spain (Peffer, 1984).

The "Hispanic" label has been controversial among Latinas/os in the United States, since it was introduced around the turn of the nineteenth century by wealthy descendants of Spaniards from New Mexico and other former Mexican territories that came under U.S. ownership in an attempt to forge alliances with American whites by shedding their Indianness and Mexicanness. According to Oboler (1995), they contended that geographic isolation from Mexico had allowed them to remain "pure-blooded" direct descendants of the original white Spaniards, unlike the "mestizo" or "half-breed" Mexicans. They adopted the term "Hispanic" to distinguish themselves from the Mexicans in the context of U.S. white society. Some sought reclassification as whites-with-Spanish-surnames (Forbes, 1992). In essence, they joined U.S. Whites in their dislike of Mexicans by claiming to be White Spanish Americans instead (Oboler, 1995).

U.S. RACISM

"Latina/o" is used here instead of "Hispanic" to refer to persons from Latin America and Spain and their compatriots living in the United States. Whereas both terms have been criticized as accentuating a connection to Europe, "Hispanic" refers distinctively to Hispanic origin, explicitly limiting the definition to Spanish-speaking white persons directly tied to Spain (Forbes, 1992). According to Forbes, this "exaltation" of whiteness was initiated by Spain to facilitate its imperialistic exploits in the Americas by installing white Spaniards as the elite superior race and as rulers. Emphasis on Hispanicism by the United States today constitutes continued promotion of this white supremacist doctrine among U.S. Latinas/os. The strategy is to create a need in Latinas/os from the various Latin American nations, with diverse ethnicities, races, languages, and cultures, to shed their individual identities and accept a new one as member of a fabricated "Hispanic" group. The idea is to shift the focus toward ethnicity in order to form a more homogeneous group that can be identified, isolated, and thus manipulated with greater ease. It is also necessary for members of this group to accept appropriate leadership, leadership that must be identified, approved, and empowered. "Appropriate" tends to mean as white as possible and preferably white. In the case of Latinas/os this leadership becomes European-based Spanish whites (Forbes, 1992). As Forbes further contends (1992), Latinas/os of color must be made to think white, internalize their own racial inferiority, and accept white domination. This strategy perpetuates the empowerment of persons of white European descent at the expense of Latinas/os of color and disguises the racial differences and racial politics that persist in Spanish-speaking and Latin American populations. "Hispanic" is, therefore, exclusive to the small ruling Spanish-speaking white elites of European descent of most Latin American nations, who exploit the vast majority of non whites, and to white Latinas/os, who are also privileged in the United States. The reality remains that to be a Latinegro, even in the United States, means to be at the very bottom of the social, economic, and political scale, because it is usually white and light skinned Latinas/os who get the positions of power and authority, hold the most wealth and economic control, and are seen as representing all Latinas/os (Fernandez, 1992).

"Latina/o" refers to groups whose languages derive from Latin but whose cultures include those of indigenous persons and those brought to this hemisphere against their will. It encompasses distinct and sovereign nations, many of which remain connected by the ensuing turmoil between the ruling descendants of the former white European colonizers and the blacks and Indians they continue to oppress. White Latin Americans have little in common with the exploited Indians and blacks who struggle for survival in a social, economic, and political structure that they control. Latinegras/os are Latinas/os who are perceived as black or of African decent in the United States (Comas-Diaz, 1996). This perception is manifested in many ways, including the oppressive denial of their Latinness by Spanish culture. According to Comas-Diaz (1996) and Zenon Cruz (1974), the use of terms such as africano latino, negro latino, and negro criollo reflects this racism. In this usage, the first word is noun and the second the adjective, making Latinegras/os Africans and blacks rather than Latinas/os, first and foremost. "You don't look Latina [or Hispanic]" is something I hear often and not just from U.S. whites. In the United States, identifiably black persons are perceived as possibly African or African American, and Latinas/os consider them inferior. Recently, I took an elevator with two white Latinos who, upon seeing me, looked away and began conversing in Spanish. When one asked for directions and I answered in Spanish, they were surprised: "You don't look Latina." Their next question, not surprisingly, was, "Where are you from?" Originally from Latin America, they had resided in the United States for several years. Once it was established that I was not also from their country, they appeared more willing to befriend me. To my dismay, one of them said, "In our country we have people who look like you." This denial of Latinegras/os, combined with public images manipulated by the media, creates the perception that Latina/o cultures do not include African ancestry. The term "Latinegra/o" is increasingly recognized as an empowering affirmation of Latinegras/os' ethnicity and race.

The United States has debated how to handle the "Spanish problem" for generations, particularly since the Mexican War (1846–1848) during and after which Texas, California, and New Mexico were annexed and later when Puerto Rico became a territory in 1898 (Oboler, 1995). Fearing a large migratory flow of Latinas/os, considered "poor material for social organization" (Toplin, 1976), the U.S. Congress saw a solution in separating them according to U.S. doctrine—by imposing the U.S. color line on them. The 1950 U.S. Census only listed "White," "Black," and "Other," and many Latinas/os classified themselves as white. In 1976 "Hispanic" was added to the categories. Today the United States officially divides the population into "Hispanic" and "non-Hispanic," subdividing whites as "of Hispanic Origin" and "Not of Hispanic Origin." "Race" in the United States is commonly used interchangeably with "ethnicity," but it is not synonymous with it, and through social practice the Hispanic designation has essentially bestowed a racial status upon a highly diverse population. Latinas/os are of various races, speak a wide variety of languages, and belong to as many different cultures. According to Forbes (1992), there appears to have been a deliberate mixing of the concepts of culture, race, ethnicity, and nationality by the U.S. Census Bureau, and several official demographic forms request racial identity while listing "Hispanic" as one of the choices. In addition, the United States has created another layer within the system of gradated Latina/o prejudices, making white Latinas/os in the United States believe that, although not white Americans, they have at least achieved a semblance of equality as White Europeans superior to other Latinas/os.

THE INTERSECTION OF LATINA/O AND U.S. RACISM

Individuals in the United States may believe that times have changed—that conditions for Latinegros have improved. After all, many U.S. educational institutions advocate multicultural education, the affirmation of diversity, and the teaching of tolerance. The sad reality is that racism continues to be part of everyday life among Latinas/os in the United States and is today confounded by U.S. racism. Latina/o racial antagonism has been transported to U.S. soil. Elite white Latinas/os, seeking acceptance by U.S. whites, quickly disown compatriots of known African lineage even when they appear white and are socially accepted as white in their home countries. In the United States these social white Latinas/os become *negros mal agradecidos* (ungrateful), *changos* (insolent), and *alzaos* (uppity) for wanting the privileges that elite white Latinas/os take for granted. Essentially, social white Latinas/os seek a closeness to elite white Latinas/os that remains simply unacceptable within the U.S. racial and social structure. In this struggle for acceptance, many social white Latinas/os fear focusing attention on themselves and their African legacy. When I moved to the mainland United States, I was told by some Latinas/os that since I would be perceived and treated as black I should identify with African Americans. Others advised me to accentuate my Latina attributes and deemphasize the black ones. Gone were most of the polite, if superficial, niceties—it no longer surprises me when I encounter Latinas/os whom I know in public places and they pretend not to see me. When U.S. Latinas/os emphasize their Hispanicism, they also tend to make sure that I understand my lack of it and the social abyss that separates us. Just three years ago, a "Hispanic" educator in Colorado told me that I was not one of them: "Hispanics are from Spain. You are not Hispanic. Everyone knows you are black." At a Latina/o educators' meeting where I raised concerns about the educational needs of African American students I was addressed scornfully: "You ought to know; you are black like 'them.'" A Latino friend explained, "Some Hispanics here don't want you to be one of them because you represent everything they don't want to be. 'How dare this black woman speak Spanish and claim to be one of us?' They see you as black, and they don't want to be black." In 1993 a "Hispanic" reader from New Mexico wrote to *Hispanic* magazine, in response to its earlier coverage of Latino major-league baseball players, including black Latinos: "I would appreciate knowing how the writer arrived at the classification of apparent Blacks as Hispanics. Does the fact that men come from Spanish-speaking countries such as Puerto Rico or Cuba automatically give them the Hispanic title designation? History shows that Africans were transported to the Americas as slaves and took the names of their slave masters."

As an educator, I have witnessed these acrimonious politics of race and racism played out at all levels. In a predominantly Latina/o middle school, a Latinegra was called "nigger" by her peers who said that it was OK to call her that because blacks had named themselves: "There is a country in Africa named after them [Niger]." I recall a high-school student of black Latino and white Latino parents coming home crying because her history teacher had taught that all black people had been brought to the United States as slaves. Her Latina/o peers called her "nigger" and "slave", pushed and shoved her, and ordered her around. I can still hear the anguished cry of another middle schooler of black Latino and white Latino parents who had left for school one morning feeling on top of the world, wearing a new outfit and with her hair professionally done for the first time. She had thought she would get compliments, but instead her peers, especially Latino boys, told her that despite what she had done to herself she was still ugly and undesirable. They threw water all over her new clothes and hair and called her "ape man," "jungle bunny," and "monkey."

A significant manifestation of Latina/o racism is the hypocrisy with which it is denied. Many Latinas/os, white and dark-skinned alike, are quick to deny the existence of racial discrimination among them. Some operate under the illusion that they are all racially mixed and racially united while regarding blacks and Indians as socially and humanly inferior. Others know the truth but do not want to answer the question "Where's your grandma?" Although not always overtly acknowledged or legally executed, Latina/o racism is covertly condoned and promoted in practice, perpetrated by all Latinas/os according to their perceived status in the hierarchy of whiteness that requires rejection of less-white persons below. *Unos tienen inga, otros mandinga. Pero muchos tienen de la banda'llá* (Some have Inga, others mandinga. But most have "from the other side"). *"Banda'llá"* is an allusion to distant and/or hidden predecessors. Many Latinas/os in the United States and Latin America, including the elite, fear opening their own family racial closets. Latinegras/os represent a reflection of Latinas/os' own blackness, a "painful mirror" that many wish to break (Comas-Diaz, 1996). The image presents a visual reminder of their relatives in *la banda'lla*. Latinas/os with racial mixing, even remotely suspected, fear that their African ancestry may come out in their children, grandchildren, or great-grandchildren if they marry other non-white Latinas/os (Comas-Diaz, 1996). There is fear of public ridicule and humiliation, scorn and rejection, of losing their privileged status. This internalized fear and systematized rejection of Blackness causes self-condemnation among dark-skinned Latinas/os. Latina/o racism and self-condemnation are so internalized that individuals cannot raise them to their consciousness. It is not uncommon to hear Latinas/os of all backgrounds say: "I am not racist. I just believe that whites are better than blacks. That's my opinion," and "I don't want blacks in my family because they are *sucios* and can't be trusted." It is heart-wrenching to hear an apparent Latinegro saying: "I am not Black. I am *indio oscuro* (dark Indian) or *quemado de sol* (sunburned)." A dark-skinned friend never dated Latinegras because: *¡Pa negro, yo! ¿Pa'que quiero mas negros?* (I'm the only black I need! Why would I want more?). I even recall hearing a very dark-skinned Latinegro proudly proclaim: "Up with Spain, my mother country," adamantly denying any connection to Africa.

One of the most insidious and pervasive forms of racism, one that appears to be escalating through globalized technology, is the promotion of images that exalt whiteness (Forbes, 1992). Historically, people of African background in Latin America have been stereotyped and vilified in popular culture in a number of ways. Media programs from Latin America and particularly Mexico are very popular among Latinas/os worldwide, especially in the United States, and are rapidly gaining other international audiences. *Telenovelas* (soap operas) and television programming are Mexico's largest export, sold throughout Latin America, the United States, and 125 other countries (Quinones, 1997). In these programs dark-skinned persons, particularly Latinegros, are presented as beggars, criminals, and servants. Latinegras are cooks, maids, nannies, and prostitutes. A term broadly used for dark-skinned Latinos in these programs is "Ladino," which also means a "liar" and a "thief." The upper class usually reflects the Nordic ideal, with light-colored eyes and hair and black and/or Indian servants. Latinegros are also promoted as either athletes or singers but are mostly depicted in a distorted way and made the object of ridicule.

CONCLUSION

Clearly, Latinas/os present a dilemma for the United States—what to do with a rapidly increasing population of mixed racial ancestry that defies categorization, resists homogenization, and cannot be readily assimilated. Today some Latinas/os mock the term as "His Panic," to signify the perceived fear of the white male–dominated U.S. government of non white Latina/o population growth. Through its racial policies and the "Hispanic" category the United States has chosen to advance Spanishness or put bluntly, whiteness, among Latinas/os (Forbes, 1992). It has established a system whereby Latinas/os are deluded into believing that they are all members of this new Hispanic group. While being reminded of my lack of "Hispanicness," I am reminded that politically my self-identification as a "Hispanic" is needed. What is concealed is that Latinas/os with uninterrupted descent from white Spaniards are glorified and established as the group's leaders. Most Latinas/os in the United States migrated in search of opportunities denied and/or made unavailable to them by the white elites of their homelands. They do not realize that the United States is recreating this power structure among them. Perhaps "His Panic" is Latinas/os' own panic—their own, even greater dilemma. The U.S. color line makes no allowance for middle groups; it is designed to disperse the middle cloud in opposite directions. Individuals are either white or "something else" (Cruz-Janzen, 1997). That "something else" may be African American, Asian American, Native American, or Hispanic, but only white Europeans—more specifically, white Europeans with the exception of Spaniards—can be white. As Hispanics, Latinas/os are spuriously classified as Europeans and white Latinas/os are deluded into believing that they are accepted as White Europeans. Latinos fail to recognize that ultimately, U.S. rejection is directed at all of them. Although their predecessors were present in this hemisphere before the arrival of the Pilgrims, U.S. Latinas/os are relegated to foreign status, forever designated as immigrants from Spain, whereas other Europeans are integrated as "Americans." Latinas/os of color are rendered invisible as only white Latinas/os are recognized.

Issues of race and racism are not talked about openly in Latina/o cultures in the United States because many Latinas/os argue that they are discriminated against as an ethnic group and discussions of internal racism divide the group and prevent coalescence against White/European-American oppression. But Latinegras/os in the United States as elsewhere resent their oppression. They are aware of the *tapujos*—the secrets, contradictions, and hypocrisy—among Latinas/os that provide fertile ground for U.S. racial policies. They express their anger and frustration over a situation that has been with them all their lives and is getting worse. Many realize that the stringent black-versus-white dichotomy is widening the racial divide that has existed among Latinas/os. What white Latinas/os fail to recognize is that U.S. racial dogma makes non white heritage unforgivable. One drop of non white blood forever taints the person and future generations. Latinas/os struggle to disclaim their convoluted background in order to gain some acceptance. The disclaimer is directed at their non white compatriots, at anyone, known or suspect, including their families, at anyone who cannot hide. Eventually the disclaimer points directly, individually, at them. Some Latinas/os in the United States today see the writing on the wall—that sooner or later all Latinas/os will be held accountable for la *mancha de platano*. Latinegras/os and all dark-skinned Latinas/os must raise their voices against their continued oppression at the hands of white and light-skinned Latinas/os. Latinas/os of all backgrounds must remove their blinders and recognize their own brand of racism and how it is being shaped by U.S. racial ideology.

REFERENCES

Andrews, George Reid. 1980. *The Afro-Argentines of Buenos Aires, 1800–1900.* Madison: University of Wisconsin Press.

Comas-Diaz, Lillian. 1997. "LatiNegra: Mental health issues of African Latinas," pp. 167–90 in Maria P. Root (ed.), *The Multiracial Experience: Racial Borders as the New Frontier.* Thousand Oaks, CA: Sage.

Crow, John Armstrong. 1985. *Spain: The Root and the Flower.* Berkeley: University of California Press.

Cruz-Janzen, Marta I. 1997. *Curriculum and the Self-Concept of Biethnic and Biracial Persons.* Ann Arbor, MI: UMI Dissertation Services.

Fernandez, Carlos A. 1992. "*La raza* and the Melting Pot: A Comparative Look at Multiethnicity/Multiraciality," pp. 126–43 in Maria P. Root (ed.), *Racially Mixed People in America.* Newbury Park, CA: Sage.

Fletcher, Richard. 1992. *Moorish Spain.* Berkeley: University of California Press.

Forbes, Jack D. 1992. "The Hispanic Spin: Party Politics and Governmental Manipulation of Ethnic Identity." *Latin American Perspectives* 19 (Fall): 59–78.

McGarrity, Gayle and Osvaldo Cardenas. 1995. "Cuba," pp. 77–108 in Minority Rights Group (ed.), *No Longer Invisible: Afro-Latin Americans Today.* London: Minority Rights Publications.

Muhammad, Jameelah S. 1995. "Mexico and Central America," pp. 163–80 in Minority Rights Group (ed.), *No Longer Invisible: Afro-Latin Americans Today.* London: Minority Rights Publications.

Nakashima, Cynthia L. 1992. "An Invisible Monster: The Creation and Denial of Mixed-Race People in America," pp. 162–78 in Maria P. Root (ed.), *Racially Mixed People in America.* Newbury Park, CA: Sage.

Oboler, Suzanne. 1995. *Ethnic Labels, Latino Lives: Identity and the Politics of (Re)presentation in the U.S.* Minneapolis: University of Minnesota Press.

Peffer, Randall. 1984. "Spain's Country within a Country: Catalonia." *National Geographic* 165: 95–127.

Quinones, Sam. 1997. "Hooked on *Telenovelas.*" *Hemispheres* (November): 125–29.

Rivera, Mario A. 1991. *Decision and Structure: U.S. Refugee Policy in the Mariel Crisis.* Lanham, MD: University Press of America.

Santiago-Valles, Kelvin A. 1995. "Puerto Rico," pp.139–62 in Minority Rights Group (ed.), *No Longer Invisible: Afro-Latin Americans Today.* London: Minority Rights Publications.

Toplin, Robert B. 1976. *Slavery and Slave Relations in Latin America.* Westport, CT: Greenwood Press.

U.S. Commission on Civil Rights. 1976. *Puerto Ricans in the Continental United States: An Uncertain Future.*

Wardle, Francis. 1998. *Definitions of Racism.* Denver, CO: National Center for the Study of Biracial Children.

Wells, Herbert George. 1961. *The Outline of History.* Garden City, NY: Garden City Books.

Zenon Cruz, Isabelo. 1974. *Narciso descrubre su trasero: El negro en la cultura puertorriqueña.* Vol. 1. Humacao, PR: Editorial Furidi.

Zenon Cruz, Isabelo. 1975. *Narciso descrubre su trasero: El negro en la cultura puertorriqueña.* Vol. 2. Humacao, PR: Editorial Furidi.

6

Haciendo patria:
The *charreada* and the Formation
of a Mexican Transnational Identity

Olga Nájera-Ramírez

> *La charrería es la reserva de la nación mexicana. Nosotros somos la reserva. Es por eso que con mucho orgullo hacemos el deporte pero también estamos haciendo patria. Estamos luchando por conservar todas las tradiciones.*

> [The *charrería* is the reserve of our Mexican nation. We are the reserve. This is why we engage in this sport with so much pride, but we are also fostering nationalism. We are struggling to preserve our traditions.]

> —Elsa López Jiménez

Even before the North American Free Trade Agreement (NAFTA) was signed, the implications of increased U.S.-Mexican integration have stirred concern over markers of differential national and cultural identity. Since its establishment over 150 years ago, the border has served as a political boundary meant to separate the United States of America from the Republic of Mexico. And yet as real as the border is—for violating the rules instituted to control movement across this space has drastic, even deadly, consequences—it has not succeeded in delimiting national culture on either side. Today more than ever, people, goods, knowledge, drugs, fashions, and culture (among other things) continue to travel back and forth across the border, muddying the sharp line that is meant to divide two cultures, two societies, two nation-states.[1]

Drawing on the cross-border scholarship pioneered by Américo Paredes, who coined the term "Greater Mexico" to express the concept of a borderless Mexican community,[2] and informed by recent studies on issues of globalization, displacement, and transnationalism,[3] this chapter examines the *charreada* or Mexican rodeo as a set of cultural practices deployed to link Mexicanos on both sides of the border symbolically as "one people." As a cultural practice that transcends national boundaries, the charreada offers an ideal site for examining the ways in which increased globalization and migration challenge but do not erase preexisting conceptions of national and cultural identity. On the basis of five seasons of ethnographic fieldwork centered in Sunol, California, but extending to other parts of the United States and Mexico, I show how the charreada helps construct a particular conception of Mexican cultural identity by invoking a set of images, landscapes, historical events, symbols, and rituals that represent the shared experiences that give meaning to Mexico as a national culture. In the words of the *charros*,[4] *haciendo patria* (engendering nationalism) and *haciendo cultura* (producing and/or practicing culture) are precisely what they intend to accomplish through their participation in the charreada.

The desire to express a sense of unity among Mexicanos within and across two nation-states acquires greater saliency when considered in the context of the history of Anglo-Mexican relations, a history fraught with (cultural) conflict and (economic) interdependence. The imposition of the U.S.-Mexican border, whereby the United States took possession of Mexico's northern provinces and transformed Mexicans living north of the border into "foreigners," became a powerful marker of U.S. domination. Constructed as a "conquered people" and viewed largely as a source of cheap labor, Mexicanos experienced a sense of cultural devaluation as a result of the racist and nativist reaction to Mexican immigration, a reaction that has recently undergone considerable intensification (Gutierrez, 1996; Vélez-Ibáñez, 1996; Zavella, 1997). Thus, for Mexicanos the border became a "symbol of separation" inscribing the processes of deterritorialization, displacement, and devaluation. In this light, as a cultural practice that predates and transcends the border, the charreada and the notion of haciendo patria can be viewed as a counterdiscourse of resistance against Anglo domination, cultural erasure, and demeaning treatment.

Operating within and across two nation-states, however, the charreada reveals some of the tensions and contradictions concerning gender, class, and national and cultural identities that crosscut this transnational Mexicano community in multiple and often subtle ways. Therefore one must be attentive to the divergent ways in which the charreada is utilized by different communities (Mexicanos and non-Mexicanos) to promote competing visions of what it means to be Mexican. In what follows, I demonstrate how the charreada gives expression to the desires, ambiguities, and contradictions of this transnational Mexican community.

THE CHARREADA IN THE UNITED STATES AND MEXICO

Even a cursory examination of its historical roots confirms that the charreada has been a part of Mexican culture since at least the colonial period, a time when most of the Southwestern United States belonged to Mexico. At that time, cattle ranching—an industry requiring extensive lands for grazing— was widespread in the Greater Mexican region, especially on its northern frontier (Arnade, 1961; Brand, 1969; Chevalier, 1972; Le Compte, 1986). Based on the skills and techniques required in cattle ranching—made evident through the periodic *herraderos* (branding events) and *rodeos* (roundups)—the charreada emerged as a seasonal social event featuring food, entertainment, visitors, and a variety of riding and roping contests (Myers, 1969; Bishko, 1952; Le Compte, 1986).

By the end of the colonial period, regional differences notwithstanding, a distinctive Mexican-style rodeo had evolved (Le Compte, 1986; Valero Silva, 1987). A century later, amid the fervor of the romantic nationalism of postrevolutionary Mexico that gave prominence to customs and practices considered unique or native to Mexico, the charreada, as an example of *lo mexicano* (Mexicanness), gained further popularity through songs, novels, paintings, and movies (see Nájera-Ramírez, 1994). During this same period it became formally institutionalized as a national sport explicitly designed to foster patriotism, promote Mexican customs and traditions, and nurture a sense of cultural pride. Created and controlled by urban middle-class professionals in Mexico in 1933, the Federación Nacional de Charros, A.C. (National Federation of Charros), assumed responsibility for governing the practice of the official charreada.

With a set of rules and regulations instituted by the Federación Nacional de Charros, the official charreada became fairly standardized throughout Mexico in the twentieth century. In the United States, in contrast, only informal charreadas, consisting primarily of bull and bronc riding (also called *jaripeos*), were widespread prior to the Chicano civil rights movement of the late 1960s and 1970s.[5] With its focus on promoting cultural pride in lo mexicano, however, the official charreada rapidly gained attention as a cultural practice that would help advance the goals of the Chicano movement. Consequently, Chicanos invited members of the Federación Nacional de Charros to come to the United States to help them cultivate the practice of charrería. Despite the fact that an American-based charro organization was established in 1991 (calling itself the Federación de Charros, United States Inc.), to date the Federación Nacional de Charros remains the largest and most influential charro organization. Claiming membership on both sides of the U.S.-Mexican border, it has achieved transnational status.

HACIENDO CULTURA IN THE UNITED STATES

La charrería, deporte de origen mexicano, es arte, es cultura y tradición, es la identidad del mexicano en el mundo entero (Reglamento Oficial Charro).

[Charrería, a sport of Mexican origin, is art, culture, and tradition; it is Mexican identity around the world] (Official Charro Regulations).

One of the outcomes of regulating the charreada through this transnational charro organization is that it has indeed become standardized throughout Greater Mexico. Typically held on Sundays, charreadas begin around noon with a parade featuring all the participants, a salute to the Mexican flag, and the playing of the *Marcha de Zacatecas,* which charros consider Mexico's second national anthem. Throughout the formal event, a *banda* (a brass and percussive ensemble) or *mariachi* (a regional folk ensemble) provides musical entertainment.

The formal competition consists of nine *suertes* or riding and roping competitive events for men: (1) *cala,* a reining competition displaying horse control; (2) *piales en el lienzo,* the roping of a running horse by its hind legs while on horseback; (3) *colas,* bull tailing; (4) *jinete de novillos,* bull riding; (5) *jinete de yeguas,* wild mare riding; (6) *terna,* team bull roping; (7) *manganas a pie,* the roping of the front legs of a horse while on foot; (8) *manganas a caballo,* the roping of the front legs of a horse while on horseback; and (9) *paso de muerte* or jumping from a bareback running horse to a running wild mare. Since 1992, the *escaramuza,* a female precision riding team that displays horse riding skills through the execution of choreographed patterns in the arena, has been formally instituted as an official competitive event.

In addition to the formal events, the charreada usually features a number of other activities that ensure wider participation. Outside the arena, the smells of Mexican delicacies such as *carnitas* (pork meat), *barbacoa* (Mexican-style barbecue), *elotes* (corn on the cob), and *menudo* (tripe stew), as well as the ubiquitous popcorn, soft drinks, and beer, attract people to the concession stands. Amid the constant flow of people circulating between the arena and the food stands, strolling musicians (usually *conjuntos norteños*)[6] offer their services for impromptu serenades and dances. As soon as the competitive events come to an end, performing artists may provide a one- or two-hour show, often followed by an open-air dance concert.

The similarities among charreadas throughout Greater Mexico help create a shared sense of community and experience for Mexicanos. As many participants have observed, attending a charreada in the United States makes them feel as if they were in Mexico. And yet, despite the uniformity that exists in elements, structures, and features of the charreada, there are important ways in which the practice is not the same in the United States as it is in Mexico. As a state-sanctioned institutionalized cultural practice requiring a significant amount of time and money of its participants, the formal charreada in Mexico has been dubbed "the Mexican polo," being largely practiced and controlled by the elite. In the United States, the charreada is situated very differently: it receives no governmental support or recognition, and it is practiced by a predominantly subordinate working class population. Hence, in the United States, the charreada, and particularly the notion of haciendo patria (engendering nationalism), assume critical importance as politically charged cultural activity. As Elsa López Jiménez, a free-lance writer for several charro magazines in Baja California and the director of an escaramuza team, astutely notes (interview, Sund, California, September 1992): *"En Estados Unidos se vive más intensamente la charrería por la nostalgia de la tierra. Y yo me quito el sombrero con los charros de Estados Unidos porque están en un país diferente, están luchando contra la adversidad y sin embargo están saliendo adelante y su lucha no va ser en vano."* (In the United States charrería is lived more intensely due to the nostalgia for the homeland. And I tip my hats off to the charros of the United States, because they are in a different country, struggling against adversity but they nonetheless are coming out ahead and their struggle will not be in vain.)

The adversity Mexicans encounter in the United States in their effort to preserve their cultural identity has a long history.[7] Educational institutions in the United States still offer little opportunity to learn about Mexican heritage and language. And although some progress has been made over the past thirty years with the establishment of the United Farm Workers Union, Chicano studies departments, and bilingual education programs, the future looks grim. Indeed, the "English only" campaign, the debates over multiculturalism, the ongoing anti-immigration sentiment, and the recent ban on affirmative action are examples of efforts to undermine the advances made in the 1960s and 1970s. These are only a few of the adverse conditions that continually threaten Mexican cultural identity in the United States. As a result, efforts to promote Mexican culture and Spanish language have been relegated to the domestic arena. Literally and metaphorically, then, the *lienzo charro* (rodeo arena) becomes an arena in which participants attempt to recover their history and heritage. Reflecting on his own motivation for becoming a charro, Fred Castro, former president of the Federación de Charros in the United States noted (interview, Las Cruces, New Mexico, October 1991):

> I just craved that [Mexican] history, and charrería has a lot of history. There is a lot of tradition, there is a lot of history from way back. Sometimes you can imagine two hundred years back and how the big haciendas used to be in México, and how the hacendados used to have their teams and invite these other groups of ranchers to come in and perform a charreada for their workers. This has got a lot of culture and history, and I love that, so I guess this is how I got interested in this sport.

The charreada not only preserves a sentimental link to the past, but also creates a concrete, if often contested, space for participants to indulge in Mexican customs and traditions. Rubén Uriarte, a first-generation Chicano (interview, Union City, California, April 8, 1989), explains why he became heavily

involved in organizing and promoting charrería in Northern California during his college years in the early 1970s:

> We all got involved in it for various reasons. It was a good way to get together
> with friends, doing something different involving the family. Our charreadas
> would start anywhere from around 1 P.M. and finish up by 4 P.M. Then we would
> have the entertainment . . . Lucha Villa or some great mariachi group would per-
> form. And there would be a dance afterwards, and there would be refreshments
> and food. . . . *I mean you go there and you feel like you're in Mexico.* You're
> like in another era, another land. I mean, that's the beauty of it.

In this short statement, Uriarte notes the importance of the charreada in
creating a social space for Mexicanos. For Uriarte, the charreada embodies a
set of practices—music, food, entertainment, sports, costume, and behavior—that creates the "feeling that you're in Mexico." The performing artists
and dance bands that entertain the crowds after the charreada attract even
those who might not be interested in the equestrian competitions going on
inside the arena. Thus the charreada encompasses an array of cultural entertainment and displays that give participants an ample sense of their Mexican
identity not readily available elsewhere. Elaborating on the special significance of charreada to Mexicans living in the United States, Henry Franco, the
founder and co-owner of the arena charro in Sunol, provides the following
commentary (interview, Livermore, California, January 27, 1990):

> In the United States, in my opinion, it's far more important [than in Mexico] be-
> cause you are surrounded with all kinds of other sports and the Mexicans have
> to find themselves that niche, the area where they can feel proud. An area
> where they are going to enjoy the food, the music, the folklore, the atmosphere,
> the language, and the feeling of saying or eating or doing anything they feel like
> because everybody's enjoying the same thing. So it's a sense of belonging with-
> out apologizing to anyone or having to explain why you eat this or why you lis-
> ten to that or trying to interpret anything because you're looking at a bunch of
> happy faces doing exactly the same thing.

Here we have a more detailed explanation about how the charreada functions to create a cultural ambiance in which individuals can fully engage in
and, indeed, nurture and preserve their Mexicanness. The underlying theme,
however, is that being Mexican outside this special environment presents
various challenges. Foremost among these is the notion of always having to
apologize, explain, or interpret your otherness to and within the mainstream
dominant society. As Stuart Hall has noted, subordinated people engage in
dual struggles—against being positioned and subjected in the dominant
regimes of representation and against being constructed by those regimes as
different and other within the categories of knowledge of the West (Hall,
1990: 225). As a practice that predates the arrival of the Anglos in the South-

west, the charreada helps disrupt the notion that Mexicanos and their cultural practices are foreign and therefore inappropriate on this side of the border. As a Mexican judge of the charreada declared, "*Cuando California pertenecía a México ya había charrería aquí en California*" (Charreria has been practiced in California since the territory belonged to Mexico). Thus, for Mexicanos who have been deterritorialized or otherwise displaced from their places of origin, the charreada provides a culturally sanctioned space in which they can experience themselves as a social body with deep cultural and historical roots on both sides of the U.S.-Mexican border.

Related to the issue of creating a sense of shared identity is the notion of counteracting the various forces that continually fragment the Mexican community and alienate its members. Omar Castro, an elderly man from New Mexico whose family has been involved in charrería for many generations on both sides of the border (interview, Las Casas, New Mexico, October 1991), shares this view: "*Lo que quisiera que comprendiera mucha gente que vive fuera del deporte es que dentro de ésto nos une un amor a la familia muy grande . . . Ya ve que la vida moderna come hace que la familia se desintegre, que las hijas van por acá, y eso nosotros no queremos. Queremos la unidad completamente.*" (What I wish everyone that lives outside of our sport could understand is that within charrería we are united by a deep love for our family. You see how modern life fragments the family, that the daughters go their own way, and we don't want that. We want complete unity). For Castro, charrería helps to counteract the fragmentation of family resulting from modern life. Divorce, unemployment, drugs, and gangs are only some of the harsh realities of modern life that contribute to the fragmentation of families. Not surprisingly, a recurring claim among my interviewees was that they involved their children in charrería in order to give them an activity that fostered a sense of family and community and *quitarlos de andar en la calle* (to keep them off the streets and out of trouble). Such sentiments resonate with those expressed by the anthropologist Carlos Vélez-Ibáñez, who cautions, "So long as there is no place or space, cultural or social, from which our youngsters can receive recognition, affection, and feelings of value, there can be no respite for those that join gangs or those that suffer their responses" (1996: 192).

Within the context of charrería, the concept of family serves as a metaphor for nation. For example, Armando Ledesma, a charro judge from the state of Baja California, states (interview, Las Cruces, New Mexico, October 1991): "[The charreada] is a great and important means of showing our children that even though in this particular case we are in a foreign country, our roots have to prevail. And through this sport our children who live in the United States learn about our tradition, learn about our ways, learn our real values." Ledesma's allusion to the charros as members of one big family is a sentiment expressed by many charros. Henry Franco emphasizes that participating in the charreada provides a sense of unity even for people who haven't met one another personally. Stating that "it is a feeling of brotherhood," he recalls how the charros rescued him once when he was robbed in Mexico. Unable to get any assistance from the local police, Franco was in state of despair after the robbery. But suddenly "a white pick up arrived across the street and a charro got out of the pick up. I felt hope at that moment, so I walked over there and I identified myself with my *credenciál,* and within fifteen minutes I had enough money to buy more gas than I could possibly need to get to Guadalajara and to eat, which I never had to pay back." He concludes, "What I'm trying to say is that if you can go to almost any city, if you're a member of the charrería, someone helps you. All you have to do is ask, 'Who are the charros in the city? Where's the lienzo?' And most generally on a Sunday there's going to be something going on and someone will help you. For me, it's been one of the biggest pleasures of my life."

The metaphor of family for nation is particularly apt in a transnational context because it evokes a sense of connection among members of community that is not tied to space or territory.[8] One's ties to the Mexican nation, like one's familial ties, are not determined by where one resides. But like other families, the charrería as practiced transnationally also contains some tensions and conflicts that merit closer attention. The first of these concerns the issue of gender. Although participation in the charreada is open to men and women, the particular roles they may play follow gender lines. In the charreada, women manage food booths, cheer as spectators, reign as queens, host visitors, and perform as e*scaramuzas.* Although the multiple roles they play unquestionably attest to their numerous skills and abilities, women have largely been confined to subsidiary roles. As noted elsewhere, the charreada, like the family unit it seeks to emulate, operates as a patriarchal system in which women are defined as men's subordinate counterparts or attachments, not as their equals (Nájera-Ramírez, 1994). Luciana Ozuna, a lifelong participant in the charreada (interview, Las Cruces, New Mexico, October 1991) observes: "I always come to the charreadas with my parents, or sometimes just with my father and it's very political. The fact that he knows a lot of the *presidentes,* a lot of the charros, that has helped me a lot. And they recognize me as his daughter. I guarantee you half of them don't even know my name. But if they see me with my father, they'll know who I am. . . . So how they see you has to do with who you are with."

Such comments reveal the heightened awareness some women have of their subordinate roles and this awareness, in turn, has led to changes, most notably in the role of the escaramuza. Now considered a fundamental component of the traditional charreada, the escaramuza is actually a relatively new phenomenon that marks the greatest inroads women have made in this male-dominated sphere. First established in the 1950s, the escaramuza was originally an exhibit rather than a competition, but in 1992 the escaramuzas finally won the right to compete within the charreada. As contestants they were guaranteed a sanctioned time within which to perform so that their presentations would not be rushed or shut down prematurely, the right to have qualified judges evaluate their skills, and the right to have formal rules established. Reflecting on this recent achievement, Elsa López Jiménez notes (interview, Elsa López Jiménez, Sunol, California, September 1992): *"La mujer en México ha logrado su lugar dentro de la charrería. Y eso lo logramos a base de tenacidad, a base de disiplina y a base de que se nos ha exejido a nosotros mismas mucha perfeción de movimientos. Y nos sentimos muy orgullosas de ser las primeras escaramuzas que se califiquen y sabemos que vamos a dejar les a nuestras hijas una herencia de deporte y una herencia de respeto asi lo nuestro."* (Women in Mexico have earned their place within charreria. We achieved that based on tenacity, discipline, and the fact that we demand of ourselves perfection of movement. We feel very proud to be among the first escaramuzas to be judged, and we know that we are passing on to our daughters this sport as well as a great respect for our traditions). But these changes are not without their critics, many of whom express concern that these inroads are indicators that the women are "refusing to stay in their place." A central point of contention has to do with who has the authority to define a woman's place. Clearly, the issue is far from settled.

Another line of tension lies between charros residing in the United States and those living in Mexico. For instance, Mexicans in the United States are often perceived as having special privileges because of their status as Americans. Commenting on an occasion in which his team won first place in a major charro competition in Mexico City, Omar Castro provides the following example:

Pasó una anécdota tan muy chistosa en la Ciudad de Mexico cuando ganamos ese trofeo. Después de que competimos otro día, ibamos del hotel al lienzo a ver una competencia pero ya no ibamos vestidos de charros. Y luego comentamos al taxista, "¿ya supo quien gano el trofeo Guadalupano?" Y dijo "sí esos méndigos gringos nos ganan con todo, pero que chiste hacen ellos, allá el gobierno de los Estados Unidos les da todo, les tienen todo." Y nosotros nos ibamos dentro de nosotros riendonos no?, sabiendo, que éste es un deporte honestamente mexicano, y que todavía no se desarrolla al grado que verdaderamente el gobierno nos apoyara y nos diera una ayuda. Al contrario, aveces luchamos contra de él para que nos deje hacer nuestra cultura aquí. [9]

[A funny anecdote occurred in Mexico City when we won that trophy. The day after we competed we were traveling from the hotel to the arena, but we weren't dressed in our charro costumes. And we asked the taxi driver, "Did you hear who won the Guadalupano trophy?" And he said, "Yes, it was those stupid *gringos* (Americans), but that doesn't really count because the United States government gives them everything." And inside, we were laughing, you know, because he didn't realize that this is truly a Mexican sport. We wish the United

States government did support us, but on the contrary, sometimes we have to struggle against it in order to practice our culture here.]

Underlying this story is the popular notion that Mexicans in the United States are somehow not "real" Mexicans. Note, for example, the taxi driver's use of the term "gringo"[10] to describe the charros residing in the United States. Anita Franco, co-owner of the charro arena in Sunol and mother of a charro family (interview, Sunol, California, September 1992), explains how she deals with these attitudes: "It inspires you when you go to Mexico, even though sometimes they look down on you because you don't speak the language that well. But I've always thought to myself it doesn't make any difference how you speak it; the thing is that you're trying. *Tienes ganas de enseñarte.* (You have the desire to learn.)"

Charro officials from Mexico, who view themselves as "guardians" of Mexican culture, consider it their responsibility to teach the charros in the United States how to be "proper" Mexicans. Mexican charro judge Miguel Jiménez explains why:

Para ellos este era un deporte pues de campo y pensaron ellos que se podría pues no llevar con mucho orden. Pero venimos nosotros con todo orden, practicando las nueve or diez suertes de la charrería. Vistiendo con propiedad, y comportandonos sobre todo con toda propiedad en los Estados Unidos, nosotros como Mexicanos era nuestra obligación poner el ejemplo de lo que era realmente nuestro deporte no subirse a un caballo y correr y gritar y, o tomar una cerveza arriba de un caballo, eso no es charrería.

[They thought that the sport was a rural activity that could be run with little order. But we came with much discipline, practicing the nine or ten events of the charrería. Properly dressed and behaving properly as well in the United States, we as Mexicans had the obligation of setting the example of what our sport is really like. Not to get on a horse galloping and screaming, or drinking a beer on horse back, that is not charrería.]

Significantly, most of the federated charros in Mexico and certainly all of the charro officials tend to be well-educated professionals, whereas in the United States the charros are typically laborers or small entrepreneurs. Controlled by urban elite professionals, the charro federation emulates an extended patriarchal family in which charro officials position themselves as the patriarchs who have both the obligation and the authority to define the proper way of being Mexican (see Nájera-Ramírez, 1994).

The class and gender differences briefly described above emphasize that although Mexicanos seek to present a unified vision of Mexican national culture through charrería, clearly class, language, geographical location, and gender are internal divisions operating within the charreada. Despite these internal differences, however, charros on both sides of the border recognize the common goal of promoting and preserving a dignified image of Mexican culture.

But this concern with presenting a "positive" image is only one indication of the extent to which Mexicanos on both sides of the border perceive that negative images of Mexicanos prevail in the United States, particularly in the media—a perception that is well supported in fact.[11] Given the importance of the charreada as a means of promoting a positive image of Mexican culture and identity, it is particularly ironic that its practice in the United States has itself become the focus of recent negative media attention that portrays charros as cruel, violent "rodeo renegades" who abuse animals in the name of tradition (see Nájera-Ramírez, 1996). Because animal-rights advocates claim that this sport—specifically the *colas* (bull tailing) and *manganas* (horse tripping)—is an act of cruelty to animals, horse tripping has been banned in California, Texas, New Mexico, and Maine, and this has threatened to prevent U.S. charros from participating in the transnational charro association.[12]

Similarly, the use and control of public and even private spaces has become another point of contention. In some communities in the United States, residents who live near the arenas have mobilized to ban the charreadas altogether, complaining of the excessive noise. Curiously, these attacks on charrería simultaneously fragment and unite charros in the United States and Mexico. On the one hand, the attacks threaten to prohibit or restrict the practice of charrería in the United States, a threat that many charros regard as disrespectful of Mexican culture. At the same time, however, the people who practice charrería in its various forms are coming together (thereby transcending social and class differences as well as national borders) to defend their right to do so.

CONCLUSION

Rooted in riding and roping skills developed in the cattle-ranching industry of colonial Mexico, the charreada is a cultural practice that predates the establishment of the U.S.-Mexican border and continues to be practiced and preserved by Mexicanos living on both sides of the border. It has therefore become an important means of fostering a sense of unity among Mexicans on both sides of the border. Operating within and across two nation-states, however, the charreada must be understood in the context of the transnational processes that integrate people in new space-time combinations that challenge preexisting conceptions of national and cultural identities. As a consequence, the charreada also becomes a site in which differences based on gender, class, and national and cultural identities are given expression. Despite these internal differences, which often produce competing visions of what it means to be Mexican, the charreada and the notion of haciendo patria offer a unifying counter discourse in a post-NAFTA climate that has witnessed the intensification of anti-Mexican sentiment.

NOTES

1. Nestor García Canclini observes that the U.S.-Mexican border is the busiest crossing point in the hemisphere (1992: 39).

2. Paredes has written extensively on the border as a site of cultural conflict and creativity. In coining the term "Greater Mexico," he was among the first to conceptualize the Mexican cultural community as extending beyond the political border of the Republic of Mexico. For a collection of some of his most significant articles as well as a complete list of his publications, see Paredes (1993).

3. The literature on these topics is quite extensive. For general overviews of the anthropological literature, see Marcus (1995), Appadurai (1991), and Kearney (1995). My work has been most influenced by scholars such as Carlos Monsivais, Norma Klan, Nestor García Canclini, Pat Zavella, and José Manuel Valenzuela, whose work has concentrated on U.S.–Mexican relations.

4. Charros is the term given to practitioners of the charreada.

5. Often combined with other festivities, jaripeos continue to be a widespread practice among the popular classes on both sides of the border.

6. A *conjunto norteño* typically consists of an accordion, a *bajo sexto* (12-string bass guitar), and a *tololoche* or contrabass.

7. For a historical overview of nativist reaction to Mexicans in the United States, see Gutierrez (1996). For a comprehensive and detailed analysis of the social, economic, and political subordination of the Mexican population in the United States, see Vélez-Ibáñez (1996).

8. The word "nation" refers both to the modern nation-state and to something more ancient and nebulous, the *nation,* a local community domicile, family, and condition of belonging (Brennan, 1990: 45).

9. Omar Castro, in an interview with the author in Las Cruces, New Mexico, in October 1991.

10. Paredes (1978) notes that "gringo" is a disparaging term applied primarily to Anglo-Americans although it has a long history among Spanish-speaking peoples as a name for a non-Spanish-speaking foreigner.

11. See, for instance, Limón (1973), Woll (1977), Pettit (1980), and Monsivais (1993). For exemplary studies on negative representations of Mexicans in the social science literature, see Romano (1968), Paredes (1977), and Rosaldo (1989).

12. Charros in the United States have managed to circumvent this threat by roping but not tripping the horses in the two manganas events.

REFERENCES

Arnade, Charles W. 1961. "Cattle Raising in Spanish Florida, 1513–1763." *Agricultural History* 35: 116–24.

Alvarez del Villar, Jose. 1968. *Origenes del charro mexicano.* Mexico City: Librería A. Pola.

Appadurai, Arjun. 1991. "Global Ethnoscapes: Notes and Queries for a Transnational Anthropology," in Richard G. Fox (ed.), *Recapturing Anthropology.* Santa Fe, NM: School of American Research Press.

Bishko, Charles Julian. 1952. "The Peninsular Background of Latin American Cattle Ranching." *Hispanic American Historical Review* 32: 491–515.

Brand, Donald D. 1969. "The Early History of the Range Cattle Industry in Northern Mexico." *Agricultural History* 35: 132–39.

Brennan, Timothy. 1990. "The National Longing for Form," in H. Bhabha (ed.), *Narrating the Nation.* London: Routledge Press.

Chevalier, Francois. 1972. *Land and Society in Colonial Mexico: The great hacienda.* Berkeley: University of California Press.

Confederación Deportiva Mexicana, A.C. 1991. Reglamento oficial charro: Reglamento de las competencias, de los competidores, damas charras y escaramuzas. Mexico City: Comisión Nacionál del Deporte.

García Canclini, Nestor. 1992. "Cultural Reconversion," in George Yudice, Jean Franco, and Juan Flores (eds.), *On Edge: The Crisis of Contemporary Latin American Culture.* Minneapolis: University of Minnesota Press.

Guitierrez, David. 1996. "Introduction," in *Between Two Worlds: Mexican Immigrants in the United States.* Wilmington, DE: Scholarly Resources.

Hall, Stuart. 1990. "Cultural Identity and Diaspora," in Jonathan Rutherford (ed.), *Identity: Community, Culture, Difference.* London: Lawrence and Wishart.

———. 1992. "The Question of Cultural Identity," in *Modernity and its Futures*, ed. Stuart Hall, David Held, and Tony McGraw (Cambridge: Polity Press), 274–323.

Kearney, Michael. 1995. "The Local and the Global: The Anthropology of Globalization and Transnationalism." *Annual Review of Anthropology* 24: 547–65.

Le Compte, Mary. 1986. "Any Sunday in April: The Rise of Sport in San Antonio and the Hispanic Borderlands." *Journal of Sports History* 13: 128–46.

Limón, José. 1973. "Stereotyping and Chicano Resistance: An Historical Dimension." *Aztlán* 4: 257–70.

Marcus, George. 1995. "Ethnography in/of the World System: The Emergence of Multi-sited Ethnography." *Annual Review of Anthropology* 24: 95–118.

Monsivais, Carlos. 1993. "¿Tantos millones de hombres no hablaremos inglés? (La cultural norteamericana y México)," in Guillermo Bonfil Batalla (ed.), *Simbiosis de Culturas.* Mexico City: Consejo Nacional para La Cultura y Las Artes.

Myers, Sandra. 1969. *The Ranch in Spanish Texas, 1691–1800.* El Paso: Texas Western Press, University of Texas.

Nájera-Ramírez, Olga. 1994. "Engendering Nationalism: Identity, Discourse, and the Mexican Charro." *Anthropological Quarterly* 67: 1–14.

———. 1996. "The Racialization of a Debate: The Charreada as Tradition or Torture?" *American Anthropologist* 98: 505–11.

Paredes, Américo. 1977. "Ethnographic Work among Minorities: A Folklorist's Perspective." *New Scholar* 6: 1–32.

———. 1978. "The Folkbase of Chicano Literature," in Joseph Sommers and Tomas Ybarra-Frausto (eds.), *Modern Chicano Writers: A collection of Critical Essays.* Englewood Cliffs, NJ: Prentice-Hall.

———. 1993. *Folklore and Culture on the Texas Mexican Border.* Austin: University of Texas Press.

Pettit, Arthur G. 1980. *Images of the Mexican American in Fiction and Film.* College Station: Texas A & M University Press.

Romano, Octavio. 1968. "The Anthropology and Sociology of the Mexican American: The Distortion of Mexican American History." *El Grito* 2: 13–26.

Romo, Ricardo and Raymund Paredes (eds.). 1978. *New Directions in Chicano Scholarship.* La Jolla: Chicano Studies Program, University of California, San Diego.

Rosaldo, Renato. 1989. *Culture and Truth: The Remaking of Social Analysis.* Boston: Beacon Press.

Sands, Kathleen Mullen. 1993. *Charrería mexicana: An Equestrian Folk Tradition.* Tucson: University of Arizona Press.

Stoeltje, Beverly J. 1987. "Making the Frontier Myth: Folklore Process in a Modern Nation." *Western Folklore* 46: 235–53.

———. 1989. "Rodeo: From Custom to Ritual." *Western Folklore* 48: 244–54.

Valero Silva, Jose. 1987. *El libro de la charrería.* Mexico City: Ediciones Gacela.

Vélez-Ibáñez, Carlos. 1996. *Border Visions: Mexican Cultures of the Southwest United States.* Tucson: University of Arizona Press.

Woll, Allen L. 1977. *The Latin Image in American Film.* Los Angeles: UCLA Latin American Center Publications.

Zavella, Patricia. 1997. "The Tables Are Turned: Immigration, Poverty, and Social Conflict in California Communities," in Juan F. Perea (ed.), *Immigrants Out!: The New Nativism and the Anti-Immigrant Impulse in the United States.* New York: New York University Press.

7

"*La tierra's* Always Perceived as Woman": Imagining Urban Communities in Chicago's Puerto Rican Community

Gina M. Pérez

Early in the summer of 1997, I visited a bakery on Division Street in one of Chicago's Puerto Rican neighborhoods, Humboldt Park, to buy some *pan de agua* (Puerto Rican "French" bread) and *quesitos* (a typical Puerto Rican pastry filled with cheese). As I walked out of the bakery, a local community leader, Juan Lanauze, approached me and asked me if I had a few minutes to see something exciting down the block.[1] As we walked across the street, he told me and another Puerto Rican couple who accompanied us about the latest *proyecto de la comunidad,* or community project. "This project is great," he told us. "It is really going to add something important to Paseo Boricua."[2] Juan led us to a vacant lot on the south side of the street where six teenage Puerto Rican boys were planting flowers, moving dirt and arranging stones to landscape the new garden. At the back of the lot was a little wooden house with a large porch, flowers, and a balcony. "This," he said, "is a typical *jíbaro casita* [Puerto Rican peasant house made of wood], you know, the ones you used to see in Puerto Rico. And we're going to inaugurate it during the mini-festival [Fiesta Boricua] the first weekend in September." I asked Juan what the lot used to be, and he said, "It was nothing. So we knew we had to buy it because, you know, if we don't, we'll lose it and then lose everything here in this area." The couple nodded in agreement as he continued to explain the importance of not only buying land in this area to resist gentrification but also building symbols of *nuestra cultura,* our culture, in these spaces: our flag, our food, our music, and, now, our own *casitas jíbaras.*

But who is going to live in this "typical," preindustrial Puerto Rican casita? The Mattel Corporation provided one possible resident for the *jíbaro* home. Recently, my sister told me that I needed to see the new international line of

Barbies at FAO Schwartz. When I found the Barbie section in the store, I dis-
covered that one of the new international Barbies is Puerto Rican Barbie, a
light-skinned, dark-haired *jíbara* in a "typical" jíbara white dress. On the
back of the box is a narrative by Barbie herself of Puerto Rican history and
culture: what she and other Puerto Ricans eat, where they live, and even
some discussion of Puerto Rico's political status. Barbie ends her narrative
with a quick pitch for tourism on the island, inviting all readers to visit her
on *la isla del encanto* (the enchanted island) to enjoy Puerto Rico's unique—
and, apparently, unchanging and rural—cultural traditions.

The peasant, the countryside, and the rich traditions associated with rural
living—simplicity, face-to-face interaction, humble, close-knit communities—are popular tropes for constructing "authentic" ethnic culture in the
context of urbanization and rapid social and economic change (di Leonardo,
1984; 1998; Ferguson, 1992; Williams, 1973). These images are also enduring
templates for apprehending the nature of this change in politically charged
contexts: Chicago School urban sociologists believed that traditional forms
of social organization based on kinship and a communal shared history were
obstacles to the assimilation and modernization that were prerequisites for
mobilizing a disciplined, modern labor force (Hannerz, 1980; Williams,
1973); politicians may invoke iconic images of an agrarian past in constructing cultural nationalist platforms (Dávila, 1997; Chatterjee, 1989); social
groups often contest hegemonic cultural practices and the negative consequences of political-economic shifts by deploying "traditional" cultural symbols (Aponte-Parés, 1997; Sciorra, 1996; Ramos-Zayas, 1997); and, more recently, the mass media frequently present images of quaint ethnic families
and culture to encourage popular consumption (Zukin, 1991; di Leonardo,
1998). These opening narratives therefore highlight an attempt to articulate
an "authentic" Puerto Rican culture that is rural, folkloric, and nostalgic; yet
they do so for profoundly different reasons. For Juan Lanauze and other
community leaders in Chicago's Humboldt Park, the casita is one of many
culturally significant objects along Paseo Boricua used to inscribe a specific
time and space, "a pre-industrial Puerto Rico of the recent past" (Sciorra,
1996: 75). These cultural symbols are strategically deployed to claim space
and create "place" as a way of resisting ongoing gentrification in the West
Town and Wicker Park neighborhoods on the city's near-northwest side and
on the eastern border of Humboldt Park. A popular bumper sticker of
Chicago's Puerto Rican flag on Division Street, for example, with the words,
"Aqui luchamos, aqui nos quedamos" (Here we fought, and here we shall
stay), is clearly a reminder of the Puerto Rican riots on Division Street in June
1966 (for details, see Padilla, 1987). But it is also a suggestion of a collective
memory of the displacement of low-income Puerto Ricans from Lincoln Park
to Humboldt Park in the 1960s and a community will to oppose further residential dislocation in the 1990s.

Mattel's use of Puerto Rican folklore is far less noble. Puerto Rican Barbie invokes an authentic Puerto Rican culture as part of a marketing plan that targets Latina/o communities, one of the fastest growing-consumer markets in the United States today.[3] Mattel's production, packaging, and distribution of cultural diversity through an international line of Barbies is troubling and is a clear example of a danger in contemporary multiculturalist thinking: It reifies culture, ignoring race and class differences, and posits an essential cultural and ethnic identity. It doesn't matter that most Puerto Ricans both on the island and on the mainland are urban dwellers and eat hamburgers and hot dogs as much as they eat *arroz con gandules*. Puerto Rican Barbie, like the casita, represents an authentic, pristine cultural past: before high unemployment, before migration, and before the development of an alleged "culture of poverty" (see Lewis, 1966) in Puerto Rican and U.S. cities.

This article is concerned with how urban life is imagined and discussed among first-and second-generation Puerto Ricans in Chicago. I shall argue that contradictory understandings of urban life are constructed transnationally and are deeply gendered; in other words, life in Chicago, past and present, is frequently apprehended by first-and second-generation Puerto Ricans in relation to popular notions of the folk and rural traditions of Puerto Rico. These folkloric cultural understandings are not only used to mobilize cultural pride and community support against the consequences of growth politics in Humboldt Park but also inflected with gendered notions of place, space, culture, and migration. By foregrounding gender I hope to contribute to a gendered understanding of transnational migration by not only exploring the role of women in transnational communities but by examining the ways in which ideas of home, place, and culture are part of gendered systems of meaning that inform how migrants themselves apprehend migration, the city, and the urban social landscape and how these understandings are employed in local-level and national politics. The opening narratives therefore provide an important window into the various ways in which gender informs popular notions of national culture and cultural identity and the contradictory ways in which Puerto Rican migrants and their children in Chicago understand migration, culture, space, and the urban social landscape in a transnational setting.

I shall begin my discussion with an examination of the burgeoning scholarship on women and migration and the different ways in which feminist scholars have advanced immigration research by foregrounding women, their social networks, and their role in the construction and maintenance of transnational communities. I shall then provide an historical narrative of Puerto Rican migration to Chicago beginning in the late 1940s that pays particular attention to gender and the shifting constructions of local knowledge about Chicago's Puerto Rican community. Since the late 1940s, politicians, academics, and the local media have constructed Puerto Rican migrants in relation to ethnic and racial others in Chicago, employing an "ethnic report card" approach to understanding and evaluating the city's minority communities (see di Leonardo, 1984: 94). Finally, I turn to women's role in the construction and maintenance of a transnational community. Working-class women are key players in local political struggles; they are also central to the construction of notions of home, place, and community. In Chicago, Puerto Rican cultural symbols and national identity, while steeped in images of rural life and folklore, are profoundly urban and are predicated, in large part, on women's cultural work both at home and on the level of local community politics.

GENDER, CULTURE, AND TRANSNATIONALISM

Transnational approaches to migration and migrant communities have correctly drawn scholars' attention to the ways in which the global circulation of commodities, people, and capital gives rise to new transnational identities, cultures, and communities within (to use Arjun Appadurai's [1990] notion) an ethnoscape marked by global plurality and cultural interconnectedness. According to the transnational model, global restructuring of capital has created economic dislocations in both the industrialized nations and the Third World sending nations (Glick Schiller, Basch, and Szanton-Blanc, 1992; 1995). In contrast to previous population movements, current migration takes place in a global context of economic uncertainty that facilitates the construction of systems of social relations that transcend national borders. In short, the circulation of goods, ideas, and information is embedded in systems of global social relations that are maintained, reconfigured, and reproduced in families and cultural, political, and economic institutions (Glick Schiller, Basch, and Szanton-Blanc, 1992; 1995; Basch et al., 1994; Rouse, 1991; 1992; Appadurai, 1990; 1991; 1993).

While transnational approaches to migration and migrant communities correctly draw our attention to the ways in which migrants construct and reproduce political, economic, and social ties in host and sending communities, feminist scholars have cogently argued for the need to gender transnational migration theories (Alicea, 1997; Hondagneu-Sotelo and Avila, 1997; Sutton, 1992). Since the 1930s, women have predominated in migration flows to the United States (Morokvasic, 1984; Houston, Kramer, and Barrett, 1984). For the past decade, feminist scholars have attempted to theorize gender in migration processes in a variety of ways. Much of the early scholarship was highly descriptive, documenting changing social and economic conditions and shifting male-female roles (Diner, 1983; Glenn, 1986). Other feminist scholars have moved beyond largely descriptive accounts of migrating women to examine the effects of male out-migration on women's employment, residential patterns, and gender ideologies (Bretell, 1987; Foner, 1978; Pessar, 1982; Grasmuck and Pessar, 1991; Pedraza, 1990; 1991; Georges, 1992; Gabaccia, 1994; Safa, 1990; 1995; Toro-Morn, 1995).

Yet another scholarly trend attempted to rethink important questions in migration theory and the role, nature, and importance of migrant social networks. Research on households "as the immediate facilitators of migration" helped to correct bias in migration research that documented the role of men's social networks and ignored how households contributed to the migration process (Pessar, 1982: 343). Considering the role of households in migration made women's reproductive work visible and redirected our attention to the important function of nonmigrants in population movements. This work, however, was predicated on unquestioned assumptions about gender relations and power in households. It assumed that the household was the unit that decided when migration was possible, who would migrate, and what economic resources would be allocated to migration (Pedraza, 1991). Furthermore, since households were considered to be mediating links between individuals at home and abroad, it was argued that when women migrated this process did not disrupt the social spheres in which they were self-actualized (Pessar, 1986). Migrating women, instead, reconstituted households in the host country, thereby preserving them as an important locus of women's activities (Pessar, 1986; Georges, 1992; Charles, 1995).

More recently, feminist scholars have argued for a transnational approach to migration that foregrounds women's active and creative roles in the construction, maintenance, and reproduction of transnational communities. Women's participation in the maintenance of such communities, however, is often fraught with contradictory perceptions of home and family (Toro-Morn, 1995; Alicea, 1997). These contradictions are complicated by the predominance of women as domestic workers (as child-care workers and housekeepers) and their reproductive labor in the United States in order to provide for children who remain in the country of origin (Colen, 1995; Hondagneu-Sotelo and Avila, 1997). This "stratified reproduction"—borrowing Shellee Colen's term—raises important issues regarding the meaning of parenting, motherhood, and reproductive labor in transnational communities.

My research among working-class Puerto Rican women uncovers yet another important way in which a gender focus pushes the boundaries of migration research: Migrant women not only are central to the construction and maintenance of transnational communities, but also serve as a template for understanding notions of home, place, culture, and migration. These ideas are part of gendered systems of meaning that inform how first- and second-generation Puerto Rican migrants apprehend the city, the urban social landscape, and cultural identity; they are also gendered notions that are strategically deployed in local political struggles to construct cultural place as a way to contest the consequences of urban growth politics. As does the work of other feminist anthropologists and geographers, this research highlights the connection of time, space, and place with constructions of gender (Hayden, 1995; Spain, 1992; Low, 1996; Massey, 1994). The space/place dualism is often conceptualized as masculine versus feminine, with place—that which is "local, specific, concrete, descriptive" and feminine—being devalued (Massey, 1994: 9). The local (or place) is associated with the feminine since "—it is said—women lead more local lives than men do." Space, in contrast, is coded masculine: global, universal, theoretical, and conceptual. Gendered dualisms also inform the ways in which rural and urban life in the United States have been imagined and analyzed over time (Hannerz, 1980; Wilson, 1991; di Leonardo, 1984). The city is frequently seen as a masculine place in which women, "along with minorities, children, the poor, are still not full citizens in the sense that they have never been granted full and free access to the streets" (Wilson, 1991: 8; see also Low, 1996). My research contributes to this scholarly trend by complicating these dualisms. Working-class Puerto Rican women do indeed lead deeply local lives, but they do so in a transnational context. How they understand urban life in Chicago is inextricably intertwined with popular constructions of Puerto Rico, a daily process that problematizes the gendered space/place antinomy in earlier migration and urban research.

For many Puerto Rican migrants in Chicago, the city is *dura y peligrosa* (hard and dangerous), a place entirely different from Puerto Rico, where life is *tranquila* (calm) and safe. The use of the cultural categories of the city as dangerous and Puerto Rico (which is usually imagined as rural) as safe is one way in which Puerto Ricans in Chicago apprehend the consequences of migration and contemporary urban life. In this context, the casita has a particular historical and gendered meaning: It is a cultural object of memory used to resist ongoing gentrification in a working-class, predominantly Latina/o neighborhood and a symbol fraught with contradictory meanings of gender, place, migration, and culture.

RESEARCH DESIGN AND METHODOLOGY

This article is based on two years of ethnographic and historical research among Puerto Rican migrants and their families in Chicago and is part of a larger study of Puerto Rican migration, gender, and poverty in Chicago and San Sebastián, Puerto Rico. The data for this study were gathered through in-depth interviews with fifteen first- and second-generation Puerto Rican families in Chicago, participant observation, and historical research. As I began my research in 1996, my intention was to explore the relationship among poverty, gender, and migration among first- and second-generation poor and working-class Puerto Rican women in Chicago. Popular and scholarly debates regarding "the persistence of Puerto Rican poverty" informed my concern to construct an ethnographic project that would counter the attribution of poverty among Puerto Ricans on the mainland to circular migration, the failure of migrants to establish roots in one place, and pathological or "underclass" behavior.[4] As a G.E.D. (General Equivalency Degree) instructor at one of the Puerto Rican cultural centers in Chicago, I worked with men and women who helped me to see the need for further examination of the meaning of culture among second-generation Puerto Ricans in Chicago. It was not uncommon for my students and others to express their desire to learn more about Puerto Rican culture and history so that they could, in turn, share this information with their families and, in particular, their children. In these conversations people frequently referred to culture, place, and identity in gendered terms. Realizing this prompted me to pay closer attention to the use of gender in speech in routine interactions with people and in formal interviews with my informants.

From the ethnographic and historical research I conducted in the Humboldt Park/West Town neighborhoods of Chicago it is clear that there are a variety of ways in which urban life has been understood and imagined over time. Stories about problems with gangs, fears of teen pregnancy, concern about cultural authenticity, and news reports that compare newer migrants with older immigrant groups figure prominently in the urban imagination. These stories also demonstrate how local knowledge about urban communities is produced (both internally by community members themselves and externally by journalists, politicians, and academics) in relation to real and imagined others in Chicago and abroad. In what follows, I will identify three pieces of local knowledge regarding Puerto Rican migrant communities in Chicago beginning in the late 1940s and demonstrate that these urban communities are imagined in a number of contradictory ways.

FROM "MODEL MINORITY" TO "UNDERCLASS": PUERTO RICAN MIGRATION TO CHICAGO

The first significant wave of Puerto Rican migration to Chicago began in the late 1940s and was regarded by elected officials in both Puerto Rico and Chicago as a win-win situation. State-sanctioned and private contract labor migration was a strategic response to rising unemployment in Puerto Rico as U.S.–led industrialization of the island displaced cane workers and subsistence farmers, leaving them unemployed (History Task Force, 1979; Meléndez and Meléndez, 1993; Pantojas-García, 1990; Rodriguez, 1991). This migration was also part of a larger political-economic strategy of planned development whereby the U.S. and Puerto Rican governments encouraged mass migration from Puerto Rico to U.S. cities to remedy the "overpopulation

problem" on the island.[5] In postwar Chicago, Puerto Rican migrants provided cheap labor for the city's expanding economy. Poor men and women
were frequently contracted in Puerto Rico to work in Chicago homes and
factories, although this arrangement was fraught with problems from the beginning (E. Padilla, 1947; F. Padilla, 1987; Maldonado, 1979). At that particular historical moment, migration was imagined as economic opportunity and
"urbanity" as progress. According to the media in both Chicago and Puerto
Rico, migration and city living meant freedom, opportunity, and prosperity.
The airplane was, according to a *Sun-Times* article of the 1950s, the
"*Mayflower*" for Puerto Rican migrants to Chicago (*Chicago Sun-Times,*
March 1, 1953).

Women figured prominently in this first wave and subsequent migrations to
Chicago and served an important ideological and material function for the
U.S. and Puerto Rican governments. Ideologically, poor and working-class
women of childbearing age were one of the principal obstacles to the implementation of Puerto Rico's modernization project, the alleged overpopulation
problem. Materially, however, these women were bundles of productive and
economic potential who could eventually contribute handsomely to the island economy by sending remittances to cash-strapped households and by
maintaining crucial economic links to the island.[6] In promoting the migration
of young, poor, and working-class women to cities such as Chicago, the
Puerto Rican government believed it could defuse the population "time
bomb" on the island, meet the increasing demand for labor in U.S. cities, and
expand the island's economic base through migrant remittances. To this end,
it established *centros domésticos* to prepare young women for domestic work
on the mainland and, in the case of Chicago, actively promoted private contract labor arrangements for women to work as domestics in city and suburban homes (*El Mundo,* August 28, 1947). Many women who had come to
work in Chicago homes and factories had worked previously in Puerto Rico
in their own stores and shops, as domestics in upper middle class homes, and
as laborers in the island's needle trades, both at home and in factories (Ortiz,
1996; Boris, 1996; Toro-Morn, 1993; 1995). Once in Chicago, women would
frequently send remittances back to Puerto Rico in order to facilitate the migration of other household members. This migration of Puerto Rican women,
however, is often reimagined by second-generation migrants and migration
scholars as a migration of *madres,* of wives and mothers joining working men
in Chicago and other mid-Western company towns.[7] Moreover, newspaper
accounts of Chicago's new migrants tended to focus on male migrants who
were "very much the head of [their families] in the manner of the Spanish culture" (*Chicago Daily News,* August 11, 1959), not only overlooking women's
pioneering role in Puerto Rican migration and the ways in which migration
challenged prevailing gender ideologies but also reproducing the notion of
machismo as an integral, unchanging component of "Spanish culture."

Through the mid-1960s, Chicago and island-based newspapers praised the city's new migrants and compared them with a number of different ethnic groups in urban America such as "hard-working" Irish, Polish, and Italian immigrants and not-so-hard-working populations such as the New York Puerto Ricans. Chicago's *Daily News* trumpeted Chicago Puerto Ricans as "an upbeat West Side Story," positing them as a kind of model minority: They were "peaceful and furiously ambitious" while New York *puertorriqeños* were violent, welfare-dependent, and involved in gangs (*Daily News,* June 5, 1965).[8] "If Horatio Alger were alive today," the article maintained, "he would sure be a [Chicago] Puerto Rican." The Chicago Puerto Rican's industriousness, his self-analysis, and his desire to "put roots here" resulted from the "modern Puerto Rican personality," which was "a mixture of Latin and North American characteristics." This news account, like many others, spotlighted hard-working Puerto Rican men and the stable nuclear families they established and (rather incorrectly) portrayed women solely as dutiful homemakers. This profile of *the* Puerto Rican migrant as a hard-working *man* not only rendered women's migration experiences and work invisible but also served to distinguish "good" Puerto Rican migrants from "bad" ethnic others in the urban imagination.

One year after they were christened the modern Horatio Alger, Chicago Puerto Ricans' status as a model minority was seriously challenged by the Division Street Riots of June 1966. On the surface, the riots were a reaction to the shooting of a young Puerto Rican man by a white police officer, and from June 12 to June 14 Puerto Rican residents looted and burned neighborhood businesses in protest (Padilla, 1987). The Division Street Riots stunned city officials, who had expected unrest in other Chicago neighborhoods but not in the Puerto Rican community. According to the commissioner of the Chicago Commission on Human Relations, "there [was] no indication that something of this type could happen [in the Division Street area]. To say that we were surprised would be a big understatement" (*Chicago Daily News,* June 13, 1966).

The Division Street Riots marked a radical shift in the history of Puerto Ricans in Chicago for two reasons. First, they impelled the creation of a number of community-based organizations to address the problems of poverty, housing discrimination, and police brutality among Puerto Ricans in the city. Second, and perhaps more important, they were key in transforming the popular perception of Puerto Ricans as hard-working, peaceable, and furiously industrious people. News articles instead began to focus on the problems of gangs, drugs, welfare dependency, and violence that now, according to media accounts, characterized the community. Humboldt Park and the West Town neighborhoods were no longer quaint ethnic neighborhoods with hard-working, noble migrants; instead they were dangerous, decaying, and ruled by local gangs. Such images of Humboldt Park continue to define the neighborhood. In 1997, for example, one journalist referred to Humboldt Park as "hell's living room" (*Chicago Tribune Magazine,* March 16, 1997). And while events in Humboldt Park and about Puerto Ricans in general are practically invisible in the local English-language television media, coverage in the local Spanish news focuses in large part on the problems with gangs and violence that "plague" the Puerto Rican community. When the English-language print and television media do feature Humboldt Park in local news coverage, they focus almost exclusively on the divisiveness of nationalist politics and the "terrorist activities" of Puerto Rican *independentistas,* which, according to these media accounts, render Humboldt Park a dangerous political space as well.[9]

I do not wish to suggest that these communities do not have serious problems. Unemployment and poverty *are* pervasive in Puerto Rican communities in the city. At 33.8 percent, Puerto Ricans have the highest poverty rate among Latinas/os—which is 24.2 percent overall—and a slightly higher poverty rate than that of African Americans, which is 33 percent (Latino Institute, 1995). Instead, I wish to highlight how local knowledge about a particular population is produced and imagined differently over time. The way in which first- and second-generation Puerto Ricans have metamorphosed from a "model minority" to members of "the underclass" is related both to their position in the local economy and to the emergence of ethnic others to replace them as hard-working, furiously ambitious people. As Puerto Ricans' structural position has changed in Chicago and in Puerto Rico, so, too, has public opinion shifted as polititans, academics, and journalists now understand the "Puerto Rican problem" to be a product of excessive migration, pathological behavior, and poor family values.

GENDER, CULTURE, AND THE URBAN IMAGINATION

The stories of Puerto Ricans living in Humboldt Park provide a second piece of local knowledge regarding how "urbanness," urban life, and migration are imagined and reproduced among Puerto Ricans in Chicago. For working-class Puerto Rican parents, urban life is *peligroso* (dangerous), uncertain, and filled with instances of violence, sexual danger, racism, and discrimination. Urban danger and uncertainty are clearly gendered, and migration is frequently believed to be a way to address actual and potential problems with children. For young women, sexual danger figures prominently in parents' concern about their daughters' future. Aida, a thirty-year-old woman, born and raised in Chicago, told me that her mother had sent her to Puerto Rico when she was thirteen "so I wouldn't be spoiled." "But you know," she told me later, "we [young girls] almost always come back and get in worse trouble than when we left." While critical of what she perceives to be her mother's overprotective approach in raising her, she expresses similar concern about raising her own teenage daughter. Afraid that her daughter might *meterse las patas* (get pregnant), she spends much of her time strategizing how to get her daughter out of a sexually dangerous environment before it is "too late." Sending her daughter to live with an aunt in Puerto Rico is one option she often considers, although, considering her own experience, she is hesitant to do so. Military service after high-school graduation is another strategy she considers both to protect her daughter and to provide her with marketable skills and discipline so that she will be able to secure steady employment in the future. At one of the Puerto Rican cultural centers where I worked in Chicago, teenagers frequently told stories about parents' threatening to send them to Puerto Rico if they did not behave differently. Sixteen-year-old Mari told one of the center's counselors that her mother wanted to send her to Puerto Rico to get her away from her boyfriend, who had recently been shot by opposition gang members. The mother was afraid that Mari and her boyfriend were "too serious" and that something might happen to Mari if they continued to see each other. She thought that the only way to protect her was to get her out of Chicago. Mari, of course, did not agree, but teenagers generally have little power to convince their parents otherwise.

For young men, urban danger takes the form of gang violence, discrimination, and problems with local police. As for young women, migration is frequently seen as a parental strategy to protect young men. Again, those sent to live in Puerto Rico frequently report that these strategies are ineffective. Fifteen-year-old twins were taken out of G.E.D. classes at the center, for example, to live with their grandmother in Puerto Rico because of their involvement with gangs. They eventually returned, they told me, because they continued to get into trouble in Puerto Rico. Celia, a second-generation migrant, explained that, while gangs are certainly a problem, problems with the police were a bigger problem and a greater source of danger for her son. "There's a lot of police discrimination here, a lot," she told me. Not only did the police stop her son and other young Latinos for little or no reason, but also responded much more slowly or failed to respond at all to complaints by "Spanish" people. "When Spanish [people] have problems with Spanish, [the police] don't care. But if a Spanish [person] would have a problem with a white person, they would go and get that Spanish or that black person wherever they're at. And that's how these police are. They don't like Spanish people *for nothing.*" She feels that her son is in constant danger of being stopped, harassed, questioned, and possibly physically harmed by a police force that discriminates against and mistreats poor and working-class Latino residents in Humboldt Park.[10]

Finally, the danger of not finishing one's education prompts many parents to send children to finish school in Puerto Rico because they believe their children will have a better chance to finish there than in Chicago public schools. One counselor at a local community organization told me that his father, a factory worker, had made sure to send him to school in Puerto Rico so that he would finish. After doing so and then serving in the armed forces, he had returned to Chicago to work as a high-school counselor. Nélida, a first-generation migrant, echoed this concern. After her daughter was attacked by a group of girls at a local high school, she immediately set in motion plans to send her back to Puerto Rico. Her daughter protested, saying that she wanted to finish high school in Chicago, and ultimately was able to convince her mother that it was better for her to stay in Chicago than to risk being held back by transferring to a school in Puerto Rico. Her mother reluctantly agreed but continued to express her doubts about the safety of Chicago public schools.

Clearly, not all parents are able to send—nor do they always send—troubled or endangered children to live with relatives in Puerto Rico. What is important is that migration is imagined as a possible solution to problems with children and Puerto Rico as a place that is fundamentally different from Chicago. Moreover, it is usually mothers who are engaged in this kind of emotional work, drawing on kin networks in Puerto Rico that they have maintained and nurtured over time. In most cases, these women—both first- and second-generation migrants—had engaged in similar transnational household strategies when they were younger. Some had been sent to Chicago to help relatives with childcare or to look for employment; others were sent to Puerto Rico because of real and imagined urban dangers. Migration is believed to be an effective way to protect children and to increase the possibility of a better life; in this way, migration understandably becomes part of a strategic repertoire for dealing with family problems. This idea is predicated on both the ways in which Puerto Rico is imagined by parents and particular understandings of the realities of life in Chicago. According to a recent report by the University of Illinois, Chicago, more than half of Humboldt Park residents over the age of eighteen lack high-school diplomas (*Extra,* September 18, 1996). Moreover, G.E.D. students at the center frequently report that problems with gangs and teen pregnancy are the greatest problems they face and one of the principal reasons they and their friends did not finish school. In sharp contrast, Puerto Rico is imagined as an utterly different world. As one young woman explained to me, "It's a better place for you to live . . . [you don't] worry about coming back home or the curfew [or] police, you know . . . it's peaceful."

While this kind of romanticization of "homeland" and patria is not necessarily new, it is important to recognize that the idea of Puerto Rico as significantly better than Chicago is, frequently, only imagined to be true. One informant told me a number of times how dangerous Puerto Rico is today. "If you're driving your car at night and the light turns red, in Puerto Rico," he told me, "you stop to look but then keep on going because of all the car-jackings going on over there." The prevailing idea of Puerto Rico as safe (because it is usually imagined as rural) and Chicago as dangerous creates a situation in which migration is a plausible solution for problems with children. In this way, migration is neither disruptive nor indicative of a lack of commitment to life on the mainland as many researchers would like us to believe (see Tienda and Diaz, 1987). Instead, it reflects a sincere concern about the effects of deindustrialization and federal neglect of inner-city schools and neighborhoods since the 1960s, which disproportionately affect poor Puerto Rican youth.

FOLK AND URBAN COMMUNITIES AND CULTURAL AUTHENTICITY

Finally, urban communities are imagined as culturally "inauthentic" places where an inferior or "Americanized" Puerto Rican culture thrives. One thirty-year-old woman, for example, is always quick to point out who is *really* Puerto Rican and the different ways in which she does not exactly fit the "authentic Puerto Rican" profile. "My husband's cousin," she told me, "she talks to you like a Puerto Rican. She doesn't got no accent, you know. . . . *no me crié asi* [I wasn't raised] with the whole Puerto Rican culture. . . . I was raised with the American, an American—I'm an *Americanized* Puerto Rican." When I asked her what she meant by this, she replied, "Well, I'm of Puerto Rican descent, but I'm with the American culture more. You know, I guess, my Spanish ain't as great—as yours is, you know." (I am completely shocked by this since I myself engage in this I'm-not-really-authentically-Puerto Rican insecurity as well). My friend's assessment of what constitutes "authentic" Puerto Rican culture and identity is largely a matter of the ability to speak Spanish "correctly." Her analysis of what is culturally authentic is a piece of linguistic ideology that takes for granted that *a* language corresponds to *a* culture; "Spanish is equated with Puerto Rican values and English with American values in ways that objectify both language and culture" (Urciuoli, 1996: 5).

What is interesting, however, is that speaking Spanish well is not sufficient. For Aida, her children need to know how to speak *Puerto Rican* Spanish and to know *Puerto Rican* culture and food. She said that she tells her daughter that she is "being raised in the Puerto Rican culture. So, that's what you are. A Puerto Rican. . . . [Your cousin] is being raised with the Mexican culture. . . . He eats his tacos and his tortillas and all that. What do you eat? . . . You don't eat *pozole*. He does. *Tú comes sancocho.* You know. He eats tamales, you eat pasteles." Aida went on to say that going to Puerto Rico is a way to affirm her own—and her children's—cultural roots through knowledge of Puerto Rican history, language, culture and food. She wants to send her children to Puerto Rico so that they can see *"que lindo es . . . como son la gente . . . las costumbres. . . .* I want [my kids] to know that they're Puerto Rican. We're not American-Americans. . . . [And that's important because], you know, *los puertorriqueños* is disappearing here in Chicago. It's becoming more of a Mexican place. Everywhere you go now, it's like, Mexican restaurants, Mexican owners and stores, you know. I don't see the Puerto Rican that much anymore."

Puerto Rico, therefore, is imagined as culturally pure, pristine and authentic. Chicago, in contrast, with all of its ethnic others, is a place of cultural ambiguity and uncertainty. Migration is frequently seen as a way to affirm the cultural integrity of *puertorriqueñidad* that many feel is threatened by Americanization and by the "Mexicanization" of the city.[11] When migration is not possible, Puerto Rican cultural centers and community organizations are seen as places of "true" cultural knowledge and information. One Puerto Rican woman in her mid-thirties, for example, went to the cultural center where I worked to find out what the national flower of Puerto Rico was. I didn't have this information, but when my coworker told her it was the *amapola* the woman smiled and said, *"Yo pensé lo mismo. Pero no lo es. Es otra flor"* (That's what I thought it was too. But it's not. It's actually another flower.) As we looked through books to find the *real* national flower of Puerto Rico, the women confessed, hesitantly, that she was relieved that neither one of us knew what the national flower of Puerto Rico was. If we who worked in Puerto Rican cultural center didn't know the name of the flower, she told us, it was OK that she didn't know either. She told us that she needed this information for her daughter, who was participating in the Miss Puerto Rico contest for the Puerto Rican Day Parade. *"Yo la metí en el concurso porque me estoy dando cuento de que ella se está perdiendo su cultura, y eso me asusta"* (I got her into the contest because I am realizing that she is losing her culture, and that scares me.) Getting her children involved in activities that involved Puerto Rican culture was important so that she would not become "too American."

Fears of being too American or not knowing Puerto Rican Spanish and culture are not exclusive to Puerto Ricans in Chicago. Concerns about language, education, and culture have existed in Puerto Rico since the U.S. occupation of the island in 1898 and the attempt to Americanize the native population not only in Puerto Rico but in the Philippines and in Cuba as well. Cultural life in Chicago, however, is significantly different, according to some, in that the city's large Mexican and African American population poses a threat to Puerto Rican cultural integrity. Many of my informants have explained that the Puerto Rican flags on Division Street are not only a sign of *orgullo boricua* but also a cultural response to what they perceive to be the Mexicanization of Chicago.[12] Such beliefs challenge Padilla's (1987) analysis of "Latinismo," a pan-ethnic formation created by Puerto Rican and Mexican community leaders, and underscore the persistence of national identities, particularly in the context of economic uncertainty and competition over scarce resources such as affordable housing, urban space, and secure employment. While nonprofit organizations such as the Latino Institute and other pan-ethnic organizations attempt to forge a Latina/o identity in order to address shared problems, this coalition building is frequently strained and smoothes over internal conflict. These different understandings of a Latina/o versus a national identity also belie important class-based cleavages among Puerto Ricans in Chicago—white-collar professionals versus working class and poor—that map onto political positions with regard to Puerto Rico's political status. As Ana Yolanda Ramos-Zayas points out, "'Puerto Ricanness'—the nationalist idea of a Puerto Rican (not Latino) identity" is an important mobilization tool in local political struggles (1997: 152). This Puerto Ricanness is also fundamental to working-class Puerto Ricans' perceptions of their own cultural identity and integrity vis-à-vis ethnic others in the city .

Not surprisingly, women engage in the cultural work necessary to promote and teach "authentic" Puerto Rican culture to their children. As staff members in community organizations, Puerto Rican women are also engaged in cultural work on the community level. Women's cultural work in households is central to the construction and understanding of "cultural tradition," and, as di Leonardo (1984: 228) argues, children and other family members lay claim to a particular cultural and ethnic identity through women's work.[13] Puerto Rican families in Chicago do this, in large part, through migration and women's "kin work" in the construction, maintenance, and reproduction of transnational household ties.[14] Women, for example, often bring sick relatives to live with them in Chicago and serve as liaisons between their kin and government agencies as they file documents, meet with social workers, and secure the necessary social services. When this is not possible, mothers send their daughters or other female family members to Puerto Rico to attend to sick relatives. Women engage in this work not only for their own families, but for their husband's extended-kin networks as well, and, as di Leonardo points out, this work is unremunerated, often overlooked, and largely culturally assigned to women (1984: 257). For Puerto Ricans in Chicago, the kin work involved in migration is crucial because it reaffirms and maintains kin networks—both actual and imaginary—between Chicago and Puerto Rico. It is also a way for Chicago Puerto Ricans to assert cultural identity and authenticity in an urban context that they believe threatens Puerto Rican cultural integrity; and, like the folkloric notions of "authentic" Puerto Rican culture that line Paseo Boricua, kin work is a deeply gendered phenomenon that is linked to shifts in the global and local economy in which it is embedded.

CONCLUSION

Both the jíbaro casita and Puerto Rican Barbie demonstrate the ways in which notions of the "folk," that which is culturally authentic, are inflected with class, race, and gender ideologies. For *puertorriqueños* in Chicago, the casita is "a metaphor of home that is both the domestic dwelling space and the national homeland" (Sciorra, 1996: 77). Images such as *casa, hogar,* home place are part of gendered systems of meanings of space and place which typically (and problematically) link woman with home/place and men with time/space (Massey, 1994: 9). One of my male informants, for example, explained that going to Puerto Rico is like "going home": "Going back to Puerto Rico is like going back to your mom, I think. . . . *La tierra's* always perceived as woman, as a female. And going back there is like, you know, that's where your mom is from." Similarly, situating the jíbara/o, Puerto Rico's white, highland agricultural laborer, as authentically Puerto Rican promotes a particular representation of national identity that excludes the blacks and mestizos on the coasts and in the cities and erases a long history of racial mixing (Dávila, 1997: 69–73; Sciorra, 1996: 77).

The jíbaro as a national symbol, however, is an historically specific construct. The original meaning of *jíbaro* in Spanish is "wild," and it was used to refer to the descendants of African slaves, Taino Indians, and European and Moor stowaways who refused to work on Spanish sugar plantations in the eighteenth and nineteenth centuries and settled, instead, in the highlands of Puerto Rico (Bourgois, 1995: 50). Throughout the twentieth century, the jíbaro has been used as a patriotic symbol by political parties in Puerto Rico to promote everything from accommodationist to anti-imperialist politics both on the island and on the mainland (Dávila, 1997; Sciorra 1996: 77).[15] It is also used to suggest that someone is "backward," "naïve," or "innocent." The meanings attached to the jíbaro and to rural communities, then, have changed over time and are informed in large part by political and economic shifts in Puerto Rico and on the mainland. Similarly, the way in which urban communities are imagined and understood is an historically specific construct that is embedded in changing political-economic contexts in Chicago and in Puerto Rico. Moreover, local-level race and ethnic politics influence the way in which urban life and Puerto Rican migrant communities are imagined both by migrants themselves and by the larger society.

For many working-class Puerto Ricans in Chicago, life on the mainland is *dura y peligrosa* (hard and dangerous). These images and understandings of urban life are often discussed in relation to *una vida tranquila en Puerto Rico* (a peaceful life in Puerto Rico) that is imagined as rural and pure. These rural and urban imagined communities, however, should not be understood simply as polar opposites. Rather, they are cultural categories for understanding Puerto Rican history and contemporary urban life produced in a context of colonialism and growing immiseration on the island and the mainland (see Hobsbawm and Ranger, 1983; Roseberry and O'Brien, 1991). The casita jíbara on Division Street is therefore not only a culturally significant object that nostalgically invokes a rural and "authentic" Puerto Rican community but also a politicized cultural symbol used to resist gentrification and to call attention to the effects of economic restructuring. In other words, it is as urban as Chicago's Sears Tower.

NOTES

The author thanks the *Latin American Pespectives'* reviewers for their helpful comments. She is especially grateful to Micaela di Leonardo and Baron Pineda for their comments and suggestions on earlier drafts and their support while conducting fieldwork in Chicago and San Sebastian, Puerto Rico.

1. All names in this chapter are pseudonyms.

2. Paseo Boricua is the part of Division Street that lies between two fifty-ton Puerto Rican flags extending across the street that were erected in 1994.

3. It is also no coincidence that Chicago is one of Mattel's markets for Latina Barbies. According to the Latino Institute (1994), one in four Chicagoans and one in ten Illinois residents will be Latina/o by the year 2000. This is a very large and young consumer market.

4. See Tienda and Jensen (1988) and Chavez (1991) for a discussion of the cause of persistent poverty among Puerto Ricans on the mainland and Wilson (1987) for a definition and explanation of underclass and "underclass behavior." Ortiz (1993; 1996) and Rodríguez (1993) provide an important critique and response to culturalist explanations for Puerto Rican poverty and the relationship among gender, poverty, and migration.

5. Promoting migration as a way to address Puerto Rico's alleged overpopulation problem has a long history beginning with the U.S. occupation of the island in 1898, but it was the Chardón Report in 1934 that formally enshrined mass migration as a policy strategy. See Puerto Rico Policy Commission (1934) for the report in full; see also Pantojas-García (1990: 36-60) and Stinson-Fernández (1996: 121-126) for more on the Chardón Plan and its implications for industrial development in Puerto Rico.

6. Maldonado cites correspondence between Donald J. O'Connor of the U.S. Department of the Interior and Puerto Rico's commissionor of labor, Manuel A. Pérez, in which the issue of women and Puerto Rico's demographic problem is addressed. According to Maldonado, O'Connor believed "that the Puerto Rican government should encourage migration for young women of childbearing age. These women would need to be helped financially because they would have less opportunity to save money to come to the mainland. Political repercussions, he felt, could be lessened if the demographic effect of female emigration was made clear in the privacy of executive session" (1979: 105). In the late 1940s, Antonio Fernos-Iserns, resident commissioner in Washington, made a cogent argument for the need to promote migration while maintaining economic links to migrants abroad: "It may come to be an added source of income for [Puerto Rico] if the proper economic relations are maintained between the Island and the emigrants in their new settlement" (quoted in Lapp, 1990: 42).

7. A notable exception is Maura Toro-Morn's important work on gender, class, and Puerto Rican migration to Chicago (1993; 1995).

8. My dissertation research also reveals that the Migration Division of Puerto Rico's Department of Labor was key in manufacturing and disseminating an image of Chicago Puerto Ricans as distinct from and more amenable to assimilation than New York Puerto Ricans. The construction of the easily assimilable Chicago Puerto Rican was the cornerstone of a public relations campaign beginning in the early 1950s aimed at facilitating the relocation of New York Puerto Ricans to Chicago and the redirection of the migrant flow from the island to places outside of New York City.

9. The most recent example of this bias in the English-language print media and television has been the ongoing controversy at Clemente Community Academy, a high school located on the eastern edge of Paseo Boricua and an important community space for Puerto Rican residents of Humboldt Park and West Town. In February 1997 the *Chicago Sun-Times* reported that Puerto Rican terrorists had used Title I poverty funds for promoting political activities in pursuit of Puerto Rico's independence from the United States. See *Chicago Sun-Times* (February 4, 1997) for early media coverage on the Clemente political scandal; see also Ramos-Zayas (1997: 380-384) for a discussion of the scandal and community reaction to it.

10. Police brutality against young Latino and black men in Chicago is a serious community issue. This is particularly the case in the gentrifying areas of West Town and the eastern border of Humboldt Park, where young Puerto Rican men complain of being policed excessively to make the neighborhood safe for "yuppies" moving into the area. Community activism with regard to police brutality was galvanized most recently around the death of Jorge Guillen, a Honduran immigrant who died while in police custody. Chicago's extremely controversial antiloitering ordinance is another example of the problem.

11. According to the Latino Institute (1995), by 1990 almost three hundred and fifty thousand Mexicans and one hundred and twenty thousand Puerto Ricans lived in Chicago. A number of my informants talk at length about the Mexicanization of Chicago and admit that they make racist comments about Mexicans. This, of course, places me in an uncomfortable position both academically and politically. No one likes to think that the community with which one works contributes to racist structures in our society. One point, however, is clear: My informants are responding to real effects of deindustrialization in Chicago—economic displacement, growing immiseration, the decline of real wages, and intense competition for adequate housing and a dwindling number of well-paying jobs. This is not to suggest that their racism is acceptable or that it can be excused. Rather, it is important to contextualize these comments to see how economic insecurity and competitition for scarce resources are inextricably linked to racist beliefs and practices.

12. The Division Street flags are multivalent symbols of national pride. Created in commemoration of the centennial of the Puerto Rican flag in 1995, they represent an important nationalist symbol of Puerto Rican independence in the context of deeply local struggles against uneven urban development, gentrification, and the negative consequences of growth politics. In Humboldt Park, Puerto Rican community activists deploy these national symbols in local political struggles. Community residents' responses, however, are more complicated, ranging from ethnic pride in demarcating a Puerto Rican cultural space to extreme skepticism of the flags and their proindependence meaning. Frequently these differing perceptions fall along class and po-

litical lines vis-à-vis Puerto Rico's political status (middle-class and professional Puerto Ricans who support statehood or Commonwealth status being more suspicious of these nationalist symbols). But even some *independentista* activists with whom I spoke expressed concern for what they believe to be a dangerous culturalist strain of Puerto Rican nationalism.

13. In her work on Italian Americans in Northern California, di Leonardo demonstrates the different ways in which ethnic identity is frequently predicated on women's work: "preparing spcial foods, planning rituals, and enforcing 'ethnic' socialization of children" (1984: 222). See di Leonardo (1984: 191-229) for a more extensive discussion of gender, ethnicity, and ideology.

14. By kin work I refer to what Micaela di Leonardo describes as "the conception, maintenance, and ritual celebration of cross-household kin ties" (1992: 48). See also Alicea (1997).

15. The most recent example of this is the Partido Nuevo Progresista's use of the jíbaro in promoting *la estadida jíbara* throughout the congressional debates surrounding the Young bill in May 1997 and renewed efforts to promote Puerto Rican statehood. According to this logic, statehood would bring the economic, social, and political benefits of being a full-fledged member of the United States while maintaining Puerto Rico's cultural and linguistic integrity.

REFERENCES

Alicea, Marixsa. 1997. "'A Chambered Nautilus': The Contradictory Nature of Puerto Rican Women's Role in the Social Construction of a Transnational Community." *Gender and Society* 11: 597–626.

Aponte-Pares, Luiz. 1997. "Casitas, Place and Culture: Appropriating Place in Puerto Rican Barrios." *Places II* (I): 52–61.

Appadurai, Arjun. 1990. "Disjuncture and Difference in the Global Cultural Economy." *Public Culture* 2: 1–24.

———. 1991. "Global Ethnoscapes: Notes and Queries for a Transnational Anthropology," pp. 191–210 in Richard G. Fox (ed.), *Recapturing Anthropology: Working in the Present*. Santa Fe, NM: School of American Research Press.

———. 1993. "Patriotism and Its Futures." *Public Culture* (4): 411–29.

Basch, Linda, Nina Glick Schiller and Cristina Szanton-Blanc (eds.). 1994. *Nations Unbound: Transnational Projects and the Deterritorialized Nation-State*. New York: Gordon and Breach.

Boris, Eileen. 1996. "Needlewomen Under the New Deal in Puerto Rico, 1920–1945," pp. 33–54 in Altagracia Ortiz (ed.), *Puerto Rican Women and Work: Bridges in Transnational Labor*. Philadelphia: Temple University Press.

Bourgois, Philippe. 1995. *In Search of Respect: Selling Crack in El Barrio*. Cambridge University Press.

Bretell, Caroline. 1987. *Men Who Migrate, Women Who Wait: The Demographic History of a Portuguese Parish*. Princeton, NJ: Princeton University Press.

Charles, Carolle. 1995. "Gender and Politics in Contemporary Haiti: The Duvalierist State, Transnationalism, and the Emergence of a New Feminism (1980–1990)." *Feminist Studies* 21: 135–64.

Chatterjee, Partha. 1989. "Colonialism, Nationalism and Colonized Women: The Contest in India." *American Ethnologist* 16(4): 622–33.

Chavez, Linda. 1991. *Out of the Barrio: Toward a New Politics of Hispanic Assimilation.* New York: Harper Collins.

Colen, Shellee. 1995. "'Like a Mother to Them': Stratified Reproduction and West Indian Childcare Workers and Employers in New York," pp. 78–102 in Faye D. Ginsburg and Rayna Rapp (eds.), *Conceiving the New World Order: The Global Politics of Reproduction.* Berkeley: University of California Press.

Dávila, Arlene. 1997. *Sponsored Identities: Cultural Politics in Puerto Rico.* Philadelphia: Temple University Press.

di Leonardo, Micaela. 1984. *The Varieties of Ethnic Experience: Kinship, Class and Gender Among California Italian-Americans.* Ithaca, NY: Cornell University Press.

———. 1992. "The Female World of Cards and Holidays: Women, Families and the Work of Kinship," pp. 246–62 in Barrie Thorne with Marilyn Yalom (eds.), *Rethinking the Family: Some Feminist Questions.* Boston: Northeastern University Press.

———. 1998. *Exotics at Home: Anthropologies, Others, and American Modernity.* Chicago: University of Chicago Press.

Diner, Hasia. 1983. *Erin's Daughters in America.* Baltimore: Johns Hopkins University Press.

Ferguson, James. 1992. "The Country and the City on the Copperbelt." *Cultural Anthropology* 7: 80–92.

Foner, Nancy. 1978. *Jamaica Farewell: Jamaican Migrants in London.* Berkeley: University of California Press.

Gabaccia, Donna. 1994. *From the Other Side: Women, Gender, and Immigrant Life in the U.S., 1820–1990.* Bloomington: Indiana University Press.

Georges, Eugenia. 1992. "Gender, Class and Migration in the Dominican Republic: Women's Experiences in a Transnational Community," pp. 81–100 in Nina Glick Schiller, Linda Basch, and Cristina Szanton-Blanc (eds.), *Towards a Transnational Perspective on Migration, Race, Class, Ethnicity, and Nationalism Reconsidered.* New York: New York Academy of Sciences.

Glenn, Evelyn Nakano. 1986. *Issei, Nisei, Warbride.* Philadelphia: Temple University Press.

Glick Schiller, Nina, Linda Basch, and Cristina Szanton Blanc. 1995. "From Immigrant to Transmigrant: Theorizing Transnational Migration." *Anthropological Quarterly* 68: 48–63.

Glick Schiller, Nina, Linda Basch, and Cristina Szanton Blanc, (eds.). 1992. *Towards a Transnational Perspective on Migration, Race Class, Ethnicity and Nationalism Reconsidered.* New York: New York Academy of Sciences.

Grasmuck, Sherri and Patricia Pessar. 1991. *Between Two Islands: Dominican International Migration.* Berkeley: University of California Press.

Hayden, D. 1995. *The Power of Place.* Cambridge, MA: MIT Press.

Hannerz, Ulf. 1980. *Exploring the City: Inquiries Toward an Urban Anthropology.* New York: Columbia University Press.

History Task Force. 1979. *Labor Migration Under Capitalism: The Puerto Rican Experience.* New York: Monthly Review Press.

Hobsbawm, Eric and Terence Ranger. 1983. *The Invention of Tradition.* New York: Cambridge University Press.

Hondagneu-Sotelo, Pierrette and Ernestine Avila. 1997. "'I'm Here, But I'm There': The Meanings of Latina Transnational Motherhood." *Gender and Society* 11: 548–71.

Houston, Marion F., Roger G. Kramer and Joan Mackin Barrett. 1984. "Female Predominance in Immigration to the United States since 1930: A First Look." *International Migration Review* 18: 908–63.

Lapp, Michael. 1990. *"Managing Migration: The Migration Division of Puerto Rico and Puerto Ricans in New York City, 1948–1968."* Ph.D. diss., Johns Hopkins University.

Latino Institute. 1994. *"A profile of nine Latino groups in Chicago."* Chicago.

———. 1995. *"Facts on Chicago's Puerto Rican population."* Chicago.

Lewis, Oscar. 1966. *La Vida: A Puerto Rican Family in the Culture of Poverty—San Juan and New York*. New York: Random House.

Low, Setha. 1996. "The Anthropology of Cities: Imagining and Theorizing the City." *Annual Review of Anthropology* 25: 383–409.

Maldonado, Edwin. 1979. "Contract Labor and the Origin of Puerto Rican Communities in the United States." *International Migration Review* 13: 103–21.

Massey, Doreen. 1994. *Space, Place, and Gender*. Minneapolis: University of Minnesota Press.

Meléndez, Edwin and Edgardo Meléndez. 1993. *Colonial Dilemma: Critical Perspectives on Contemporary Puerto Rico*. Boston: South End Press.

Morokvasic, Mirjana. 1984. "Birds of Passage Are Also Women . . ." *International Migration Review* 18: 886–907.

Ortiz, Vilma. 1993. "Circular Migration and Employment Among Puerto Rican Women." *Latino Studies Journal* 4(2): 56–70.

———. 1996. "Migration and Marriage Among Puerto Rican Women." *International Migration Review* 30: 460–84.

Padilla, Elena. 1947. *Puerto Rican Immigrants in New York and Chicago: A Study in Comparative Assimilation*. M.A. thesis, Department of Anthropology, University of Chicago, Chicago

Padilla, Felix. 1987. *Puerto Rican Chicago*. Notre Dame, IN: University of Notre Dame Press.

Pantojas-García, Emilio. 1990. *Development Strategies as Ideology: Puerto Rico's Export-Led Industrialization Experience*. Boulder and London: Lynne Rienner.

Pedraza, Sylvia. 1990. "Immigration Research: A Conceptual Map." *Social Science History* 14: 43–67.

———. 1991. "Women and Migration: The Social Consequences of Gender." *Annual Review of Sociology* 17: 303–25.

Pessar, Patricia. 1982. "The Role of Households in International Migration: The Case of U.S.–Bound Migrants from the Dominican Republic." *International Migration Review* 16: 342–62.

———. 1986. "The Role of Gender in Dominican Settlement in the United States," pp. 273–94 in J. Nash and H. Safa (eds.), *Women and Change in Latin America*. South Hadley, MA: Bergin and Garvey.

Puerto Rico Policy Commission. 1934. *Report of the Puerto Rico Policy Commission*. San Juan, PR.

Ramos-Zayas, Ana Yolanda. 1997. "La patria es valor y sacrificio: Nationalist Ideologies, Cultural Authenticity, and Community Building among Puerto Ricans in Chicago." Ph.D. diss., Columbia University.

Rodriguez, Clara. 1991. *Puerto Ricans: Born in the U.S.A.* Boulder, CO: Westview Press.

———. 1993. "Puerto Rican Circular Migration." *Latino Studies Journal* 4(2): 93–113.

Roseberry, William and Jay O'Brien. 1991. *Golden Ages, Dark Ages: Imagining the Past in Anthropology and History.* Berkeley: University of California Press.

Rouse, Roger. 1991. "Mexican Migration and the Social Space of Postmodernism." *Diaspora* (1): 8–23.

———. 1992. "Making Sense of Settlement: Class Transformation, Cultural Struggle, and Transnationalism Among Mexican Migrants in the United States," pp. 25–52 in Nina Glick Schiller, Linda Basch, and Cristina Szanton-Blanc (eds.), *Towards a Transnational Perspective on Migration, Race, Class, Ethnicity, and Nationalism Reconsidered.* New York: New York Academy of Sciences.

Safa, Helen. 1990. "Women and Industrialization in the Caribbean," pp. 72–97 in Sharon Stichter and Jane L. Parpart (eds.), *Women, Employment, and the Family and the International Division of Labor.* London: Macmillan.

———. 1995. *The Myth of the Male Breadwinner: Women and Industrialization in the Caribbean.* Boulder, CO: Westview Press.

Sciorra, Joseph. 1996. "Return to the Future: Puerto Rican Vernacular Architecture in New York City," pp. 60–92 in Anthony King (ed.), *Re-presenting the City: Ethnicity, Capital, and Culture in the 21st-Century Metropolis.* New York: New York University Press.

Spain, D. 1992. *Gendered Spaces.* Chapel Hill: University of North Carolina Press.

Stinson-Fernández, John. 1996. "Hacia una antropología de la emigración planificada: El Negociado de Empleo y Migración y el caso de Filadelfia." *Revista de Ciencias Sociales* (1): 112–54.

Sutton, Constance R. 1992. "Some Thoughts on Gendering and Internationalizing Our Thinking About Transnational Migrations." *Annals of the New York Academy of Sciences* 645: 241–50.

Tienda, Marta and William Diaz. 1987. "Puerto Ricans' Special Problems." *New York Times* (August 28).

Toro-Morn, Maura. 1993. "Class and Gender Dimensions of Puerto Rican Migration to Chicago." Ph.D. diss., Loyola University, Chicago.

———. 1995. "Gender, Class, Family and Migration: Puerto Rican Women in Chicago." *Gender and Society* 9: 712–26.

Urciuoli, Bonnie. 1996. *Exposing Prejudice: Puerto Rican Experiences of Language, Race, and Class.* Oxford: Westview Press.

Williams, Raymond. 1973. *The Country and the City.* New York: Oxford University Press.

Wilson, Elizabeth. 1991. *Sphinx in the City: Urban Life, the Control of Disorder, and Women.* Berkeley: University of California Press.

Wilson, William J. 1987. *The Truly Disadvantaged: The Inner City, the Underclass, and Public Policy.* Chicago: University of Chicago Press.

Zukin, Sharon. 1991. *Landscapes of Power: From Detroit to Disney World.* Berkeley: University of California Press.

III

TRANSFORMING WORK, LABOR, COMMUNITY, AND CITIZENSHIP

One of the principal hallmarks of globalization during the past twenty years has been the shrinking manufacturing base and the concomitant growth in service and light industrial work. These changes not only reflect a shift in domestic consumer tastes but are a prominent outcome of trade agreements such as NAFTA and a host of policy adjustments aimed at reducing the size of government and increasing the efficiency of multinational corporations. While these adjustments have introduced unprecedented wealth to certain segments of the United States and Latin America and a surge in employment, they have also exacerbated enduring stratifications in the region.

It is this shifting labor context that serves as the centerpiece of the chapters in this section. Zamudio examines the work of the Hotel Employees' and Restaurant Employees' Union in organizing service workers in the New Otani Hotel in downtown Los Angeles. The results of her study challenge traditional labor theory and strategies and highlight the complex interethnic and interracial schisms and alliances that have become common in the various centers of Latina/o labor.

Palerm moves the discussion of these changing labor structures to more rural environments, discussing the impact of shifts in agricultural production from cattle, milk, and citrus to specialty products such as strawberries and grapes and the intensification of labor that accompanies this shift. His examination of the new labor patterns provides us with insights into the changes in migration and a typology of the migrant communities working in the fields.

Zavella artfully bridges the gap between the urban and rural regions explored in the previous two selections by following a major manufacturing company in California as it leaves the largely Mexican community that has been its home base for more than twenty years and relocates to a small community in

Mexico. Zavella's research proves to be a pivotal contribution both for its application of a processual approach and for the wealth of detailed ethnographic information it provides regarding the plant's relocation—a phenomenon that has become all too frequent in working-class communities across the country. Ultimately, this chapter goes a long way toward enhancing the methodological possibilities for studying Latina/o communities and demonstrating how seemingly disparate populations have been reconfigured and woven together in the age of globalization.

The shifts in occupation and opportunities described here alter both our understanding of labor and our view of the relationship between states and citizens. In the same way that globalization has transformed the shape of our national economy, the scaling down of traditional state functions (particularly as they relate to regulation of the economy) has transformed the way in which we operate as a nation and who is included within the bounds of citizenship. Thus, in the final selection of this section, Rocco examines theories of civil society that promote new explorations of citizenship and reframes the discourse of contemporary political participation. Central to his discussion is the argument that, while class and the distribution of capital are still fundamental to our understandings of globalization, current political and social theorists have not appreciated the fact that the nature of class itself has been altered and have subsequently undervalued issues such as immigration and ethnicity in their analysis of globalization. Rocco turns to a case study of Latina/o associational organizations in Southeast Los Angeles as a means to build new theories around the experiences of citizenship practices of emerging Latina/o communities.

What makes these contributions notable is that they all draw upon experientially based fieldwork, with the result that their "thick description" of events, persons, and processes constrains and stimulates their analyses. They have a basic analytical honesty and modesty that emerges from the ethnographic processes that have produced them. Ethnography forces us to recognize the awful responsibility each of us has to the people with whom we work. These chapters express differing versions of this dynamic.

Each contribution provides important examples of the megascripts imposed on Latina/os over time: poorly paid "service" workers in Los Angeles, the "natural" movement of transnational capital regardless of the cost to localities, the wholesale exploitation of agricultural workers as low paid labor regardless of return on investments, and the national definitions of "citizenship." These scripts are little debated and become an accepted part of "progress" and development. At the same time, each of the examples in this section illustrates the ways in which new scripts may transform unwelcome and unwelcoming environments without benefit of institutional or national support. Indeed, it is at the most grounded level that transnational processes can best be understood—without physical borders, without theoretical borders, and mostly without the borders of the mind that we inherit as "normal" or "common sense."

8

Segmentation, Conflict, Community, and Coalitions: Lessons from the New Labor Movement

Margaret Zamudio

Organizing immigrant Latina/o workers concentrated in the segmented labor markets of the secondary sector in a global economy is central to the success of democratic unionism. While in the past unions have contributed to the relegation of immigrant Latina/o workers to the lowest rungs of the economy, the emergence of a new labor movement promises to empower workers traditionally treated with contempt. Three decades of union decline to some extent reflect the fact that unions historically colluded with employers in need of a pool of vulnerable workers for the unstable and seasonal segment of the secondary sector in exchange for maintaining the dominance of native white workers in the primary sector (Laslett and Tyler, 1989; Quadagno, 1994). The lack of an organized base in the secondary sector has been particularly devastating to organized labor given the huge growth in service-sector jobs. According to Cobble (1996), 90 percent of the new jobs created in the past decade are located in the service sector. As in the past, immigrants and women continue to be overrepresented in the competitive, unorganized sector of the service economy. Wilson (1996: 32) suggests that the 15 percent growth in jobs in Los Angeles obtained by those with less than a high-school education, for example, "reflects the large immigration of Hispanic and other minorities." He reports that the increased labor participation of low-skilled women reflects the growth of entry-level service jobs. Thus, today more than ever, the success or failure of organized labor rests on the ability of unions to organize women and immigrants in the service sector.

In order to assess the viability of unionism in this until recently ignored sector of the economy, this study will focus on the labor activity of immigrant Latina/o workers at the New Otani Hotel and Gardens in the Little Tokyo area of Los Angeles, California. The expansion of the hotel industry in general and the activity at the New Otani Hotel in particular reflect the dramatic industrial and demographic changes taking place in major global centers. To the extent that the New Otani case captures some of these general trends, this study is strategically situated to illuminate how labor confronts these new challenges and provides us hints on whether these new players on a new terrain can make a difference for the future of the working class.

The New Otani workers represent the major structural transformations that have taken place with respect to industrial and demographic changes. In contrast to the traditional focus on organizing white industrial workers in the primary sector, today's unions depend for their survival on an ability to organize in industries previously neglected—service industries concentrated in the secondary sector. In Los Angeles and other cities featuring large-scale immigration, the focus of the unions' organizing efforts must be Latina/o immigrants if unionism is to be a viable option for working-class organization. Responding to changed conditions in the working class, Local 11 of the Hotel Employees' Restaurant Employees' International Union (HERE) represents another major transformation in the terms and conditions of the class struggle. Local 11, with María Elena Durazo at the helm, represents a departure from old-guard conservatism and often racist, sexist, and nativist unionism and a return to grassroots organizing. This new brand of union activism has revitalized the labor movement and propelled insurgent activists like Durazo to the head of Local 11 and John Sweeney to the presidency of the American Federation of Labor–Congress of Industrial Organizations (AFL-CIO). In sum, as Sweeney points out in a recent *Los Angeles Times* (February 5, 1996) article, these changes render the New Otani campaign "one of the most important efforts to organize low-wage workers in Southern California today, as well as one of the highest-profile current organizing campaigns in the United States."

This chapter examines the case of the New Otani Hotel where for the past few years Local 11 and the working-class leadership in the hotel have been unionizing workers and struggling for a union contract. Their struggle has gained the support of the majority of workers in the hotel and has resulted in an international boycott of the New Otani. The labor activity and the social composition of the New Otani workforce make this a prime case for examining the relationship between organized labor and immigrant Latina/o workers in a historical moment in which the globalization of the economy has made these workers major players in the class struggle. Three questions may be useful for evaluating the potential for a new labor movement that is grassroots, antiracist, antisexist, and antinativist: (1) How does the relationship between organized labor and immigrant Latina/o workers today differ from past relationships? (2) How do the present structural conditions and the globalization of the economy influence this relationship? And (3) What strategies has labor developed to overcome the problems of the past and to take on the conditions of the present? Examining these three questions in relation to the case of the New Otani provides insight into the new relationship between organized labor and Latina/o workers. This study suggests that, while the historical concentration of immigrant Latina/o workers in the secondary sector of the economy as a result of the nativist and racial practices of unions and employers has undermined the organization of these workers, the structure of a global economy transforms seasonal jobs into stable ones and creates the conditions for group identification and working-class solidarity. In addition, the flow of immigrants with political experience and the emergence of a union leadership born out of struggles for democratic unionism have created a leadership with the ability to channel ethnic and racial solidarity into working-class formation.

This study will be organized into four sections and a conclusion. The first section provides background information about the present organizing campaign and an overview of the composition of the workers. The second section establishes a historical context for the relationship between Latina/os and organized labor and describes the process of relegating Latina/o workers to the most unstable and vulnerable sector of the economy. The third section analyzes the structural and demographic transformations produced with the emergence of Los Angeles as a global city. The final section suggests the possibilities for forging a strong relationship between Latina/o workers and unions.

This study relies on two related sets of data. The first comes from a yearlong ethnographic study of Local 11's campaign to organize the New Otani Hotel, an effort that continues today. The study was conducted between February 1995 to January 1996 using participatory research methods such as attending meetings, rallies, participating in the picket, and traveling with organizers and workers as they attempted to build support for the union. During this period, interviews were conducted with hotel workers, Local 11 organizers working on the New Otani campaign, and Local 11's president, María Elena Durazo, and Local 11 staff director, Jennifer Skurnik. In order to maintain confidentiality, the names of workers who continue to work at the hotel have been changed. In addition, forty in-depth interviews with hotel employers in the Los Angeles area provide a second and complementary source of data for this project. The interviews are part of an unrelated study of the attitudes of employers toward various groups of workers including immigrant Latina/os.

THE NEW OTANI: HISTORY AND SOCIAL FEATURES

The luxury New Otani Hotel sits in the middle of Little Tokyo in downtown Los Angeles. City Hall and Parker Center, the home of the Los Angeles Police Department, are a short walk away and supply the hotel and its restaurants with a regular walk-in clientele. In January 1996, HERE, along with a long list of supporters including several elected officials, called for an international boycott against the hotel. Within three weeks, this action seemed to be having an effect. On any given Friday during the lunch and dinner hours picket lines of about fifty workers, union organizers, and community supporters shouting boycott slogans lined the main entrances to the hotel. The workers were mostly Latina/o while the community supporters were split between Asian Americans and Latina/os, accompanied by smaller numbers of black and white supporters. When I arrived to join the multiethnic picket line during the height of the lunch hour, one of the hotel's main restaurants appeared deserted. I signed in and got my picket sign from Manuel and joined Ana, a thirty-five-year-old mother of three who had immigrated from El Salvador in 1978 and who had been fired from the hotel after working there for seventeen years.

Ana was one of three lead organizers in the hotel and was fired two years before on trumped-up charges that she had allowed another worker to punch out her time card. She is now a union organizer for Local 11 and a symbol for the New Otani struggle. A 10-by-5-foot photograph of Ana alongside two other fired women makes up one of the three panels in the "Wall of Shame" erected outside the hotel to protest its unfair labor practices. Another panel depicts Chinese slaves imprisoned during World War II by the Kajima Corporation, the Japan-based corporate owner of the New Otani. The third panel is a picture of some of the Japanese-Americans who, after a long struggle with the New Otani owners, were displaced from their low-income homes in the 1970s to make way for the construction of the hotel. Many of the community activists involved in fighting the New Otani over thirty years ago have returned to support the hotel workers.

Workers say that the best organizers are the hotel's management. In fact, Local 11 had very little to do with the formation of a core group of pro-union activists from the "back of the house" of one of Los Angeles's luxury hotels. As workers tell the story, the attempt to form a union started in 1993. Marcos, an employee in the purchasing office, was being harassed and was eventually forced out. His mother worked in housekeeping and sought the help of the union. A worker explains what occurred in those early days of the union campaign.

> They were pressuring him. When they want to get rid of you they put on the pressure. They start by increasing your work, and then they continue to criticize what you do, no matter how good of a job you're doing. They stay on top of you and don't let up. They transferred him to dishwashing from his office job and cut his hours to only two days a week. And then they gave him one day during the night shift and the other during the day. That's pressure, no?
>
> He asked me and others what he should do. His friend in Purchasing said that without a union this is going to keep happening, but we didn't know what union. My brother-in-law worked at the Hilton and was in a union, and the

monthly union letter was delivered to my address. I wrote the name of the union down and called. We went to the union and talked to someone named Patricia. She said to gather those interested but don't tell anyone else and come back. Then she gave me her card. Marcos's mom called to make an appointment. Six of us showed up. At that time we met with María Elena [the president of Local 11] and Jennifer [the chief of staff]. They told us that we had to organize. We had to talk to our *compañeros* and form a leadership committee and work hard at organizing others.

This happened three and a half years ago. We thought that just by showing up, the union would take over and the problem would be resolved. No, it doesn't work that way. It's been a difficult fight, but we're getting there. We were thinking that we were just going to tell others and that was that. They told us that it wasn't going to be easy, but if we wanted it, we could do it. They never told us anything different. They are the same people that we met that first day. María Elena asked us if we knew who the union is. She answered, "You are the union. We're only going to represent you."

While we were working on the workers, they [the union] began introducing us to Japanese community members—Glen, David, Art. They told us that they had a reason to help us because the construction of the New Otani involved destroying parts of the community significant to them. We met at the cultural center, Jennifer, Beti, and me. We told them why we wanted a union. We wanted better treatment, and we were tired of the injustices. Glen offered to work together with us. He's got determination and commitment. We've had a lot of support.

The workers' activities over the next three years led to an increase in involved workers from a small group of six into a leadership committee of thirty-five who meet every other week at the union hall to plan organizing strategies. The committee's efforts have been fruitful, and in spite of the aggressive resistance from hotel management, it has gained the support of the majority of its coworkers. As of November 1995, the majority of the 270 New Otani workers had signed a card pledging their support for the union. The hotel, in turn, has put up quite a fight against the union, but the very existence of a large, vocal group of workers who challenge the hotel on a daily basis is a victory in and of itself.

The effort at the New Otani is especially impressive given that historically unions have neglected organizing low-wage immigrant workers. The majority of workers at the New Otani can be classified as low-wage service workers. Housekeeping makes up the majority of these service jobs, and the majority of the housekeepers are Latina immigrants, mostly from Mexico with a large minority from El Salvador and Guatemala. Immigrant Latina/os also fill the remaining "back of the house" jobs in the laundry and the kitchen. The union estimates that 70 percent of the workers at the New Otani are Latina/o, the vast majority of them immigrants. Twenty percent are Asian immigrants, the majority of them Japanese, with a significant minority from the Philippines and a few from Korea and other Asian countries. The remaining 10 percent of the workforce is made up of native whites and native blacks. The workforce reflects the dominant trend in the industry except for its large Asian immigrant segment. Whereas the management and administration of the majority of the hotels in Los Angeles are held by native white employees, with a significant representation of native blacks, the New Otani has a significant Japanese presence and little black representation in these management positions. In its up-scale Thousand Cranes restaurant, the servers are exclusively Japanese women who work in traditional costume, and the chefs are also of Asian descent. Immigrant Filipinos make up almost the entire accounting department. The few black workers are most likely to be in service occupations.

LATINA/O WORKERS AND UNIONS

Historically, the position of unions with regard to Latina/o workers has ranged from hostile to indifferent. At different points the AFL has been actively hostile. It sought to restrict Mexican immigration in the 1920s, arguing that "Mexicans would take jobs from white workers, break strikes, and lower wages" (Lazo, 1995: 25; see also Gómez-Quiñones, 1994). An AFL delegate to the 1919 convention stated that "Mexican immigrants were detrimental to the best interest of the nation . . . un-American in their ways . . . non-union, . . . aliens, owing their allegiance to another country" (Lazo, 1995: 25). In 1928, Congressman John C. Box expressed the racial ideology fueling the restrictionist movement. He argued that the mixing of Mexicans with whites threatened "America's racial integrity." Of Mexicans he said, "this blend of low grade Spaniard, peonized Indians, and Negro slave mixes with Negroes, mulattoes, and other mongrels, and some sorry whites, already here. The prevention of such mongrelization and the degradation it causes is one of the purposes of our laws which the admission of these people will tend to defeat" (Lazo, 1995: 25-26). In the 1930s, the AFL rallied for a repatriation of Mexican workers that led to the deportation of one hundred thousand workers, many of them U.S. citizens, in California alone (Lazo, 1995; Gómez-Quiñones, 1994).

When Latina/o workers were organized under the AFL, they often faced discrimination in training programs and in job referrals. Until the Civil Rights Act of 1964, unions also segregated them in Latina/o locals with lower pay rates and unfair seniority lines (Lazo, 1995). The union's hostility toward Latina/o immigrant workers often undermined the work of young Latina/o organizers. For example, the failure of the International Ladies' Garment Workers' Union (ILGWU) to support the work of its Latina/o organizers in the post–World War II period eventually led to the union's decline. The hostility toward Latina/o organizers and union members took the form of limiting the use of Spanish during local meetings (Laslett and Tyler, 1989). Even more destructive to the ILGWU was its failure to organize the sportswear segment of the industry in which Latina immigrants were concentrated. This neglect proved very damaging to the union during the 1950s when casual clothing became the fashion and this sector of the industry expanded while the unionized traditional sector vastly declined. The union's failure to focus on workers industry-wide rather than on just white workers, augmented by its lack of insight into the economic shifts at the time, was costly for everyone involved. The ILGWU has yet to recover from these mistakes.

While racism, nativism, and sexism (particularly in the case of the ILGWU) motivated much of the relationship between unions and immigrant Latina/o workers, employers seized on the division. The need for cheap labor placed employers at odds with the restrictionists. Employers argued that Mexican workers were needed to fill jobs that native workers shunned. The emergence of a booming agricultural sector in California that depended on large numbers of seasonal laborers served to lock immigrant Latina/o workers into the most backward segment of the economy (Guerin-Gonzales, 1993). The union backlash coupled with employers' stereotypes of the docile immigrant worker facilitated the segmentation of immigrant labor into the most exploitative positions. The Bracero Program, in effect from 1942 to 1964, exemplified the ways in which unions and employers found common ground. The program facilitated a steady pool of labor, stripped of political rights, that employers could easily exploit and white workers could easily exclude. It also promoted a system of seasonal migration that gave workers who worked intensely a few months out of the year before returning home very little incentive to organize.

It is from these conditions that the image of the unorganizable immigrant Latina/o worker with an affinity for unstable low-wage secondary-sector jobs has developed. This image, rooted partly in myth and partly in the reality of political and economic disenfranchisement propagated by both unions and employers, is best captured in Michael Piore's analysis of the dual labor market in his book *Birds of Passage* (1979). According to Piore, immigrants have an affinity for the secondary sector of the economy because it gives them access to easily acquired temporary jobs. Piore's argument rests on the assumption that the orientation of immigrants predisposes them to lower wages and the secondary sector. He argues that the logic of the internal labor market makes migrants unlikely candidates to meet the stable basic demand of a capital-intensive firm in the primary labor market. The fact that immigrants are often sojourners makes them costly to train and unlikely candidates for the stable primary sector, but their instrumental orientation to work and wages make them perfect for intensive, seasonal labor. Piore characterizes migrants as *homo economicus*. In the host country solely to earn enough to increase their status in the country of origin, migrants can easily

cast off the social aspects of work and engage themselves in the types of economic activities normally avoided at home. Given their willingness to take
jobs that native workers shun, their temporary status in the labor market, and
their instrumental orientation toward wages, Piore argues, migrant workers
make prime candidates for the secondary sector and are reluctant to involve
themselves in labor disputes.

Surely immigrants are affected by the same conditions that have undermined the organization of native workers, and just as do native workers they
may accept substandard working conditions for all sorts of different reasons.
Given the history of nativism in this country and the limited rights of immigrant workers, it is not unexpected that immigrant workers have historically
been more compliant than others. But to suggest that these conditions are inherent in the orientation of immigrant workers simplifies the problem. In
fact, the data from the New Otani suggest that immigrant workers have the
same orientation and desires for the future as native workers. As one worker
stated, "Contrary to what others think, in our countries unions exist. We also
know what we want. We want respect for our rights, for the rights of all
workers. We are organizing for our children, who are the future, for other immigrants yet to come. We want the industry organized so that no one is
treated badly, and we will continue to organize so that others aren't fright-
ened." It is not the orientation of immigrants that has concentrated them in
the secondary sector. Rather, the precarious position in which they found
themselves as employees limited them to the most exploitative of jobs and
the representatives of the working class largely complied has historically
placed immigrant Latina/o workers in the sector of the economy that is difficult to organize, seasonal, and labor-intensive.

In fairness to Piore it must be acknowledged that his theory is not always
empirically wrong, but too general. Economic refugees who plan on returning to their country of origin will of course have a different posture toward
unionism than immigrants who plan on staying in the host country. However, *who* plans on returning is structurally and historically influenced, not
merely a product of individual desire.

Thus, hostility, neglect, and indifference color much of the historical relationship between the dominant elements of organized labor and immigrant
Latina/o workers. Gwendolyn Mink (1986) has effectively argued that much
of the conservatism of organized labor was formed in its reaction to immigrants. However, numerous instances of union militancy among immigrant
Latina/o workers are part of the historical record. From the 1903 labor strikes
in Oxnard, California (Almaguer, 1984), to the radical organization of cannery workers in the 1940s by the communist-led United Cannery, Agricultural, Packing, and Allied Workers of America (UCAPAWA) (Ruiz, 1987) to the
current activities of immigrant Latina/o workers, there is ample evidence that
under the right conditions immigrant workers do organize. Thus, to general-

ize from a few instances that immigrant labor cannot be organized fails to consider the context that facilitates organizing and tends to reify the role of immigrant workers in national economies.

In the case of the New Otani, the picketers on the line, the speakers at the rallies in support of the hotel workers, and the working-class leadership that meets every other Tuesday at the union hall all challenge the stereotype of the unorganizable immigrant worker. In light of this new militancy, it is important to examine what conditions have changed to facilitate organizing and what conditions remain the same.

ECONOMIC GLOBALIZATION AND THE NEW WORKING CLASS

Working-class formation in the first seventy years of the twentieth century was forged by rapid industrialization and dramatic technological advancement. In the latter part of the century, technological advancement continued while heavy industry took its last breaths in the country it had made the center of the world economy. It is these economic shifts that drive the new era of capitalist expansion, a period of globalization that has dramatically transformed relations between labor and capital in the emerging global cities.

Going beyond the thesis of deindustrialization and restructuring (Wilson, 1987; Kasarda, 1989) that describes the loss of a manufacturing base and high-paying union jobs in the major urban areas of the United States, Saskia Sassen (1988; 1991) links these events to global shifts in capital that have not only transformed production but altered the demographic characteristics of the working class in the global cities. Los Angeles, New York, London, Tokyo, and other major urban areas have experienced an influx of foreign investment into the emerging service sector. The development of highly concentrated financial management centers in these core cities has led to unprecedented growth in the specialized services needed to maintain the financial industry. This new growth at the top requires an infrastructure of services to maintain the owners, managers, and well-paid servants of the new economy. Service facilities such as restaurants and hotels, which require a large low-wage workforce, expand to meet the new needs.

At the other end of this movement in capital is the transfer of manufacturing overseas to underdeveloped countries where labor costs are low and control over the labor force is perceived to be high. This foreign investment in underdeveloped economies has led to the disruption of the traditional economy in these countries and the disappearance of means of subsistence, creating a surplus of labor whose only option is to migrate in search of work. While one would expect investment in labor-intensive manufacturing to absorb displaced workers, the disruption often forces women and children into the same labor market to compete with the traditional male wage earner. Thus, the disruption often creates a larger labor pool than can be absorbed.

The mobility of capital between the financial centers of the developed countries and the emerging manufacturing sites in the underdeveloped countries paves the way for the migratory flows of labor. The push and pull factors determining migration are built into the process of foreign investment in underdeveloped economies and the consolidation of financial capital in the global cities. Sassen (1988) shows that the recipient areas of foreign investment are the ones with the highest rates of out-migration, while the global cities experience the highest rates of immigration. Jobs are being lost at one end and created at the other. With this movement of labor and capital, globalization changes the conditions and possibilities for organizing immigrant Latina/o workers.

The New Otani Hotel is a product of globalization as is its immigrant workforce. The hotel was built in 1977 as part of the first wave of the expansion of services in Los Angeles. An overview of the trends between 1970 and 1990 in the Los Angeles hotel industry (U.S. Department of Commerce, Bureau of the Census, 1970; 1980; 1990) indicates that the hotel industry has grown tremendously in the past thirty years. In 1970 hotels employed about twenty-eight thousand people. By 1990 hotel employment had grown to almost seventy-two thousand. Dramatic changes in the composition of the industry accompanied this tremendous growth. In 1970 foreign-born Latina/os were 9 percent of the industry. In 1990, their share of the industry had increased to almost 38 percent. The percentage of foreign-born Asians also climbed, from less than 2 percent in 1970 to almost 9 percent in 1990.

This expansion of the hotel industry and the creation of thousands of new jobs filled by immigrant Latina/o labor has profound structural implications for the organization of workers. Unlike the seasonal jobs in agriculture that encourage return migration, the jobs created at the low end of the services sector are quite stable. In general, secondary-sector jobs like the "back of the house" positions in the hotel industry have traditionally been considered unstable, with high rates of turnover (Piore, 1979). However, the data from my interviews with hotel employers suggests that the immigrant workforce is quite stable and employers actually prefer immigrants over native workers because of their lower rate of turnover. The need for stability is especially acute in Los Angeles, which not only has expanded services because of the consolidation of the financial sector but also caters to a year-round tourism industry that makes the hotel industry a central part of the economy.

While the transformation from an industrial to a global economy presses forward, the employers' traditional practices of segmenting the workforce by race and gender remains constant. The majority of employers in my Los Angeles sample preferred immigrant labor, particularly Latina/o, for "back of the house" jobs. This preference was based on the perception that immigrant workers were more controllable than native workers. One hotel employer stated, "My experience is that most Latinos have a much better work ethic than the whites and blacks I've employed here. . . . There is less complaining. More or less tell them what has to be done and they do it in a rather happy manner." Another employer stated, "Immigrants are good workers. They do the job. They are like soldiers—work and go home without knowing what's going on around them." An employer at a large airport-area hotel expressed the industry's view of immigrants: "I have to say that employers tend to think that they'll be good workers and keep quiet. It is what it is, I have to say. . . . People think that way. Hire them and there won't be no problems." The perceptions of today's employers suggest historical continuity in attitudes toward immigrant Latina/o workers and in the role these attitudes play in maintaining a segmented labor market with Latina/o immigrants concentrated in the most exploitative positions.

As in the past, racial and ethnic segmentation leads to conflict between workers and creates an obstacle for working-class solidarity. This type of conflict is salient within the New Otani Hotel and to some extent has been an obstacle to the struggle for union representation. In fact, the segmentation at the New Otani has made it difficult to get all workers on board in a union campaign. The most significant divisions are between immigrant Latina/o and Asian workers. The Filipinos in accounting, for example, do not support the union drive, nor has any great progress been made in organizing the Japanese workers concentrated in two of the hotel's Japanese-theme restaurants. According to one Local 11 organizer, six out of the approximately twenty-five to thirty Japanese workers support the union. As of 1996 only two had actually signed a union card. According to a Local 11 organizer, the general attitude of the Japanese workers toward Local 11 is that "the union is for lazy Mexicans. I work hard, therefore I don't need a union."

The attitude of Asian immigrant workers toward the union changes depends on the distance between the groups. For example, in contrast to the Filipinos in accounting, the Filipinos in housekeeping have signed in support of the union. The distance imposed by occupational segmentation leaves room for the emergence of ethnic/racial stereotyping and for employers' manipulation of employee attitudes toward their coworkers, thereby establishing a basis for intergroup conflict. As in the past, employers tend to treat workers differently depending on their ethnic or racial background. The unequal treatment of workers at the New Otani is particularly salient and leads to hostility and misunderstanding between Japanese and Latina/o immigrant workers.

Latina/o workers believe that the Japanese workers' higher status gives them little reason to rebel against the company. In addition, they feel that racial/ethnic ties between the hotel management and the Asian workers override worker solidarity. Ironically, Latina/o workers also carry with them stereotypes of the unorganizable Asian immigrant. They say that Asian workers are conformists and consider conformity inherent in Japanese culture. As a result, the organizers ignored Japanese workers for the first two years of the campaign, and in doing so, they gave the hotel a two-year head start in capturing the support of a crucial segment of the workforce. As one organizer said, "Nobody in the Japanese workers' lives was talking about the union. Instead they were bombarded daily with antiunion propaganda. They are told that the union is Mafia, that unions are for lazy Mexican workers, and so on." Conditions of segmentation that kept the working class divided in the earlier part of the century continue to be an important obstacle to working-class solidarity.

The segmentation of workers has unintended consequences when coupled with the conditions of globalization. While the seasonal nature of the secondary sector that Piore (1979) identifies as an obstacle to unionism encouraged the pattern of sojourning in the past, the current globalized structure facilitates settlement rather than return migration. In turn, segmentation and settlement facilitate solidarity as workers see "their group" consistently being treated unfairly. The worker consciousness developed during the settlement process is directly rooted in racial and ethnic discrimination. Thus, ethnic and racial consciousness drives the process of class formation. It is the perception of racial and ethnic discrimination inherent in the process of segmentation that leads to greater awareness of workplace inequities and nurtures the drive to resist. The disparities found in segmented labor markets are a product not only of wages and workloads but also of the way groups are treated. Treatment is a somewhat intangible measure and difficult to isolate, but we can grasp it in the words of workers when they say they are fighting for "dignity and respect." The fact that employers treat workers according to immigrant stereotypes has pushed workers to organize. For example, a Latina worker from Mexico who has been at the New Otani for nine years explains,

> If you're a person, regardless of your race or where you're from, you deserve respect. But here they see you're from somewhere else and they disrespect you. They don't care about the worker. They want robots. They don't care how we feel. They intimidate us. They tell us if we're not satisfied with our job there are plenty of others who want it, and then they show us a stack of applications. I rebel when I get treated like that.

According to immigrant Latina/o workers, the hotel treats Asian workers with greater respect. Several workers pointed to their small or nonexistent raises in comparison with the higher increase another worker received as an indication of favoritism. Although no one knew for certain that the Asian workers in other departments received substantial raises, many assumed that they did. Instances of favoritism such as allowing the Japanese workers to park in the hotel lot or giving them vacation time were generalized to mean that favoritism occurred constantly. Thus, the perception of unequal treatment is compounded by segmentation of groups and is articulated through racial and ethnic solidarity.

Taken at face value, the notion of organizing based on ethnicity appears antithetical to class formation, but the point is that ethnicity and race inform the experience of exploitation. For example, a Latina housekeeper explained that when she started working the manager gave her only three days of training and had her cleaning a sixteen-room load by her fourth day. The experience in itself was exploitation that came with the territory of being a worker. However, a week later a Filipina worker was hired and given two weeks of training and a month before she had to clean sixteen rooms. Although both women were exploited as workers, the Mexican employee's experience was compounded by racial discrimination. Unequal treatment based on ethnicity and race intensified the worker's class experience. As a result of her heightened awareness, she joined the union leadership committee even before her probationary period was over.

Once resistance is fostered, settlement strongly influences the decision to struggle for better work conditions. The struggle is often cast in terms of hope for a better future in the immigrant worker's new home. Unlike Piore's (1979) sojourner, who had little incentive to commit to a potentially long-term labor dispute and who faced hostility and discrimination from both employer and union, the immigrants of today have a much greater stake in improving their conditions and the political experience to do so. The dimension of political experience is central in understanding the conditions that have driven the new labor movement. While globalization largely explains the structural conditions that have influenced mass immigration and patterns of settlement, political experience and background of the working-class leadership at the New Otani explains its ability to harness the alienation of the workers and foster the transformation of a "class in itself" into a "class for itself."

The pattern of Latina/o immigrants in the twentieth century is reminiscent of earlier immigrant groups. Polish immigrants of the nineteenth century were difficult to organize because their rural peasant background did not provide them with the political experience to engage in class politics and their pattern of return migration undermined any incentive to do so. John Bukowczyk (1984: 65) explains how heightened politicization subsequently shifted the organizational potential of Polish immigrant workers:

> While migrants from rural Poland had little acquaintance with radical ideologies or progressive politics in the 1880's, the opposite held true for post-1890 migrants. Leaving a rural society now gripped by popular agitation for peasant land reform, strikes by agricultural wage laborers, and a full fledged rural socialist

movement, they carried an assortment of democratic and egalitarian notions which hardly fitted contemporary—and latterday—stereotypes. . . . Blending Polish nationalism with a radical social and economic program, these Polish leftists appealed strongly to other working-class Poles and helped galvanize workplace tensions and class resentments into an upsurge of labor militance in the 1910's.

More than a hundred years later, history repeats itself—this time politicized with Latina/o immigrants from Mexico and war-torn Central America asserting their own role in U.S. ethnic and labor history.

The workers at the New Otani are better equipped to take on a union struggle than earlier immigrant Latina/o workers for the same reasons that set the post-1890s Poles apart from their predecessors. The majority of the New Otani workers I interviewed had had prior political experience in their home country. For example, a housekeeper from El Salvador had worked with her husband to organize the country's ten thousand power plant workers. An undocumented worker from El Salvador described how he had organized a campesino group to work with the moderate Christian Democrats. He added, however, that his family had often hosted meetings of the Fronte Farabundo Martí de Liberación Nacional (Farabundo Martí National Liberation Front—FMLN) as well. A Mexican immigrant showed me a scar on her arm where she had caught a soldier's bullet during the 1968 massacre of students in Mexico City. Another worker with relatives in the canneries of Northern California had inherited a union tradition from the struggles of workers there. She explained that her mother had worked in a cannery and earned $14 an hour whereas her sister did the same work in a nonunion cannery for minimum wage.

Like the post-1890 Poles, the recent wave of immigrants includes political refugees from war-torn countries and immigrants who for one reason or another do not plan on returning. A worker who had been part of the teachers' union in El Salvador described her experiences with war. She said that one day when she was walking home, there was a group of women and children further up the road, and she heard an explosion and saw the mother of a toddler screaming and running around in the field picking up the pieces of her dead child and placing them in her apron. One worker from El Salvador stated, "We have the war in our head. There was shooting and bombs daily. That's why we're here. We have these memories. We don't want to live over there anymore." Another worker who had fled El Salvador during the height of the war explained that the displacement of home and family had changed the Salvadoran landscape to such an extent that "it's not the same anymore." He had worked on a cotton farm owned by an officer in the military in an area that the FMLN had penetrated. The war had made it impossible to continue working in the countryside, and he had fled with his family to the city. His sister had stayed behind but lost her son and husband to the war. He said, "I had to leave my life back there. My family had to move from the *campo* to the city. We talk about it here. It's the same story for all of us. They sometimes ask if I think I'll ever return. I don't know. I don't think so. I can't go back to the *campo* after working in the city for fifteen years." The fact that these immigrants see their future in the United States influences the way they construct their entitlement to fair treatment. This is now their home, and their entitlement is based on a notion of human rights instilled in them by political experience.

Characterizing immigrants as unorganizable fails to consider the social and historical context that shapes the possibilities for political activity. In the case of the New Otani, globalization, segmentation, and the political experience of the working-class leadership create the conditions that make working-class formation a possibility.

STRATEGIES OF THE NEW LABOR MOVEMENT

The other essential factor in shaping the new labor movement is the union itself. While the history of organized labor in the United States, with the exception of the CIO (see Arroyo, 1995), has actively promoted the vulnerability of immigrant labor, there has been a resurgence of progressive unionism dedicated to the empowerment of immigrant workers. Local 11 embodies this dedication and has played a major role in the transformation of the union's organizing strategies.

The leadership of Local 11 emerged as a result of struggles for union democracy. The previous leadership, headed from 1975 to 1987 by Andrew Allen, had refused to establish guidelines for full participation for the growing Latina/o membership (Gómez-Quiñones, 1994) and declined to introduce Spanish translation during meetings. Its neglect of organization as industry expanded had allowed membership to decline by 50 percent (Gómez-Quiñones, 1994). Having survived several rank-and-file challenges from Latina/o workers, Allen resigned under the pressure of a new opposition led by María Elena Durazo. The Durazo camp was made up of mostly Latina/o workers, with significant representation of blacks, Asians, and whites. With Allen's resignation, the international stepped in to reorganize the local. A new election in 1989 made Durazo the new president (Gómez-Quiñones, 1994), and since then Local 11 has increased its membership and won several high profile labor disputes. The most recent victory includes a contract with six of the major downtown hotels that has set a new standard for the industry. The new pact announced in January 1998 includes large wage increases (from $8.15 an hour to $11.05 an hour over six years for housekeepers), protection against the subcontracting of jobs, and protection of the jobs of immigrant workers who have to leave the country to renew their work permits. The commitment to organize in the interests of all workers, including immigrants, reflects the activities of a new kind of union activist.

The new union faces the daunting task of dealing with the legacy of segmentation. It is a problem that Local 11 has taken on directly. In the process of building a grassroots union, it has actively recruited the support of target communities. In order to get the Japanese workers on board, or at least minimize the conflict between Latina/o and Asian workers, it has appealed to the Japanese-American community. The coalition between New Otani workers and the surrounding Little Tokyo community has helped lessen the impact of racial and ethnic segmentation.

In 1996 the union launched an aggressive campaign aimed directly at the Japanese workers. Two organizers were brought in to work specifically with Japanese workers, and the union has continued to pursue a community-based strategy to help overcome the barriers that the social division of labor reinforces. Central to the effort to gain the support of the local Little Tokyo community is the work of the New Otani Workers Support Committee. This committee is made up of local activists with strong ties to the Japanese-American community, among them clerics, clergy, lawyers, professors, and students. Many of its members had been active in the campaign for government reparations for the Japanese Americans interned during World War II. In a position statement dated June 9, 1995, Glen Omatsu, a Japanese American community activist, said,

> For the past year-and-a-half, Asian American community groups and individuals have participated in the New Otani Workers Support Committee. The mission of the support committee is threefold: (1) to build solidarity in the Asian American community for workers' efforts to form a union; (2) to educate the Asian American community about the significance of the workers' campaign, especially relating to interethnic relations, protection of immigrants rights, and the community demand for corporate accountability; and (3) to monitor and counteract management's attack on workers. Thus, the support committee defines the Asian American community, especially the local Japanese American community, as directly involved in the workers' campaign. The organization of a union at the hotel will benefit not only workers employed there; it will also raise the quality of life in Little Tokyo.

The formation of coalitions within communities has proven to be an effective strategy whenever the potential for racial and ethnic antagonisms exists (see Horton, 1989; 1995). The hope of community activists, workers, and Local 11 is that community support will undermine the hotel's attempt to write off the struggle at the New Otani as mere racial/ethnic conflict. As Omatsu put it,

> The New Otani is managed and owned by Japanese corporations, while the workforce is predominately immigrant Latinos. Thus, conflict regarding union-

ization at the hotel can easily be perceived as interethnic conflict. Asian American community groups are acutely concerned about the state of race relations in Los Angeles in this period following the Los Angeles Uprising. Corporations from Japan often take actions that inflame racial tensions; unfortunately, local Asian American communities usually become the targets of righteous anger of others upset by the racism of corporations from Japan. Thus, in this period, Asian American community groups have a special responsibility to directly confront corporations from Asia.

Another aspect of the support from the Asian American community comes in the form of endorsements for the boycott from prominent Asian American organizations. At this point, it is not clear how effective the support committee will be in terms of helping to organize the Japanese workers. It is clear, however, that without the coalitions formed between workers and the community the boycott could have never gotten off the ground and the perception of racial/ethnic conflict would have dominated the scene. The important lesson here is that in multiethnic communities, multiethnic coalitions overcome the perception that hostilities are racially based and emphasize the reality of a class-based struggle.

The assumption underlying the formation of interethnic coalitions is that race and ethnicity play an important role in influencing divisions or solidarity among workers. This is not a novel idea, but the history of organized labor suggests that the decline of union strength in the United States reflects how often the ethnic and racial dimension is ignored. Rather than treating the status of immigrant workers as problematic, Local 11 draws on the experiences of workers as a resource for class formation. In doing so, it actively organizes with the understanding that it must take community and culture into account to achieve universal ends.

The emerging union leaders on the national as well as the local level seem to have learned their historical lessons and to be working hard not to make the old mistakes. The lessons are reflected in the composition of the union leadership and front-line organizers and in their mode of communication. Local 11 actively recruits a cadre of multiethnic organizers who are sensitive to the issues central to the community, and much of the organizing is done in Spanish. The important role that language plays in organizing workers is suggested in the admiring comments that workers often make about the white organizer, who did not know any Spanish when she started on the campaign but was almost fluent after three months on the job. In addition to having ethnic and racial representation in union organizing, the union also learns where ethnic bonds exist and attempts to organize around them. In an interview, the president of Local 11 explained,

> We try to be very aware of those situations where there are family relations in order to have them help organize. You get the right people that are related to

each other, then you get the whole network. That network runs through not only within the hotel but within the whole industry. That network is there, and we try to uncover the relationships. For example, at the Sheraton Grande Downtown and at the Intercontinental there were some relations between the stewards, the dishwashers, in those two nonunion hotels. They would recruit from their families so that they would make sure that in the union organizing drive they would have the loyalty of their family members. To break through that network is almost impossible.

The role of networks in organizing the New Otani has been of great importance. There is an understanding that the bonds between people are often based on family membership or friendships established in their native country. It is through these networks that ethnicity comes to play a role in influencing class formation and to represent a strong basis for worker loyalty. Understanding of these networks has helped the organizers to win over central groups in the hotel. For example, the majority of banquet workers live in the Lennox community and come from the same town in Mexico. At first, these workers were ambivalent toward the union. The union recognized the importance of Armando within the network and concentrated on recruiting him. They learned that the group met every morning at a neighborhood donut shop. One of the union organizers approached him there to talk to him about the union. Once Armando was won over, the rest of the group also signed in support of the union. This kind of maneuvering is possible only with a real understanding of the dynamics of the immigrant Latina/o community. It is an understanding that appears to arise from the union's commitment to go beyond merely organizing the workplace to organizing communities.

Local 11 attributes its success in organizing immigrant workers to its reliance on grassroots organizing. Of course, this reliance demands that the union understand the community it serves. As with the CIO of the late 1930s and early 1940s, there is a movement today toward organizing groups traditionally ignored, and contrary to conventional wisdom, immigrants, women, and members of ethnic minorities are more than willing to organize. The strategies of Local 11 suggest that they are willing to move away from reified understandings of race, ethnicity, gender, and citizenship to build a union based on the understanding that the social division of labor can be overcome and can even serve to facilitate the organization of workers.

The struggle at the New Otani Hotel has yet to be resolved. There has been no letup since the boycott began in earnest. The informational picket lines have been extended from one to two days a week. The union continues to add to its long list of community supporters. The hotel has been put on the defensive and is fighting back. It has gathered its own list of supporters and its own workers' petition. It is not clear whether the workers will win or lose. The hotel shows no sign of meeting the union at the bargaining table, but optimism prevails.

Whether the workers at the New Otani win or lose, they have already made history. The high-profile case has captured the attention of labor leaders and become a model for interethnic organizing. The message that the workers at the New Otani send out is clear. Immigrants do organize. Race, ethnicity, and citizenship status do not necessarily undermine labor organization. Latina/os will fight for their rights. There are still lessons to be learned and obstacles to be overcome, but the unionization process at the New Otani has paved the way for a more complex understanding of the role of race, ethnicity, and citizenship in class formation.

CONCLUSION

An examination of the organizing efforts at the New Otani hotel suggests the potential for the success of a new labor movement in revitalizing unionism in the United States. Historically, the anti-immigrant strategies of unions and employers' strategies for maintaining a seasonal and vulnerable supply of workers have led to the segmentation of Latina/o workers into the secondary sector of the economy. The instability of this sector has traditionally undermined the settlement of immigrant Latina/os and created an obstacle for working-class organization. The globalization of the economy and the expansion of a service sector to meet the needs of the new economic structure have stabilized the jobs that Latina/o immigrants are segmented into and facilitated the settlement process. Settlement coupled with the influx of immigrant workers with political experience has increased the opportunity for the organization of immigrant Latina/o workers. As the rank and file has struggled for greater union democracy and representation in the workplace, a new cadre of organizers has emerged. Local 11 and the workers at the New Otani Hotel reflect this new movement, and their activities shed light on the potential for a new labor movement.

REFERENCES

Almaguer, Tomas. 1984. *Racial Faultline: The Historical Origins of White Supremacy in California*. Berkeley: University of California Press.

Arroyo, Luis Leobardo. 1995. "Chicano Participation in Organized Labor: The CIO in Los Angeles, 1938–1950: An Extended Research Note," pp. 47–62 in Antoinette S. Lopez (ed.), *Latinos in the United States: History, Law, and Perspective*. New York: Garland.

Bukowczyk, John J. 1984. "The Transformation of Working Class Ethnicity: Corporate Control, Americanization, and the Polish Immigrant Middle Class in Bayonne, New Jersey 1915–1925." *Labor History* 25(1): 53–82.

Cobble, Dorothy Sue. 1996. "The Prospects for Unionism in a Service Society," in Cameron Lynne Macdonald and Carmen Sirianni (eds.), *Working in the Service Society*. Philadelphia: Temple University Press.

Gómez-Quiñones, Juan. 1994. *Mexican American Labor, 1790–1990.* Albuquerque: University of New Mexico Press

Guerin-Gonzales, Camille. 1993. "The International Migration of Workers and Segmented Labor: Mexican Immigrant Workers in California Industrial Agriculture, 1900–1946," pp. 155–175 in Camile Guerin-Gonzales and Carl Strikwerda (eds.), *The Politics of Immigrant Workers: Labor Activism and Migration in the World Economy Since 1830.* New York: Holmes and Meier.

Horton, John. 1989. "The Politics of Ethnic Change: Grass-Roots Responses to Economic and Demographic Restructuring in Monterey Park, California." *Urban Geography* 10: 578–592.

———. 1995. *The Politics of Diversity: Immigration, Resistance, and Change in Monterey Park, California.* Philadelphia: Temple University Press.

Kasarda, John. 1989. "Urban Industrial Transition and the Underclass." *Annals of the American Academy of Political and Social Science* 501: 26–42.

Laslett, John and Mary Tyler. 1989. *The ILGWU in Los Angeles 1907–1988.* Inglewood: Ten Star Press.

Lazo, Robert. 1995. "Latinos and the AFL-CIO: The California Immigrant Workers Association as an Important New Development," pp. 100–123 in Antoinette S. Lopez (ed.), *Latinos in the United States: History, Law, and Perspective.* New York: Garland.

Mink, Gwendolyn. 1986. *Old Labor and New Immigrants in American Political Development: Union, Party, and State 1875–1920.* Ithaca, NY: Cornell University Press.

Piore, Michael. 1979. *Birds of Passage.* New York: Cambridge University Press.

Quadagno, Jill. 1994. *The Color of Welfare: How Racism Undermined the War on Poverty.* New York: Oxford University Press.

Ruiz, Vicki L. 1987. *Cannery Women, Cannery Lives: Mexican Women, Unionization, and the California Food Processing Industry, 1930–1950.* Albuquerque: University of New Mexico Press.

Sassen, Saskia. 1988. *The Mobility of Labor and Capital: A Study in International Investment and Labor Flows.* New York: Cambridge University Press.

———. 1991. *The Global City: New York, London, Tokyo.* Princeton, NJ: Princeton University Press.

U.S. Department of Commerce, Bureau of the Census. 1970. *Census of Population and Housing, Public Use Sample, 5 percent 1 in 100 Sample.* Washington DC.

———. 1980. *Census of Population and Housing, Public Use Microdata Sample (A Sample) (MRDS).* Washington, DC.

———. 1990. *Census of Population and Housing, Public Use Microdata Sample (A Sample) (MRDS).* Washington DC.

Wilson, William Julius. 1987. *The Truly Disadvantaged: The Inner City, the Underclass, and Public Policy.* Chicago: University of Chicago Press.

———. 1996. *When Work Disappears: The World of the New Urban Poor.* New York: Alfred A. Knopf.

9

Engendering Transnationalism in Food Processing: Peripheral Vision on Both Sides of the U.S.–Mexican Border

Patricia Zavella

Theorists of the "new transnationalism" have shifted our thinking about immigration, which previously involved a linear model of change in which migration is typically toward the First World and settlement entails discernible stages of liminality, transition, and adaptation to the host country. Instead, these theorists argue that we should examine transnational circuits, spaces, or networks as people migrate from one country to another. Glick Schiller and her colleagues argue that the current connections between immigrants and home societies are of a different order from those of previous generations. Migrants are pushed into the migrant stream by new circuits of capital that are sustained by transformations in technologies of transportation and communication and the inability of migrants to become fully incorporated into the countries in which they resettle. Thus transnational theorists make the useful suggestion that we adopt a "bifocal" orientation and examine "the processes by which immigrants build social fields that link together their country of origin and their country of settlement," including familial, economic, social, organizational, religious, and political relations that span national borders (Glick Schiller, Basch, and Blanc-Szanton, 1992: ix; Rouse, 1992: 25–52; Glick Schiller, Basch, and Blanc-Szanton, 1995: 48–63).

Too often, however, analysts of transnational migration focus on the cultural phenomena occurring within the United States, which embody a poetics of nostalgia, with regard to the cultural formations from which the migrants came. Appadurai (1996), for example, analyzes transmigrants' "politics of return"—that is, how they construct new spatial sites so as to "reterritorialize" and counter the feeling of being displaced from their home countries. Rouse (1992) suggests that transmigration includes changing class and gender relations in production. The ethnographic data presented by these transnational theorists, however, are often about the experiences of men and the loss of male privilege in the United States. Certainly these processes are occurring, but the picture is more complex. These theorists ignore gender relations, the ways in which men and women experience the changing relations of production in their migration, the link of changing relations of production to reproduction (often culturally constructed as the domain of women), and the specific globalization processes that shape transnational migration. They draw upon Saskia Sassen's framework calling for a transnational perspective but ignore her admonition about analyzing "the particular historical and political context of the current migration phase," which shifts over time and involves social actors from multiple social locations (1988: 3).

Taking Sassen's framework seriously allows us to see what is new about transnationalism in the Mexican context. Mexicanas/os have been migrating across the border ever since it was established at the close of the Mexican War in 1848. During the nineteenth and the early twentieth century, prior to the establishment of the Border Patrol (in 1924), they crossed the border little noticed by state officials. Mexican families often spent considerable time in sites on both sides of the border, and therefore notions of "reterritorialization" are fraught with the history of Mexico's having lost one-third of its territory to the United States and the multiple economic, kin, and political ties Mexicans have established in both countries.[1] And U.S. immigration history includes periods (notably during the Great Depression and the 1950s) when hundreds of thousands of Mexicans, including some U.S. citizens, were repatriated involuntarily (Hoffman, 1974; Sánchez, 1993). It was only at the end of the century, beginning in earnest during the 1970s, that migration from Mexico became a massive social phenomenon that resulted in the passage of the Immigration Reform and Control Act of 1986 with the aim of curbing immigration. Given this long and troubled history, Mexican migration includes a rich infrastructure of settlement—social networks that provide access to knowledge about successful migration and communities in the United States that provide housing and support to Mexican migrants. Some Mexican communities have experienced more than a century of transnational migration to the United States (Massey et al., 1987).

I will examine the transnational migration occurring in the food-processing sector (freezing, canning, and packing), which includes the migration of Mexican workers to the United States and the migration of capital from the United States to Mexico. This case study focuses on two regions: the Pájaro Valley, which has experienced deindustrialization in food processing (its major industry), and the Bajío, which has experienced an expansion of food processing.[2] These linked processes form one example of the linking of U.S. and Mexican agricultural economies, in what Palerm and Urquiola (1993) call a "binational system of production and reproduction," with Mexican workers being reproduced in Mexico but servicing California's agricultural economy. I extend this framework by showing how production and social reproduction in food processing generate complex, contradictory, and ironic cultural changes on both sides of the U.S–Mexican border. I agree with Ginsburg and Rapp's (1995:1) suggestion that we make reproduction central to social theory so as to understand how people's local cultural logics and social relations "incorporate, revise, or resist the influence of seemingly distant political and economic forces."

Michael Peter Smith's (1994) notion of transnational social and cultural formations is useful here. Although he focuses on grassroots political activities, I want to extend this view to quotidian struggles within families, social networks, and work sites. Weaving together feminist, materialist, and cross-border interpretive frameworks, I will show how transnational social formations include ways in which actors in different social locations—bourgeois entrepreneurs and plant managers, local state officials, and predominantly female workers— on both sides of the border reveal localized experiences and constructions of social meaning of the new world order.[3]

The restructuring of food processing illustrates the intersection of the local and global as capital moves from California to Mexico, abandoning one site and expanding in another in order to produce for export to the global economy (Borrego, 1997). These processes are fueled by market forces that began prior to but were facilitated by the passage of NAFTA and complicated by recurring Mexican economic crises. But this is more than the story of capitalist vampires satisfying their inexhaustible need for cheap labor. By imposing global standards of quality and developing new markets, agroindustry has become oriented toward the international requirements in the global food chain, and production for global markets has established profitable specialized niches (Little and Watts, 1994). Moreover, through global standardization, processors have established particular relationships with local growers and, ultimately, with the workers who harvest the produce and labor in the factories. I will argue that what is new about transnationalism, in the context of globalized food processing, is the way in which gender is embedded in processes of economic restructuring. The engendering of transnationalism can be seen in the feminization of the labor force on both sides of the border, the feminization of the infrastructure of migration, and the unexpected consequences of women's and men's quotidian struggles for the process of transnationalization itself.

AGROINDUSTRIAL PRODUCTION AND REPRODUCTION IN THE PÁJARO VALLEY

The story begins in Watsonville, California, a city of 37,000, that grew by 38 percent between 1980 and 1997, mainly as a result of Mexicana/o settlement.

Watsonville was one of many California communities that had become "Latinized," increased migration and settlement by Mexicans (beginning with the Bracero Program, 1942–1964) having eventually made whites the minority (Palerm, 1991; Takash, 1990). It is an agricultural hub, providing the system of coolers and distributors for strawberries, lettuce, and other agricultural products, and the city in which many laborers who work in the Pájaro Valley live and shop. After the 1965 immigration reform bill, women migrating from Mexico increased to 20 percent of all migrants, while the percentage of women who migrated within Mexico—an indicator of possible future transnational migration—increased to 27 percent. Thus women who settled in this region were part of larger demographic changes in the migrant stream and political-economic forces that pushed Mexicans to leave their home regions, attracted to jobs in agriculture (Durand, 1992: 121; Cardenas and Flores, 1986). Watsonville growers and processors, seeking a more stable workforce, recruited women. Women used their own social networks to facilitate migration—some coming to the region by themselves and others accompanied by female friends or kin. Watsonville has strong ties to several villages in Jalisco, Michoacán, and Guanajuato and on both sides of the border, and social networks from these regions are replicated there.

Jobs in food processing were plentiful in the late 1960s, when settlement locally began in earnest, and because women could combine seasonal cannery work with family responsibilities they returned to the canneries season after season. The industry was unionized by the International Brotherhood of Teamsters, and therefore wages were relatively good and the benefits package included medical insurance. Given the availability of unemployment benefits during the off season, women could provide support to their families even when they were not actually on the job. According to Joe Fahey, president of the Teamsters local (interview, October 25, 1996), in its heyday in 1982 there were eight thousand peak-season food-processing jobs in Watsonville, filled mainly by Mexicanas and Chicanas, and Watsonville called itself the "Frozen Food Capital of the World."[4] One out of four Watsonville residents were Teamsters, and more Mexicans voted in union elections, which required only union membership, than in city elections, which required citizenship (see also Takash, 1996). Whether male or female, however, once they arrived in Watsonville Mexicans often experienced discrimination on the basis of their race and, for women, their gender, so they were entering a highly segregated labor force and community.[5]

Despite individual struggles with supervisors or landlords, women's work in canneries contributed to long-term settlement and upward mobility by Chicanas/os and Mexicanas/os (see Takash, 1996).[6] Some were able to purchase homes or work their way up to becoming supervisors in large production sites (particularly if they were bilingual), while a sizable number of former farmworkers and cannery workers were able to lease or purchase land themselves and become small growers. By 1997 there were five hundred Latino strawberry growers in the Pájaro Valley, part of a $600 million world market.[7] As one local journalist observed, "In Watsonville, perhaps more than anywhere else in the state, the Latino growers' success is historically significant. Latino pickers, who toil long hours for low wages, have been the backbone of the strawberry industry for decades. Now Latinos make up about a third of operators in Santa Cruz and Monterey Counties" (Cha, 1997: 1).

Even as agriculture was expanding in acreage and moving into new crops, the food-processing sector—which produced mainly vegetables for freezing—began restructuring globally and downsizing locally beginning in the 1980s. The first cannery had opened in the Bajío in 1959, and by 1967 several others had begun production. The growth of this sector in Mexico was fueled by profits to be made through cheap labor costs (especially after the 1976 Mexican devaluation), a year-round agricultural season, and the availability of fertile land and well water. The Bajío increasingly became a competitive place to grow and process fruit and vegetables, especially after Watsonville workers were able to retain their costly benefits after the well-publicized 1985–1987 cannery strike. Initiated by Mexican workers and then supported by the Teamsters and other labor organizers, the strike maintained its picket line, and women in particular developed into key leaders (Bardacke, 1987; Flores, 1997).[8] Even though strikers eventually took wage cuts, wages in Mexico were even lower. During and after the strike, the industry began relocating in earnest to the Bajío. Some factories were literally packed up and trucked there, while many new factories were constructed in Mexico—often equipped with machinery made in Watsonville.

The effects of the plant closures on Watsonville have been devastating. Ten years after the end of the strike, local unemployment rates remained high: in 1997 the seasonal low was 12 percent while the high was 23 percent. According to a city council member (interview, August 20, 1996) and affected workers, retraining programs after the plant closures, funded through the county, lacked direct links to new jobs, and there was a general displacement of food-processing workers into the expanding service sector or agricultural jobs or out of town. Approximately three thousand unionized food-processing jobs remained in Santa Cruz County in the late 1990s (Joe Fahey, interview, October 25, 1995). The majority of displaced workers were Mexican women, ironically often migrants from the states in central and western Mexico in which the new factories opened up. These displaced workers experienced increased poverty and instability and competed with more recent migrants for the jobs available locally.

Workers had responded to the strike and other problems experienced by migrants by organizing a series of community-based organizations, advocating for education and neighborhood safety for their children and freedom from harassment by *la migra* (the Immigration and Naturalization Service). When the factories began closing down, workers mobilized their political contacts and informal social networks to form the Comité de Trabajadores Desplazados. During the NAFTA hearings in 1993, members of the Comité joined the Teamsters' anti-NAFTA demonstrations around the state. The Teamsters also organized several trips to Irapuato to meet with the Frente Auténtico del Trabajo (Authentic Labor Front—FAT), an opposition labor organization. Their purpose was to explore whether there was a basis for common struggle between food-processing workers in Irapuato and in Watsonville, to engage in dialogue, and to impart the message that globalization under NAFTA could hurt workers in Irapuato as well. Joe Fahey recalled, "We had a broader message, which was, 'These companies are not your salvation. They left us for a particular set of reasons and they will leave you for other reasons, but they will leave when they are good and ready to.'" While in Irapuato they protested the low wages and poor working conditions in transnational food-processing factories. María Cabañas (interviewed July 19, 1993), who was a member of the Comité, noted: "We confronted the fact that we needed to unite ourselves and struggle for justice not only personally but locally and internationally. Because what affects them there [in Mexico] affects us here, too." While all parties saw the transborder dialogue as successful, in the end there was no organizational follow-up, mainly because of lack of resources.

Supporters of this group also produced a video on the water problems in the Bajío, "Dirty Business," that was shown during the NAFTA hearings. Through innuendo the video alleges horrific health problems and environmental pollution by food processors in the Bajío. Despite the lack of hard evidence linking food processing to these problems, enough political controversy was generated by the video that the Mexican government passed a water treatment law and built the first municipal treatment plant in Irapuato.[9]

Long after the cannery strike, Watsonville remains politically polarized around racial issues. The overwhelming majority of elementary school children are Spanish-speakers and the children of immigrants. With the loss of 25 percent of low-income housing units after the 1989 earthquake, housing is dense, especially during the peak harvest season (city council member interview, August 20, 1996). In 1989, Latinas/os won a racial discrimination suit challenging city-wide council elections, that was fought "tooth and nail" by the local power structure, and in 1991 the first Latino city council member was elected through a district election (Takash, 1990; 1996; city council interview, February 5, 1997). There is bitter conflict over land use, with developers seeking to annex prime agricultural land for development while farmworker advocates push to retain the land in agricultural production and provide continued employment (Bardacke, 1994; *San Jose Mercury News*, August 29, 1997). Farmworker advocates include the United Farmworkers Union (UFW), which has waged a long battle for unionization of the predominantly Latina/o workers. The UFW staged a demonstration in 1997 that attracted between fifteen thousand and twenty thousand supporters, mostly from out of town, and the national political figures Jesse Jackson and Dolores Huerta (Woolfolk, 1997; Barnett, 1997).[10] Growers fought back with accusations and lawsuits, and three to four thousand local strawberry workers marched against the UFW (Barnett, 1996). According to the workers I interviewed, the anti-UFW organizing occurred with the aid of Latino growers, some of whom used their kin and village networks to recruit seasonal workers from Mexico who were then reluctant to join an organization of "outsiders." Mexican residents and their supporters continue to agitate for better education, social services, and housing. Thus polarization in Watsonville has centered around the strike, the district elections, the UFW unionization drive, efforts to make the schools more accountable, and the conflict over land use and is particularly visible in city politics.

Local political officials have little recourse for coping with the multiple problems in Watsonville. The city has embarked upon a development strategy based on attracting large stores in an attempt to increase sales tax revenues and stop the leakage of about $150 million in retail sales to surrounding areas. The projected job growth is in food services, retail sales, tellers, clerks, accounting, and farm work. With the exception of the latter, all these jobs require educational levels and bilingual skills that many cannery workers lack. As one local official remarked (interview, August 22, 1995), "Because they have Third World skills and have to live in the United States, that no longer means you're going to be guaranteed an income that's feasible." Efforts at attracting a satellite campus for the local community college have been successful. but this is a long-term strategy, as are the efforts by the Latino Strategic Planning Collaborative to secure more funds from the county for social service agencies and community-based organizations.[11] In exasperation, a city council member noted that "there are solutions [to Watsonville's problems] but they are not within the logic of capitalism." A city official, recognizing the magnitude of problems, described the need for a new perspective: "In the world today, we are not living within our own borders. If Watsonville wants to be successful economically and provide for its people who are here, then it needs to look beyond its own prejudices, beyond what happened ten, fifteen years ago. It needs, frankly, to look beyond the very narrow-mindedness of this county government. It needs to look beyond its borders."

In mobilizing their social networks and working with local activists and sympathetic city officials, migrants have helped shape the debate about how corporations conduct business and the conditions under which Mexicanas/os live. An unexpected consequence of transnational migration, then, is the ability of Mexican women and men to talk back to the processes of globalization, even though the corporations continue their relocation to other regions.

AGROINDUSTRIAL PRODUCTION
AND REPRODUCTION IN THE BAJÍO

Mexicans in the Bajío have also contended with transnational pressures. The Mexican government had long protected privately held parcels and communal lands from market forces. Nevertheless, in the past thirty years, several transnational food-processing plants have opened in the Bajío, which is also a center of textile, leather, auto production, and agriculture. Global market prices, technological innovations, recurring economic crises, and the federal government's neoliberal export-oriented strategy have changed Mexican systems of production and trade in agriculture. In 1992 President Carlos Salinas de Gortari pushed through a constitutional amendment, Article 27, that ended the land distribution program and opened the way for ejido privatization. The government also established neoliberal policies that cut subsidies for agricultural inputs such as fertilizers and seeds, reduced farm credit, and liberalized prices so they would drop to international levels. These policies enabled transnational corporations as well as Mexican firms to establish contractual relationships with small growers who have abandoned traditional agricultural practices to grow products for processing and sale in international markets (Barry, 1995). Growers were also pressured into moving into the fresh market and increasing the technology used on their farms so as to deliver products to the United States and Canada. Thirty-six thousand trucks, many of which carry fresh and frozen agricultural products, cross the border at Laredo every day on the "NAFTA highway," which includes three bridges spanning the U.S.–Mexican border. Trucks from Mexico generate more than $20 million a year in revenues from crossing fees (Schrader, 1996: 20; Carroll, 1995). According to the plant managers I interviewed, there also has been consolidation, with some large food-processing firms buying out the smaller plants (indicating the maturation of this sector), and some firms are expanding current plants or constructing new ones. Agroindustry is big business in the Bajío.

The food-processing factories utilize predominantly women's labor; increasingly growers who supply the factories are using women's labor in the fields for planting, weeding, and, depending on the crop, occasionally harvesting as well.[12] With high inflation and devaluation of the peso, women's wages in the food-processing factories were about the same in 1995 as they had been in 1985—the equivalent of about $3 a day (Moulton and Runsten, 1986; Borrego and Zavella, 1999).[13] Moreover, women's incorporation into the labor force draws on and often reinforces traditional notions that women's place is in the home, despite their contributing to household income (Fowler-Salamini and Vaughan, 1994). Thus women's lower wages are central to the process of development in this sector as in many regions of the world.

Despite their competitive advantage in producing in Mexico, managers presented narratives of overcoming adversity, particularly contending with First World perceptions that Mexico is "backward." A factory manager took pains to explain the importance of public relations and marketing Mexico's competitive edge (interview, December 14,1995): "We the Mexican processors have the conditions of lower salaries, climate, laborers, and technology high enough to guarantee the best quality in the world. We are not taking advantage of the image that Mexican products deserve. On the contrary, it's almost as if we are embarrassed when a product says made in Mexico. That should not be; we have to change that." Other challenges included weather problems or pests, the lack of government-subsidized research stations, the high tolls on the new highway system, the delay in border crossings because of the search for contraband, competition from lower Guatemalan wages, demanding global standards, and inadequately trained or slow workers. Producers and processors overcame these problems best when they had a transnational organization of production, which meant maintaining close contact with their U.S.–based managers so as to refine production processes.

Similarly, state officials in Guanajuato see themselves as being in the "vanguard" of export-oriented production and education. The state's official slogan is "Land of Opportunities," and its economic development plan includes promoting world-class industries, linking related businesses, providing training for workers, generating permanent employment, attracting investment, promoting industrial parks, and supporting small businesses. Potential foreign investors are the main audience for this program. The aim is to increase foreign investment and hope for a trickle-down effect. Armando Servin de la Mora, a subsecretary in the Ministry of Economic Development (interview, March 28, 1996), explained that the strategy was to construct "a culture of quality and productivity." While the plan is ambitious, in interviews with Vicente Fox, then governor and leader of the conservative opposition, Partido Acción Nacional (National Action Party—PAN), and his high-level staff, it was clear that there are not enough resources to implement the plan, particularly providing quality public education and infrastructure. Anticipating running for president, Fox (interview, September 12, 1996) took pains to position himself against the power of the Partido Revolucionario Institucional (Institutional Revolutionary Party—PRI) by asserting that he was contending with decades of "an all-powerful presidency, a dictatorship of the party. It has pursued development that has destabilized the country and made it very centralized." The governor admitted that, despite the growth of export-oriented agriculture, unemployment in Guanajuato had increased, 40 percent of the population lived in dire poverty, and illiteracy was widespread. He saw the only path for change as "creating mechanisms that unite and integrate the vanguard [industries] with the rear guard [workers]. Those are the means to resolve

[the problems] of neoliberalism." Thus, although, according to Javier Us-
abiago Arroyo of the Ministry of Agricultural and Rural Development (interview, March 28, 1996) food processing represented only about 7 percent
of total agriculture-related output in Guanajuato, local government officials
saw it as a key sector that should be supported.

Three years after the 1994 devaluation of the peso, the Mexican economy
began experiencing growth. President Ernesto Zedillo refinanced $6 billion
in loans and created 495,000 new jobs, and the peso gained strength. More
important for the working class, inflation was down to 19.7 percent (from 31
percent in 1996), contract wage increases exceeded the rate of inflation, foreign investment flowed into Mexico, and consumer buying power stopped
declining. President Zedillo acknowledged that the common people had not
benefited from the country's economic gains, and he initiated a $155 million
program to attack poverty, which he called Mexico's "gravest shortcoming."
The program, which partially replaced previously dismantled subsidies,
would help four hundred thousand families by providing subsidies for food
and regular visits to doctors (DePalma, 1997). Despite these modest improvements, Guanajuato state officials struggled to solve entrenched economic and social problems that were national in origin and seen as beyond
their control.

Workers also struggled in this economic and social context. Women who
worked in the transnational food-processing plants were trained to produce
quality based on the destination of the finished product. Women were concentrated in tasks requiring manual labor—cutting vegetables or repacking
after inspection. The work was arduous and strained their bodies, leaving
them with sore hands, necks, or backs. Compared with working in the fields,
however, these were good jobs. Women appreciated that they were paid
above the minimum wage, that they were working indoors and did not have
to endure the hot sun, and that the work seasons were longer than those for
fresh products.

Young women often found themselves the sole or major support of very
large households, particularly when there was no land and men were un-
or under employed. In rural areas, women employed in agroindustry usually stopped working after they got married, but in the working-class
neighborhoods of cities they often stayed on the job even after marriage
(Arias, 1994). Young women were well aware that their families were struggling economically and if they were to marry the loss of their wages would
devastate the household economy. Older women were also in a vulnerable
situation, often being the major source of support for their families even
when husbands or sons were employed. The strategy of "work intensification," in which multiple household members, particularly women, participated in the labor market, was increasingly common in rural areas
(González de la Rocha, 1994). Further, the difficulties generated by lack of

running water or transportation meant that the double day for working women in rural areas was extraordinary.

With the exception of a few very high-paying blue-collar jobs, men also experienced working in food processing as economically debilitating. The work itself was hard, and it paid about $5 a day; workers estimated this was about two-thirds what it would take to support a family well. Thus men's jobs in food processing generated the need for additional sources of income, each of which was physically and emotionally taxing and disrupted traditional notions of men's work. After a full day on the job at the factory, when men often expected to relax over a meal, they were trying to figure out how to augment their incomes—perhaps by raising animals or finding a service or product to sell. Work, then, was no longer fixed in a particular site, job or employer, and men performed other income-generating activities when they were off the job. These experiences disrupted the notion of being *jefe de familia* (head of the family), traditionally providing for one's children and wife and even one's widowed mother.

In response to these conditions, the FAT embarked on the organization of women food-processing workers. An FAT organizer (interview, September 14, 1995) told me: "I am developing a project especially for women. Not just for women workers, but a general problematic: women and the family, at work, in politics, women and human rights." Impeded by company unions at the plants, the FAT served as a shadow union, informing workers about their legal rights and advocating with them for health benefits when they were injured on the job.[14]

Food-processing workers often considered the possibility of getting outside the constraints of their lives through migration to the United States, which would help them earn dollars and significantly increase family income. Indeed, the Bajío includes states with high emigration rates (Massey, et al. 1987). Workers often felt deeply ambivalent about this prospect, however, and considered family constraints as well as their reception in the United States before deciding to leave. For example, when I asked Javier if he had he ever thought of going to the United States to work, he replied (interview, September 13, 1995): "Well, yes, I have thought about it, but right now is when the children need me the most. One day the oldest will work and stay here helping his mother—then I could go. And it is very difficult if one does not have documents, and it is difficult to arrange everything. Some say that when one goes then bad luck will strike. That's why I have not thought about going, at least not now. Perhaps one day later on." Even those who had concrete plans worried about possible failure and the costs to their families. Their vision of the family was disrupted by economic constraints. No longer did it contain traditional notions that families should live together, children should be nurtured by both parents and complete their schooling, and women should dedicate themselves to their homes and families rather than the labor market. Rather, families had to rely on multiple sources of income and increasingly flexible gender expectations—a process that began much earlier in the United States.

Potential migrants were well aware of the passage of California's Proposition 187 (1994). Over 90 percent of Mexican households have access to television, and news programs focus on the plight of migrants (Castañeda, 1995). People asked me repeatedly, "Why don't they want us? We only want to do the work that Americans don't like." Further, potential migrants worried about the possible negative influences on their children of American culture. The dangers of crossing the border illegally were more chilling, for there were stories of migrants' being robbed or assaulted or dying on the journey *al norte*. In 1997 the U.S. Immigration and Naturalization Service began broadcasting a "Stay Out, Stay Alive" campaign, featuring television commercials and newspaper advertisements in Mexico and other countries warning of the dangers of evading immigration checkpoints.[15] For all of these reasons, migration was not a viable option for many. Those who remained often felt defeated, as did María Gonzáles (interview, September 13, 1995): "With those wages in the factories, we can't do anything. There is no recourse but to remain here, working."

Workers, then, presented narratives of overcoming adversity and struggling to maintain their families. Young women took pride in their ability to *aguantar* (persevere) in the face of difficulties, and were relieved that they no longer had to work in the fields. Whatever dreams or fantasies young women might have had—to continue their education, to marry and raise a family—were often held in check. Married women's and men's desires—often centering on dedicating themselves to their children's well-being—were frustrated as well. Increasingly, the family, considered part of the cultural bedrock of Mexico, was becoming something that working-class Mexicanas/os mourned the loss of as they considered the possible disruptions of migration and cultivated transnational social networks.

LAS CASAS TRISTES

In an attempt to look more closely at the sending communities, I visited several villages in Guanajuato, Michoacán, and Jalisco. I had interviewed Ester Mora in her modest home in Watsonville, and her mother, Doña Isabel, from the village of San Pedro in Jalisco, happened to be visiting and caring for her youngest child during the interview. Ester had five children, all born in the United States, and after years of working in the fields and then the canneries, had been laid off and received training as a hairdresser. She was employed full-time at a local beauty shop and hoped to continue studying English. Ester found the pressures of working full-time very intense. An especially trying time had been when she was a checker in the fields and had to begin work at 6:30 A.M. and then spent her evenings studying English. It had been hard on the whole family but especially on her children, for whom she had little time. When her oldest daughter was thirteen years old, she began expressing rebellion over her lack of freedom, and Ester and her spouse decided that she and her daughter would return to San Pedro. The women remained for a year, living in the house the Moras had built with wages from working in the fields and to which they hoped to return eventually. After they returned to Watsonville, the daughter calmed down, hoping to avoid another tour in the old country, and appreciated the many freedoms she had compared with young women in the village. Ester and her spouse, who worked in light manufacturing making over $10 an hour, were able to purchase their home in Watsonville and had achieved economic stability. They were becoming increasingly ambivalent about the possibility of returning to San Pedro. Ester's husband wanted to return there when he retired, but Ester (interview, September 16, 1996) said: "I told him, 'Why now? You are going to keep the doctor busy here.' And over there life is more regulated. It could be because I have spent more time here, in this house also, than the time when I was single [living in San Pedro]." The people I interviewed estimated that about three hundred homes remained in San Pedro, while over six hundred people from San Pedro lived in Watsonville. Ester noted: "Almost everyone from San Pedro is living in Watsonville now. Only the houses remain behind, with the elders and the children." Ester would have a hard time persuading her U.S.–born children to move permanently to San Pedro, especially after the experience of the oldest daughter.

A year and a half after I interviewed Ester, I looked up Doña Isabel in San Pedro. I found her in a cool brick house, spacious and well furnished, with running water and electricity, modern appliances, lovely arched windows, and a center courtyard filled with fruit trees, herbs and flowers, and song birds. Her spouse had built the home during the years in which he traveled to Texas as a bracero beginning in 1946, originally to pick cotton. Later he would travel to California, to Watsonville in particular, to pick other crops through the early 1970s. His position as a low-waged farmworker had generated enough income to pay for the small tortillería and grocery store that the family still ran as sources of income and much prestige for him as *jefe de familia*. The couple eventually had twelve children. In the late 1970s their eldest son began migrating, following the path set out by his father. Eventually eight of the children would migrate and settle permanently in the United State, two in Los Angeles and six in the Watsonville area. Doña Isabel's home was very nice compared with some of her neighbors'—she had her own "*norte*" there in San Pedro.

Ester's sister showed me the two small businesses, and then took me to see what she called *la casa triste*, Ester's house. The house was situated on the lakeside; the living room had a view of the lake and the green hills surrounding the village, bathed in sunshine. It was modern, with running water, electricity, two bathrooms, and three bedrooms partially furnished with hand-carved wooden tables and beds. A relatively new washing machine sat idle. Outside were fruit trees, flowering bougainvillea, herbs, and roses, all carefully tended. As we walked through the empty rooms that echoed our footsteps, I was overwhelmed by *tristeza* (sadness). "Why can't the family live here in this paradise?" I wondered. How sad that Ester and her spouse worked so hard in the fields and canneries to save for a beautiful home in which they cannot live!

There were other *casas tristes* in the village, as well as *familias* saddened by the permanent migration of kin. I visited another woman whose son and daughter-in-law (Lucio and María Cabañas) I had interviewed in Watsonville. Without a telephone and with very limited funds, Señora Cabañas could not maintain frequent communication with her children in the United States. Thus we became an important conduit of knowledge, informing her about her son's new, better job and the well-being of his children, and when I returned to Santa Cruz County I took them a recent photograph of her. The village felt abandoned.

Doña Isabel explained that she spent several months each year visiting her children in California. That was how I had met her the previous year. She always returned home to stay with her two youngest children, however, who were in their early twenties. Thus her family lives in a *casa dividida* (divided home), with some members in the United States and some in Mexico in frequent communication and social exchange.[16] Her son rented land to grow corn and from experience knew that one day's work in the United States was more than a week's in San Pedro. Her daughter ran the grocery store. They, too, wanted to migrate but had to wait for their papers, and they carefully monitored television reports on possible changes in U.S. immigration law. As did many others, they asked me about immigration politics in California. Doña Isabel would prefer to live in San Pedro. Although her income from the two businesses was small, so were her needs; her house was paid for, and she preferred her own village to the United States. Still, she was resigned to the prospect of leaving San Pedro once her youngest children left. Meanwhile, her family—like many others—was a transnational imaginary. Her kin on the U.S. side and those living in San Pedro constantly worried about each other, considered possibilities for migration (the younger siblings to California, Ester and her family back to San Pedro), and crossed the border many times.

PERIPHERAL VISION

Whether they lived in the Bajío and had never migrated to the United States or lived in Watsonville after "successful" migration, workers imagined their work situations and their family lives in terms of a comparison with what was on *el otro lado* (the other side)—across the U.S.-Mexican border. I call this "peripheral vision," for it originates in the periphery, in the power imbalance between Mexico and the United States and the disempowerment of Mexicans in the United States. This peripheral vision includes frequent reminders that one's situation is unstable in comparison with others'—that life is contingent upon the vagaries of the two economies. It occurs when a migrant son or daughter leaves for *el otro lado* (the other side), full of hope and trepidation, or returns, triumphant or defeated, and compares home with the second home. In Watsonville during the peak of the harvest season, the community is flooded with migrant workers from Mexico, and workers know that they can easily be replaced. In the Bajío there are plenty of unemployed women who can join the food-processing labor force. Thus when a supervisor on either side of the border tells a protesting woman, "The door is wide open, we can replace you with others," workers must consider their options. Peripheral vision occurs when a television program announces the possibility of a better economic situation in the United States, another crisis in Mexico, which might encourage more people to migrate, or a worsening immigration climate in California or gains in the Mexican economy, which might stem migration. Workers experienced peripheral vision through their participation in transnational social formations, in which production was geared toward a global marketplace and the organization of reproduction took place in fluid, flexible ways.

Guanajuato state officials also had to contend with being in a relatively marginal position. In comparison with other Mexican states and regions, Guanajuato was conservative. Enmeshed in the conservative PAN, they attempted to position themselves with an aggressive neoliberal economic development plan despite its negative effects on social policy. They were aware of competition from other regions in the world and knew that unexpected shifts in the world economy—particularly in U.S. consumption of agricultural products—could threaten the state's uncertain position. Politicians and state officials, then, also experienced peripheral vision as they recognized the tenuousness of their efforts at leadership from the periphery.

Similarly, managers experienced peripheral vision as they attempted to establish a presence in the marketplace. Mexico was in a somewhat marginal position, with an expanding economy recovering from the 1994 peso devaluation but facing increasing competition from other countries, including Guatemala next door. In this context, managers and owners of farms and food-processing plants struggled to remain profitable and saw the low cost of labor as one of their advantages. They were aware that their relative advantage was contingent upon precarious political maneuvering by federal and state officials and fluctuating markets, particularly in the United States.

Meanwhile, Watsonville struggled with an economic development policy that was attracting service-sector jobs and an overburdened educational system with high dropout rates, portending the continuation of relatively low-paying jobs for the predominantly Latina/o labor force even as the state of California moved into economic recovery. Increasingly the city was becoming a bedroom community for the Silicon Valley and City of Santa Cruz engineers, managers, and professionals attracted by its ambiance and its relatively low housing prices. Watsonville city officials and social activists found themselves pushing for equitable allocation of resources for social services, well aware that they had to accommodate continued migration of agricultural workers from Mexico over which they had little control. They, too, experienced peripheral vision.

CONCLUSION

Transnationalism is engendered by multiple processes set in motion by an integration of the U.S. and Mexican economies that began generations ago and increasingly depends on women workers on both sides of the border. This is a binational system of flexible accumulation for specialized market niches in which everyone feels the pinch. It is workers, however, who are affected the most, displaced by unstable local economies in Mexico and the United States and pushed into the transnational migrant stream. Communities, work sites, social networks, community-based organizations, and even families have become transnational social formations as Mexicanas/os construct lives in response to the labor needs of global capital and their own struggles to survive and create social meaning. Thus transnationalism is socially constructed through the efforts of many social actors working at cross-purposes in a particular historical context. Perhaps what is new about transnationalism is that in this increasingly global economy and culture, the moments of uncertainty brought on by peripheral vision are becoming more frequent for Mexicanas/os of all classes on both sides of the border.

NOTES

I thank John Borrego, Micaela di Leonardo, David Runsten, Ana Sampaio, Carlos Vélez-Ibáñez, Manolo González-Estay, and Enrique Ochoa for their helpful comments on this chapter. I am grateful to the California Policy Seminar, the University of California Consortium on Mexico and the United States (UC MEXUS), and the Chicano/Latino Research Center, University of California, Santa Cruz, for providing support for the research.

1. For discussions of changing immigration restrictions and Mexican repatriation, see Gamio (1930), Portes (1979), Hoffman (1974), and Sánchez (1993). For discussions of cross-border family migration, see Alvarez (1987) and Vélez-Ibáñez (1996). For other studies of Mexican transnational migration, see Chávez (1991), Hondagneu-Sotelo (1994), Kearney (1990), Nagengast and Kearney (1990), and Zabin et al. (1993).

2. The Bajío is a large agricultural valley located in central Mexico, mainly in the state of Guanajuato but reaching into the states of Jalisco, Michoacán and Queretero. Watsonville is located in the Pájaro Valley in southern Santa Cruz County and northern Monterey County on the north-central coast of California.

3. This chapter is a précis of a larger work in progress. The methodology is historical and ethnographic, primarily based on in-depth interviews with 125 persons of various class backgrounds—plant managers, growers, technical staff for food-processing plants, other technical consultants (e.g., a chemical engineer on water use), labor organizers and union officials, elected officials and heads of governmental agencies, professionals in social service agencies and community-based organizations that assist workers, and workers themselves. Of the 56 life histories of Mexicano workers, half were recorded in the Bajío and the rest in the Pájaro Valley. Except for public figures, subjects' names are pseudonyms. I also did participant observation in Watsonville and the Bajío during four field research trips made to Mexico (see Borrego and Zavella, 1999).

4. Segal (1988: 120) says that there were approximately 11,500 workers in the California frozen fruits and vegetables industry in 1982, but those were full-time jobs.

5. For example, over 90 percent of the farmworker population is Latina/o (see Santa Cruz County Farmworker Housing Committee, 1993). According to interviews with workers and farm managers, in contrast to the situation in other regions in California, there is not a significant presence of indigenous people from Mexico in the farmworker labor force (see Zabin et al., 1993). For a discussion of poverty in the farmworker population, see Griffith, Kissam, et al. (1995).

6. For a discussion of similar processes occurring in the Northern California canning industry, see Zavella (1987). I use "Chicana/o" to designate people of Mexican origin born in the United States, noting that people's own terms of identification vary tremendously depending on social setting, region, generation, etc.

7. Between 1982 and 1992, the number of California farm operators declined by 6 percent, that of Asian/Pacific Islander farm operators by 1 percent, and that of black operators declined by 29 percent, while that of Latino farm operators increased by 28 percent (see Cha, 1997). For an analysis of the strawberry industry in the Pájaro Valley as a whole, see Wells (1996).

8. This strike was immortalized in the award-winning documentary "Watsonville on Strike," directed by Jon Silver.

9. According to a government official, the plant was not functioning as late as September 1996.

10. This demonstration undoubtedly strengthened the UFW, which won an historic contract with the grower Bruce Church to cover lettuce workers, mainly in the nearby Salinas Valley (see *San Jose Mercury News*, April 20, 1996; Rodebaugh, 1996).

11. Its plan, "Unidos Para Nuestro Futuro/United for Our Future: Strategic Plan for the Latino Community of Santa Cruz County, May 1997," provides an analysis of social problems experienced by Latinas/os and makes policy recommendations regarding the economy, education, health, leadership, public safety, and the social environment.

12. For a discussion of feminization of the agricultural labor force throughout Latin America, see S. Flores (1996).

13. The decline in real wages is noticeable and difficult to manage. Mexico suffered an inflation rate of 17.9 percent in 1996 (see Béjar Álvarez and Mendoza Pichardo, 1993).

14. Independent labor unions often have ties to the universities in Mexico and are in opposition to PRI policies and official unions (see Barry, 1992).

15. The INS launched "Operation Gatekeeper" in 1994, deploying more resources to make it more difficult for illegal migrants to enter the United States. The campaign has tripled smuggling fees and only pushed migrants to different locales for crossing the border (see *San Jose Mercury News*, September 8, 1997). According to a recent study, between 1993 and 1997, 1,185 people had drowned, died of exposure or dehydration, or been hit by automobiles while they were attempting to cross the border away from designated checkpoints (Eshbach, Hagan, and Rodríguez, 1997; Verhovek, 1997).

16. A research team based at El Colegio de Michoacán and local news stories documented the relationship between migrants and settlers between Watsonville and the nearby village of Gómez Farias (see López Castro, 1986; Biasotti, 1996a; 1996b; and 1996c).

REFERENCES

Alvarez, Robert. 1987. *Familia: Migration and Adaptation in Baja and Alta California, 1800–1975.* Berkeley: University of California Press.

Appadurai, Arjun. 1990. "Disjuncture and Difference in the Global Cultural Economy." *Public Culture* 2: 1–24.

———. 1996. *Modernity at Large: Cultural Dimensions of Globalization.* Minneapolis: University of Minnesota Press.

Arias, Patricia. 1994. "Three Micro Histories of Women's Work in Rural Mexico," in Heather Fowler-Salamini and Mary Kay Vaughan (eds.), *Women of the Mexican Countryside, 1850–1990.* Tucson: University of Arizona Press.

Bardacke, Frank. 1987. "Watsonville: How the Strikers Won." *Against the Current* (May/June): 15–20.

———. 1994. *Good Liberals & Great Blue Herons: Land, Labor and Politics in the Pajaro Valley.* Santa Cruz, CA: Center for Political Ecology.

Barnett, Tracy L. 1996. "Orders Issued Against UFW." *Santa Cruz Sentinel*, June 19.

———. 1997. "Thousands Rally for UFW." *Santa Cruz Sentinel*, April 15.

Barry, Tom. 1995. *Zapata's Revenge: Free Trade and the Farm Crisis in Mexico.* Boston: South End Press.

Barry, Tom (ed.). 1992. *Mexico: A Country Guide.* Albuquerque: Inter-Hemispheric Education Resource Center.

Béjar Alvarez, Alejandro and Gabriel Mendoza Pichardo. 1993. "Mexico 1988–1991: A Successful Economic Adjustment Program?" Translated by John F. Uggen. *Latin American Perspectives* 20 (Summer): 32–45.

Biasotti, Marianne. 1996a. "A Tie That Binds: Watsonville's Sister Village." *Santa Cruz Sentinel,* January 14.

———. 1996b. "They Send Money From Watsonville, When Able." *Santa Cruz Sentinel,* January 14.

———. 1996c. "Going North Means Survival to Gomez Farias Residents: Region Sends More Workers to U.S. than Any Other in Mexico." *Santa Cruz Sentinel,* January 15.

Bivings, Leigh and David Runsten. 1992. "Potential Competitiveness of the Mexican Processed Vegetable and Strawberry Industries." Report Prepared for Ministry of Agriculture, Fisheries and Food, British Columbia, July.

Borrego, John. 1997. "A Tale of Two Cities in North America: Global Capitalism and Revolutionist Accumulation." Unpublished manuscript.

Borrego, John and Patricia Zavella. 1999. "Policy Implications of the Restructuring of Frozen Food Production in North America and Its Impact on Watsonville, California." Report to the Latina/Latino Policy Research Program, California Policy Seminar.

Cardenas, Gilberto and Estevan T. Flores. 1986. "The Migration and Settlement of Undocumented Women." Unpublished manuscript, Center for Mexican American Studies, University of Texas at Austin.

Carroll, Paul B. 1995. "Speedier U.S.–Mexico Traffic Is Sought." *Wall Street Journal,* September 19: A18.

Castañeda, Jorge G. 1995. *The Mexican Shock: Its Meaning for the U.S.* New York: The Free Press.

Cha, Ariana E. 1997. "Immigrants Alter Face of State's Farms, Minorities Reap Success in a Field Long Dominated by Whites." *San Jose Mercury News,* August 25.

Chávez, Leo R. 1991. *Shadowed Lives: Undocumented Immigrants in American Society.* New York: Harcourt Brace Jovanovich College Publishers.

DePalma, Anthony. 1997. "Mexico's Recovery Just Bypasses the Poor." *New York Times,* August 12.

Durand, Jorge. 1992. "Mas allá de la linea: Patrones migratorios entre México y Estados Unidos." Ph.D. diss., Colegio de Michoacán.

Eshbach, Karl, Jacqueline Hagan, and Nestor Rodríguez. 1997. *Death at the Border.* Center for Immigration Research Working Paper 97–102.

Flores, Sara María Lara (ed.). 1996. *Jornaleras, temporeras y boias-frias: El rostro femenino del mercado de trabajo rural en América Latina.* Venezuela: UNRISA–Nueva Sociedad.

Flores, William V. 1997. "*Mujeres en huelga*: Cultural Citizenship and Gender Empowerment in a Cannery Strike," in William V. Flores and Rina Benmayor (eds.), *Latino Cultural Citizenship: Claiming Identity, Space, and Rights.* Boston: Beacon Press.

Fowler-Salamini, Heather and Mary Kay Vaughan. 1994. "Introduction," in Heather Fowler-Salamini and Mary Kay Vaughan (eds.), *Women of the Mexican Countryside, 1850–1990.* Tucson: University of Arizona Press.

Fox, Vicente. 1997. "Mexican Politician Warns of Peso Catastrophe." *Reuters Limited,* February 25.

Gamio, Manuel. 1930. *Mexican Immigration to the United States.* Chicago: University of Chicago Press.

Ginsburg, Faye D. and Rayna Rapp. 1995. *Conceiving the New World Order: The Global Politics of Reproduction.* Berkeley: University of California Press.

Glick Schiller, Nina, Linda Basch, and Cristina Blanc-Szanton (eds.). 1992. *Towards a Transnational Perspective on Migration: Race, Class, Ethnicity, and Nationalism Reconsidered.* New York: New York Academy of Sciences.

Glick Schiller, Nina, Linda Basch, and Cristina Blanc-Szanton. 1995. "From Immigrant to Transmigrant: Theorizing Transnational Migration." *Anthropological Quarterly* 68: 48–63.

Gónzalez de la Rocha, Mercedes. 1994. *The Resources of Poverty: Women and Survival in a Mexican City.* Oxford: Blackwell.

Griffith, David, Ed Kissam, et al. 1995. *Working Poor: Farmworkers in the United States.* Philadelphia: Temple University Press.

Hoffman, Abraham. 1974. *Unwanted Mexican Americans in the Great Depression: Repatriation Pressures, 1929–1939.* Tucson: University of Arizona Press.

Hondagneu-Sotelo, Pierrette. 1994. *Gendered Transitions: Mexican Experiences of Immigration.* Berkeley: University of California Press.

Kearney, Michael. 1990. "Borders and Boundaries of State and Self at the End of Empire." *Journal of Historical Sociology* 4(1): 52–75.

Little, Peter D. and Michael J. Watts. 1994. *Living Under Contract: Contract Farming and Agrarian Transformation in Sub-Saharan Africa.* Madison: University of Wisconsin Press.

López Castro, Gustavo. 1986. *La casa dividida: Un estudio de caso sobre la migración a Estados Unidos en un pueblo michoacano.* El Colegio de Michoacán, Asociación Mexicana de Población.

Massey, Douglas S., Rafael Alarcón, Jorge Durand, and Humberto González. 1987. *Return to Aztlan: The Social Process of International Migration from Western Mexico.* Berkeley: University of California Press.

Moulton, Kirby and David Runsten. 1986. *The Frozen Vegetable Industry of Mexico.* Berkeley: University of California Cooperative Extension.

Nagengast, Carole and Michael Kearney. 1990. "Mixtec Ethnicity: Social Identity, Political Consciousness, and Political Activism." *Latin American Research Review* 25 (2): 61–91.

Palerm, Juan Vicente. 1991. "Farm Labor Needs and Farm Workers in California, 1970–1989." Unpublished manuscript, State Employment Development Department.

Palerm, Juan Vicente and José Ignacio Urquiola. 1993. "A Binational System of Agricultural Production: The Case of the Mexican Bajío and California," in Daniel G. Aldrich Jr. and Lorenzo Meyer (eds.), *Mexico and the United States: Neighbors in Crisis.* Berkeley, CA: Borgo Press.

Portes, Alejandro. 1979. "Illegal Immigration and the International System: Lessons from Recent Legal Mexican Immigrants to the United States." *Social Problems* 26: 425–38.

Rodebaugh, Dale. 1996. "UFW, Lettuce Grower to End 17-Year Battle." *San Jose Mercury News,* April 29.

Rouse, Roger. 1992. "Making Sense of Settlement: Class Transformation, Cultural Struggle, and Transnationalism among Mexican Migrants in the United States." *Annals of the New York Academy of Sciences* 645 (July): 25–52.

Sánchez, George J. 1993. *Becoming Mexican American: Ethnicity, Culture and Identity in Chicano Los Angeles, 1900–1945.* New York: Oxford University Press.

Santa Cruz County Farmworker Housing Committee. 1993. "Santa Cruz County Farm Worker Housing Needs," Unpublished manuscript.

Sassen, Saskia. 1988. *The Mobility of Labor and Capital: A Study in International Investment and Labor Flow.* New York: Cambridge University Press.

Schrader, Esther. 1996. "Of Time and the River." *San Jose Mercury News,* October 13, 20.

Segal, Sven William. 1988. "Economic Dualism and Collective Bargaining Structure in Food Manufacturing Industries," Ph.D. diss., University of California, Berkeley.

Smith, Michael Peter. 1994. "Can You Imagine? Transnational Migration and the Globalization of Grassroots Politics." *Social Text* (Summer): 15–33.

Takash, Paule Cruz. 1990. "A Crisis of Democracy: Community Responses to the Latinization of a California Town Dependent on Immigrant Labor." Ph.D. diss., University of California, Berkeley.

———. 1996. "Remedying Racial Inequality in California Politics: Watsonville Before and After District Elections." Report to the California Policy Seminar.

Vélez-Ibáñez, Carlos G. 1996. *Border Visions: Mexican Cultures of the Southwest United States*. Tucson: University of Arizona Press.

Verhovek, Sam Howe. 1997. "Silent Deaths Climbing Steadily as Migrants Cross Mexico Border." *New York Times*, August 24.

Wells, Miriam J. 1996. *Strawberry Fields: Politics, Class, and Work in California Agriculture*. Ithaca, NY: Cornell University Press.

Woolfolk, John. 1997. "Thousands Take Part in UFW March." *San Jose Mercury News*, April 14.

Zabin, Carol, Michael Kearney, Anna García, David Runsten, and Carole Nagengast. 1993. *Mixtec Migrants in California Agriculture*. Davis: California Institute for Rural Studies.

Zavella, Patricia. 1987. *Women's Work and Chicano Families: Cannery Workers in the Santa Clara Valley*. Ithaca, NY: Cornell University Press.

10

Immigrant and Migrant Farmworkers in the Santa Maria Valley

Juan Vicente Palerm

Agriculture in California is a growth industry. In fact, the nearly $20-billion business was recently characterized by the *Los Angeles Times* as one of the few healthy parts of the state's wounded economy (Woutat, 1993). California's expanding farm economy is fueled by a healthy and growing worldwide appetite for fresh fruits and vegetables and is integrated by its ability to supply markets year-round because of a benign climate, a reliable irrigation infrastructure, and an effective corporate structure.

The production of high-value but labor-intensive specialty crops has increased both farm revenues and farm employment (Martin, 1988; Palerm, 1991; Villarejo and Runsten, 1993). Recent estimates reveal that nearly 1 million workers are employed by California farms, 20 percent more than fifteen years ago (Villarejo and Runsten, 1993: vii). The vast majority of these workers, 90 percent, are foreign-born; most come from Mexico.

Although a large and growing number of Mexican-origin farmworkers have settled permanently in California with their families (Palerm, 1989; 1991), many continue to travel from their home communities in Mexico to farm employment locations in California on a regular schedule (Massey et al., 1987; Palerm and Urquiola, 1993). Save a select few, most farmworkers—both settled and migrant—habitually experience seasonal and intermittent farm jobs and, as a result, must race from employer to employer, from crop to crop, and from county to county in order to enjoy some modest degree of continuous employment and a regular source of income or, more correctly stated, to diminish the deleterious effects of seasonal unemployment and chronic underemployment.

Finally, despite the fact that special provisions included in the Immigration Reform and Control Act of 1986 allowed many undocumented immigrant

247

farmworkers to legalize their presence in the United States, unauthorized migration continues unabated. Farmworker dependents who either did not qualify for the special amnesty provisions or were subsequently imported and a new wave of aspiring farmworkers continue to stock the pool of unauthorized immigrants in the countryside. As a result, California's farmworker community contains a substantial and growing number of undocumented migrants, mostly from Mexico.

Because many farmworkers in California lead delocalized lives—incessantly changing jobs and addresses, maintaining migratory practices, being undocumented and/or harboring the undocumented, and crowding into unusual housing arrangements—they challenge conventional theoretical and methodological constructs and data-gathering procedures and elude efforts to identify and enumerate them (Gabbard, Kissam, and Martin, 1993). Yet their growing numbers, needs, and problems require that accurate information be collected in order to design and implement appropriate public policy.

This chapter focuses attention on one California location, the Santa Maria Valley, where the above-mentioned farm intensification process has taken place and where, as a result, immigrant and migrant farmworkers gather to tend and harvest premium fruit and vegetable crops. Although the Santa Maria Valley cannot claim to be fully representative of California's very diverse agricultural economy, it does serve to highlight some of the major social, economic, and demographic events that are rapidly overtaking the state. It is also an important point in the itinerary followed by migrant farmworkers in their annual trek for farm jobs on the West Coast as well as a preferred site for permanent settlement. Consequently, it offers an excellent opportunity to observe both migrant and immigrant populations and their interactions.

The examination of the Santa Maria Valley and its burgeoning farmworker community therefore allows us to glimpse and garner intelligence on the demographics of contemporary rural/agricultural California. This chapter devotes special attention to several matters that are germane to the issues in question:

1. It examines the forces that have impelled agricultural change in the valley by focusing attention on the crops and production cycles that, ultimately, are responsible for stimulating both immigration and migration.
2. It enumerates and characterizes the valley's current farmworking population, including immigrants and migrants, and distinguishes and describes the basic types and behaviors of itinerant laborers.
3. Finally, it describes migrant farmworker behavior as observed during the 1993 agricultural campaign, highlighting the dynamic mobility of agricultural populations.

Much of the information included in this work regarding agriculture and farm employment is derived from ongoing long-term ethnographic field research conducted in the area under the auspices of the Center for Chicano Studies, University of California, Santa Barbara. Data on current migrant-farmworker behavior were elicited in 1993 through interviews specifically designed to capture information for the above-mentioned Center for Survey Methods.

SANTA MARIA VALLEY AGRICULTURE AND FARM EMPLOYMENT

Santa Maria is a rich, alluvial coastal valley located in the northwestern corner of Santa Barbara County, some 160 miles north of Los Angeles. The 260-square-mile area is endowed with excellent natural conditions that, reinforced by a substantial man-made farming infrastructure, yields a bounty of crops year-round. In recent years most of the available farmland has been conditioned to raise a variety of fruits and vegetables, and cooling plants, storage facilities, shipping depots, and crop-processing installations have been erected throughout the valley to handle the crops. Farm employment has, consequently, grown incessantly, almost exponentially, since 1985, doubling numbers for the peak spring and summer employment seasons and growing by at least half for the slower winter months.

The rapid, unprecedented growth of the Hispanic population reported for two of the valley's principal population centers reflects, in great measure, the boom in agriculture: The cities of Santa Maria and Guadalupe are, respectively, a hub of agroindustrial activity and a farmworker community. Santa Maria's overall population, for example, grew by 54.4 percent, from 39,685 to 61,284, during the 1980–1990 intercensus period. A substantial part of this growth, almost 70 percent, is attributable to Hispanics, who increased in numbers from 13,281 to 28,014 in the same period. Meanwhile, the city of Guadalupe's 4,546 Hispanics accounted for 83 percent of the city's 1990 population and were, moreover, responsible for all the city's reported growth between 1980 and 1990. Many of the valley's new inhabitants were, in effect, enticed to settle by the new jobs created by agriculture and related businesses.

The valley has always been an important agricultural employer. In the past, however, most farmworkers remained in the area only while jobs were available and quickly moved on to other locations as soon as work was completed (Garcia, 1992; Palerm 1993). As recently as the 1960s, the valley's principal crop (sugar beets) employed a large number of workers but only during relatively short periods of time, to thin and harvest in the spring and fall respectively. Ernesto Galarza (1978: 87) describes the valley in the 1950s as a place that relied heavily on bracero labor; up to 30 percent of all hired workers were actually contracted in Mexico.

Until 1964, when the Bracero Program was canceled, farmworkers were not encouraged to settle in the area but, as a matter of course, were asked to return to participate in the forthcoming campaign (Palerm, 1993: 87). In the early 1970s, however, many of the valley's traditional field crops, including sugar beets, were replaced by more valuable fruit and vegetable crops, which not only required a larger number of workers to plant, till, and harvest but also expanded employment seasons. As a result, migrants were for the first time enabled and even encouraged to settle in the valley to provide a constant, stable, and reliable labor supply. At the same time, the flow of migrants increased to satisfy increased seasonal demands (Palerm, 1993: 33).

Elsewhere I have documented how, when, and to what extent traditional field crops and livestock were overtaken and displaced by specialty fruit and vegetable crops (Palerm, 1991). It is sufficient for the purpose of this work to indicate that while in 1960 more than half of Santa Barbara County's $67-million farm value was generated by a variety of field crop and livestock products, its import dwindled to a mere 11 percent in 1992. Meanwhile, the combined value of fruits and vegetables grew from 40 percent in 1960 to 75 percent of the county's current $500-million farm value (Palerm, 1991: 46; Gilman, 1993). In 1960 cattle, lemons, and milk were listed as the county's top-value crops. Today broccoli, strawberries, and lettuce have replaced them. Finally, while 61,000 acres of the county's farmland devoted to field crops in 1960 has diminished to 20,000, fruit and vegetable acreage has expanded from 40,000 to nearly 90,000 acres.

Although an array of seventy-five different commodities occupies the valley's fruit and vegetable acreage, only a handful are actually responsible for the transformation of local agriculture. These crops are broccoli, strawberry, lettuce, cauliflower, wine grapes, and celery. In 1992 they yielded 79 percent of the county's fruit and vegetable value and 54 percent of the county's total farm value. Together they occupy 62,763 acres—56 percent—of the county's cropland and engage nearly 80 percent of all the farm labor employed in the county (Palerm, n.d.). These six principal fruit and vegetable crops consequently determine and define the valley's farm labor market. Among other things, their acreage and production requirements establish the number of workers that will be needed at any given moment and clearly demarcate when and for how long farmworkers will be employed. Thus each crop in conjunction one with the other determine the employment cycle of the migrating populations, undocumented or not, necessary for their production. Each of these crops has its own employment patterns and peculiarities.

Broccoli, for example, relies heavily on a local, stabilized, and skilled labor force that has settled permanently in the area. Even the sporadic, odd part-time jobs are filled by locals, usually by relatives (spouses and children) of regular employees. A recent review of Santa Maria broccoli crews revealed not a single nonresident seasonal migrant. Most strawberry acreage is relatively recent, and most of the employment it has occasioned in the Santa Maria Valley represents new jobs. Strawberries are hand-planted from late October to early December, after meticulous and costly soil preparation, and hand-harvested from as early as February to as late as October. The peak harvest, however, occurs from March/April through July/August. Most of the spring-to-early-summer yield supplies domestic and foreign fresh-produce markets, but as the summer sets in a larger proportion of the harvest is destined for local processing plants. Employment is, therefore, highly seasonal.[1]

Considering their production and employment circumstances, Santa Maria strawberry farms rely heavily on nonresident migrant workers who settle in the valley only while harvest activities are in progress. Many expert pickers, moreover, stay only during the peak, high-yielding periods, when good earnings can be obtained through piece-rate wages, and quickly move on to other berry-producing locations in California and Oregon when yields begin to fall.

Strawberry crew surveys conducted in April—just when the 1993 harvest season was beginning to unfold on the aforementioned fifty-eight-acre farm—revealed that only nineteen of seventy-eight employees, 24 percent, were local permanent residents; the remaining 76 percent were migrants, most of them with a permanent home base deep in the interior of rural Mexico. Further scrutiny of the fifty-nine migrants, moreover, revealed that twenty-six of them, 44 percent, were regular return migrants who had been employed by Santa Maria berry farms during the past three seasons, while the remaining 56 percent were there for the first time.

Despite strawberry farming's unquestionable dependence upon migrant, sojourner labor, the remarkable proliferation of strawberry plantations also favored, in some measure, the settlement of former migrant farmworkers. For instance, some one thousand regular, stable jobs have been created for those who work the strawberry harvest and the winter planting activities. Other settled strawberry pickers obtain local off-season jobs in other crops, a common practice being, for example, to seek employment in the wine grape harvest during the autumn and tend vineyards in the winter. Another circumstance contributing to the settlement of strawberry workers in the Santa Maria Valley was the establishment of special sharecropping arrangements with local growers. This practice was subsequently banned by a State Supreme Court ruling in 1989 but only after a considerable number of immigrant families had settled in the area. All in all, assuming that my 1993 harvest crew samples are accurate, nearly one-fourth of the ten thousand strong strawberry labor force has settled permanently in the valley.[2]

The lettuce companies that are also present in Santa Maria have established a highly specialized harvest labor force, *lechugueros*, that moves about the extended lettuce geography reaping and packing the vegetable. Although some lechugueros have settled permanently in the Santa Maria Valley, most maintain a home base in the U.S.-Mexican border area (e.g., Calexico, El Centro, Yuma, Mexicali, and San Luis Rio, Colorado), near winter employment sites and in communities where the cost of living, especially housing, is comparatively low. Santa Maria lettuce farms employ some fifteen hundred workers during a large part of the year. About one-third are locals who belong to planting-thinning-weeding crews and machine operators and irrigators. The remaining workers, about one thousand, are lechuguero migrants from the border area who remain in the valley only during the lettuce harvest but enjoy near year-round employment by moving from one company production site to another. Lettuce-harvest crew surveys conducted in 1993 confirmed that few local residents were included in them and that most of the lechuguero migrants, 90 percent, had been employed by the same employer for at least the past three years. Although highly mobile, lechugueros represent a much more stable labor force than, for example, migrant strawberry pickers.[3]

As a close relative to broccoli, cauliflower presents similar production and employment characteristics. It is, for example, farmed nearly year-round and, as a result, offers a relatively steady source of employment to a number of local farmworkers. Demanding 96.5 man-hours per acre to produce (Kumar, Chancellor, and Garrett, 1978: 192), Santa Maria's current cauliflower acreage consumes 860,000 man-hours. Two-thirds of the labor requirement is used to harvest and field pack and the remainder to plant and cultivate. Some eight hundred workers are employed regularly but intermittently by local cauliflower farms to complete these tasks. Harvest crews surveyed in 1993 revealed that all employees are local permanent residents. Weeding and thinning crews are in large measure made up of the same local workers who perform these tasks in the broccoli fields.[4]

Because Santa Barbara wine grapes are used to craft premium wines, the fruit must be picked at its prime, that is, during a narrow window of opportunity when a large number of workers must labor in a frenzy to gather the grapes and transport them to the wineries for processing. Although mechanical means are currently available to harvest wine grapes and, in fact, most Santa Barbara vineyards have been designed and trellised with this in mind, growers continue to hand-harvest their crops in order to ensure a product of the highest possible quality.

Santa Barbara vineyard acreage, according to available man-hour/acre computations, requires some 1 million man-hours to cultivate and harvest. Some three hundred workers, employed intermittently during the course of the year, supply the labor needed to complete all the production tasks except for harvesting. The grape harvest itself employs as many as three thousand workers for approximately twenty to thirty days. All nonharvest employees are local resident workers, and many combine intermittent employment in the vineyards with employment in other local crops. Harvest crews, in contrast, are made up of both local and migrant workers. My 1993 survey of grape harvest crews revealed a prevalence of transient migrants with a smattering of local residents, including many who had participated in other valley crops, especially strawberries, during the course of the summer.[5]

The celery industry, like the lettuce, has established specialized harvest crews that move about California coastal celery-growing sites (between Ventura and Monterey counties). In contrast to the lechugueros, who tend to live in the U.S.-Mexican border area and enjoy a relatively stable relationship with their employers, celery cutters are typically migrants from the interior of Mexico and suffer high attrition rates. The celery harvest offers young men an excellent opportunity to make good money, but few workers remain in its employment for more than a few years. Nursery employees and celery cultivators (transplanters, weeders, irrigators, etc.) are mostly derived from the local, settled farmworking population and enjoy stable employment.[6]

The six fruit and vegetable crops described above create a 15-million-man-hour labor demand in the Santa Maria Valley. However, to estimate the valley's entire fruit and vegetable labor demand it is necessary to make two additional adjustments. First, a myriad of other labor-intensive vegetable crops (e.g., asparagus, cabbage, peas, cilantro, artichokes), occupying 11,230 valley acres and generating $41 million in 1992, augment the valley's labor demand by at least 1.5 million man hours. Second, because one-fifth of the Santa Maria Valley belongs to neighboring San Luis Obispo County and these estimates have been based on crop data from Santa Barbara County alone, it is necessary to augment the first estimate by 20 percent. With these two adjustments, the valley's fruit and vegetable labor demand rises to nearly 20 million man-hours.

If the aforementioned labor demand were to be evenly distributed throughout the year, it would create approximately ninety-five hundred full-time jobs. Because farm employment is not uniformly distributed, Santa Maria's fruit and vegetable farms employ as many as twenty-three thousand different workers during the course of the year. Controlled field observations and work crew interviews conducted in 1993 suggest that in the Santa Maria Valley (1) only 10 percent of all farm employees enjoy full time, year-round employment; (2) 20 percent experience regular but intermittent employment during eight to ten months of the year; (3) 45 percent attain continuous employment during an extended season of four to six months and, hence, encounter long periods of unemployment; and (4) 25 percent are employed only during a short, intense work season of two months or less. Finally, 43 percent of Santa Maria's strong fruit and vegetable workforce of twenty-three thousand are immigrants who have established themselves permanently in the valley with their families. The remaining 57 percent (thirteen thousand) are migrants who maintain a home base either in the border area or in the interior of Mexico.

The number and mix of immigrant and migrant farmworkers in the Santa Maria Valley has been in constant flux ever since I initiated my observations there several years ago. This is, in part, the logical outcome of an agricultural economy undergoing rapid, profound change. Two other conflicting forces, however, have also exerted considerable influence in recent times: (1) the Immigration Reform and Control Act's special provisions for farmworkers, which, while encouraging many former migrants to settle permanently in the valley, have helped to increase the number of both authorized and unauthorized immigrants and (2) the increasing prominence and rapid proliferation of farm labor contractors, whose preference for new sojourners over established immigrants has stimulated migratory practices while displacing immigrants from their jobs. Nevertheless, in light of these 1993 observations, the trend seems to be for both immigration and migration to continue growing unabated, probably at a rate that exceeds the creation of new farm jobs.

Although most immigrants were in the valley at the time of the survey, only half or fewer of the migrants were present. By early April the strawberry and lettuce harvest was just beginning, and most migrants were still in the process of making their living arrangements for the season, creating havoc in the local housing situation and probably producing the worst possible conditions for the completion of a sound and accurate population count. Finally, in April the wine grape harvest was still six months away and, as a result, most of the migrant workers who participated in it were missed as well.

IMMIGRANTS AND MIGRANTS

The immigrant and migrant farmworking population of Santa Maria, continues to grow because of: (1) the farm employment opportunities the valley continues to offer, (2) the dynamics of migration itself as settled migrants draw family and friends from their home communities in Mexico, and (3) ongoing reverberations of immigration reform. There is no reason to assume that the flow will cease or diminish any time soon, despite the fact that the valley already suffers a considerable labor oversupply.

Farmworkers in the Santa Maria Valley are not a homogeneous lot. The stereotypical view of the California farmworker as a nomadic, young, single male campesino (peasant) from Mexico is of little value today. Among the valley's numerous farmworkers are young and old, male and female (in fact, as many as 30 percent of the valley's farm laborers are women), single and married. Some, as we have seen, are settled, while others move about.

Farmworkers continue to come from traditional sending communities located primarily in the Mexican central states of, for example, Guanajuato, Jalisco, Michoacán, and Zacatecas but also from new sending communities located in the southern states of, for example, Oaxaca and Guerrero, and some are from as far south as Central America, especially from Guatemala. Work crews in the Santa Maria Valley include mestizo campesinos, Mixtec and Zapotec Indians, and Mexican urbanites from, for example, Mexico City, Guadalajara, and Monterrey. I have in fact identified schoolteachers and university graduates laboring in the fields.

Examining the valley's agricultural labor force from the perspective of crops as I have done above provides vital information regarding the number and flow of workers but reveals little about the labor force itself. To capture meaningful information on behavioral regularities, educe patterns, and formulate typologies, it is necessary to observe and interrogate farmworkers directly. Here I will focus on three fundamental circumstances of the farmworkers' lives: where their permanent home is, the nature of the family that inhabits that home, and the role they play in the household. The answers to these three queries elicited from farmworkers observed and interviewed in the valley's fruit and vegetable fields during the 1993 campaign allow the distinction of five types of farmworkers: (1) the immigrant worker, who has settled permanently in the valley and severed most economic ties and responsibilities with the home community in Mexico; (2) the binational worker, who maintains two functional homes, one on each side of the border, and constantly moves back and forth between them; (3) the Mexico-based migrant, who periodically leaves home and family in search of employment and wages; (4) the border migrant-commuter who, using a home base in the U.S.-Mexican border area, accesses an assortment of job opportunities in both countries; and (5) the seemingly single, unattached, "homeless" migrant, who spontaneously and unsolicited appears in the valley looking for work.

A review of the circumstances that govern the lives of these farmworkers, aside from providing interesting insights and improved understanding, allows us to highlight the way in which the economic and political ecology of a region is organized by international and national market demands that in turn create the dynamic processes by which human beings are integrated into a continuous mobile stream.

Before undertaking the description and examination of the five categories of farm workers enumerated above, two clarifications are necessary. First, although the five types may suggest the logical stages of a migration-immigration continuum, they are most definitely not. Each, in fact, represents an outcome in itself—an arrangement arrived at by design on the part of the farmworker and not a step in a process leading to settlement. Second, the outcomes described are at best temporary, adjustments to an ever-changing and highly unpredictable environment, one that is the product not only of agriculture's inherent uncertainties but also of recent momentous developments. Among the most obvious of these are the rapid transformation of California agriculture and its employment practices, the never-ending changes in immigration laws and vacillating if not contradictory enforcement measures, and the changing conditions in Mexico and in the farmworkers' home communities, which can either inhibit or foster migratory practices. It would therefore be inappropriate to claim that the proposed characterizations represent more than current adaptations to current conditions.

IMMIGRANT WORKERS

Many of the above immigrant farmworkers who have settled in the Santa Maria Valley have done so permanently, relinquishing their place and position in the home community, severing economic ties and responsibilities with the home-based family, and transplanting their dependents (at least spouses and children) to the valley. Immigrant farmworkers often travel to Mexico to visit family and friends, sometimes on a regular annual schedule, but their roots are now in Santa Maria. Permanent settlement can be said to have taken place when the producer and consumer components of a given domestic group (family) are living (reproducing) together in the valley on the basis of locally derived income and wages.

The vast majority of Santa Maria's immigrant families (65 percent) come from just three states located in the central part of Mexico: Michoacán, Jalisco, and Guanajuato. The others are from northern border states such as Durango and Chihuahua (20 percent), Mexico City (10 percent), and the southern state of Oaxaca (5 percent).

Starting in 1964, a succession of at least three immigration waves populated the valley with its current mass of settled farm workers. Although prior to 1964 (the year when the Bracero Program was cancelled) some farm workers had already settled in the valley forming small, marginal *colonias* or *barrios* within the towns of Guadalupe and Santa Maria, it was the elimination of the program that actually precipitated the first important movement of ex-braceros towards settlement. This action was enthusiastically urged and even abetted by local growers who feared they would otherwise lose access to their labor supply and, especially, their most skilled, trusted, and reliable workers.

A second wave in 1975–1985 accompanied the expansion of high-value, labor intensive, specialty crops which, as already discussed, created a bounty of new farm jobs with longer employment seasons. Growers once again encouraged and helped migrant employees to settle in order to ensure the presence and availability of a stable, reliable labor supply to tend valuable and highly perishable farm commodities.

The third and most recent wave was prompted by IRCA and its special provisions for farm workers which were designed specifically to accommodate the interests and needs of the agricultural industry. IRCA accomplished two things in the Santa Maria Valley: On one hand, it created a unique opportunity for many settled yet undocumented/unauthorized immigrants from earlier waves to legalize, and, on the other, it encouraged a new cohort of migrant farm workers to emulate the experience of preceding generations by also settling down.

Surveys conducted in 1991 and 1993 among fruit and vegetable workers in the valley reveal that immigrants enjoy the best farm jobs, either as skilled full-time employees (e.g., machine operators, field managers, labor foremen, irrigators) or in vegetable harvest crews which offer nearly year-round intermittent jobs. In fact, 74 percent of all immigrant farm workers are employed by the vegetable industry. Typically, for example, a broccoli cutter earns $1,000 to $1,200 monthly during at least nine to ten months of the year; while, in contrast, a strawberry picker earns $500 to $800 monthly during, at best, five to six months of the year. Vegetable employment and wages, in short, allow workers to minimally provide for a family living in the valley, while strawberry employment and wages do not.

Immigrant families, moreover, are typically large and contain multiple wage earners who can assemble a sizable annual income by sharing resources. A preferred arrangement is to place the household head in year-round employment (e.g., in a broccoli harvest crew) while the spouse and other family members find occasional part-time jobs weeding and thinning vegetable crops and perhaps harvesting strawberries in the spring and summer. An immigrant family who cannot place one or more workers in year-round or near year-round jobs, in contrast, must deploy all its available workers, including children, during the short but intense strawberry harvest to amass sufficient income to carry them over into the next employment season. Valley immigrants only rarely leave the area to seek employment elsewhere during both expected and unexpected periods of high unemployment and underemployment but rely on unemployment insurance and occasional odd jobs to tide them over.

Immigrant families are not only large, but nearly 45 percent of them are extended; that is, they are made up of one nuclear family (one couple with children) and at least one *arrimado* (houseguest)—usually a live-in relative. Many extended groups include two or more nuclear families with arrimados who share income, expenses, and household responsibilities. About one-third of the settled families, particularly those who arrived with the first waves, own their homes, while one-half of the families who rent have lived at the same address for at least three years. It is, therefore, a relatively stable population. Newcomers, those who arrived with the last wave, experience a more precarious existence and, as a result, frequently change domicile. There is, for instance, an observable annual concentration-dispersion cycle which corresponds with periods of high and low employment; that is, in bad times several families will converge, actually crowd, into a shared apartment, dispersing into separate homes as soon as better times return.

Immigrant homes, finally, contain a considerable number of "visitors" who are either family and friends from the home community in Mexico or paying boarders. Settled families, in fact, represent a sort of haven for seasonal migrants, especially kin, who receive shelter and assistance while they remain in the valley during their annual trek from Mexico. On the other hand, by letting rooms, converted garages and other home facilities to non-kin during the farm employment peaks, immigrant families earn additional revenue with which to supplement an always insufficient farm income.

Settled immigrant families, in contrast with all other farm workers, lead relatively stable existences in the valley. They, in fact, enjoy a greater degree of employment security, and many have set up permanent residences. As such, it would appear that settled families should not pose serious difficulties or obstacles to enumeration efforts. To accept this as a sound conclusion, however, would be a grave mistake.

Settled families, to begin, harbor a significant number of unauthorized/undocumented immigrants who need to be protected from detection. Although IRCA amnesty provisions allowed many long-term undocumented immigrants to legalize, it forced many others who did not qualify for any of the programs, who were unable to assemble the required documents, or who just simply did not understand the new law to remain undocumented. IRCA also enticed many regular sojourners who already spent a great part of the year in the Santa Maria Valley to settle there permanently and to subsequently transplant their families from Mexico. Although these recent settlers received authorization to remain in the United States thanks to the Special Agricultural Workers (SAW) program, the imported dependents (mostly women and children, and some elderly) have not been authorized. Finally, as indicated above, settled families habitually provide kin with sanctuary during their seasonal sojourn from Mexico to the valley and, hence, add to the growing number of undocumented aliens to be found in their midst. Because many of the undocumented are close kin, immigrant families will not readily or voluntarily reveal their presence to anyone; they are, rather, quite determined to shield them from detection and possible deportation.

It is necessary to note that immigrants' dogged determination to conceal undocumented relatives, even from innocuous surveyors, increases exponentially as the anti-immigrant sentiment we have witnessed in recent times swells. Local, state, and federal "get tough with immigrants" measures which, among other results, propose to bar children from school, deprive workers from access to basic health services, and rescind citizenship from the children of undocumented parents born in the United States are all unmistakable signs that the risk factor of detection is greater than ever. Cautious suspicion, as a result, is heightened to near paranoia when it is rumored that, among others, teachers, doctors, social workers, and "good" citizens at large will be asked, if not required, to report the presence of undocumented aliens to proper government authorities.

Finally, because many immigrant families lease parts of their dwellings to non-kin sojourners, violating in the process local housing ordinances and rental agreements, they are not inclined to reveal or report their presence to anyone. Moreover, they can become particularly apprehensive about this matter because boarders provide an income that probably goes unreported to the Internal Revenue Service.

BINATIONAL WORKERS

Easy to confuse with the growing ranks of settled immigrant families described above are some 3,000 workers who, although they appear to have settled permanently in the Santa Maria Valley, really have not. That is, though they display evidence of settlement by having both consumers and producers living in stable and well organized domiciles in the valley, they also continue to maintain a principal place of residence in the Mexican home community. Some actually own and maintain two homes, one in Mexico and the other in the Santa Maria Valley. Members of these families move back and forth between the two homes incessantly, some at regular intervals following, for example, farm employment cycles and school schedules, and others seemingly at random.

Binational workers, to be sure, own property in their home communities (i.e., farmland, homes, businesses, and livestock) and view Mexico as their principal residence even when most household members may be in Santa Maria during the greater part of the year. Their domestic economy integrates resources and earnings on both sides of the border to, on one hand, support all family members and, on the other, to improve homes, farms, and businesses in Mexico. Typically, they save and accumulate earnings in Santa Maria to invest in Mexico in the hopes of developing a resource base that will eventually allow the family to live there permanently with security and in comfort. A few, however, are inadvertently becoming deeply rooted to Santa Maria and will likely end up forming part of the valley's burgeoning community of immigrant farmworkers.

Most binational workers interviewed in 1991 and 1993 are from the same central states of Mexico in which most of the immigrant settlers originate; only a few, 16 percent, are from the southern state of Oaxaca and none from the northern border states. Binational workers were at one time braceros who during the program years used earnings in California to assist their rural homes and families in Mexico. Even after the Bracero Program was cancelled, they continued to participate in the annual journey despite the increased costs and risks brought about by the illegality of the practice. In fact, it is because travel and illegal border crossings became burdensome, expensive, and risky that some former braceros who did not own farmland in Mexico decided to settle in the Santa Maria Valley with their families (the first immigration wave); in contrast, former braceros who did own farmland at home or had been awarded an *ejido* plot (land grant) by the government's land reform programs continued to migrate seasonally to California in search of earnings to improve their holdings in Mexico.

In the mid-to-late 1970s, when high-value specialty crops took off, migrant former braceros began to remain in the Santa Maria Valley for considerably longer periods of time—up to nine or ten months rather than the former three to five. In fact, under favorable climatic conditions it was not unusual for a closing farm season to nearly overlap with the opening of a new one, forcing migrant farmworkers to shorten their visits home or forgo them altogether. The successful development of specialty crops also created more job opportunities, which were quickly filled primarily by relatives, often by the grown children of former braceros themselves. Although all this was a boon to migrant workers' earning capacity, it was a hardship because of the prolonged family separations it entailed.

Regularly employed migrant farmworkers, as a result, began to establish temporary second homes in the valley to accommodate several related workers and cut costs during the annual sojourn. They transplanted other family members, mostly women, to provide a home environment and infrastructure, as well as to increase family wage earnings by taking occasional part-time farm jobs. Once installed in Santa Maria, children were also transported, among other reasons, for access to better schools than those available to them in rural Mexico. An outcome of this behavior the establishment of binational families that manage and share two sets of resources, one in each country, with members who shuttle back and forth between them with remarkable ease and frequency.

Surveys conducted in 1991 and 1993 reveal that binational workers share the valley's best farm jobs, especially with the older, more experienced workers, like settled immigrants, who know the job market well and have developed good relations with local employers. Individual monthly earnings, as a result, range from $1,000 to $1,200. Although many are involved with vegetables, a sizable number are employed by strawberry farms as part of a core group of "privileged" workers who are the first to be hired when the harvest season begins in March/April and the last to be dismissed when the season ends in September/October.

Binational families are large and complex. All of them form extended family groups that operate as an economic unit. Typically, they include three to six nuclear families, three to four distinct generations, and as many as twenty-five to forty individuals, more than half of them being children under fifteen years of age. Theses families work in teams; while one part, usually the least productive, remains in Mexico managing the homestead and caring for both the very young and the very old, the most productive members and some school-age children journey to Santa Maria for variable periods of time.

During spring and summer a sizable number are employed in the valley, but in the autumn, when farm jobs begin to taper off, unemployed members immediately return home to assist in the corn harvest there and to help keep costs down in Santa Maria. In late November only a skeleton group, along with some schoolchildren, remains in the valley, and by Christmas it is often possible to find the whole extended-family group gathered in Mexico for an instant. Soon afterward, however, workers begin to drift back. In February, the northward movement begins in earnest, and by May all employable members are back in Santa Maria.

Binational families need to coordinate the deployment and employment of their workers to ensure a maximization of the resources (labor) at their command. Because they place a large number of workers in the job market and, in the process, keep expenses down by maintaining a rural homestead in Mexico and temporary living quarters in Santa Maria, they are able to assemble a considerable family income even when individual wages are low or negligible. It is uncommon for binational workers to seek employment outside the Santa Maria Valley; rather, they return to Mexico as soon as jobs become scarce.

Binational households in Santa Maria contain a surprisingly large number of legal, documented migrants. Many of the first-generation former braceros still carry and use the *micas* (ID cards) issued to them in the late 1960s by the INS for commuting across the border; others have subsequently exchanged these micas for green cards and, in the process, become legal residents. Many of the undocumented, especially those who had evidence of employment, were able to legalize their status and obtain work authorization through the SAW program before the end of the 1980s. The fact that so many workers are documented has not diminished their binational involvement; rather, documentation has just made it easier for them to shuttle between the Mexican homestead and the Santa Maria extension. Many, nonetheless, remain illegal. This is especially the case of women and children who did not qualify for the SAW program and, as a result, continue to cross the border clandestinely. It is not unusual for authorized workers to share their documents (green card, Social Security, and work authorization papers) with undocumented kin to facilitate border crossings and to seek employment.

The exact enumeration of binational migrants faces two complications: First, the extraordinary and often unpredictable mobility of household members may easily cause a house-to-house survey to elicit as few as three to five members one day and as many as eighteen to twenty on another. Second, because their households contain a substantial number of undocumented or unauthorized residents, who need to be concealed and protected, binational migrants are always apprehensive about providing correct, complete, and reliable information regarding the size and composition of their households.

MIGRANT WORKERS

Not to be confused with the above-described binational workers are the approximately six to seven thousand migrants who regularly sojourn in the Santa Maria Valley to harvest fruit and vegetable crops. These are migrant workers who are firmly rooted in their Mexican home communities, where they maintain permanent domiciles, but regularly migrate to California looking for seasonal farm jobs and wages to send back home. They are, in a sense, braceros (guest workers) without a Bracero Program. Many originally became involved in this annual trek in the 1940s when the Bracero Program was first established and have maintained the practice ever since by passing it from one generation to the next. Families that participate in this tradition have organized their lives and households in such a way as to enable workers to migrate, and wage remittances have become an intrinsic and indispensable part of their household economy (Palerm and Urquiola, 1993).

A key distinction of the seasonal migrant vis-à-vis the binational worker is that only the most productive and employable workers migrate. Less productive workers and dependents (women, children, and the elderly) are always left behind in the home community to tend the family farm or simply survive on the basis of a steady flow of wage remittances arriving from the United States. Migrants' stays in the United States also are considerably shorter than those of binational workers. Many will return home as soon as the employment season ends or, if a pre-set earnings goal is accomplished, sooner. They come only to work and earn wages, and they are with few exceptions always in a hurry to return home.

Seasonal migrant workers occupy a particular niche in the farm-labor market and production cycle of Santa Maria Valley agriculture. They serve as a labor reserve that intermittently complements year-round vegetable harvest crews during the peak spring and summer months when crops tend to mature faster or even bolt with the arrival of longer days and warmer temperatures. And they especially supply the bulk of the peak harvest labor for strawberries and wine grapes during the spring-to-summer and early autumn months, respectively.

Although the members of seasonal migrants in Santa Maria diminished considerably during the 1980s as immigrant workers settled permanently in the valley, they began to increase again in the 1990s as strawberry acreage expanded and farm employment practices changed with the immigration reform. The recent proliferation of farm labor contractors has often placed migrant workers in direct competition with the stable but more expensive local immigrant laborer. Nonetheless, migrant workers do not enjoy the better-paid, more stable, and skilled farm jobs, which continue to be largely monopolized by immigrant and binational workers. Migrants hold the most seasonal, insecure, and intermittent farm jobs, with monthly earnings that range from $500 to $800 during the peak employment season.

Interviews conducted among seasonal migrants during the 1993 campaign, especially among strawberry harvest crews, revealed that there are two distinct subtypes of migrants: the descendants of braceros, those who have established a tradition of migration from sending communities in Guanajuato, Jalisco, Michoacán, and Zacatecas, and new immigrants, mostly from Oaxaca and Guerrero.

Traditional migrants have established effective networks and accrued experience that facilitate travel, border crossings, and employment. Some have kin and friends established permanently in the Santa Maria Valley who provide sanctuary and assistance during the annual trek. Others rent apartments or rooms for the season and share them with other migrants to cut living expenses during their stay in the valley. They have considerable personal access to farm employers (growers, labor foremen, and farm labor contractors) who hire them year after year. Many come to Santa Maria only to perform a specific job (i.e., strawberries) with a specific employer and return home with their savings as soon as the season is over. Although many, especially those who have kin in the valley, travel from Mexico alone, it is quite common to find cohort groups travelling together, either groups of friends and neighbors of a similar age or multigenerational kin-based groups. The presence of women workers among migrants is not uncommon, especially among family groups, but men continue to predominate. In 1993 approximately 40 percent of the migrants interviewed fit the description of traditional migrants.

New migrants account for the remaining 60 percent of the migrant labor force observed in the Santa Maria Valley in 1993. As stated above, most come from Oaxaca and Guerrero and many are Mixtec and Zapotec Indians. Few have a California migration history of more than ten years, though most have lived the lives of migrants as seasonal farmworkers in Sinaloa, Sonora, and Baja California in Mexico. In recent times they have included the U.S. West Coast as part of their itinerary.

New migrants' short U.S. experience translates into a less-developed network to assist their mobility and employment. As a result, they hold the worst and lowest-paid jobs and are usually the last to be hired and the first to be fired as the harvest seasons run their course. In Santa Maria's strawberry harvest, for instance, they typically occupy the crest of the high-employment season and move on to other production sites before the season is over. Many find daily employment with a variety of employers to fill momentary gaps, aid short-handed crews, or meet special urgent contracts. Most secure employment through farm labor contractors.

New migrants are much more mobile and versatile than traditional migrants. They travel up and down California and in and out of Oregon and

Washington following a variety of crops. Some chase the berry harvest, starting on the Mexican border in February and ending up in Washington by mid-June, always striving to remain on the crest of the peak harvest season when piece-rate earnings are at their best. Others become involved in other highly seasonal crops, such as cherries, asparagus, pickle cucumbers, raisin grapes, oranges, and apples, which are spread out both in space and in time. In the Santa Maria Valley, new migrants are especially numerous during the peak strawberry season, April–June, and again in September to participate in the short but intense wine grape harvest.

Since most new migrants come from impoverished rural regions of Mexico, they travel in large family groups without children or other unemployable dependents who could slow them down or hinder full employment in the course of their trek. It is not uncommon for these families to leave children and other dependents behind in shantytowns and camps located on the Mexican side of the border (i.e., Tijuana, Mexicali, or San Quintín) while the most productive and employable members seek jobs and wages in the United States. Many of the new migrants interviewed enter California in February and return to their home communities in southern Mexico by mid-November. During their stay in the Santa Maria Valley they typically crowd into local hotels and small unfurnished apartments. In 1991 and 1993 I observed as many as eight workers sharing a double hotel room and up to sixteen jammed into a small one-bedroom apartment.

The incidence of undocumented workers among both traditional and new migrants is quite high. Data collected in 1993 reveal that as many as 50-60 percent of traditional migrants are undocumented. Moreover, those who do possess appropriate authorization to work in the United States have received it only recently through the SAW program. In contrast, only 10-15 percent of the new immigrants are undocumented, although all of them hold some sort of paperwork for obtaining employment.

The high incidence of unauthorized or undocumented workers, compounded with the fact that many actually hold counterfeit documents, makes migrants especially vulnerable. By April of every year the vast majority of migrants are either just starting off on their annual treks from their home communities in Mexico or are busy harvesting strawberries in other southern producing areas such as Baja California, northern San Diego County, and the Oxnard-Ventura plain where the fruit matures earlier.

BORDER COMMUTER WORKERS

Approximately one thousand members of Santa Maria's sizable agricultural labor force maintain a permanent home base in the U.S.-Mexican border area, either in small colonias in or near El Centro, Calexico, and Yuma or in

Mexico itself, especially in or near the city of Mexicali. From these communities they regularly commute to the Santa Maria Valley, where they participate in the lettuce harvest.

Most of the border-area commuters are employed by a few large corporations that have come to monopolize the lettuce industry partly by maintaining production sites in different parts of the state: in Santa Maria and other coastal valleys in the summer and in the Imperial Valley in the winter. Some of these companies regularly transport farm equipment, vacuum cooling plants, and office facilities over great distances from summer to winter producing sites and back. Large lettuce producers have also developed a highly specialized and stable labor force that travels from site to site as needed. These are the lechugueros or specialized lettuce harvesters (cutters, wrappers, and machine operators), who maintain a permanent home base in the border area, near winter production sites, and migrate seasonally to summer production sites such as the Santa Maria Valley.

Lechugueros explain that in the border area they find affordable housing, a lower cost of living, and a more favorable sociocultural environment. Few of them are originally from the border area itself, but after the Bracero Program was cancelled they settled there in what they saw as an ideal location from which to access U.S. employment. Many of them can be traced back to the traditional sending communities of Central Mexico. Professional lechugueros are a breed apart among California's agricultural laborers in that they enjoy nearly year-round employment, always with the same employer, by following the crop from production site to production site. They also earn relatively high wages, $1,200 to $1,500 monthly with some benefits.

At home on the border and during the winter months, while lechugueros are busy with the winter harvest, other family members also find part-time, intermittent employment in local agricultural endeavors. During the summer, however, only lechugueros migrate to the distant production sites, leaving behind dependents and other family members, who continue to seek part-time occasional farm jobs near home. Migrants return home occasionally, every two or three weeks, for a few days to visit family and friends and to rest. During their stay in the Santa Maria Valley, lechugueros rent apartments that they share with other commuters to cut down expenses. A few experienced commuters have installed small, dilapidated trailers in the area that they use as temporary second homes.

Most of the lechugueros I interviewed in 1991 and 1993 are documented and have been so for some time. A few who do not possess either green cards or citizenship use commuter border passes issued to them years ago by the INS that entitle them to work in the United States while living on the Mexican side of the border. Those who before 1986 lacked adequate documentation were subsequently able to make their status legal through the SAW program with the encouragement, sponsorship, and assistance of their employers.

Because lechugueros, relatively speaking, lead fairly conventional lives, they are much less apprehensive about being identified and counted and, as a result, offer little resistance to census takers and other surveyors. Nonetheless, those who maintain a permanent home base on the Mexican side of the border are likely to be missed during the census count, while those who live on the U.S. side risk being counted twice because in the early spring they typically occupy two homes.

SINGLE UNATTACHED WORKERS

The four types of workers described thus far have established some degree of routine or recurrent behavior over the years in accordance with the opportunities created by their farm jobs and/or the arrangements they have made with the larger family group (in Santa Maria, the home community in Mexico, or the border area) to which they belong. These four categories account for approximately 85 percent of the farmworkers employed by Santa Maria farms during the course of a complete agricultural cycle. There is, in addition, an undetermined number of single unattached workers, mostly young males, who spontaneously show up in the valley during peak employment seasons and who remain there only as long as employment is available, quickly moving on to other work locations.

Although it is difficult to ascertain the exact number of these transients, I estimate that there is a pool of three hundred to five hundred such workers in the Santa Maria Valley at any given time. Overall, up to two or three thousand individuals may pass through Santa Maria during the course of the year; some remain in the valley only for a few days, while others may stay there for several months. Interviews conducted in 1991 and 1993 reveal that some of these workers follow a preconceived itinerary designed to land short-term jobs in especially demanding crops (i.e., celery, strawberries, asparagus, and raisin grapes) through a network of farm labor contractors. Indeed, a few of the transients interviewed were originally recruited by farm-labor contractors in the border area and in their home communities deep in Mexico to perform a specific job in California and then were referred to other labor contractors in other work locations. Most, however, are on their own and seek out farm labor contractors upon arriving at a new location to inquire about work and shelter.

Single transients land the worst possible jobs and receive rock-bottom wages, often at rates below the minimum wage. They are usually employed as day laborers, and they rarely know for how long or for how much. In a good week a transient worker can earn as much as $200, but typically monthly earnings rarely exceed $400. They also experience long and frequent periods of unemployment between jobs.

Despite their erratic and transient lives, these workers continue to be strongly attached to their families in their home communities in Mexico, to which they send part of their wages whenever they can spare them. Many, in effect, aspire to return home before Christmas with presents, new clothes, and $1,000 in cash in the pocket. It is, however, not uncommon for transients to remain in the United States for several consecutive seasons, to return home only when they are broke, homesick, and/or ill.

As would be expected, few transient workers are documented, but most have acquired fake documents. While in Santa Maria, they find shelter either in one of the few labor camps still open or in garages, toolsheds, shacks, and trailers offered by their employers (usually farm labor contractors) at a price. Many camp out in the fields, in boxcars, or in their cars. Only when the weather forces them to will they choose to stay in one of the local hotels that caters to migrant farmworkers.

CONCLUSION

We have examined the forces that attract immigrant and migrant farmworkers from Mexico to the Santa Maria Valley and the various forms and behaviors of this labor force. Megatheories dealing with such questions as hybridity, transnationalism, and alleged delocalizing cultural identity should be appreciative of the complex relations that emerge in the political economy analyzed here. One conclusion from this field research is that a considerable number of immigrant and migrant farmworkers are under constant stress because of extreme temperatures in the fields, backbreaking work, constant planning and strategizing, the physical dangers of insecticides and pesticides, the incessant presence of immigration authorities, the lack of medical and hygienic support, the crowded and sometimes nonexistent housing arrangements, and speed of aging among men, women, and children under such conditions. Grand theories that focus simply on issues of personal identity amount to no more than self-gratifying intellectualizing. Therefore, although the persons considered in this study are part of a political economy that emphasizes mobility, rapid redeployment, delocalization, and transient living arrangements, these cannot be considered to be populations whose cultural identity or social engagements are of the same quality. If anything, these populations seek desperately to regain stability, determinacy, and certainty for the long term while suffering greatly from short-term survival tactics.

NOTES

1. These figures are based on the analysis of acreage production labor needs. Occupying 24,757 acres of the valley's prime farmland and yielding a gross value of $68,588,744, broccoli became Santa Barbara's number-one value crop in 1992

(Gilman, 1993: 8), deposing strawberries, which had enjoyed the top ranking since at least 1987. Although broccoli is produced for both fresh produce and frozen vegetable markets, local growers strive to supply the former, which offers a premium price for premium products. The green vegetable has thrived because of changing dietary practices of the American consumer; acreage, in fact, has doubled since 1975. Varietal and farming improvements have boosted yields from four thousand three hundred pounds per acre in 1979 to nearly fifteen thousand in 1989 (People's Self-Help Housing Corporation, 1990). A result of both acreage expansion and improved yields is that broccoli labor requirements have increased considerably.

Experts report that broccoli farming consumes some 80 man-hours per acre (Kumar, Chancellor, and Garrett, 1978; Mamer and Wilkie, 1990), half of them for harvest activities alone. Because it is possible to farm broccoli year-round in the Santa Maria Valley and because plantings are strategically staggered, the harvest is almost continuous. Specialized broccoli harvesters consequently enjoy reliable but intermittent employment. Although machines typically accompany harvesters in the field, the reaping of the crop continues to be done by hand. This is essential to maintain a high-quality product. The purpose of the machines is actually to facilitate field packing rather than to ease or replace harvest labor.

Santa Maria broccoli acreage requires an estimated 2 million man-hours to sow, till, harvest, and pack, occupying, in varying degrees, some two thousand workers in the course of the year. This labor requirement is approximately 25 percent greater than in 1990, when broccoli acreage was smaller. From field observations, I estimate that, at most, one-fifth of these workers (mostly machine operators, irrigators, and crew foremen) enjoy regular year-round employment, while three-fifths (mostly harvesters and packers) enjoy regular but intermittent employment. The remaining one-fifth are employed only occasionally to perform odd, seasonal, and sporadic part-time jobs such as hoeing and weeding.

2. From 1985 to 1991 strawberries were the uncontested top-value farm commodity of Santa Barbara County. Its current spread of 5,280 acres is located entirely in the Santa Maria Valley. In both 1989 and 1991 strawberry value surpassed the $80-million mark, accounting for nearly 18 percent of the county's total farm value extracted from only 4 percent of the farmland. Although strawberry acreage increased in 1992, crop value fell precipitously from $82.3 to $56.7 million owing to low market prices and poor climatic conditions that affected both crop quality and yields (Gilman, 1993: 3). Much of the acreage currently devoted to strawberries is converted irrigated pasture that not long ago supplied a now-defunct dairy industry. County records indicate that strawberry acreage never exceeded one thousand acres before 1982.

Farming and varietal improvements have increased crop yields from less that ten to more than thirty tons per acre. Moreover, the introduction of day-neutral varieties such as Selva is extending the fruit-bearing season from five to nine months of the year, and the recent development of genetically altered varieties promises to offer a frost-resistant strawberry plant capable of producing fruit year-round. Although cutting-edge science and technology have in a short time transformed strawberry farming, the delicate fruit continues to be harvested by hand, consuming an inordinate amount of labor.

Mamer and Wilkie (1990: 189-190) report that strawberry production in Ventura County requires 1,612 man-hours/acre. Given the proximity of the two locations, it is safe to assume that Santa Maria strawberry farms have similar labor needs. Nonetheless, calculations based on field observations conducted in Santa Maria reveal that as many as 2,150 man-hours/acre may be necessary (Palerm, 1991: 75). Local growers judge that they need one and a half to two full-time workers per strawberry acre throughout the five-month peak harvest season. This calculation elicits a range of 1,200-1,600 man-hours/acre for harvest activities alone. Using the more conservative figure proposed by Mamer and Wilkie, I estimate that Santa Maria strawberry farms annually consume some 8.5 million man-hours, more than all Santa Maria vegetable acreage combined.

The 8.5 million man-hours devoured by local strawberries would represent nearly four thousand full-time jobs if employment were distributed evenly throughout the year. In actuality, Santa Maria strawberry farms employ as many as ten thousand individual workers, many of them intermittently, during a four-to-five-month period and some for even shorter periods of time. From field observations I estimate that about one-tenth of the workforce enjoys nearly year-round employment while the remaining nine-tenths are seasonal employees.

A local fifty-eight-acre strawberry farm, for example, maintains a permanent skeleton crew of some ten full-time workers, keeps on standby a similar number of regular employees who enjoy year-round occasional jobs, and hires as many as one hundred seasonal harvesters in a good production year. The hiring of seasonal harvesters builds up quickly following the opening of the season, peaks in June, and gradually tapers off soon afterwards. The pronounced fluctuation of the county's 1990 farm employment curve is accentuated by the strawberry's seasonality.

3. Generating $45 million in 1992, head and leaf lettuce is Santa Barbara County's third-highest-value crop (Gilman, 1993). Most of the current 11,553 acres devoted to lettuce is located in the Santa Maria Valley. After experiencing a bonanza in the 1960s, acreage has remained relatively stable since the mid-1970s (Palerm, 1991: 68), at least until recently when it rebounded by adding 34 percent more acreage between 1989 and 1992. Although head lettuce accounts for most of the lettuce acreage and value, the leaf variety seems to be making significant headway. Lettuce enjoys a vigorous consumer demand as a staple for salads stocked by fresh produce markets and as an indispensable garnish in most fast-food outlets.

Lettuce requires 143.8 man-hours/acre to produce, 96 of them just to harvest (Mamer and Wilkie, 1990: 118-124). As with other important vegetable crops, farming and varietal improvements have increased lettuce yields significantly while labor use has remained largely unchanged (People's Self-Help Housing Corporation, 1990). Lettuce is therefore another heavy consumer of labor. Available man-hour/acre estimates suggest that Santa Maria lettuce growers require 1.7 million man-hours to plant, cultivate, harvest, and field pack, two-thirds of which is used to perform the last two tasks alone.

Lettuce has an extended but well-defined harvest season. In the Santa Maria Valley plantings are staggered from January through the summer, and therefore lettuce is harvested continuously from early spring to late autumn. Harvest activities begin in March, build up to a peak in May through September, and subsequently slow down to end in November. Planting, thinning, and weeding crews are regularly but intermittently employed from January to August, while specialized lettuce harvest crews are employed from March through November.

A defining property of the lettuce industry in California is that it has come to be virtually monopolized by a handful of large corporations, such as Bruce Church and Dole (Friedland, Barton, and Thomas, 1981; Thomas, 1985). These corporations own and/or manage lettuce production sites throughout California and Arizona with the specific purpose of supplying nationwide markets year-round. Coastal sites like Santa Maria are designed to supply summer demand, while interior sites like the Imperial Valley are designed to satisfy winter markets.

4. Santa Barbara County's fourth-highest-value crop is cauliflower. It engaged 8,920 acres of the Santa Maria Valley's prime farmland and generated $29.5 million in 1992 (Gilman, 1993: 1). Cauliflower boomed from under one thousand five hundred acres in the late 1970s to nearly nine thousand today (Palerm, 1991: 71), and yield has risen from under nine thousand pounds per acre to fifteen thousand in the same period (People's Self-Help Housing Corporation, 1990).

5. Wine grapes are Santa Barbara County's sixth-highest-value crop. Vineyards yielded $28 million in 1992 and occupied 9,532 acres (Gilman, 1993: 3). Prior to 1970 there were no commercial vineyards in Santa Barbara, but soon afterward the industry took off as a result of a growing national demand for wine, especially for the premium varieties that Santa Barbara is capable of producing (Haley, 1989). In 1975 some 7,000 acres had been appropriated by the crop, and by the early 1980s growth had leveled to the current acreage (Palerm, 1991: 65). Although many of Santa Barbara's vineyards are located in the neighboring Santa Ynes Valley, much of the new growth has occupied the hills and slopes that surround the Santa Maria Valley. Moreover, much of the labor employed by the county's vineyards finds temporary or permanent lodging in the Santa Maria area.

Wine grapes require approximately 110 man-hours/acre to cultivate and harvest (Haley, 1989). Much of the vineyard work is spread throughout the year and consequently requires only small crews to prune the vines, till the soil, inspect and repair trellises and drip irrigation lines, fertilize and spray, and complete preharvest leaf removal. Harvest, in contrast, claims half of the annual labor requirement during a brief and intense moment in the early fall.

6. With just 2,724 acres, celery yielded an impressive $16.9 million in 1992, making it the county's seventh-highest-value crop (Gilman, 1993: 1). Celery acreage and value are both down relative to 1989 production, when 3,478 acres yielded $23.6 million. Nonetheless, it represents another vegetable crop with a healthy consumer demand. Most Santa Maria celery is grown for premium markets and therefore pampered during cultivation and then hand-harvested.

Celery is essentially a cool-temperature crop that thrives in the temperate winters of the California coast. In the Santa Maria Valley, plantings are established during the late summer and early autumn to be harvested from November to July, when the long summer days and increased temperatures cause the plant to bolt. The cultivation of celery actually begins in nurseries where seedlings are started and prepared for transplantation to the fields. Growers stagger transplanting activities in a way that will ensure an extended but steady harvest.

Although mechanical planters are normally used, work crews are also needed to feed and assist the machine and to correct frequent planter errors. When the ground is too wet, owing to rain or irrigation, the use of the mechanical planter must be forgone altogether. Weeding is intense, and harvest constitutes a major enterprise. Depending on whether mechanical planters are used or not, celery requires from 240 to 320 man-hours/acre to produce, much of this (about 150 man hours) during the harvest alone (Kumar, Chancellor, and Garrett, 1978; Palerm 1991: 75).

The celery harvest is arduous, back breaking, and, considering the presence of a large number of workers swinging razor-sharp instruments in a fairly restricted space, dangerous. Harvest crews are therefore made up almost exclusively of young men.

Available man-hour/acre computations suggest that Santa Maria celery acreage requires some 800,000 man-hours to produce. From field observations I estimate that harvest crews employ about 400 workers who enjoy a seven-to-eight-month season of reliable but intermittent employment. Transplanting and farming crews employ about 175 workers on a fairly regular schedule during at least six months of the year, while nursery work employs some 50 workers year-round.

REFERENCES

Friedland, William H., Amy Barton, and Robert J. Thomas. 1981. *Manufacturing Green Gold: Capital, Labor, and Technology in the Lettuce Industry*. New York: Cambridge University Press.

Gabbard, Susan, Edward Kissam, and Philip L. Martin. 1993. *The Impact of Migrant Travel Patterns on the Undercount of Hispanic Farm Workers*. Washington, DC: Research Conference on Undercounted Ethnic Population. Bureau of the Census.

Galarza, Ernesto. 1978. *Merchants of Labor: An Account of the Managed Migration of Mexican Farm Workers in California 1942–1960*. Santa Barbara, CA: McNally and Loftin, West.

Garcia, Victor. 1992. "Surviving Farmwork: Economic Strategies of Chicano/Mexican Households in a Rural California Community." Ph.D. diss., University of California, Santa Barbara.

Gilman, Ronald M. 1993. *Santa Barbara County 1992 Agricultural Production Report*. Santa Barbara, CA: Agricultural Commissioner.

Haley, Brian. 1989. *Aspects and Social Impacts of Size and Organization in the Recently Developed Wine Industry of Santa Barbara County, California*. Santa Barbara, CA: Center for Chicano Studies, University of California.

Kumar, R., W. Chancellor, and R. Garrett. 1978. "Estimates of the Impact of Agricultural Mechanization Developments on In-field Labor Requirements in California Crops," in John Mamer and Varden Fuller (eds.), *Technological Change, Farm Mechanization and Agricultural Employment*. Berkeley: Division of Agricultural Sciences, University of California.

Mamer, John W. and Alexa Wilkie. 1990. *Seasonal Labor in California Agriculture: Labor Inputs for California Crops*. Sacramento, CA: Employment Development Department.

Martin, Philip L. 1988. *Harvest of Confusion: Migrant Workers in U.S. Agriculture*. Boulder, CO: Westview Press.

Massey, Douglas, Rafael Alarcon, Jorge Durand, and Humberto Gonzalez. 1987. *Return to Aztlan: The Social Process of International Migration from Western Mexico*. Berkeley: University of California Press.

Palerm, Juan Vicente. 1989. "Latino Settlements in California," in *The Challenge: Latinos in a Changing California*. Riverside, CA: University of California Consortium on Mexico and the United States.

———. 1991. *Farm Labor Needs and Farm Workers in California, 1970–1989*. Sacramento, CA: Employment Development Department.

———. n.d. *Farm Worker Enumeration, Santa Barbara County: A Preliminary Report*. Santa Barbara, CA: Resource Management Department.

Palerm, Juan Vicente and Jose Ignacio Urquiola. 1993. "A Binational System of Agricultural Production: The Case of the Mexican Bajío and California," in Daniel G. Aldrich, Jr. and Lorenzo Meyer (eds.), *Mexico and the United States: Neighbors in Crisis*. San Bernardino, CA: Borgo Press.

People's Self–Help Housing Corporation. 1990. *San Luis Obispo County Farm Worker Housing Needs Study: Farm Labor Hiring Patterns*. San Luis Obispo, CA.

Salo, Matt T. n.d. "Statement of Purpose and Need." Washington, DC: Center for Survey Methods Research, Bureau of the Census.

Thomas, Robert J. 1985. *Citizenship, Gender, and Work: Social Organization of Industrial Agriculture*. Berkeley: University of California Press.

Villarejo, Don and Dave Runsten. 1993. *California's Agricultural Dilemma: Higher Production and Lower Wages*. Davis: California Institute of Rural Studies.

Woutat, Donald. 1993. "A Growth Industry: State's Agribusiness Rides Out Recession, Insects, and Bad Weather." *Los Angeles Times*, July 26.

11

Citizenship, Civil Society, and the Latina/o City: Claiming Subaltern Spaces, Reframing the Public Sphere

Raymond A. Rocco

For those attempting to understand the nature, scope, and significance of the dramatic changes in the characteristics and dynamics of Latina/o communities in the United States, the issues configured around the idea of civil society are particularly important. Although the discourses about civil society have various contested organizing themes, I take them to be fundamentally about the conditions that foster and sustain democratic social relations. In particular, the relationship between the nature of associational relations and the functioning of, access to, and inclusion in the institutions of power is one of the major axes of this literature. Because the specific historical context and trajectory of Latina/o communities are most appropriately understood as centered around the concern with institutional inclusion and exclusion, the relevance and importance of these civil-society discourses is apparent.

Latina/o urban communities throughout the United States have undergone extensive and profound changes during the past thirty years. Dramatic increases in the size and rate of growth of Latina/o populations have played a fundamental role in transforming the configuration of political, cultural, spatial, and economic characteristics and relations of major cities. These increases are both cause and effect of processes of social restructuring embodied in a broad variety of institutional strategies, policies, and practices at both the regional and the international level. As globalization and transnationalization have unfolded, the issues around which political and social inclusion and exclusion revolve have shifted considerably. Prominent among these is the reemergence of citizenship as a focus of political and cultural relations, discourse, and policy agendas. This is in large measure a direct consequence of the fact that the policies and practices that constitute economic restructuring have served as a catalyst for massive increases in migration from Latin America, Africa, Asia, and the Caribbean. In particular, the demand for low-wage labor in the major cities of the United States and Europe has acted as a magnet for immigrants from these regions seeking economic opportunity and progress. In contrast to the immigrants of the late nineteenth and early twentieth century, however, these new immigrants come from cultural and social backgrounds and contexts dramatically different from those of the countries in which they settle. This disjunction has generated a qualitatively different set of political issues and alignments and corresponding discourses, including contestation over the rights, responsibilities, obligations, entitlements, and other privileges of being a member of the national community, and these are precisely the factors that constitute the meaning of citizenship.

The form or pattern that these elements should take has become one of the most contested terrains in the new politics both in the capitals of Europe and in the major cities of the United States. The depth, divisiveness, and intensity of this issue have been clearly evident in the recent campaigns in California to promote English-only requirements, to limit immigrants' access to state-provided services, and to abolish affirmative action. This debate has also found expression in a wide-ranging scholarly literature that acknowledges the need to retheorize citizenship in the context of the new social formations. Approaches range from philosophical analysis of the theoretical foundations of democratic citizenship to empirical sociological studies of the conditions and correlates of citizenship practices.[1]

Despite the obvious relevance of these issues to the political and economic empowerment of Latina/o communities, there have been few serious attempts to conceptualize the articulation between the transformation of these communities and the issue of citizenship. In this chapter I argue that the changes in Latina/o community formations brought about by the processes of restructuring, and the collective strategies developed in response to them, require a reformulation of the concept of citizenship that is rooted in a particular model of civil society. The first section reviews some of the theoretical dimensions of citizenship and civil society; the second discusses the development of a range of social and cultural practices revealed by ethnographic and life-history studies in the Latina/o "hub" cities of Southeast Los Angeles (Fulton, 1997) that in effect constitute a type of rights—claims activity, an alternative articulation of new claims to citizenship.

CITIZENSHIP, COMMUNITY, AND DIFFERENCE

A number of scholars have commented on the recent reemergence of citizenship as the subject of analysis, indicating that it is one of the most contested theoretical terrains across the political spectrum (Kymlicka and Norman, 1995; Beiner, 1995b; Mouffe, 1992a; 1992b). Not only are the substantive differences considerable but the way in which the problematic is framed varies widely. As with most theoretical positions, the elements and issues emphasized typically reflect the specific problems one is attempting to understand and the context in which they are inscribed. It follows, then, that the most productive approach to the problematic of rethinking citizenship in a way that is salient for Latina/o communities is to focus on the particular factors that have characterized their experiences and affected the articulation between these communities and the major institutions of power in the United States.

Clearly one of these defining factors throughout the history of these relations is the ethnic and cultural disjunction inscribed in class relations, political access, and the nature of participation in the economy. Recent scholarship has refined our understanding of the dynamics of exclusion and the cultural, economic, and political processes that have marginalized and systematically disempowered significant sectors of Latina/o populations. Thus, while cultural difference is not the determinant of relations of power, it has played a fundamental role in the configuration of institutional relations and social locations affecting Latina/o communities. The debates over the nature of multiculturalism have revealed the highly politicized dynamic of cultural difference in redefining the broad political and policy agenda of the past thirty years.

Until a few years ago, mainstream discourses in social and political theory were relatively silent regarding the rise of multiculturalism in the United States and Europe. However, the impact of the lived reality of differences was so pervasive and the issues were so persistently raised by scholars on the margins that the meaning of radical cultural differences has become a major theme in theoretical debates across the social sciences and humanities. Of particular relevance to the issue I want to examine here are works on citizenship in contemporary political theory and the sociology of citizenship that have focused on cultural difference among groups.

In his *Multicultural Citizenship*, Kymlicka (1995) seeks to demonstrate that the two seemingly irreconcilable perspectives on citizenship can be reformulated to advance a theory of citizenship that can account for the reality of multiculturalism. The first of these, the liberal approach, is organized around the primacy of individual rights, and citizenship is construed in terms of the individual as the bearer of these rights. These rights ensure that private individuals can pursue their self-interest through the protection of the state, whose primary function is to mediate conflict and regulate activities. The opposing view is that proposed in the communitarian formulation, and what is common to the various versions of this approach is the conception of rights as a function of membership in a historically specific society, community, or state and the emphasis on the formative role of cultural context in defining the nature and significance of claims to rights. It is only within a specific configuration of social relations, institutions, and culture that the idea of rights can be understood and realized.

Kymlicka's purpose is to advance a new "distinctively liberal approach to minority rights" that preserves the basic principles of individual freedom but is not limited by the traditional liberal notions that all rights must be "difference-blind" and that there are no group rights (1995: 7). He notes that modern societies are increasingly multicultural but the ways in which this is formulated are exceedingly vague and ambiguous, primarily because the concept has not been grounded in an analysis of "how the historical incorporation of minority groups shapes their collective institutions, identities, and aspirations" (11). In order to overcome this lack of specificity, he identifies four types of difference: separate nations within an existing state, immigrant ethnic groups, refugees and exiles, and the special circumstances of African Americans. The rights claims of distinct cultural groups need to be understood and evaluated in terms of the different institutional articulations that define these categories, but it is the first two that are really the focus of concern.

Examining the diversity that arises from the multination situation, Kymlicka sees the nation as a "historical community, more or less institutionally complete, occupying a given territory or homeland, sharing a distinct language and culture" (1995: 11). In the case of immigration, groups seek affirmation of their ethnic identity but do not intend to establish a separate nation, instead aiming to "modify the institutions and laws of the mainstream society to make them more accommodating of cultural differences" (11). Kymlicka argues that to acquire effective citizenship status these multinational and polyethnic groups require three forms of group-differentiated rights: self-government rights, polyethnic rights, and special representation rights. Far from rejecting the cultural distinctiveness of these groups as a basis for rights claims, he suggests that the meaning of liberal freedoms can only be realized in a cultural context of choice. Central to the concept of freedom that is the basis of the liberal tradition is the premise that individuals have the right to choose how to live their lives, to live according to their beliefs about what gives meaning and value to their existence. But determining the value and meaning of different options depends on the existence of a societal culture that provides the context without which these determinations cannot be made (83). It is "a matter of understanding the meanings attached to it by our culture" (Kymlicka, 1995a: 83). Thus the cultural disjunction that characterizes the historical incorporation of multinational and immigrant groups requires that they be given certain group-differentiated rights (different for each type) that protect their cultural distinctiveness as indispensable to their pursuit of the freedom that is the foundation of the liberal form of citizenship.

Other works argue for these group-differentiated rights as the basis for citizenship claims on substantially different theoretical grounds (see, for example, Young, 1990; Taylor, 1994). These works represent a significant advance in the attempt to formulate conceptions of citizenship that can accommodate the challenges of diverse cultural identities, but they have certain problems. While they acknowledge the institutional dimensions of the problematic they confront, their theorization of the structural changes that constitute the context for it is so general and abstract that it is difficult to assess its validity. Thus, for example, Kymlicka acknowledges the vagueness of the ways in which the notion of multiculturalism has been used and even alludes to the processes of "globalization" as having a determinative effect on the issue: "Globalization has made the myth of a culturally homogeneous state even more unrealistic, and has forced the majority within each state to be more open to pluralism and diversity. The nature of ethnic and national identities is changing in a world of free trade and global communications, but the challenge of multiculturalism is here to stay" (Kymlicka, 1995: 9). Yet nowhere in the exposition is there a systematic analysis of multiculturalism as a set of specific *institutional social practices* that are part of a broader process of social transformation. Even more problematic is the lack of specification of the processes of globalization. It is not simply that a more complete analysis of these phenomena would fill out the argument. An accurate understanding of globalization at the level of the institutional practices that constitute it would in fact alter the way in which the issue of citizenship in a multicultural context must be conceptualized.

This is position that underlies the argument of the urban theorist Saskia Sassen, who, after concentrating on the dynamics of globalization for several years, has joined the growing number of scholars focusing on the implications and consequences of these processes for both the discourse and the institutional arrangements of citizenship (Sassen, 1996a; 1996b; Garcia, 1996; Holston and Appadurai, 1996).[2] One of the major objectives of Sassen's work is to use the notion of situated space, or "place," as she calls it, to ground the processes that constitute globalization. Adopting such a position, she argues, "allows us to recover the concrete, localized processes through which globalization exists and to argue that much of the multiculturalism in large cities is as much a part of globalization as is international finance" (Sassen, 1996a: 206). Examining the practices that constitute globalization, she demonstrates that it is defined by a very specific pattern of transnational relations and actors but also that only part of the relations and activities of transnational capital are generally considered constitutive of globalization in many analyses. This is understandable in that the new forms of transnational legal regime "privilege the reconstitution of capital as an internationalized actor and the denationalized spaces necessary for its operation" (217). What is obscured by these formulations is that not only has the configuration of capital changed but the spaces that serve as the basis of their practices and activities have also been fundamentally altered by changes in what binds people and places together in these spaces and in the claims made on their economic, social, political, and cultural dimensions.

Thus these conceptualizations of globalization have overvalorized the role of capital and undervalorized that of labor as constitutive elements. The phenomena of immigration and ethnicity that are in fact constitutive of globalization are positioned theoretically in ways that make it difficult to perceive the reconstituted spaces that emerge from the process wherein different types of claims to citizenship are pressed by the cultural others that typically inhabit these spaces (Sassen, 1996c: 218). What we still narrate in the language of immigration and ethnicity, I would argue, is actually a series of processes having to do with the globalization of economic activity, of cultural activity, of identity formation. Too often immigration and ethnicity are constituted as otherness. Understanding them as a set of processes whereby global elements are *localized*, international labor markets are constituted, and cultures from all over the world are de- and reterritorialized puts them right there at the center along with the internationalization of capital as a fundamental aspect of globalization. Thus while the new claims on the state of transnational capital are represented as a major component of globalization, both the spaces and the claims being made in them by immigrants and other disempowered sectors are either erased, ignored, or construed in terms of a discourse anchored in social and economic relations long since eclipsed by the forces of globalization. The spaces created by globalization have become strategic sites for the formation of transnational identities and communities and for the emergence of new types of claims in these transformed spaces.

Although they do not emerge from the same detailed analysis that grounds Sassen's position, other works argue for the similar notion that this process involves new types of citizenship claims, claims that are difficult to reconcile with the liberal assumptions that underlie efforts like Kylmlicka's. In their introduction to an issue of *Public Culture* devoted to citizenship, Holston and Appadurai assert that the transnational processes constitutive of globalization have generated claims to "new kinds of rights outside of the normative and institutional definitions of the state and its legal codes" (1996: 197). And in an introductory essay on "Cities and Citizenship," Garcia reviews the debates on the "rapid changes in the practice of citizenship" and argues that these require the development of new forms of conceptual and empirical analysis (1996: 7). From this perspective, then, it is crucial that attempts to reformulate our conceptions of notions of citizenship incorporate the contending claims of all the actors occupying different spaces in the new globalized city, a process of political contestation that is likely to change the boundaries and components of the discourse of sovereignty.

That this is the case should not be unexpected since the history of the development of citizenship is characterized by contestation resulting in the reformulation of both the conceptualizations and the practices of citizenship. Despite this clear pattern, there is a tendency, particularly in the discourses that focus on rights claims, to treat citizenship in static rather than dynamic terms, as concepts and arrangements that somehow float above the concrete social formations in which they are rooted. The work of T. H. Marshall (1964) on the sociology of citizenship and recent theoretical and empirical work by sociologists like Margaret Somers (1993) and by the political theorist Kirstie McClure (1992) have demonstrated the complex ways in which different and historically changing social configurations have enabled new rights claims and demands for expansion of the operative notions of citizenship. The need to rethink these in the current period, with its dramatic institutional changes, seems clear.

The challenge that emerges from these analyses, which either suggest or explicitly call for the reformulation of citizenship, is to develop a theoretical framework that allow us to examine these new types of claims and their relationship to the processes of globalization, one that enables us to ground the social practices of these sectors and the processes that produce them in specific institutional sites, "spaces" or "places." I believe that such a framework can be developed by drawing on some of the insights found in the discourse on civil society with regard to the relationship between citizenship, the state, and democracy.

Civil Society and Associational Citizenship

Despite its rather substantial historical legacy and trajectory, the notion of civil society has until recently been a neglected theme in social and political theory (see Cohen and Arato, 1992; Seligman, 1992; Chandhoke, 1995; Alexander, 1997). Although it has been applied extensively in discussions of the revolutionary transitions and grassroots politics of Eastern Europe and several countries in Latin America, Africa, and parts of Asia, my focus here is on explorations of the role of civil society in promoting more inclusive and responsive forms of democratic governance and citizenship (see, for example, Hann and Dunn, 1996; Axtmann, 1996: chap. 2).[3] Walzer (1992) proposes that civil society describes "the space of uncoerced human association and also the set of relational networks—formed for the sake of family, faith, interest and ideology—that fill this space." Although there are considerable differences on many of the dimensions of civil society, there is no question that the central focus of the concept is associational activity and practices taking place outside the sphere of the official mechanisms of the state. There seems to be agreement that at least some of these networks of social action can constitute a "public sphere" that is concerned with both the form and the content of collective life. What is contested is the particular forms, institutional contexts, and types of activity that should be included in this construct (Fraser, 1990).

The relationship between associational activity and the political realm broadly conceived has been explored in a number of different areas of study. In a recent volume on social movements in Latin America (Alvarez, Dagnino, and Escobar, 1998), several reviews of case studies rely heavily on civil-society arguments to argue for an expanded and enlarged conceptualization of citizenship and rights-claiming activity. In particular, they focus on the central role of associational behaviors and practices based on relations of trust, reciprocity, and exchange in the development of new forms of rights claims and modes of citizenship. The introductory essay states that these chapters "call attention to the cultural practices and interpersonal networks of daily life that . . . infuse new cultural meanings into political practices and collective action. These frameworks of meaning may include different modes of consciousness and practices of nature, neighborhood life, and identity" (14). These practices have come to articulate claims about rights within society and not solely against the institutions of the state. Sites normally construed as apolitical are transformed in these cases into rearticulated public spaces in which "market stalls, local bars, and family courtyards" serve as localities where processes of political affirmation and contestation were enacted and resulted in rights-claiming practices (Rubin, 1998: 155). Similar conclusions are advanced in a recent volume that focuses on examining civil society in non-Western societies, arguing that "there is . . . a need to shift the debates about civil society away from formal structures and organizations and towards an investigation of beliefs, values, and everyday practices" (Hann, 1996: 14).

This dimension is represented in what is perhaps the best-known attempt to link these associational behaviors and sites to democratic practices, found in Robert Putnam's work, which contends that "networks of civic engagement" and norms of reciprocity are crucial to promoting the expansion of democratic participation and "good" government (1993; 1995). "Networks of civic engagement, like the neighborhood associations, choral societies, cooperatives, sports clubs, mass-based parties . . . are an essential form of social capital: the denser such networks in a community, the more likely that its citizens will be able to cooperate for mutual benefit" (1993: 173). Thus social capital, which Putnam defines as "features of social organization, such as trust, norms, and networks" (167) that establish relations of reciprocity, is activated by social trust, which arises from "two related sources—norms of reciprocity and networks of civic engagement" (171). Thus, as in the social-movements literature referred to above, the fostering of democratic social relations and forms of government requires a broad network of activities and practices rooted in "the submerged networks of daily life" (Alvarez, Dagnino, and Escobar, 1998: 14). This of course argues for a much broader concept of the political than that found in much traditional political science and sociology, where it is defined primarily in terms of the primacy of a formal, institutional apparatus for governing. The implications for understanding the dynamic nature of the processes that define the boundaries of the "political" are summarized by Roniger (1994: 8): "The 'construction of reality' hinges on so-cial interaction and exchange as a contextual, pragmatic phenomenon. It is at this level of interplay between the logic of modern constitutional democ-racy and the praxis and pragmatics of everyday life and social action that moral obligations and commitments are enmeshed and can be reformulated in recurrent patterns of action and exchange through a complex web of movements, communities, associations, and interpersonal relations."

Adopting the general perspective of these works, I propose that "civil so-ciety" refers to practices based on norms of reciprocity, trust, and exchange that take place within the institutional spaces that mediate the relationship between the household and the institutions that control the primary re-sources of economic, political, and cultural power. Referring to the political significance of the relationship between the state and civil society, Chand-hoke (1995: 9) says that states invariably seek to control and limit the politi-cal practices of society by constructing the boundaries of the political. The state attempts in other words to constitute the political discourse. However, politics as articulatory practices which mediate between the experiential and the expressive are not only about controls and the laying down of bound-aries. They are about the transgressions of these boundaries and about the reconstitution of the political. The site at which these mediations and con-testations take place, the site at which society enters into relationship with the state can be defined as civil society. I would amend this position to include mediation not only with the state but with the macroinstitutions of economic and cultural power. These sites of mediation are the spaces of everyday life, in which individuals and groups engage and encounter the norms, boundaries, customs, and networks that define institutional relation-ships and experience the effects of economic and political policies. Schools, churches, the workplace, and parks are all sites in which the activities of everyday life are carried out and the effects of the practices of power are ex-perienced—in which the boundaries set by privilege, status, and access are encountered as the limits of action. But they are also the sites of association, in which individuals and groups establish a wide variety of relatively stable networks of activity that not only sustain their survival, identity, and sense of worth but also serve as the basis for the development of practices and activ-ities that are concerned with the direction of community and collective life—with the constitution of a "public sphere."[4]

There are, however, several aspects of this construct of civil society that need to be clarified. First, the emphasis here is on linkage between institu-tional power and the *activities* or *practices* that constitute civil society. It is the nature and purpose of activities that constitute the mediating sites as civil society. However, in Putnam's formulation, vastly different types of associa-tional behavior are treated as if they were equally valuable in contributing to democratic practices, with the Boy Scouts apparently being on the same level as more explicitly political forms of relationship. Since not all activities have the same public character or political significance, it is necessary to differentiate these activities. In order to focus on the different ways in which these different activities might promote democratic citizenship, Young (1997: 7) has proposed distinguishing private, civic, and political associations. She uses these to examine levels of associational activities, since it is often the case that the same site can accomodate different forms of association in different circumstances. Private association refers to activity that constitutes the sociality of personal networks that sustain the individual on a personal level, such as the family, friends, and social clubs. Civic associational activity is made up of practices that are concerned to promote and attend to the collective life of the larger group, be it a neighborhood, a city, or a region. Political association is distinct in that its activities self-consciously aim at forming networks to give voice to public issues, to promote particular interests, principles, and values, to hold institutional decision makers accountable, and to influence the direction and/or content of decisions that affect the well-being of a community.

Both the process and the content dimensions of the activities of civil society are important in delineating the linkage to the claims to democratic citizenship. Claims to citizenship always take place within a specific ensemble of relations that *enable* them, not as isolated phenomena. Thus, for example, forms of civic association that strengthen solidarity and trust in a community may not in themselves constitute citizenship claims but may be vital in leading to the activities that do. Hence forms of association that support the development of strong identities, enhance trust and solidarity, and promote a sense of participatory rights and responsibilities in nonpolitical spheres, while not themselves being citizenship claims, provide the necessary conditions for these to emerge.

Despite the advantages and insights that this and related conceptualizations of civil society may provide, there are clearly problems and difficulties that can weaken or distort analysis. One of the primary problems with promoting the development of relations of trust and reciprocity as a means of fostering political inclusion is that, when placed in societal context, these ties can easily deepen the divisions between communities and actually lead to greater political instability and social division. Putnam (1993: 175) alerts us to this difficulty: "Dense but segregated horizontal networks sustain cooperation *within* each group, but networks of civic engagement that cut across social cleavages nourish wider cooperation." But this points to another weakness of analyses like Putnam's, which never really recognize the "political compromise, restraint, and accommodation necessary for reconciling competing interests in a peaceful and more or less orderly way" (Foley and Edwards, 1996: 47). And as Alvarez and colleagues point out, civil society is not unambiguously a positive force for democratization but "also a terrain of

struggle mined by sometimes undemocratic power relations and the enduring problems of racism, hetero/sexism, environmental destruction, and other
forms of exclusion" (Alvarez, Dagnino, and Escobar, 1998: 17). Thus I am not
proposing that the practices that deepen and/or thicken the networks of civil
society are unproblematic or that they inevitably lead to a broadening of
democratic inclusion. Rather, I argue that these practices have the potential
for the political empowerment and collective action that are necessary but
insufficient conditions for expanding the basis of rights claims and the
boundaries of citizenship.

GLOBALIZATION, LOCAL TRANSFORMATION, AND SOUTHEAST LOS ANGELES: LOCAL SPACES/LANDSCAPES IN THE TRANSNATIONAL POLITICAL ECONOMY

As should be clear from this brief review of the complex issues that characterize the relationship between globalization, citizenship, and civil society,
there is considerable disagreement about which frameworks or approaches
are most useful and/or valid in advancing our understanding of these configurations. One way to shed light on this is to examine these theoretical considerations in the context of the local manifestations of globalization in a particular community or region. The remainder of this chapter is an effort to do
so with regard to the so-called hub cities of Southeast Los Angeles.

This area, which encompasses the cities of Bell, Bell Gardens, Commerce,
Cudahay, Huntington Park, Maywood, South Gate, and Vernon, played a pivotal role in the economic development of the Los Angeles metropolitan area.
It was the principal site of the growth of Fordist manufacturing industrialization between the 1920s and the early 1970s, occupying a strategically key
physical space only a few miles south of downtown Los Angeles. This was the
result of decisions made during the 1920s by the economic and political leadership to extend the industrial base of Los Angeles through a process of sub-
urbanization, promoting the growth of different industrial sectors in outlying
areas. Thus the development of the aircraft industry was concentrated in the
area extending about ten miles south along the coast from Santa Monica,
while the growth of the movie industry took place primarily in Hollywood
and parts of Burbank, and, as Fulton (1997: 72) describes it, "Cars and tires
went to the lowlands, creating an industrial belt south and east of downtown,
along the Los Angeles River and the major rail lines that followed the river
from the rail yards south to the ports near Long Beach." The coherence in the
Southeast region lies in the mutual dependence of these cities. Vernon, Cudahay, and Commerce developed as the sites of the industrial plants, with few
residents. South Gate, Huntington Park, and, to a lesser degree, Maywood reflected a mixed pattern, having a significant number of industrial sites but also

large residential areas and strong commercial districts. Bell and Bell Gardens were and continue to be primarily residential. The residential tracts through-out the area developed to house the new white working class that was mi-grating to the region, much like today's Latina/o immigrants, to fill the labor demand of the developing industries. Thus there was a clear pattern of co-herence in the region that revolved around housing, jobs, and commercial de-velopment, a pattern that continues, in form at least, to this day.

Until recently, Los Angeles was not thought of as a major manufacturing center. The fact is, however, that the economic expansion that took place during and after World War II converted the region as a whole into the largest manufacturing center in the United States. The 1950s and 1960s were decades of unprecedented economic growth in the area, and Southeast Los Angeles was a key site of this expansion of jobs, income, and economic op-portunity in general. This growth "machine" came to an end as the area was affected by the global restructuring that began in the late 1960s. U.S. indus-trial corporations initiated a series of strategies and policies in response to steadily declining profits and the loss of a competitive edge to the more effi-cient and productive emerging economies of countries such as West Ger-many and Japan.

These strategies and policies eventually forced the closing of the major plants in Southeast Los Angeles that had sustained the economic prosperity enjoyed by the white working class, and this was only one component of a major restructuring of the economic configuration of Southern California. Four interactive processes constituted the local expressions of the forces of globalization, a relationship now often referred to as "glocalization" (Swyn-gedouw, 1997; Robertson, 1994; 1995): deindustrialization, reindustrializa-tion, expansion of the service sector, and a shift in the role of the state (see Soja, 1987; 1989a; 1989b; Wolch, 1996). By the 1980s a large number of firms in the large-scale manufacturing sectors of Los Angeles, particularly in durable goods such as steel, autos, rubber, and glass, had relocated either offshore or in other parts of the country. Despite the dramatic loss of jobs in the Fordist sector, other industrial sectors in the region expanded. The growth of the key industries reflected a bipolar pattern, with the production of high-wage, skilled jobs in high-technology firms and an explosion of low-wage, unskilled and semiskilled, nonunion jobs in the low-technology and service industries.

These local expressions of globalization were clearly visible in the cities of Southeast Los Angeles, whose growth and development had been driven by their key role in sustaining Fordist expansion. While closing of plants was one of the dimensions of restructuring in the region, finding a source of cheaper labor for the new low-wage, low-technology small firms that were replacing them was another. The closing of the major Fordist manufacturing plants resulted in the loss of the primary job source for the residents of the area. In combination with other factors, this resulted in a rapid exodus of the mostly white working class, who were unwilling to take the remaining, much lower-paying jobs. This demand for low-wage manufacturing and ser-vice labor became a magnet for immigrants from Latin America. Much as had the white working class before them, they settled in the residential areas nearest the sites of the new wage growth industries, renting and buying in neighborhoods in which housing costs had declined dramatically. Thus, by 1980, the local dynamic of globalization in Southeast Los Angeles had brought about a complete economic and cultural transformation of the re-gion into an extensive network of Latina/o communities. The proliferation of low-wage jobs, the demographic transformation of the area, and the spatial clustering of Latina/o communities are all the result of globalization, and at the same time they define the new cultural and social matrix within which associational activities give rise to new patterns of interaction, different struc-tures of needs, and distinct strategies of institutional articulation, all of which define a dramatically different civil society.

TRANSFORMING THE PUBLIC SPHERE: THE DEVELOPMENT OF THE ASSOCIATIONAL BASIS OF CITIZENSHIP

The effects of globalization are clearly visible throughout Southeast Los An-geles. The signs of restructuring and of transnational linkages are inscribed in the physical spaces of commerce and industry, the cultural sites of social-ity, and the spheres of commercial and economic interaction. An integral and constitutive dimension of these social figurations is the associational prac-tices that make up civil society. In the following I want to focus on the ac-tivities that I believe form the basis of claims about rights to inclusion, access, or goods and services in various dimensions of collective life. These claims have emerged from the economic, cultural, and political changes that have characterized globalization in this region, and they arise from the strategies developed by households to deal with the impact of these changes.

The nature of these claims and the processes that give rise to them can best be understood by examining several illustrative cases. Associational ac-tivities were observed in an informal-economy network, a workplace net-work, a grammar school, a soccer association, a social club, and a women's household network. Because the latter instance provides such a clear exam-ple of the types of conditions that enable rights and citizenship claims, I will turn to it first.

In one of the residential communities adjacent to the principal commercial area of Huntington Park, an informal network of between thirty and forty-five women emerged in 1989. The majority of these women were Latina immigrants from Mexico, with a smaller number from Peru, El Salvador, and Nicaragua. About 25 percent of the women had been born and raised in the United States, several of them coming from third- and fourth-generation families. However, despite their differences, the great majority of the women had lived in the area for several years, and those in the smaller group that began to meet in members' homes on a regular basis and establish stronger ties had all known each other for between two and ten years. Their neighborhood activities overlapped considerably—having children in the same schools, attending the same church, frequenting the same park and local restaurants, shopping at the same nearby stores for staples, and visiting the same medical clinic on the edge of their neighborhood. These women, in other words, shared experiences, and this led to the development of ties or bonds of reciprocity; exchanging child care, washing, and ironing; exchanging clothing, especially for growing children; and shared strategies for coping with low incomes, obtaining medical treatments, and securing information about (primarily part-time) employment. Thus these became fairly thick networks of exchange and reciprocity based on mutual trust, familiarity, shared experiences, and a sense of solidarity.[5]

Since the group gatherings originated as social occasions to develop these relations of reciprocity, part of the discourse naturally had to do with problems the women tended to have in common: child care, low-income, temporary jobs, household management and budgets, drug- and gang-related problems, poor education, and the inadequacy of the health care available in the area. From these discussions emerged a shared sense of their economic and political marginalization, which in turn led to critiques and expressions of entitlement to certain basic rights, including the right to participate in or at least have an impact on the decisions that affected them, their families, and their local community. Expressions of this were found in their efforts, for example, to develop a set of proposals (handwritten as a guide and not a formal document) that they argued for in PTA meetings in the grammar and middle schools. At one of their gatherings, one of the women indicated that she had read an article in the local newspaper describing proposed redevelopment plans for the area and pointed out that these did not include any provision for improving local health care. She was severely critical of the city council for responding only to the interests of the local merchants and not being concerned with addressing the needs of the residents. This led to a relatively short-term but well-organized campaign to gather support for a confrontation with the city council on the matter, which took place at two council meetings. Although they were unsuccessful in their effort to have the health care issue incorporated into the immediate plans, the women did increase the visibility of the issue among the residents of other neighborhoods and it was addressed in a number of church- and school-related meetings.

Three aspects of this case are particularly relevant to the issue of civil society as I have framed it. The processes, practices, and activities that led to the citizenship claims were as follows: First, the women organized and became active on a situational basis to improve conditions for their families and their community. Secondly, their participation in more public and political activities was based on existing relationships of familiarity, friendship, mutual trust, and solidarity rather than on membership in a formal organized group. Third, these networks were based not on individualistic contract types of linkage but on relations of reciprocity that included exchanges of information, labor, various goods and services, food, and emotional and psychological support. These exchanges were not made with the goal of immediate reciprocity, however. Instead, the general expectation was that when the reciprocal support was needed it would be provided.

A second case that exhibits similar characteristics also occurred in Huntington Park. By the mid-1980s, the school population in this area was overwhelmingly Latina/o, and most schools were severely overcrowded. One of the grammar schools had a parents' organization formed in the mid-1970s that was very active in working with administrators and teachers to help meet student needs with limited resources. The overcrowding was due in part to declining tax revenues and in part to a rapid increase in the number of students with no corresponding increase in funds. Most of the leadership of the organization had been elected in the early 1980s and consisted of a number of second-, third-, and fourth-generation Latinas and several Anglo men and women who were relatively long-term residents of the area. In 1989 there had been no turnover in the elected leadership for several years, despite the fact that some of these individuals no longer had students in that school.

Huntington Park had undergone one of the most dramatic demographic transformations in California between 1970 and 1990. Many of the immigrants were either monolingual Spanish-speakers or had difficulty expressing themselves effectively in English. Some parents attended the monthly meetings despite the fact that they understood only a fraction of the discussions and usually relied on acquaintances to provide them with brief summaries. Several of the parents already knew each other and had established some overlapping networks, including social gatherings in the home, and the subject of the poor education they believed their children were receiving came up during their informal gatherings. They talked about strategies for conveying their concerns to the leadership and to school officials, and during one of these discussions someone suggested that they request a brief summary of the proceedings in Spanish during the meeting so that they could understand the issues and be able to respond. When they made this request at the next meeting, the response was not only negative but abusive. A number of the board members were indignant that such a request was made at all and told the petitioners that they had no right even to make this suggestion, expressing the none-too-novel opinion that they were in America now and needed to learn English, and if they were not so inclined, they should go back to where they came from. Only one member of the board, the only male Anglo member of the leadership, suggested that the request had some merit and indicated that they needed the support of all the parents and perhaps this measure should be considered. There was an emotional debate for over an hour that was joined by the normally passive parents, and there was a clear split in opinions. The measure was finally moved as a formal proposal and rejected by an eight-to-one vote.

Immediately after the meeting, about a dozen or so of the Spanish-speaking parents met informally in the parking lot and agreed to organize a meeting to discuss how to respond to the situation. About two weeks later, a group of some thirty parents met for the first time in one of their homes for what was to be a series of meetings over the next month. Through these dialogues, they concluded that rather than try to fight the board of the existing association they should form their own organization of Spanish-speaking parents, which they called Padres para la Promoción de Educación (Parents for the Promotion of Education). Within a year their meetings, which had moved to one of the small meeting rooms at the school, were regularly attended by over sixty parents, considerably more than attended the meetings of the original association, and as a result of a series of meetings with school officials and teachers they were able to participate much more effectively in the education of their children.

As was the case with the informal associational activity of the women's group discussed earlier, the activities that at least the leaders of this group engaged in to address the education of their children emerged from informal associational relations that already existed, networks based on the same factors of trust, friendship, common experiences, and exchange relations. Some of the men had worked together, others were members of a soccer association, and several spent time helping each other with household projects or repairs. And several of the families knew each other through their common membership in a patriotic cultural association of individuals from the state of Michoacán in Mexico that sponsored a variety of activities, such as dances and parties, fund-raisers, citizenship-qualifying courses, and counseling on amnesty and other immigration-related issues. In the course of the meeting to form this alternative association, discussion revolved around the idea of their having certain rights despite the fact that most were not formal citizens. This was a theme that was reiterated in different ways and registers, with the main rationale, although not articulated in these terms, being that they had a stake in their communities and their welfare and that of their children which required their participation in decisions that affected them collectively. One of the women summarized these citizenship claims as follows:

> All of us came to this country to work for a better life for ourselves and our children. And we do work. I have never asked for welfare or any help from the

government, and I know that is true of you as well. So I don't see why we were told to go back to Mexico. This is our community. We work here, we keep their business going because we buy from them, so I am not a foreigner here. We keep this community alive; it depends on us. Without us to do their work and to pay rent and buy houses, what would happen to them? And I believe that because we are the community, we have every right to make sure that our desires are considered by these people who are making decisions not only about our children's education but about so many other things as well. I may not be a citizen, but as long as I don't ask anything from anyone and don't harm or bother anyone else, I don't deserve the insults we heard at that meeting. I'm proud of what my husband and I have accomplished here, and no matter what, we are human beings who deserve respect and have a right to be part of the decisions that affect us.

What these cases illustrate, I suggest, is the existence in Latina/o communities of precisely the kind of associational practices, activities, and values, located within the sites of civil society, that are concerned with the welfare of the entire community and therefore constitute a community public sphere. The deliberations that characterize some of the meetings fit the criteria proposed by those who argue for the need to revitalize the public sphere. These activities were a coming-together of members of a community to discuss what constituted the collective "good" for them, not primarily on the basis of narrow self-interest but with a concern for the quality of life for the entire community. They were, in other words, engaged in promoting collective democratic participation as a means of considering what was in the collective interest. Even more important for the argument I am making here is that certain social preconditions made it possible for these activities to emerge. Without the preexisting networks based on mutual trust, common experience, reciprocal relations, solidarity, and friendship, it is unlikely that the new claims to citizenship would have been made. These substantive relations in effect serve an enabling function for the assertion of the rights claims and practices of an emerging citizenship. What remains to be examined is the extent to which institutional conditions and established political alignments and agendas determine whether these claims can become transformative practices that broaden the boundaries of citizenship and strengthen democratic relations.

NOTES

1. A sense of the variety and complexity of this literature can be gleaned from: Beiner (1995a), Axtmann (1996), Turner (1993), Spinner (1994), Soysal (1994), Bauböck (1994), and van Steenbergen (1994).

2. The growing concern to understand the implications of globalization and restructuring for the concepts and practice of citizenship is reflected in special issues of

several scholarly journals: *Public Culture* 8 (1996), *International Journal of Urban and Regional Research* 20 (1996), *Environmental and Planning A* 26 (1994), *Theory and Society* 26(4) (1997).

3. Because of the limitations of space, I do not review the various issues that are contested in the extensive literature on civil society. Instead, I offer a brief grounding for the particular formulation that I have found most useful in the analysis of the new claims to citizenship.

4. This formulation of the concept of the "public sphere" deviates fundamentally from the discussions informed by Habermas's original analysis and is subject to a range of objections and criticisms. While I believe that it can be defended, again, space limitations lead me to present it simply as an assertion and hope that its application here will convey some general idea of the reasons for my adoption of it. See Habermas (1989 [1962]) and Cohen and Arato (1992: esp. 211-231, 241-251).

5. For a detailed discussion of the fundamental role of these relations of reciprocity in creating the conditions for collective action, see Vélez-Ibáñez (1983; 1988; 1996).

REFERENCES

Alexander, Jeffrey C. 1997. "The Paradoxes of Civil Society." *International Sociology* 12: 115–133.

Alvarez, Sonia E., Evelina Dagnino, and Arturo Escobar. 1998 "Introduction: The Cultural and the Political in Latin American Social Movements," pp. 1–29 in Sonia E. Alvarez, Evelina Dagnino, and Arturo Escobar (eds.), *Cultures of Politics—Politics of Culture: Re-visioning Latin American Social Movements.* Boulder, CO: Westview Press.

Axtmann, Roland. 1996. *Liberal Democracy into the Twenty-First Century: Globalization, Integration, and the Nation-State.* Manchester, U.K.: Manchester University Press.

Bauböck, Rainer. 1994. *Transnational Citizenship: Membership and Rights in International Migration.* Brookfield, VT: Edward Elgar.

Beiner, Ronald. 1995a. "Introduction: Why Citizenship Constitutes a Theoretical Problem in the Last Decade of the Twentieth Century," pp. 1–28 in Ronald Beiner (ed.), *Theorizing Citizenship.* Albany: State University of New York Press.

Beiner, Ronald (ed.). 1995b. *Theorizing Citizenship.* Albany: State University of New York Press.

Chandhoke, Neera. 1995. *State and Civil Society: Explorations in Political Theory.* Thousand Oaks, CA: Sage.

Cohen, Jean and Andrew Arato. 1992. *Civil Society and Political Theory.* Cambridge, MA: MIT Press.

Cohen, Joshua and Joel Rogers. 1995. *Associations and Democracy.* New York: Verso.

Foley, Michael W. and Bob Edwards. 1996. "The Paradox of Civil Society." *Journal of Democracy* 7(3): 38–52.

Fraser, Nancy. 1990. "Rethinking the Public Sphere." *Social Text* 25/26: 56–80.

Fulton, William. 1997. *The Reluctant Metropolis: The Politics of Urban Growth in Los Angeles.* Point Arena, CA: Solano Press Books.

Garcia, Soledad. 1996. "Cities and Citizenship." *International Journal of Urban and Regional Research* 20: 7–21.

Habermas, Jurgen. 1989 (1962). *The Structural Transformation of the Public Sphere.* Cambridge, MA: MIT Press.

Hann, Chris. 1996. "Introduction: Political Society and Civil Anthropology," pp. 1–26 in Chris Hann and Elizabeth Dunn (eds.), *Civil Society: Challenging Western Models.* New York: Routledge.

Hann, Chris and Elizabeth Dunn (eds.). 1996. *Civil Society: Challenging Western Models.* New York: Routledge.

Holston, James and Arjun Appadurai. 1996. "Cities and Citizenship." *Public Culture* 8: 187–204.

Kymlicka, Will. 1995. *Multicultural Citizenship: A Liberal Theory of Minority Rights.* Oxford: Clarendon Press.

Kymlicka, Will and Wayne Norman. 1995. "Return of the Citizen: A Survey of Recent Work on Citizenship Theory," pp. 283–322 in Ronald Beiner (ed.), *Theorizing Citizenship.* Albany: State University of New York Press

Marshall, T. H. 1964. "Citizenship and Social Class," pp. 65–123 in T. H. Marshall, *Class, Citizenship, and Social Development.* New York: Doubleday.

McClure, Kirstie. 1992. "On the Subject of Rights: Pluralism, Plurality, and Political Identity," pp. 108–127 in Chantal Mouffe (ed.), *Dimensions of Radical Democracy: Pluralism, Citizenship, Community.* London: Verso.

Mouffe, Chantal. 1992a. "Preface: Democratic Politics Today," pp. 1–16 in Chantal Mouffe (ed.), *Dimensions of Radical Democracy: Pluralism, Citizenship, Community.* London: Verso.

———. 1992b. "Democratic Citizenship and the Political Community," pp. 225–239 in Chantal Mouffe (ed.), *Dimensions of Radical Democracy: Pluralism, Citizenship, Community.* London: Verso.

Putnam, Robert D. 1993. *Making Democracy Work: Civic Traditions in Modern Italy.* Princeton, NJ: Princeton University Press.

Putnam, Robert D. 1995. "Bowling Alone: America's Declining Social Capital." Journal of Democracy 6 (1): 65–78.

Robertson, Roland. 1994. "Glocalization: Space, Time, and Social Theory." *Journal of International Communication* 1.

———. 1995. "Globalization: Time-Space and Homogeneity-Heterogeneity," pp. 25–44 in Mike Featherstone, Scott Lash, and Roland Robertson (eds.), *Global Modernities.* London: Sage.

Roniger, Luis. 1994. "The Comparative Study of Clientelism and the Changing Nature of Civil Society in the Contemporary World," pp. 1–18 in Luis Roniger and Ayse Günes-Ayata (eds.), *Democracy, Clientelism, and Civil Society.* Boulder, CO: Lynne Rienner.

Rubin, Jeffrey. 1998. "The Cultural Politics of Ethnicity, Race, and Gender," pp. 141–164 in Sonia E. Alvarez, Evelina Dagnino, and Arturo Escobar (eds.), *Cultures of Politics—Politics of Culture: Re-visioning Latin American Social Movements.* Boulder, CO: Westview Press.

Sassen, Saskia. 1996a. "Whose City Is It? Globalization and the Formation of New Claims." *Public Culture* 8: 205–223.

———. 1996b. *Losing Control? Sovereignty in an Age of Globalization.* New York: Columbia University Press.

Seligman, Adam B. 1992. *The Idea of Civil Society*. Princeton, NJ: Princeton University Press.

Soja, Edward W. 1987. "Economic Restructuring and the Internationalization of the Los Angeles Region," pp. 178–189 in Michael Peter Smith and Joe R. Feagin (eds.), *The Capitalist City: Global Restructuring and Community Politics*. New York: Basil Blackwell.

———. 1989a "It All Comes Together in Los Angeles," pp. 190–221 in Edward W. Soja, *Postmodern Geographies: The Reassertion of Space in Critical Social Theory*. New York: Verso.

———. 1989b. "Taking Los Angeles Apart: Towards a Postmodern Geography," pp. 222–248 in Edward W. Soja, *Postmodern Geographies: The Reassertion of Space in Critical Social Theory*. New York: Verso.

Somers, Margaret R. 1993. "Citizenship and the Place of the Public Sphere: Law, Community, and Political Culture in the Transition to Democracy." *American Sociological Review* 58: 587–620.

Soysal, Yasemin Nuholu. 1994. *Limits of Citizenship: Migrants and Postnational Membership in Europe*. Chicago: University of Chicago Press.

Spinner, Jeff. 1994. *The Boundaries of Citizenship: Race, Ethnicity, and Nationality in the Liberal State*. Baltimore: Johns Hopkins University Press.

Swyngedouw, Erik. 1997. "Neither Global nor Local: 'Glocalization' and the Politics of Scale," pp. 137–166 in Kevin R. Cox (ed.), *Spaces of Globalization: Reasserting the Power of the Local*. New York: The Guilford Press.

Taylor, Charles. 1994. "The Politics of Recognition," pp. 25–73 in Amy Gutmann (ed.), *Multiculturalism: Examining the Politics of Recognition*. Princeton, NJ: Princeton University Press.

Turner, Bryan S. (ed.) 1993. *Citizenship and Social Theory*. London: Sage.

Twine, Fred. 1994. *Citizenship and Social Rights*. Thousand Oaks, CA: Sage.

van Steenbergen, Bart. (ed.) 1994. *The Condition of Citizenship*. Thousand Oaks, CA: Sage.

Vélez-Ibáñez, Carlos G. 1983. *Bonds of Mutual Trust: The Cultural Systems of Mexican/Chicano Rotating Credit Associations*. New Brunswick, NJ: Rutgers University Press.

———. 1988. "Networks of Exchange Among Mexicans in the U.S. and Mexico: Local Level Mediating and International Transformations." *Urban Anthropology* 17 (1): 27–51.

———. 1996. *Border Visions: Mexican Cultures of the Southwest United States*. Tucson: University of Arizona Press.

Walzer, Michael. 1992. "The Civil Society Argument," pp. 89–107 in Chantal Mouffe (ed.), *Dimensions of Radical Democracy: Pluralism, Citizenship, Community*. London: Verso.

Wolch, Jennifer. 1996. "From Global to Local: The Rise of Homelessness in Los Angeles during the 1980s," pp. 390–425 in Edward Soja and Allen J. Scott (eds.), *The City: Los Angeles and Urban Theory at the End of the Twentieth Century*. Berkeley: University of California Press.

Young, Iris Marion. 1990. *Justice and the Politics of Difference*. Princeton, NJ: Princeton University Press.

———. 1997. "State, Civil Society, and Social Justice," in Ian Shapiro (ed.), *Rethinking Democracy*. Cambridge, MA: Cambridge University Press.

Conclusion

New Projects and Old Reminders

Carlos G. Vélez-Ibáñez and Anna Sampaio

Globalization and the transnational networks established by economic integration have produced a context in which the gathering of knowledge about Latina/o and Latin American communities is largely devoid of any processual perspective. This means that we must construct an alternative methodology to capture the international and transnational social fields and arenas of this multinational population. Nowhere does this type of dialogue appear more necessary than in studies of immigration from Latin America to the United States. In particular, we maintain that the integration of Latin American and Latina/o studies requires viewing these new waves of migrants as part of a synchronic flow of capital, goods, and resources back and forth between the United States and their countries of origin. We have shown in our discussion of remittances that multiple levels of economic dependency result.

In particular, with the shift toward regional economic integration it is no longer sufficient to depict migrant communities simply as either temporary sojourners or permanent settlers. Rather, these communities, like their U.S.-born counterparts, must be seen in terms of a larger economic framework in which traditional identities wedded to a single nation-state or the traditional patterns of national economic development have been replaced by a more heterogeneous construction of identity that is drawn from specific social locations and speaks to global/regional economic changes.

While imagining a Latina/o political subjectivity that operates in a multinational context is not entirely new (important contributions exist in the growing literature on Puerto Rican and Dominican politics and the migration between mainland and island communities and on Cuban American political groups seeking to direct U.S. foreign policy and alter the political environment of Cuba), this construction of political citizenship has begun to engage

293

more publicly with the dominant paradigms in Latin American studies, in particular with regard to the way in which globalization has aggravated inequalities and facilitated a discussion on linking populations of Latina/os across state boundaries. It is this framework of creativity, resistance to hegemonic economic consolidation, and insistence on national "coherences," coupled with the specificity of our own day-to-day struggles, that promises the most fruitful analyses.

At the same time, we must caution against an overemphasis on transnational identities and global cultural references. We are very much aware of the importance of the effects of migratory and circulating population movements and the increasing spatial diffusion of cultural scripts not necessarily tied to a single physical space and place. However, we must continue to conduct careful local-level fieldwork with an emphasis on the relational aspects of daily living and the manner in which the basic funds of knowledge that are crucial to daily survival develop, emerge, and change over generations and in multiple sites. We must engage in more longitudinal research involving not only multiple sites and locations but also multiple generations.

To emphasize identity within a single cohort in Latina/o studies would reduce our research on the basis of material and social existence to a snapshot of what we think others think about the way they think. We simply cannot afford the luxury of failing to examine a representative series of time slices of the same population or cross-sections of populations. This approach should concentrate on the changing material relations of power, economy, and the provisioning process in which Latina/os participate on a daily basis.

Ultimately, to appreciate the value of this type of research we need only return to the communities described in the introduction to this collection. The forty-some households mentioned there are totally engaged in simple survival—where to get money for a quart of milk, how the recurrent fevers of a two-year-old can be resolved, how to keep out the horseflies from the local dairy that infest any leftover crumb, how to balance the need for children's books against the need for sufficient food for the week, how to send remittances to an aging aunt in Guanajuato, and how to prevent a son from joining the local smugglers to bring over even more relatives. At the same time, there are actions and behaviors reflecting passion and relationships gone awry, physical and emotional abuse, borrowing from the local money lender at exorbitant interest, or finally buying a small truck to try truck-farming in order to escape from the fields only to have it break down under too much weight. Yet they seek an alternative to urban rents and dangers, to the crossing of dangerous borders, to lack of medical care and decent housing, and, above all to the helplessness of working three jobs and still not making enough for two days' food, much less amenities. So they build from nothing, scratching for a few extra dollars for paint and mortar, scavenging for used concrete blocks, and jury-rigging electric conduits, water mains, and cesspool drains from neighbors whom they trust. In a few short years they have built extensive networks of persons from the same *colonia* in Guanajuato, Zacatecas, Chihuahua, or Ciudad Juárez. They return to visit, to bring more relatives, to pay off loans, to buy land, or to help in the local rituals. They may also participate in community action groups designed to create pressure, for example, for the construction of a small park for children to play in. Finally, they relocate and build and create scripts that mostly contradict the ongoing megascripts of institutions, government, economy, and surrounding communities. They test the physical and ideological frontiers of existence and make borderless the basis of social life and cultural expectations. These are realities and the way in which these dynamics change from one generation to another is a crucial problem that we simply cannot overlook.

Our research, then, needs to be grounded in the actual physical sites where much of the transnational negotiation of relationships and relations occurs, whether in the United States, in the Caribbean, Central and South America, and Mexico, or between these states. Such grounding provides the basis for processual analysis and, more important, constitutes a constant check on grand theorizing that may be unrelated to the life needs of the populations about which we write.

Index

About the Editors

Carlos G. Vélez-Ibáñez is a professor of anthropology and Presidential Chair in Anthropology at the University of California at Riverside. He was awarded the Bronislaw Malinowski Award for 2003 by the Society for Applied Anthropology. He is also director of the Ernesto Galarza Applied Research Center and former dean of the College of Humanities, Arts, and Social Sciences in the same institution. He is the author of three major monographs and two edited books as well as numerous articles. He is an elected fellow of the American Association for the Advancement of Science and a former fellow of the Center for Advanced Study at Stanford. He was raised in Tucson, Arizona, and received his undergraduate and graduate degrees at the University of Arizona and his Ph.D. in anthropology at the University of California at San Diego.

Anna Sampaio is assistant professor of political science at the University of Colorado at Denver, where she teaches and researches in the areas of ethnic and gender politics, critical race theory, and postcolonial theory. Her work has been published in the *American Political Science Review, New Political Science, Women Studies Quarterly*, and *Latino Studies*. Her most current research on the intersections of gender, globalization, and transnational resistance focuses principally on areas of conflict in Latin America and their links to Latina/o communities in the United States.